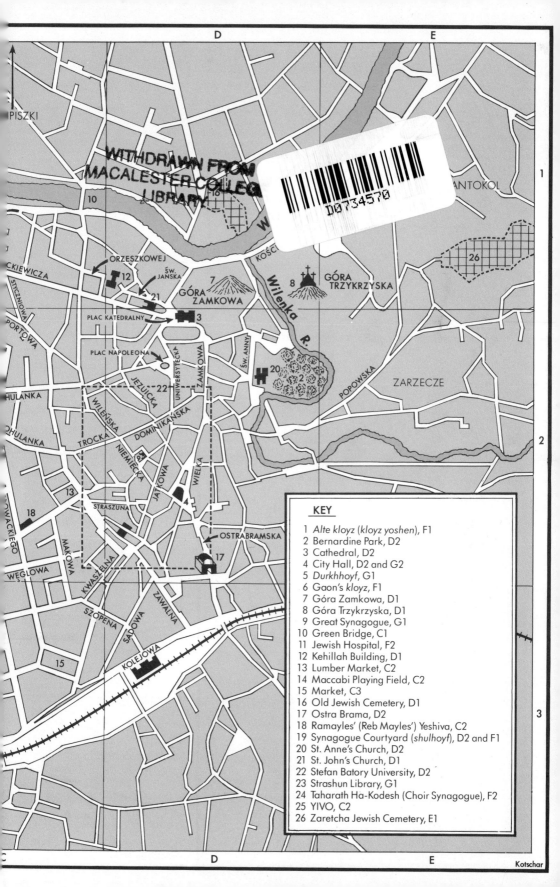

PISZKI

ANTOKOL

10

ORZESZKOWEJ

12 ŚW. JAŃSKA

5 21

3 PLAC KATEDRALNY

GÓRA ZAMKOWA

7

8 GÓRA TRZYKRZYSKA

Wilenka R.

KOŚCI

16

W

CKIEWICZA

STYCZNIOWA

PORTOWA

HULANKA

PLAC NAPOLEONA

UNIWERSYTECKA

ZAMKOWA

ŚW. ANNY

20

2

ZARZECZE

POPOWSKA

26

JEZUICKA 22

WILEŃSKA

TROCKA

DOMINIKAŃSKA

NIEMIECKA

JATOWA

WIELKA

2

HULANKA

13 STRASZUNA

18

WACKIEGO

STRASZUNA

4

OSTRABRAMSKA

17

WĘGLOWA

KWASZELNA

MAKOWA

SZOPENA

SADOWA

ZAWALNA

15

KOLEJOWA

3

KEY

1 *Alte kloyz (kloyz yoshen)*, F1
2 Bernardine Park, D2
3 Cathedral, D2
4 City Hall, D2 and G2
5 *Durkhhoyf*, G1
6 Gaon's *kloyz*, F1
7 Góra Zamkowa, D1
8 Góra Trzykrzyska, D1
9 Great Synagogue, G1
10 Green Bridge, C1
11 Jewish Hospital, F2
12 Kehillah Building, D1
13 Lumber Market, C2
14 Maccabi Playing Field, C2
15 Market, C3
16 Old Jewish Cemetery, D1
17 Ostra Brama, D2
18 Ramayles' (Reb Mayles') Yeshiva, C2
19 Synagogue Courtyard (*shulhoyf*), D2 and F1
20 St. Anne's Church, D2
21 St. John's Church, D1
22 Stefan Batory University, D2
23 Strashun Library, G1
24 Taharath Ha-Kodesh (Choir Synagogue), F2
25 YIVO, C2
26 Zaretcha Jewish Cemetery, E1

Kotschar

**Macalester
College
Library**

FROM THAT PLACE AND TIME

Also by Lucy S. Dawidowicz

The Golden Tradition: Jewish Life and Thought in Eastern Europe

The Holocaust and the Historians

A Holocaust Reader

The Jewish Presence: Essays on Identity and History

On Equal Terms: Jews in America

The War Against the Jews 1933–1945

FROM
THAT PLACE
AND TIME

A MEMOIR

1938 - 1947

Lucy S. Dawidowicz

W·W·NORTON & COMPANY

New York   London

Copyright © 1989 by Lucy S. Dawidowicz
All rights reserved.
Published simultaneously in Canada by Penguin Books Canada Ltd.,
2801 John Street, Markham, Ontario L3R 1B4.
Printed in the United States of America.
The text of this book is composed in 12/13.5 Bembo,
with display type set in Bernhard Modern Bold.
Composition and manufacturing by The Haddon Craftsmen, Inc.
Book design by Margaret M. Wagner.
Cartography by Vincent Kotschar.

First Edition

Library of Congress Cataloging-in-Publication Data

Dawidowicz, Lucy S.
From that place and time : a memoir, 1938-1947 / by Lucy S.
Dawidowicz.
p.   cm.
Includes index.
1. Jews—Lithuania—Vilnius.   2. Dawidowicz, Lucy S.—Journeys—
Lithuania—Vilnius.   3. Yiddish language—Lithuania—Vilnius.
4. Vilnius (Lithuania)—Ethnic relations.   I. Title.
DS135.R93V523 1989
947'.5—dc19   88–28858

ISBN 0-393-02674-4

W. W. Norton & Company, Inc.
500 Fifth Avenue, New York, N. Y. 10110
W. W. Norton & Company, Inc.
37 Great Russell Street, London WC1B 3NU

1 2 3 4 5 6 7 8 9 0

In memory of
the murdered Jews of Vilna

אֵלֶּה אֶזְכְּרָה. . . .

These I remember. . . .

Contents

PART III

Sometimes a man seeks what he hath lost; and from that place, and time, wherein he misses it, his mind runs back, from place to place, and time to time, to find where, and when he had it. . . .

—THOMAS HOBBES, Leviathan

Preface

One of the last people to have seen Vilna before its destruction in the fire of the Holocaust, I long wanted to write about that fabled city as it had been in 1938, when I lived there for a year as an American studying Jewish history and the Yiddish language. It was then still known by the name which Napoleon was said to have given it in 1812—the Jerusalem of Lithuania.

Vilna no longer exists. On its site stands a place identified on the map as Vilnius, capital of Lithuania, a constituent republic of the Soviet Union. Like Troy, the Vilna I knew, the Vilna described in Jewish annals, now lies buried beneath the debris of history, beneath layers of death and destruction. When the Soviets first occupied Vilna in 1940, they Sovietized it, destroying its historic identity and its Jewish particularity. The Germans who followed destroyed Vilna altogether, murdering nearly all of its 60,000 Jews—men, women, and children. Since then, nothing has remained of Vilna's Jewish culture and spirit. Hardly anything has remained of its buildings—the sticks and stones of Jewish architecture. What little the Nazis had left standing, the Soviets, who returned after the war, erased. A visitor to today's Vilnius can no longer find a trace of what had once been the Jerusalem of Lithuania.

Vilna exists now only in memory and in history. I wanted to reconstruct, as best I could, the Vilna I knew, the world capital of the realm of Yiddish, as I had seen it in that last year of its authentic life. I wanted to bestow upon it and its Jews a posthumous life.

The idea of my memoir began with the wish to bring Vilna back to life, but without documentary support I could not write about my year in Vilna with enough richness of detail to interest an American reader. All I had at my disposal were memories and a bare handful of souvenirs. The memoirist would appear not to need documentary sources, for he relies on the authority of his memory. Yet memory alone is not dependable. For, as all of us can testify, though we remember, we also misremember and we forget. We have all experienced those moments when, as the saying goes, memory deceives us. Even when memory can be prompted, as Proust has shown, by a taste, smell, sound, touch, or sight, the memoirist may still have to contend with gaps in his remembrances. Andre Maurois once said that "memory is a great artist," for who knows where authentic memory ends and imaginative reconstruction begins. A contemporary psychologist put it this way: "We fill up the lowlands of our memories from the highlands of our imaginations."

A few years ago my lifelong friend, Evelyn Konoff Bromberg, and my sister, Eleanor Schildkret Sapakoff, exhumed the letters which I had written from Vilna and which they had saved for nearly half a century. I came into a treasure of nearly a hundred letters, richly detailed and charged with the wonder of my experiences in Vilna. There is no adequate way I can thank them for having made this book possible.

While I was writing, I turned often to Dina Abramowicz, Librarian at the YIVO Institute for Jewish Research, and Leyzer Ran for their help in confirming or correcting my recollections of their native city. They were patient in answering my questions and generous with their time and knowledge. All my friends encouraged me in the course of my work. I am especially grateful to Adele Dulberger Bowers, my friend from college days, who read part of the manuscript, and to Thomas C. Wallace, friend and editor, whose faith in this book sustained me.

In writing about Vilna, I set myself the task of trying to reconstruct that beloved past without sentimentality, even though that past was brutally destroyed. The terrible finality of the murder of the European Jews and the virtual disappearance of Ashkenazic Jewish civilization from the European continent color our memories. By relying on the discipline of history, I have tried to portray that past truthfully, as it was in life. I have not wanted to retouch it. That was my obligation as one of the last witnesses.

PART I

CHAPTER 1

From New York to Vilna

On August 10, 1938, I sailed from New York on the Polish liner *Batory* on my way to Vilna. Nineteen thirty-eight was not an auspicious year to travel to Eastern Europe for business or pleasure. All that year the premonitions of war poisoned the air as if the suffocating aroma of sulfur had already been unloosed. In March Adolf Hitler had invaded Austria and annexed it. Then he turned on Czechoslovakia under the pretext of protecting the "rights" of the German-speaking population who had lived for centuries in a part of Bohemia called Sudetenland.

The Czech government resisted the Nazi demands and late in May the Germans responded with a massive concentration of troops on the Czech border. The Czechs, in turn, ordered a partial mobilization of their army, and the British then warned Germany that they would intervene in the event of a European conflict. Hitler backed down and the first Czech crisis petered out. The war, which had seemed imminent and inevitable, did not erupt. It was suspended for only a moment in historical time. In August, when I left New York, the second Czech crisis was beginning to heat up. The summer of 1938 was definitely not an auspicious time to go to Poland.

Indeed, the Jewish traffic had long been moving in the opposite direction. Central and Eastern Europe had become a vast prisonhouse from which Jews wished to escape. Those lucky enough to get visas headed for Europe's exits. Just then I started out on my contrary journey. Years later, Isaac Bashevis Singer tried to fathom my state of mind. He himself had fled Poland in 1935 and come to the United States. Puzzling over my perversity or recklessness, as he saw it, he at last found an explanation that satisfied him. "I," he said, "was a Polish Jew and I thought anything could happen. You were an American Jew and you thought nothing could happen."

Singer was saying that American Jews believed they were immune from the terrors that beset European Jews, exempted from the humiliations of anti-Semitism, and safe from the dangers of war, that American Jews weren't possessed by those ancient fears and forebodings with which history and experience had burdened the European Jews. Perhaps Singer also had in mind the temperament of Americans in those days. Even during the depression they thought their country was the best in the world. An American abroad knew that if ever he'd be in trouble, his passport would shield him like a suit of armor. Being an American then was enough to give anyone a bushel of courage.

Yet my traveling to Poland was not a case of historical forgetfulness or of mere youthful bravado. More akin to the traditional passage from youth to adulthood, it was a journey to seek one's purpose in life, an uncommon journey, to be sure, to a place from which most Jews, if only they could, would have fled.

What had set me on this seemingly perverse course from New York to Vilna? The explanation lies in the way I was brought up and how the disordered times of my youth shaped me. Here I have tried to set down those clues, hints, and indirections—Walt Whitman's words about his autobiography—that make up my particular history. Yet, however anomalous my story may appear to be, it is merely another variation on a familiar theme—how American-born children of East European Jewish immigrants came to terms with themselves as Americans and as Jews.

My parents arrived in New York from Poland, then a province within czarist Russia, around 1908, when they were in their teens. My father had been born in Warsaw, Poland's capital and major city. When he was still a small boy, his father abandoned wife and children in Warsaw and ran away to America with another woman. My father was raised by his grandfather, a learned and pious man, who insisted on the strictest observance of all 613 commandments of Jewish law. Sixty years later, his resentment still persisting, my father used to recall the tyrannical regimen which the old man imposed on him. He would tell me how his grandfather would waken him, a child of about four or five, in the dark dawns of wintry Warsaw to go to shul for morning services. He could evoke his sleepiness, the biting cold, the sleet and snow, the gnawing hunger that accompanied early morning prayers on an empty stomach. As soon as he was old enough, he fled his grandfather's loveless household.

For the rest of his life, even in his old age, my father hated the synagogue and its rituals, which he associated with his draconic grandfather. But he still remembered the Hebrew prayers and, being musical, liked to listen on the phonograph to famous cantors singing liturgical music. He even sang along.

My mother was born in Siedlce, a medium-sized city east of Warsaw. She, too, had been brought up in an observant household, but one not nearly so disciplined as my father's. She used to boast that her mother was related to the Gerer *rebbe,* the head of a famous hasidic dynasty, though the relationship was quite distant. Judaic learning in her home was apparently in scant supply, at least among the three daughters, for my mother never demonstrated any particular knowledge of traditional Judaism.

In 1905 Siedlce was caught up in the revolutionary ferment of that time. Back in 1900 the Jewish Socialist Labor Bund had organized a branch there. Somehow or other, perhaps through her older brother, my mother, who was then about fifteen, became involved in those Bund activities. In May 1905, with a few hundred others, she attended a clandestine Bund meeting held in the woods outside of town. Czarist police, reinforced with three squadrons of the czar's dragoons, charged the assembly, wounding many of the participants and arresting them all, my mother included. Her family got her released from prison. Soon afterward she emigrated, following an older sister to New York. For the rest of her life, her one revolutionary experience in 1905 remained vivid in her memory.

My parents met in New York. They worked in the shops, living frugally on their slim wages. Together they attended lectures in Yiddish and went to the Yiddish theater. About a year later they married and lived unhappily ever after. I was born in 1915. When I was a child, my father had a small umbrella-manufacturing shop of his own on the East Side. It prospered for a while, but after 1921, just before my sister was born, we became poor and stayed poor.

First my parents bought a candy store in the Bronx. A few years later, they set up a women's hat shop in Glendale, in Queens, where the only Jews in the neighborhood were the few shopkeepers. After a while, my mother resumed her seasonal work as a millinery operator and my father became a salesman of cheap pieced fur skins which he sold to small-scale furriers. Then in 1927, my parents bought a brand-new four-family house in a developing section of the Bronx, hoping thereby to improve the family fortunes. Because they continued working in order to pay off the mortgage, I was given the responsibility of checking the furnace and hot-water boiler as well as looking after my little sister, when I came home from school.

During the years of the Great Depression I couldn't notice much difference in our hard times before 1929 or after. But by 1937 my parents could no longer keep up the payments on the mortgage, despite the help that Roosevelt's New Deal then gave to small homeowners. The bank foreclosed on the house and that summer we moved to a dismal apartment in a dilapidated East Bronx neighborhood.

My parents constantly quarreled about money, but I don't remember that we ever lacked for what we needed. In 1926, when we still lived in the small apartment behind the hat store, we had the first radio on the block and all the neighbors came to hear of Gertrude Ederle's progress as the first woman to swim the English Channel. Even through those bad years I was given piano lessons and, except for the period in Glendale which afforded no such opportunity, I attended a Jewish school in the weekdays after public school was out, for which my parents had to pay tuition.

Ours was a distinctly Jewish household, even though we never attended a synagogue, even though my sister and I were never taught the rudiments of the Jewish religion. On Jewish festivals my parents closed the store, not only in deference to what the neighbors might say but also out of a sense of Jewish solidarity. My sister and I stayed home from school. My mother fasted on Yom Kippur, the Day of Atonement, on the ground that it was healthy to fast once in a while, but she never appreciated the solemnity of that day. On Passover we got new clothes to wear, mostly sewn by my mother, and our observance of the festival seemed like a Jewish version of the Easter Parade. I don't remember that we ever had a traditional seder at home, though we sometimes went to one in a relative's house. The one practice of Judaism my mother strictly followed was to buy kosher meat and poultry, which she never cooked in butter or milk. Sabbath observance was reduced to a general house cleaning on Fridays. After she washed the kitchen floor, my mother spread the previous day's Yiddish newspapers over it to keep it from getting dirty right away.

Our sense of being Jews and therefore being different from non-Jews was nurtured in me and my sister from infancy. We were raised to know that the world was divided into two irreconcilable groups: We and They. *They* were the non-Jews, who hated us and wished to destroy us. But *We* would prevail, largely because of our moral virtues and mental endowments. We took pride in being Jewish despite—or perhaps be- cause of—the tragic circumstances of our history.

My parents were Yiddishists, believing that the Yiddish language was the cementing force that united the Jewish people and would ensure its continued existence. In those days, when every idea became elaborated into an ideology, Yiddishism was not widely accepted as a philosophy of Jewish survival, probably because the commitment to a national language seldom inspired the transcendent dedication that the appeal of a nation or religion could arouse. Chaim Zhitlowsky (1865–1943) was the theoretician who formulated the Yiddishist philosophy of Jewish existence. He was a Russian Socialist-Revolutionary who had settled in the United States in 1908, after having earned a doctorate in philosophy at the University of Bern. An eclectic thinker and enthusiast for diverse causes, he evolved a theory of Jewish nationalism which integrated his socialist convictions and his anti-religious views with the idea that the Yiddish language, as the language of the common people, could serve as the basis for Jewish national existence. Zhitlowsky's ideas surely shaped my parents' notions of their Jewish identity. My father wor- shipped him, read all his books and articles, and attended his lectures.

At that time New York had four Yiddish daily newspapers. The socialist *Forverts* (*Jewish Daily Forward*) had the largest circulation, but my parents sneered at it for its low intellectual level. The *Morgn Zhurnal* (*Jewish Morning Journal*) was Orthodox in religion and Republican in politics, both anathema in our home. The Communist *Morgn Frayhayt* (*Morning Freedom*) didn't get much regard from my parents. In our house, we read *Der Tog* (*The Day*), whose masthead identified it as "the newspaper of the Yiddish intelligentsia." My father was then something of an *inteligent,* the East European definition of an intellectual. My mother was all her life a voracious reader. *Der Tog* prided itself on being a nonpartisan liberal paper and boasted an array of regular contributors comprising the elite of Yiddish writers and thinkers in the United States, among them Zhitlowsky.

The Jewish school my parents chose for me was affiliated with the Sholem Aleichem Folk Institute, an educational agency named after the Yiddish classic writer. It sponsored and supervised a network of about twenty schools with an enrollment of some 2,000 pupils in New York City. (The late twenties and the thirties were a low point for any kind of Jewish education.) The Yiddish schools were the most recent addition to the Jewish educational establishment, having come into existence in Eastern Europe as well as in the immigrant cities of the United States about the time of the First World War. They were the products of secularist Jewish ideologies. Four separate secular Yiddish school systems operated in those days in New York. One was Zionist and socialist; another was socialist but anti-Zionist; a third was Communist affiliated. Only the Sholem Aleichem Folk Institute was nonpartisan. All four school systems shared a secular view of Jewish identity and offered what they believed was a modern alternative to the *heder* and the Talmud Torah, the traditional Jewish schools where children were taught to read and memorize the Hebrew prayers without understanding them.

In my neighborhood Sholem Aleichem school, we were taught to read and write Yiddish and to sing Yiddish songs. We were instructed in the rudiments of Jewish history. The major Jewish festivals were celebrated as national holidays, with emphasis on folk elements—customs and traditions—rather than liturgy, ritual, and expressions of religious faith. There was a touch of anthropology to this approach, as we were taught which delicious foods were appropriate to each festival.

Though my parents were principled Yiddishists, we nevertheless spoke English at home as frequently as Yiddish. This was largely my mother's doing. She prided herself on her own extensive English vocabulary and her knowledge of world literature in English translation, but even more compelling was her determination to have her children succeed, first in school and later in the world. For that, she realized, they would need a good command of English.

Meanwhile, in 1928, I entered Hunter College High School, then an all-girls' elite high school, known for its rigorous curriculum which required four years of English, three years of mathematics and Latin, two years of French or German, as well as biology and physics. As for history, all I can summon up is the unhappy memory of an American history course which consisted of tables of railroads (names, dates, and mileages) and of tariffs (names, dates, and the imports on which duties were imposed).

The English courses mattered most to me and they nurtured my love for literature, poetry especially. We had some splendid teachers, who introduced us to the English poets from Shakespeare to Swinburne. All women, a few of them became the objects of those prelesbian crushes endemic to all-girls' schools. On our own, we discovered contemporary poets, notably Edna St. Vincent Millay, whose verses fed my romantic imagination. T. S. Eliot was then still an unknown name to me.

Reading spurred me to writing, especially to poetry. I was soon admitted into the school's literary clique, and joined the staff of *Argus,* the school's literary journal, becoming its editor in my senior year. Through *Argus,* I was introduced to the excitement of printing, the clutter of the printing shop and the clatter of its linotype machines and presses. I felt very important as I read and corrected galley proofs, my fingers smudged with printer's ink.

From Monday to Friday I went to classes at Hunter College High School, and on Saturday and Sunday, from early morning until mid-afternoon, I attended the Sholem Aleichem Mitlshul, a Yiddish high school operated under the auspices of the Sholem Aleichem Folk Institute. When I first enrolled, probably around 1929, the Mitlshul was housed in a run-down four-story rented building on East 15th Street, whose original flats had been converted into classrooms and one floor into an auditorium. The paint was always peeling off the walls, the wooden floors were grimy and discolored, the staircase narrow and rickety. At the time we didn't pay attention to such things, perhaps because we were used to the shabbiness of our elementary Yiddish schools. But its dingy appearance didn't matter, for the Mitlshul was where most of us made friendships that would last a lifetime and where romances blossomed into enduring marriages.

It was there I realized that other worlds existed besides that of Keats, Shelley, and the romantic poets. The passion for learning which some of my teachers communicated was catching and their erudition dazzled me. They opened the door to an exciting universe of scholarship that until then had been outside my ken. I didn't realize it at the time, but the Mitlshul became a decisive factor in my life.

The Mitlshul's director, Leibush Lehrer (1887–1965), born in Poland, had come to the United States in 1910. A man of medium height and build, his most distinctive physical feature was the shiny bald expanse of his head, ringed at the sides and back with dark brown hair. Behind the black-rimmed glasses were eyes that appraised you knowingly and kindly. His humor had bite. About human frailty, he'd say: "A man is only human and sometimes not even that." But about politics he was always serious, being one of the few in that milieu in the middle thirties who hated the Bolshevik regime and its American apologists.

Specializing in psychology and education, he had earned his bachelor's and master's degrees at Clark University, a few years after Freud had lectured there on psychoanalysis. Lehrer thereafter applied his knowledge to the practice and theory of Jewish education. Unlike the radical Yiddish secularists who rejected Judaism as superstition and unlike the Marxists who believed that religion was the opium of the people, Lehrer saw Judaism as the product of a folk culture. He reinterpreted its religious traditions and beliefs in ethnic-national terms. Aware of the profound emotional power which long-lasting traditions and their symbols played in shaping and strengthening Jewish identity, he tried to retain as many as were compatible with the pervasive antireligious temper of the time.

Besides being the Mitlshul's director, he was also the founder and lifelong director of a Yiddish-speaking summer camp, Boiberik, named for one of Sholem Aleichem's fictitious towns. There Lehrer had even more leeway in putting his educational ideas into practice. Most Mitlshul students had been campers at Boiberik and then camp counselors. (I hadn't because my family was too poor for that.) In addition, Lehrer pursued his scholarly interests by serving as research secretary of the Psychology/Education Section of the Yiddish Scientific Institute in Vilna and was active in its branch in New York.

Teaching at the Mitlshul provided additional income for most of our teachers, some of whom taught at Yiddish elementary schools during the week. A few had higher aspirations and had already carved out reputations as writers or scholars. One such was the Yiddish poet and critic Nochum Boruch Minkoff (1893–1958). Born in Warsaw, he had come to New York when he was about twenty. In 1921 he earned a law degree at New York University, but instead of practicing law, he chose to be a Yiddish poet and became a leading member of the Introspectivists, a school of modernist Yiddish poets. His teaching helped to support his poetry. In later years, he taught at the New School for Social Research. He was more rigorously intellectual than our other teachers and less comradely, but we respected him and struggled to understand his poetry.

We became accustomed to knowing the most celebrated Yiddish poets and novelists of the time, because their children were our classmates. Yiddish literature had become, as it were, familiar and personal. I knew Daniel, the elder son of the Yiddish poet H. Leivick; David—or Doodle, as we called him—the only son of the novelist and short-story writer Joseph Opatoshu; Adah, the daughter of the poet Menahem Boraisha. That intimacy with the writers and their families stimulated our desire to read their work. We must have represented to those Yiddish writers, and especially to the modernists among them, the hope of a future readership among native-born American Jews.

Another literature teacher was Israel Knox (1907–1986), who had been a disciple of Zhitlowsky. He was good-looking in a kind of brooding Byronic style and knew it. I was one of several adolescent girls who used to languish in his presence. As a teacher, he combined an academic literary approach with a melodramatic delivery, being partial to overwrought rhetoric. He was then completing his doctorate on Kant's philosophy of aesthetics. In later years, he taught philosophy at New York University, but all his life retained his commitment to Yiddish.

The most engaging and impressive of my teachers was the historian Jacob Shatzky (1893–1956). He was a stocky man, with a head that seemed disproportionately large to his short body, perhaps because of his exceptionally high forehead. His hair was brown and curly, his eyebrows heavy, visible over his eyeglasses often perched low on his nose. He loved to pun and did so bilingually, even trilingually. Though he was often acerbic, the students loved his wit and his endless store of anecdotes.

Born in Warsaw, he received a traditional Jewish education, attended trade school for about two years, and then, after his father's death, worked in a tea store. His passion for books, languages, and historical studies brought him to the attention of a wealthy patron, who undertook to sponsor his university education. In 1922 Shatzky received a doctorate from the University of Warsaw with a dissertation about Jews in nineteenth-century Poland. During the First World War, he served as an officer with the Polish Legion commanded by Marshal Józef Piłsudski. Poland was bred in Shatzky's bone, even though he left the country soon after he received his doctorate and lived the rest of his years in New York. His ardor for Poland, its language and culture, remained undiminished all his life. Polish Jewish history became his field of specialization. He was, as long as I knew him, extremely productive, the author of numerous books, monographs, articles, and an endless stream of reviews. In the last years of his life he saw the publication in Yiddish of the first three volumes of his never-completed history of the Jews in Warsaw.

Soon after he came to New York, Shatzky taught Jewish history at two institutions which trained teachers for the Yiddish schools. When the Yiddish Scientific Institute was established in Vilna in 1925, he became a cofounder of its American branch and thereafter an active member of its Historical Section. In 1929, Shatzky became librarian at the New York Psychiatric Institute, a position that provided his livelihood for the rest of his life. He used to do a lot of his Yiddish writing, especially reviews, on the reverse side of the Psychiatric Institute's colored mimeograph paper.

It was he who advised and persuaded the Institute to purchase, shortly before war broke out, a collection of books which, as he had suspected, had been part of Freud's library. Shatzky had received a catalogue from a Viennese book dealer, detailing a collection of books on neurology and psychiatry, purporting to be the nucleus of a library that had belonged to a famous Viennese scientist. From the catalogue, Shatzky deduced that those books must have been part of Freud's library. He described to me the tension he endured until the books arrived. What if he were wrong? When the wooden crates had been brought up to the library and pried open, he reached in to pull out a book. The first one bore an inscription to Freud. Some books had marginal notations in Freud's hand. Shatzky had been right after all.

Later I learned that Freud had made a gift to the book dealer of these books, which were only a small part of his whole library and less valuable to him than the books he took with him when he moved to London in 1938. The collection, called the Freud Memorial Library, is now part of the library of Columbia University's medical campus.

Shatzky introduced me to modern Jewish history first in Mitlshul and then in the Mitlshul graduate courses, which I attended during the years I was in college. History had been a discipline of which I was ignorant except for those American railroads and tariffs, but from Shatzky I learned that history was more than dates and tables. As he taught it, Jewish history became denser and more complex than the usual litany of Jewish suffering from the Crusades through the Inquisition to the Russian pogroms. From him I first learned about the problems of Jewish emancipation during the French Revolution and about Napoleon's obsessive interest in the Jews. Still, notwithstanding my reverential regard for Shatzky and the new perspective on history which I had gained, English literature, poetry especially, continued to be my passion and my chief academic interest through my college years.

In September 1932 I entered Hunter College. The United States was then in the depths of the Great Depression and President Herbert Hoover could do nothing about it. America's landscape was dotted with bread lines, apple vendors, and hunger marchers. All across the country, people were on the move, drifting from place to place, looking for work. They were the dust-bowl farmers, the bankrupt businessmen, unemployed coal miners and steel workers, high school and college graduates whose skills no one needed. Some became boxcar hoboes. In the big cities, the dispossessed slept in the parks and the subways. On the outskirts of cities the homeless erected shantytowns called Hoovervilles or Hoover villas. The jobless demonstrated for work, the hungry for relief, the war veterans for their cash bonuses. Workers in the shops and factories of the big industrial cities were lucky if they worked a couple of days a week so they could feed their children.

People had run out of money, out of food, out of patience. Most impatient of all were the intellectuals, the writers, poets, and artists. They took their watchword from a new book by a young Yale graduate, John Chamberlain, which was called *Farewell to Reform.* It was time, they thought, for revolution. In November 1932, when Franklin Delano Roosevelt ran for the presidency on the Democratic line against Herbert Hoover on the Republican line, most of America's intellectuals were on the left. Chamberlain himself wrote in September 1932 that the only choice was between Norman Thomas, the Socialist Party candidate, and William Z. Foster, head of the Communist Party, United States of America, running on its ticket.

In October 1932, a group of fifty-three artists, writers, and intellectuals issued a manifesto, in which they announced that they were aligning themselves "with the frankly revolutionary Communist Party, the party of the workers." They rejected the Republicans, the Democrats, and even the Socialists, concluding: "It is capitalism which is destructive of all culture and Communism which desires to save civilization and its cultural heritage from the abyss to which the world crisis is driving it."

That was what the mood in the United States was like when I entered college. Until then, I had not thought much about the real world around me. Keats and Wordsworth and lyric Yiddish poetry had provided me with a refuge into which I could escape from my parents' quarrels, the hot-water boiler, and the constricted world of the East Bronx in which we lived. But reality soon confronted me with its brutal politics.

At the end of January 1933, when I had just finished my first semester in college, Adolf Hitler became chancellor of Germany. The anxieties about life in depressed America paled before the dread we all felt. It was one of those moments which everyone recognized as a dangerous crossing in history. Just weeks later, on March 4, 1933, Roosevelt was inaugurated as president of the United States. He promised "action, and action now" and within the month, he had succeeded in rousing the country from its despair. At that moment, too, we knew we had arrived at yet another historic juncture. Overnight the world in which I had grown up had changed. Poetry still mattered to me, but now politics occupied first place in my consciousness. It would soon claim my time and commandeer my energy.

At seventeen I knew little of politics, but I had inherited something of my parents' outlook. My mother's girlhood experience of 1905 had been integrated into our family history. My parents' politics had been shaped largely by their hatred of the repressive czarist regime and its anti-Semitic excesses. Like tens of thousands of secularized East European Jewish immigrants, my parents were used to taking an adversarial political posture. They had cheered the February 1917 revolution which overthrew the czar and established a provisional government. They continued to cheer after the Bolsheviks overthrew the moderates and the Socialists. It didn't matter to my parents who ruled Russia, as long as the czar had been overthrown.

My parents didn't belong to any political organization. They had voted Socialist in the old days, but in 1932 they voted for Roosevelt and continued to vote Democratic the rest of their lives. Like most secular immigrant Jews, they lived within the fellowship of the left and they were familiar with Communist politics and Communist ideas, even if they usually didn't agree with them. My father's cousins, whom we often saw, were aggressive Communists who had raised their children in their Communist faith. Owners of a small shop which manufactured leather handbags, they were themselves employers, yet they were fierce in their hostility to the blood-sucking capitalists. They used to accuse the Socialists of being insufficiently revolutionary and therefore unable to solve the problems of the times.

In the 1930s, my parents became members of the Workmen's Circle, a fraternal society that provided medical benefits and burial plots. They chose the Workmen's Circle, an American offshoot of the Jewish Social-

ist Labor Bund in Poland, in preference to a similar Zionist society or
a Communist one. My mother, being a millinery worker, was a loyal
union member. I grew up at a time when workers in the shops and
factories were underpaid and overworked, when their unions, weak and
often impotent, were their only shield against the bosses' exploitation.
Two summers, in 1933 and 1934, I worked in the hat factory where my
mother was employed. The conditions were barely tolerable, the work
excruciatingly boring. But I was making some money. That shop experience gave me the authority later to write verses which extolled "the
humble people" with "their silent strength," in contrast to the weak-
willed intellectuals who couldn't make up their minds to join the
struggle on the barricades.

By going left I went in my parents' footsteps, yet I also rebelled
against them, by joining the Young Communist League (YCL) instead
of the more moderate Young People's Socialist League (YPSL). My
decision to do so must have been all passion and the desire for risk, for
at that time I knew nothing of Marx or Marxism, nothing of Leninism
or Communist Party theory, and little about the Soviet Union. But I
had become a true believer. Lincoln Steffens's ringing words after his
interview with Lenin in 1919 continued to reverberate down the decades
into the thirties: "I have seen the future and it works."

During the Great Depression, the idea of a workers' state to which
each person would contribute according to his ability and from which
each would receive according to his need captured the imagination of
intellectuals and writers. Having been converted to communism by the
gospel of St. Marx, the intellectuals sustained their faith with the good
news brought by the returning pilgrims from Russia. Those visitors
reported on the miracles they had witnessed, the remarkable accomplishments of the workers' society which, they assured everyone, heralded
a New Age and a New Man.

In those days some people knew that Russia was not the paradise that
the travelers advertised, but few Americans knew—or cared—much
about the Soviet drive to collectivize the farms, the liquidation of
millions of kulaks in the process, and the consequent great famine in the
Ukraine in 1933. Since the Bolshevik overthrow of the Kerensky regime
in 1917, the United States had had no diplomatic relations with Russia
and it was only in November 1933 that the United States, under
Roosevelt, finally recognized Russia. During those sixteen years without diplomatic contact, Americans learned little of what was happening
in the Soviet Union. Already the Soviet Union was secretive about its
bad news; already it was evolving into a police state. In 1934 the curtain

had not yet gone up on the great show trials. The mass purges and mass arrests were still to come. The horrors of the Gulag lay ahead.

Of course we heard the constant drumbeating against Russia which came from the right, the reactionaries, the red-hunters and red-baiters, and especially from William Randolph Hearst's yellow press. They denounced Lenin, Stalin, collectivism in the Soviet Union, and they warned of the specter of Bolshevism that would haunt the world. We, children of immigrants who had fled the oppression of czarist Russia, would never give credence to those voices from the right, for they were our enemies, just as the czarist regime had been our parents' enemy. They were reactionaries who obstructed the passage to a socialist future; they were anti-Semites who for decades had inveighed against Jews and Jewish immigrants.

Joining the YCL was my way of righting the world's wrongs and working for a society in which the Jews could thrive, for a world free from hatred and prejudice. I was in search of a utopian solution for our earthly ills, and my goal was nothing less than a secular version of the eternal Jewish striving for a Messianic world. My particular vision was colored red, the color of blood and of revolution.

At Hunter, the students on the left—the YCLs and the YPSLs, the sectarian Trotskyists and the Lovestoneites—were a tiny minority among the student body. Most students kept their noses in their books and tried to have a little fun. Hunter had the traditional student entertainments, notably the Senior Hop and SING, an annual festivity for which students prepared all year, composing songs and skits, which they later performed. Hunter even had sports teams—hockey, fencing, basketball—and, surprisingly for a public college with a subway student body, as many as eighteen sororities. We, intellectual snobs and aspiring writers, thought those activities were frivolous, even irresponsible. We had fun in our own bohemian way, but we dedicated ourselves to changing the world.

For me and my circle, the YCL took precedence over our classes, especially required courses, which we cut a lot. We joined various student organizations and discussion clubs to spread our ideas and to "bore from within." In the fall of 1934, as a junior, I was appointed to the editorial board of Hunter's literary journal *Echo.* Some of my friends worked on the school paper, *Hunter College Bulletin,* and others on the college yearbook, *Wistarion.* We were deep in the campaigns and causes of the National Student League, a Communist-front organization. We sat through endless meetings in our own cell and in all sorts of committees up the YCL hierarchy to citywide and national bodies.

We attended lectures and courses at the Jefferson School, the Communist Party's indoctrination center, camouflaged as a school. We picketed, rallied, and demonstrated for whatever causes were then on the Communist Party's agenda. We marched in the Communist contingent of the May Day parade. We believed that the future was ours.

We didn't do much about Hitler and fascism in Europe. In fact until late in 1935 we devoted an extraordinary amount of energy to spreading Communist propaganda for peace and disarmament. The Communists then took the position that the capitalist nations constituted a military threat to the Soviet Union, that munitions makers were inherently corrupt and evil, and that wars served only imperialist ends. In those days we even joined with religious-minded pacifist students of the Oxford Group who sponsored the Oxford Pledge to refuse to fight in any war.

But no matter what we did or how we were used, our commitment to the Communist movement was reinforced by the growing fascist presence in Germany, Italy, and Japan. We believed we were engaged in a fundamental conflict between the evil Nazi universe and communism, the hope of mankind as exemplified in the Soviet Union. As Germany's anti-Jewish policies accelerated without resistance from inside the country or out, that success encouraged anti-Semitic movements everywhere else. The Western democracies seemed to be paralyzed, unable to halt Hitler's terror. Every day it became clearer to us, in our increasingly polarized world, that the Jews had no choice but to side with the left against the Nazis and the Fascists. That conflict between Jew and Nazi was enacted on our very doorstep, as it were, in the corridors of Hunter College. Dr. Ernst Riess, German Jew and professor of Latin, confronted Dr. Otto Koischwitz, Nazi sympathizer and professor of German. We watched at a distance in open-mouthed dismay. The elderly Riess vehemently protested Koischwitz's anti-Semitism and his defense of Germany. Koischwitz became abusive. We were afraid he would strike the older man. They never spoke to each other again. A few years later, Koischwitz returned to Germany. There, during the war, he broadcast Nazi propaganda in English beamed to American soldiers in North Africa and on the European continent.

Nineteen thirty-five turned out to be so eventful a year in my history and the history of the Communist Party that I hardly noticed the bad news from Hitler's Germany. In January *The New Masses,* the party's cultural weekly, published a "Call for an American Writers' Congress," directed to the politically engaged writers who "recognize the necessity of personally helping to accelerate the destruction of capitalism and the establishment of a workers' government." The Congress would deal with the "struggle against war and fascism" and the obligations of the revolutionary writer.

There could have been no greater thrill for me, an aspiring writer who had already introduced "social consciousness" in her verses. The American Writers' Congress met in New York on April 26–27, 1935. An acknowledged Communist enterprise, its participants lauded Soviet culture and denounced America. Mike Gold, the most gifted writer the Communists ever completely captured, spoke of a future Soviet America. The Writers' Congress was my literary guidepost when, in the fall of 1935, I become editor-in-chief of *Echo*. The first issue which I and my staff published was faithful to the Congress's spirit. My editorial pronouncement addressed itself "to the artist's position and function in society." In a society "threatened by war and the imminence of fascism," the artist, so I exhorted my readers, "must take sides not only for his own self-preservation, but for the enlightenment and redemption of all of society." And so on and on. That issue contained antiwar poems and eulogies of Soviet literature. To make sure that our message would be delivered, we printed our cover in bright red. That red *Echo* created a sensation, particularly in the dean's office. In those days, the college administration was outraged by the publication of Bolshevik propaganda within its own precincts and at its own expense. Thenceforth, I was always under the dean's vigilant eye.

Precisely when I was enjoying the notoriety of my literary-political coup, the Communist Party line changed. Late in July 1935, the Communist International (Comintern) opened its seventh—and last—congress in Moscow. Its secretary general, Georgi Dimitrov, in a major address on August 2, announced the party's new line, calling upon the Communist parties throughout the world to abandon their policy of class against class. Party members were now directed to establish "united" or "popular fronts" with all political forces, whatever their particular positions, so long as they opposed German Nazism and Japanese militarism.

The change had been introduced in deference to the new Soviet strategy, prompted by Hitler's increasingly aggressive military posture. In March 1935 Hitler had denounced those clauses of the Versailles Treaty which had prohibited Germany's rearmament; clearly he was starting to prepare Germany militarily for war. The Soviet Union had consequently decided to halt its propaganda against the Western countries and, instead, to advocate a system of collective security with them. That about-face in Communist policy was one of those abrupt and opportunistic transitions which had already become the hallmark of the Communist movement, though at that time none of us knew enough of party history to appreciate the long perspective.

We, young Communist militants, considered the new line a betrayal of our revolutionary principles, for we were afflicted with "left-wing Communism," a disease which, in an earlier period of party-line about-face, Lenin had branded as an "infantile disorder." In the fall of 1935, all Communist Party and YCL cells were instructed to study the texts explaining the new line, to discuss them, and to vote for their adoption. Our cell held intense discussions, since many of us opposed the new line, resolved to preserve our revolutionary commitments intact. How could we unite with those whom we had only yesterday vilified and who continued to obstruct our path to a utopian society? We voted against accepting the Dimitrov policy. We didn't know that zigs and zags were a standard feature of Communist Party history, that the party had already been through such a back-and-forth shift in the 1920s. Nor did we appreciate the system of party discipline imposed from above, which Communists called "democratic centralism." Afterward we learned that all the YCL college cells had voted against the new line.

Early in 1936, our cell was officially informed that the YCL and Communist Party had approved the united-front policy, that thenceforth we were to follow that line. I was outraged, for I knew that my cell had voted against the Dimitrov line and so had the other college cells. That was the moment of truth, my blinding revelation that the YCL was not a democratic organization. And so I quit the YCL. (Years later, a friend who stayed told me: "You didn't quit; you were expelled.") In a grand gesture of revenge, I resigned from the editorship of *Echo,* allowing apolitical students to take it over. A few days later I wrote to a friend about these events and signed my letter: "Now an unaffiliated student and a free agent." Nonetheless, my infatuation for the Soviet Union continued to linger like a low-grade fever.

The gloom of European politics darkened my last semester at Hunter. While I had been preoccupied with the Comintern Congress and my red *Echo,* I hadn't paid much attention to other matters, including the Nazi Party Congress held in Nuremberg in September 1935. There the Nazis adopted the so-called Nuremberg Laws which stripped the German Jews of their citizenship and branded them as an alien race with whom German Aryans were forbidden to have social contact. History had catapulted the Jews back to the center of world politics and back to my notice. More bad news came in March 1936, when Hitler's army reoccupied the Rhineland, violating the terms of the Locarno pacts. At just that time, a series of pogroms erupted in several Polish cities, the most violent in Przytyk, where two Jews and one Pole were killed. In May, when I was studying for my final exams, Mussolini completed his invasion of Ethiopia, annexing it to Italy.

That semester I no longer had anyone at Hunter to talk to about these events or about anything else for that matter. My former comrades treated me as a pariah. Once, on a street corner just outside Hunter, a former friend was delivering a soap-box oration about the menace of fascism. As I passed, she raised her voice to the pitch of hysteria and in the hyperbole of Communist rhetoric denounced the traitors who had turned their backs on the working class. Unmistakably, she meant me.

It was a relief to be graduated, though nothing awaited me in the outside world. No jobs were to be had in those days. I filled out applications at employment agencies and was interviewed in countless offices from 14th Street to 59th Street. I took Civil Service exams and Board of Education tests, with no practical results.

After I quit the YCL at Hunter, I spent more time with my friends at the Sholem Aleichem Mitlshul, where I had all along been attending its graduate courses. When we had exhausted all the courses, we formed an alumni association to give our friendships an institutional form. Then, in a surge of ambition in 1936, we turned the alumni association into a Yiddishist organization to propagandize young American Jews for Yiddish and its culture. We called ourselves the Sholem Aleichem Yugt Gezelshaft (Sholem Aleichem Youth Organization) and began to publish a small bilingual journal, *Shrift* (*Writing*), which we sometimes called "short shrift." We advocated biculturalism, cultivating our dual heritage of American culture and secular Yiddishism. Yiddish culture, I argued in a *Shrift* editorial, was as rich and authentically American as any ethnic or regional subculture. To prove it all, I'd even begun writing Yiddish verse.

Most of us in the Sholem Aleichem Yugt Gezelshaft were on the left, though only a few were actually Communists. We were impressed that the Soviet Union gave Yiddish official recognition, that elementary and secondary schools with Yiddish as the language of instruction were accredited and state supported there. The Soviets sponsored two institutes for advanced Jewish studies, in Yiddish linguistics and Yiddish literature, at the Universities of Kiev and Minsk. Yiddish newspapers and books were published in large editions. A Jewish State Theater maintained a network of Yiddish theaters throughout the Soviet Union.

We even liked the idea of the Yiddish-speaking settlemênt in Birobidzhan, which had been established in the late 1920s. It was called the Jewish Autonomous Region and was expected someday to become an autonomous Jewish republic in the Union of Soviet Socialist Republics. Admittedly, Birobidzhan was somewhat out of the way—in the Khabarovsk territory in the Soviet Far East, bordering on Manchuria, but that didn't seem much more remote to us than Palestine with its forbidding deserts inhabited by Bedouins and camels.

Birobidzhan attracted us and others like us because it offered an ideological alternative to Zionism. To me and my Yiddishist friends, Palestine was a far cry from the Yiddish world of Eastern Europe. Besides, Zionism drew upon the beliefs and symbols of Judaism and, given the hostility to Judaism which I had inherited from my father, it was natural that Zionism should be alien to me. Furthermore, in Palestine, the Zionists denigrated Yiddish and demanded that Hebrew alone be the national language of the Palestinian settlement. In those days the Zionists considered Yiddish, which was much more familiar and accessible to most European Jews than Hebrew, as a dangerous competitor to be eliminated. In Birobidzhan, in contrast, we were happy to learn, Yiddish was an official language. There the street signs, postage stamps, and names of railroad stations were printed in Yiddish. It didn't take very long before we discovered that the idea of Birobidzhan as an autonomous Jewish Soviet Republic was a fraud, that it had been conceived as a way to settle that distant vacant territory in the event of a war with China or, in our time, with Japan.

Since I couldn't find a job, except for occasional part-time work at Macy's, my mother thought I should study for a master's degree. That would be a big step toward a teaching career. Somehow she managed to scrape together enough money and I enrolled at Columbia University in September 1936, choosing courses on the art of poetry, the aesthetics of poetry, and the philosophy of art. After two weeks I realized I was wasting my mother's hard-earned money and my own less valuable time. Keats and Wordsworth no longer interested me. I needed a job and this ethereal pursuit of aesthetics wouldn't get me one. I dropped out while I could still get a refund.

Lassitude and depression enveloped me, but instead of giving in to my private miseries, I began to look for a job and absorbed myself in the public sorrows of the European Jews. Every day I read the *New York Times* and, more avidly, the Yiddish newspapers, as I tracked the daily woes and indignities which the European Jews had to endure. Everywhere on the Continent they were beleaguered. Hitler's successes inside Germany and on the diplomatic front encouraged the rise and spread of fascist movements throughout Europe. In Poland, Rumania, and Hungary, in Lithuania and Latvia, right-wing governments had become more aggressive in their anti-Jewish policies, enacting laws to limit the economic and political rights of their Jewish subjects.

The optimism which the promise of a Communist utopia had once generated in me now turned into despair. The Moscow show trials of 1936 had shaken me with their fraudulence. It was near the end of 1936 and I no longer believed that the Soviet Union represented the kind of future I looked forward to. As I watched the political drama unfolding in Europe, it seemed more likely that fascism would be the wave of the future. The struggle for the future had already begun; its testing ground was in Spain. There—so everyone in my generation believed—the prelude to the "final conflict," as the Communist anthem had it, would be played out, prefiguring the Armageddon to come between the right and the left for the control of Europe and then the world.

Like other disillusioned radicals, I was caught in a political bind. Only the Soviet Union was resisting Hitler and Mussolini. The rapidly escalating war in Spain had become a tragic object lesson. In November 1936, soon after I dropped out of Columbia, Germany and Italy recognized the insurgent government under Francisco Franco, who had led the revolt of the generals against the then newly elected leftist Republican government in Spain. The United States, hamstrung by the isolationists, opted for a policy of nonintervention, with Britain and France following suit. Germany and Italy began supplying Franco with planes, tanks, and weapons, and tens of thousands of "volunteers" to defeat the Republic's Loyalist defenders. The only military and financial support reaching Loyalist Spain came from the Soviet Union. In the West, thousands of young men volunteered to fight for the life of the Spanish Republic, enlisting in International Brigades, which were operated by the Communists. A few I knew as YCL members joined the Abraham Lincoln Battalion to fight in Spain.

Because the Soviet Union was defending the Spanish Republic and was involved in the struggle against the Fascists, I believed, as I had in 1933—though now with little enthusiasm and many reservations—that I had no choice but to side with the Soviet Union, however bizarre the Moscow trials, however duplicitous the Communist Party. In my mind, the fate of the Spanish Republic had become coupled with the fate of the Jews. The fall of Spain would presage the fall of the Jews everywhere, once the Nazis and Fascists gained ascendancy throughout Europe. At home and with my Mitlshul friends, we talked ceaselessly and obsessively about the European Jews.

The Jews in Poland were at the center of our preoccupations. In 1936, Poland was an even more degrading place for Jews to live than Hitler's Germany. The 3,300,000 Polish Jews had been forced into poverty and deprived of opportunity by the economic policies of the Polish authorities. Outbreaks of anti-Jewish violence had recently spread across the country, in several places taking on the proportions of full-blown pogroms. It was the way the Polish people showed their support for the government's anti-Semitic policies. The Jews had no political options, outnumbered and isolated as they were in the Polish political arena. Polish government circles had recently seized on an idea first broached by anti-Semitic extremists—that the most effective way to solve Poland's economic problems was to drive the Jews out of Poland. A campaign was launched advocating the "evacuation" of the Jews from Poland. In our Yiddish-English journal *Shrift,* we published articles and editorials, even poetry, condemning Poland. "You shall not drive them out," we shouted into the wind.

Late in October I told Jacob Shatzky that I had abandoned my studies at Columbia, that English literature no longer attracted me. He asked if I'd consider studying Jewish history instead. The idea didn't come as a surprise to me, perhaps because it had been afloat in my subconscious. But I protested that I was academically unprepared. The Mitlshul graduate courses in Jewish history were the only history I had ever studied, besides those high school tariffs and railroads. I would have to start once more from the beginning. Furthermore, it was even more impractical than studying English literature, for in those days, except for the rabbinate, the possibility of a career in Jewish studies was little more than a daydream.

Still, Shatzky's suggestion lodged in my mind. My only useful occupation then was a temporary job at Macy's and I had the luxury of time to brood about my gloomy prospects. It occurred to me that I might connect my English courses with a piece of research on Jews in England. Shatzky even proposed a topic—the Yiddish press in England. My adviser at Columbia approved. Then it first occurred to me that my destiny might lie in history rather than poetry, that my portion was not to be the English Romantic poets, but the European Jews. In February 1937, I reentered Columbia, enrolling in those courses in English literary history and methods of research which the History Department accepted for credit.

Even so, my mind was elsewhere that semester—in Spain, in Germany, in Poland, even at home, where things had come to a crisis and my parents were about to lose that four-family house on which they couldn't pay even the interest on the mortgage. I remember sitting in a classroom in Columbia, hardly hearing the professor drone on about Romantic literature in England as compared to Germany. It was early spring and from the window I could see the pale sunshine and yellow-green of new leaves on the trees. Why was I sitting here? What did Wordsworth matter to me at such a time? But it was too late to get a refund. I stuck it out and got credit for my courses.

In the summer of 1937 my family moved from the house with the unpaid mortgage to the dingy fourth-floor walk-up in the East Bronx. My mother was depressed and I was now saddled with many household responsibilities. There was no talk of continuing my graduate studies. But since I had no full-time job, I planned to use my free time for research on my master's essay.

Besides being depressed by the state of our family fortunes, I was depressed also because my last illusions about the Soviet Union were then unraveling. It turned out that the Soviet Union, instead of being Spain's savior, had been exacting a terrible price for its military aid. Spain had to pay Stalin with its gold reserves. Soviet commissars were fighting their Spanish allies behind the lines more savagely than they fought Franco's forces and Hitler's proxies on the battlefronts. The Russians in charge of the war in Spain and their Spanish puppets were murdering the leaders of the very people they had supposedly come to rescue. They had disarmed the non-Communist Loyalist militias and even bombed non-Communist Loyalist troops. Republican Spain had ceased to exist and was in the process of becoming a Soviet puppet state. George Orwell, who a year earlier had hailed the Spanish Republic and its defenders, now lamented that the Communists had themselves destroyed it.

Those shocking revelations of Moscow's double-dealing in Spain interconnected with the stream of faked confessions which emanated from Moscow's continuing show trials. What rational person could believe the implausible confessions of dedicated Communists who had conceived the revolution, fought for it, and created the socialist state? It strained the imagination to think that they had plotted diabolical conspiracies with their enemies to overthrow the very system they had given their full devotion to. My lingering illusions about the Soviet

Union finally expired. "The Soviet trials have worked wonders," I wrote to a friend about the current wave of defections from the party and disillusion among the party's fellow travelers. We had sobered up from our intoxication with Communist messianism, but we felt little exhilaration at the return to our senses. A line from a poem by John Donne haunted me: " 'Tis all in pieces, all coherence gone." We no longer had faith in sweeping ideological solutions or utopian promises. No other generation had been so beguiled, so gulled, and so betrayed.

Taking Shatzky's advice, I started my research on the Yiddish press of England. I was soon immersed in another world. Besides the Yiddish press in Europe, I began to get acquainted with nineteenth-century English history and to thread my way through the parliamentary and press debates on restricting Jewish immigration into England at the turn of the century. Meanwhile, I had gotten free-lance work with a some-what shady ghost-writing agency that specialized in writing disserta-tions for graduate students with more money than talent. The New York Public Library at 42nd Street became my workplace and my rendezvous.

With increasing frequency I turned to Shatzky for guidance, eager to learn from him the rudiments of historical research. He was patient and encouraging, pleased to have so earnest a disciple. Yet he must have been disappointed at my inexperience; I needed more systematic training than he could give me. One day, late in 1937, he said to me: "You should study Jewish history. You should go to Vilna to study at the Yiddish Scientific Institute."

I already knew what the Yiddish Scientific Institute—YIVO—was. It had been established in 1925 in Vilna, based on an idea originally formulated in Berlin among East European Jewish intellectuals and scholars, refugees from the violence in Eastern Europe following the Bolshevik Revolution. They had proposed establishing a Yiddish acad-emy that would serve as a center for research and study in Yiddish linguistics and literature, Jewish history, social studies, and pedagogy. That idea took hold in Vilna and there it was realized. Vilna, with its unique history as the seat of both traditional and secular Jewish learning, was the ideal place for an institution of higher learning to be conducted in Yiddish.

The YIVO soon won a reputation in the Yiddish world for its high scholarly standards and the merit of its publications. It established branches in France, England, and the United States. (The scholars associated with the YIVO in Berlin had fled in 1933.) In Poland, the YIVO became the authoritative body to which the Yiddish school systems throughout the country looked for guidance in matters of Yiddish orthography, grammar, and style, as well as in the field of pedagogy. In these matters the YIVO had in fact begun to function as an academy, setting standards for the usage of the national language. In 1935, the YIVO inaugurated a new program, called the *aspirantur.* The word *aspirant,* as it was used in Polish and Yiddish, referred to a person in training. It was the equivalent of our "research fellow." The Aspirantur trained aspiring scholars in the methods of research in modern Jewish studies. It was something like an elite graduate school of a nonexistent Yiddish university.

Still, despite what I knew about the YIVO, I laughed at Shatzky's preposterous proposal. The times were unsettled. It was absurd for an American who had studied at Columbia to go to Poland for advanced study. My family had no money to subsidize me. Besides, who wanted to go to Poland? Everyone wanted to run away from there.

Shatzky didn't think his idea was at all preposterous. To begin with, he said that I wouldn't need money, for I'd get a fellowship from the YIVO in Vilna which would support me for a year. The American branch would pay my fare to and from Poland. I was a native American and my American passport would stand me in good stead in case of trouble. He stressed the YIVO's superior scholarly standards and the unique research training that I would get. Then he challenged me. If I were really as interested in the Jews as I claimed to be, I'd realize that I'd be spending a year in a fabled Jewish city, that I'd be exposed to living Jewish history amid the relics of an ancient past. I'd witness Polish anti-Semitism, observe Jewish poverty, live in the world capital of Yiddish. It would be the experience of my lifetime.

When I told my parents about Shatzky's idea, my father responded with his habitual indifference. If I wanted to go, so be it. My mother reacted with her customary seismic intensity. She was certain that I'd be murdered in a pogrom, I'd be trapped by a war. She forbade me to go.

It was not hard to reach a decision. Shatzky had given me two powerful incentives for going—the opportunity to get a unique education and the experience of living in a city layered with Jewish history and studded with Jewish culture. My private agenda was equally compelling. By going to Vilna I would escape from the dead end I was trapped in. I would leave behind the dreariness at home, the difficulty of finding a suitable job, the uncertainty of a career. Even more alluring was the idea that I was about to embark on a great adventure, that I stood at the threshold through which I would cross into an exciting and exotic world. It was easy to decide to go to Vilna.

Early in 1938, after the American branch had approved Shatzky's proposal, I applied to Vilna for admission to the Aspirantur. My mother now looked at things in a different light and she began sewing a wardrobe for me.

Meanwhile, events in Europe continued on their violent course. The threat of war hung in the air. In February Hitler intensified his pressure on Austrian chancellor Kurt von Schuschnigg to legalize the Nazi Party and even to appoint its leaders to his cabinet. But that wasn't enough. Hitler then forced Schuschnigg to resign in favor of a Nazi. Finally, on March 12, the German army invaded Austria and annexed it to Hitler's Reich.

Just a day later, a Polish soldier was killed in a clash with Lithuanian border guards and for a moment it seemed that there might be a war right around Vilna. The Polish-Lithuanian crisis caused a run on the Polish Bank on March 18 and 19 and the Poles, as was their wont, let their frustration out on the Jews. Anti-Jewish violence broke out in Warsaw and other cities. A month later, anti-Jewish riots rocked Vilna. I worried not only about the Jews, but that my journey would be canceled.

At the beginning of May I received official notification from Dr. Max Weinreich, a director of the YIVO in Vilna, that I had been accepted for the academic year beginning September 1938 and that my research topic, "The Yiddish Press in England," had been approved.

By August the several European crises had quieted down, at least for the time being, and on August 10, 1938, I embarked on the Polish liner *Batory,* whose destination was the Polish port of Gdynia. Mine was Vilna and Jewish history.

CHAPTER 2

Vilna: A City of the Past

To an American visitor in 1938, Vilna was definitely not the Paris of the North. Nor was it the Rome of the East, despite its cathedral and its many Catholic churches. Even by Polish standards, Vilna was just a provincial city, its population only about 200,000. It lacked the bustle and tingle of Warsaw, Poland's political and cultural capital. It was wanting in the energy and entrepreneurship that animated Lodz, Poland's industrial metropolis. Nor could it measure up to the aristocratic ancestry and prestige of Cracow, a bishopric since the eleventh century and the residence of the Polish kings long before Vilna ever existed.

Yet Vilna had much to charm and engage an American tourist. It reposed in a bucolic romantic landscape, its center nestling in a narrow valley carved out by its two rivers—the graceful Wilenka River winding around wooded hills just before it entered the larger Wilja, which led to the Baltic Sea and had once been an important waterway. From its center Vilna spread outward in all directions, across both rivers, upon a range of undulating sandy hills affording splendid views to those who lived on their heights. The hilliness of Vilna and its environs earned it the reputation of being a Lithuanian Switzerland. Beyond the city stretched fields spotted with lakes and dense dark forests of pine and fir.

Even more attractive to the American tourist smitten with history were Vilna's medieval relics, visible everywhere in its streets as on its hills. It was a city whose history receded into the mists of time. To me Vilna was the very epitome of the Old World, a storied place with a storied past. Its crooked streets, with their worn cobblestones and their picturesque medieval arches, were the ubiquitous landmarks of Vilna's early origins and of the past's persistence into the present. Before I had embarked on this journey across the Atlantic, I had scarcely traveled anywhere beyond the limits of New York. Once I had gone to Philadelphia to visit a cousin and there I gaped at the crack in the Liberty Bell, the New World's claim to a historic past. Vilna, in contrast, had existed for centuries before anyone had ever imagined a New World.

Legend has it that Vilna was founded early in the fourteenth century by Grand Duke Gedimin, who ruled over the Grand Duchy of Lithuania. While hunting near the site that would become Vilna, he dreamed of a howling wolf with an iron shield. Gedimin's bard interpreted the dream. The wolf and the shield, he said, represented a mighty fortress near which a great city would arise. And so Gedimin built his fortress castle upon the highest hill between the two rivers and he named the city which he established Vilna, after the rivers. This legend of Vilna's founding has been memorialized by Adam Mickiewicz, Poland's greatest poet, in his national epic, *Pan Tadeusz*. Gedimin

> By Wilja's stream and murmuring Wilenka
> Enchanted, of the wolf of iron dreamed;
> And wakening, by the gods' command it seemed,
> Built Vilna city like a wolf that broods
> Mid bears and boars and bison in the woods.

In 1322 Gedimin made Vilna the capital of his Grand Duchy. His fortress castle gave the hill its historic identity. It came to be called Góra Zamkowa, Castle Hill. In 1938, the ruins of Gedimin's ancient castle and the remains of an octagonal tower atop the hill were Vilna's most notable landmark, a place for tourists from far and near, with a park and landscaped paths for outings, walks, and lovers' trysts.

The Lithuanians were a pagan people who had settled in the Baltic area long before the Common Era. During the later Crusades, after the Teutonic Knights had conquered the Estonians and the Latvians and imposed Christianity on them, the Lithuanians, who wished to avoid a similar fate, began to strengthen their positions aggressively by taking their neighbors' territory. Gedimin extended Lithuania's frontiers to the east and south at the expense of Russian principalities and shaped a strong unified state. His son and successor, Olgerd, continued his father's policy and during Olgerd's reign Lithuania stretched from the Baltic all the way to the Black Sea.

In 1386, to ensure the integrity of the Lithuanian empire, Olgerd's son, Grand Duke Jagiello, married Jadwiga, daughter of Louis I of Poland and Hungary, thus uniting Lithuania with the Polish kingdom. Jagiello became Władisław Jagiello, king of Poland, and monarch of one of the great powers that then dominated the European continent. At his marriage, Jagiello at last accepted Christianity and agreed to introduce it into his kingdom. Thus, Vilna, a creation of pagan Lithuania at the start of the fourteenth century, became at the century's end a Polish and a Christian city.

After 1569, when a fully united and integrated Polish-Lithuanian state was created by the Union of Lublin, Polish language and Polish culture soon prevailed over the territory. The Lithuanian aristocracy and the middle class became Polonized. The peasantry, languishing in servitude and illiteracy, eventually ceased to speak Lithuanian and instead took up White Russian as their vernacular. Lithuania lost much of its distinctive identity, becoming little more than an administrative unit, a geographic designation, a name to invoke a particular landscape.

At the end of the eighteenth century, after more than a century of recurrent invasions by the Swedes, Cossacks, Russians, and Prussians, a time of wars and decline, Poland was three times partitioned by its rapacious neighbors—Prussia, Austria, and Russia—first in 1772, and then in 1793 and 1795. Some of Lithuania was incorporated into Prussia, but most of it, including Vilna and its environs, became part of czarist Russia.

In the part of Poland which Russia ruled, the czarist authorities imposed Russian upon the educated classes as the official language and a stern policy of Russification. Chafing under Russian rule and czarist autocracy, perhaps especially in the matter of culture, the population, as everywhere in partitioned Poland, found comfort and strength in their devotion to the Roman Catholic Church and in their Polish national consciousness. They dreamed of a Polish national revival and took part in romantically futile uprisings against Russia, first in 1794, then in 1830–1831 and 1863. The rise of Polish national consciousness might even be attributed to Vilna, for it was Adam Mickiewicz, banished by czarist political police from Vilna in 1823, in his Paris exile along with other émigré Polish patriots, who nurtured the idea of Polish nationalism. After the unsuccessful Polish uprising of 1830–1831, it was he who created the legend of Poland as the martyred Christ among nations, some day to be resurrected.

Still, the Polish language never quite took commanding control in Vilna and the Lithuanian area, no doubt because the ethnic mix of population—Lithuanians, Poles, White Russians, Russians, and Jews—worked to the advantage of the Russifiers.

The First World War and the revolution in Russia brought about the collapse of the czarist empire. At last the Poles could realize their dreams of independence. In 1918 Poland proclaimed itself an independent republic. In 1919 the Treaty of Versailles affirmed Poland's new status and fixed its borders, but gave Vilna to the newly created state of Lithuania.

The idea of an independent Lithuania, according to the wits of the time, was invented by German army officers during the First World War, who wanted to encourage the Lithuanians to assert their independence. That way they hoped to weaken czarist Russia, splinter its empire, and ensure a German military victory. Events didn't work out that way, but the Paris Peace Conference nevertheless carved out a small territory on the Baltic to become an independent Lithuania. It even recognized the Lithuanian claim to Vilna since it had once been Gedimin's capital.

But early in 1919, the Red Army seized Vilna, on the ground that since it had once belonged to czarist Russia, it should now belong to Bolshevik Russia. Three months later, on April 19, 1919, to everyone's astonishment and to the chagrin of the Red Army, Marshal Józef Piłsudski, chief of the newly independent Polish state and commander of its army, captured Vilna and returned it to Poland. The Poles contended that territory which had belonged to Poland before its first partition rightfully still belonged to it in 1919. After another round of fighting against the Bolsheviks in 1920, the Poles succeeded in keeping Vilna for the brief lifetime of their independent republic. When I was in Vilna, I watched a big parade on April 19, 1939, to celebrate Vilna's twentieth anniversary as a Polish city.

On my walks in Vilna, my guides would point out the memorials and monuments to Vilna's past whenever we passed them. To my New World eye, there were many, but given Vilna's long-livedness, there were fewer testimonials to the Polish national past than one might have expected. Vilna's history explained it, for in accordance with the principle that the past belongs to those who own the present, the czars were the ones who decided what and whom the Poles could memorialize. In czarist times Vilna had no monuments to honor their heroes who had taken part in the struggles to liberate Poland from czarist tyranny in the uprisings of 1794, 1830, and 1863. Quite the contrary. The czarist authorities in Vilna had erected a statue of the man who had suppressed the uprising of 1863—Count Michael Nikolayevich Muravyov, nick-named by the Poles as Muravyov the Hangman. (In 1915, when the Russians left Vilna, they took Muravyov's statue with them, as well as monuments they had erected to Catherine the Great and Pushkin.) Then, under German occupation, Vilna's local authorities set out to erase the Russian names from their streets and name them for Polish notables—Adam Mickiewicz, Piłsudski, Chopin, and others.

After Vilna was incorporated into independent Poland, the local authorities began to erect monuments to commemorate the history of the suppressed Polish nationalist past. In January 1920, a large stone with the inscription "1863" was set in the ground on Piłsudskiego Square, where it was planned to erect a "Memorial to Liberation" to honor the patriots who had fallen in the failed uprising of January 1863, but the Poles never got around to it. Nor did they ever put up a monument to Mickiewicz. In May 1939, when I was there, the Vilna City Council voted to erect such a monument. Though the municipality was strapped for money, they authorized a budget of 1,336,826 zlotys for it. But they never had time to start on it.

On April 19, 1922, on the third anniversary of Piłsudski's seizure of Vilna from the Red Army, the Vilna city authorities set a tablet into the wall of the Vilna railroad station: "In remembrance of the liberation of Vilna from the Bolsheviks on April 19, 1919." The Bolsheviks retook Vilna in 1939; I suppose that they removed the tablet and erased the event from history.

In my sightseeing, I found all sorts of remembrances of Polish history in tablets, statues, and monuments. Though Piłsudski's body was buried in Wawel Castle in Cracow, his heart was interred, in accordance with his wishes, in the Piłsudski Mausoleum in the Vilna military cemetery. There, encased in a silver urn, it was set at the foot of the casket containing his mother's bones. The crypt was something of a national shrine.

Vilna's university, founded in 1578, was named after Poland's king Stefan Batory. Tablets marked the places where Polish heroes, poets, composers, scholars, and other men of achievement had lived and worked. On Napoleon Place, on the exterior of a grand building which had once been the bishops' residence, later the property of the czars, and finally of the Polish government, the Vilna city fathers in 1921 installed a marble tablet to commemorate a presence whom the czars had not highly valued:

Here resided

NAPOLEON

28. VI–16. VII

MDCCCXII

(On his retreat from Moscow, Napoleon stopped in Vilna on November 23, 1812, but then he stayed only twenty minutes.)

Though Vilna's political history was seldom evident in its monuments, Vilna's history as a Catholic city was faithfully preserved through the centuries. In 1938, the commanding presence of the Catholic Church was everywhere visible, audible, palpable. The spires, gables, belfries, crowned towers, and crosses of the churches dotted the horizon. They could be seen on the hills, from the riverbanks, and in the dense web of the streets. The sounds of chiming and pealing church bells seemed always to fill the air.

The most conspicuous symbol of Vilna as a Catholic city was Trzy Krzyże, the Hill of the Three Crosses, on the far side of Góra Zamkowa. Atop this hill stood a monument of three white crosses, made of concrete and iron. In the sunlight their whiteness against a blue sky was dazzling. At night the illuminated crosses shed an eerie luminescence on the dark sky. According to legend, Olgerd had put seven Franciscan monks to death here. Jagiello, after he became a Christian, erected three crosses as a monument to their martyrdom. Half a millennium later, in 1864, Muravyov the Hangman, representing the authority of the czar's Orthodox Church, ordered the crosses torn down. But in 1916, after the Russians had left Vilna, the local authorities erected a new monument to restore this symbol of Vilna's Catholicism. The Soviets, in the tradition of their czarist forebears, have—so I've heard—removed the three crosses.

Vilna emerged as a Christian city literally out of the ashes of Lithuanian paganism. Shortly after Grand Duke Jagiello had become king of Poland and had been baptized a Christian, the whole Lithuanian people, the last heathen holdouts of Europe, adopted Christianity. From the descriptions that have been handed down to us, the ceremony, held in Vilna on February 17, 1387, must have been impressive. A procession of nobles and prelates, led by King Władisław Jagiello and his brother Skirgiello, the new Grand Duke of Lithuania, entered an ancient grove of oaks, the deities of Lithuanian pagan worship. There Władisław himself chopped down the trees, destroyed the idols, and triumphantly raised the cross over the heathen altars.

It's said that on that very site, facing Góra Zamkowa, in that very year, 1387, Jagiello built a cathedral made of timber. After a fire early in the fifteenth century, it was rebuilt in stone in the prevailing Gothic style. Many reconstructions followed, as Vilna was ravaged by fires and wars through the centuries. In 1801 it was restored, but quite altered, its earlier facade of lancet windows replaced by an imposing colonnade in Classic Revival style. The original Gothic spires atop the pediment were supplanted by three lofty Renaissance-like sculptures—the figure of Queen Helena, at the top, bearing a tall cross, flanked on either side by statues of Casimir and Stanislaus, early kings of Poland who were later beatified. (The Soviets have since removed those sculptures.) What impressed me most about the Cathedral was its art—splendid paintings of the Twelve Disciples and a series of oils of Christ's progress. Like most secular New York Jews in those days, I regarded cathedrals as museums and concert halls rather than as places of worship. In New York, my friends and I, Bach aficionados, used to go to St. Patrick's Cathedral on Christmas Eve to listen to the mass.

The Cathedral of Vilna was just one of about twenty-five Catholic churches and chapels in the city. It was outclassed in architectural beauty by the Church of St. Anne, whose original timber structure was said to have been nearly as old as the Cathedral. St. Anne was rebuilt in stone in the sixteenth century in French-Flemish Gothic style and preserved that way in later restorations. Slender, tall, exquisitely graceful, it resembled Paris's Sainte-Chapelle. No wonder that Napoleon was said to have wanted to take it back to Paris.

Most of Vilna's Catholic churches were a riot of baroque. Their architecture and art were testimonies to the influence of the Jesuits in Vilna since 1565, when a Polish-Lithuanian chapter had been established to halt the spread of Protestantism. Like earlier Christian orders, the Jesuits emphasized the function of preaching in their churches, but, unlike the mendicant orders, they wanted their houses of worship to project the splendor and glory of the Church in Rome. They employed the most gifted Italian architects and artists of the time to carry out their grand conceptions. As the Society of Jesus expanded and spread across Europe, its Roman headquarters supervised the design of the churches in places even as distant as Vilna, thus introducing into northern Poland the art and architecture of the Italian *cinquecento*.

The bishop of Vilna, who had invited the Jesuits to his city, gave them a gift of the Church of St. John, erected early in the fifteenth century. Thereafter, St. John's was many times rebuilt. Its original Gothic plan was retained, but its facade was redesigned and a new gable added. The church was transformed into a baroque structure of lightness and grace. Other notable early baroque churches were the Jesuit St. Casimir, built at the start of the seventeenth century, and St. Ignatius, erected two decades later. In Antokol, an outlying area of Vilna, the Church of Peter and Paul, built in 1668, whose modest exterior belied the splendor of its Italian-Polish baroque interior, boasted no fewer than 2,000 elegantly carved figures. When I went sightseeing there, my guide described each one in unbearably tedious detail.

The University of Vilna began as a Jesuit creation, adjoining St. John's, when, in 1570, the Jesuits established the St. John Collegium as an institution of Catholic learning, to help them solidify their triumph over Protestantism. In 1578 King Stefan Batory, who often visited Vilna, elevated the school to the status of an academy and in the following years, as it thrived, a complex of buildings constructed around three courts was erected. Two centuries later, after the first partition of Poland, the Russian regime reorganized the academy and reopened it in 1803 as the University of Vilna. It continued to expand and eventually comprised a network of buildings grouped around ten courts, elegantly designed and beautifully landscaped.

The interior courtyards, when I saw them in 1938, enclosed by three-story arcaded buildings and planted with trees and flowerbeds, were oases of serenity and elegance. But the serenity resided only in the architecture and the gardening. For the University of Vilna in 1938 was still what it had been in its earliest days as a Jesuit seminary—a hotbed of anti-Semitic hooliganism and the spearhead of anti-Jewish violence in Vilna. It had changed little in 1938 in this regard, though it had expanded academically beyond its original faculty of theology, offering degrees in law, medicine, mathematics and science, humanities, and fine arts.

The most commanding Catholic presence in Vilna's everyday life was the Ostra Brama, the Pointed Arch. The only surviving tower of nine which had been part of the original city rampart built early in the sixteenth century, Ostra Brama, with its arched passageway, had once been the gateway to Vilna and the site of battles for its defense. Later on, in the customary evolution of medieval towns, the entryway to the city became its major market site, the first place where the procession of wagons stopped to unload the food brought from the nearby countryside.

In the 1670s the Carmelites built a chapel over this arched passageway. On a recessed balcony over the archway, they displayed a stunning gold image of the Madonna, probably of Byzantine origin, which became known as Our Lady of Ostra Brama or the Virgin of Vilna. This shrine soon attracted pilgrims from all over Poland. The marketplace was moved elsewhere and traffic was diverted to other streets. When I was in Vilna, the image was unveiled only during the hourly masses held in the mornings and evenings. At those times, kneeling worshippers lined the narrow sidewalks and cobbled street. No vehicular traffic was permitted and pedestrians were cautioned to respect a tradition which had once been enforced as law—to remove their hats. If the far pavement was not occupied by worshippers at their prayers, you could walk past, advisedly on tiptoe. But if the throng was dense, you just had to wait until the service was over. A reverential hush always enveloped the place.

About sixty percent of Vilna's population were Catholic—Poles and Lithuanians. Barely 5 percent, White Russians and Russians, belonged to the Orthodox Church. Their chief place of worship was the Romanov Church, on ulica Wielka Pohulanka, atop Pohulanka Hill. It was built in 1913 to commemorate the 300th anniversary of the Romanov dynasty. Its four golden onion domes added a touch of flamboyance to the Vilna horizon. There was also an older Orthodox church in the center of town, on the original site of the first Orthodox church in Vilna, where Peter the Great was said to have worshipped and, in later times, Czar Alexander II, when he came on official visits. Vilna also had two Protestant churches—one Lutheran, one Calvinist—but they were altogether obscured by the massive Catholic presence.

The massive Catholic presence in Vilna did not, however, obscure the conspicuous and distinctive Jewish presence which gave the city its particular character and its uniqueness. After the Poles, the Jews were the largest ethnic and religious group in Vilna—60,000, making up nearly 30 percent of the population. To be sure, the space which the Jews occupied in Vilna's history had never been as extensive as that of the Catholics, nor could the Jews boast anything comparable to the impressive architectural monuments which were the legacy of the Church and the nobility. Yet the Jewish presence was as palpable as any architectural relic and as audible as the Catholic church bells. The Jewish quarter and its antiquities were part of the tourist route, along with Góra Zamkowa, St. Anne's, and the University. The sound of Yiddish resonated throughout the city. According to official Vilna statistics of December 1933, nearly 50,000 people in Vilna, about 85 percent of all the Jews and a quarter of the city's population, gave Yiddish as their mother tongue. You heard Yiddish in the streets, the shops, and the marketplaces. (Those who gave Russian, Lithuanian, White Russian, or German as their mother tongue accounted for less than 10 percent of Vilna's population.) You could live a full life in Vilna for a year, as I did, or even a lifetime, as many Vilna Jews did, speaking only Yiddish, without knowing much Polish or knowing it well.

The Vilna Jews had even given Vilna's streets Yiddish names, mostly translations from the Polish. Góra Zamkowa, Castle Hill, was called *shlos barg,* the Yiddish equivalent. Ulica Wileńska, Vilna Street, was called *vilner gas;* ulica Wielka, "broad" in Polish, was *breyte gas.* A few streets had Yiddish names which were quite different from the Polish ones. For example, Św. Mikołaja (St. Nicholas), just an alley in the heart of the Jewish quarter, was called *gitke toybe's zavulek,* "alley of Gitka Toba," named for the widow of a wealthy Lithuanian Jew, who early in the nineteenth century had held the lease on property there.

In pursuit of a Jewish past beyond the limits of my immigrant parents' experience, I found a rich historical landscape in Vilna, where the Jews had lived for over half a millennium. Vilna's streets and buildings were emanations of the past, visible evidence that the past continued to exist in the present. Except for the house I lived in, which had just been built, every place in Vilna had been touched by a historical spirit. The cobblestones had been traversed by the carriages of the world's notables and trodden by the advancing and retreating hosts of many European nations. Every place had its history, even if I didn't always know it at the time.

Napoleon was reputed to have exclaimed on seeing the Great Synagogue that Vilna was "the Jerusalem of Lithuania." Vilna had been the residence of the Vilna Gaon, one of Jewry's great moral and scholarly figures. Here Israel Salanter, the founder of the *musar* movement, which stressed the moral-ethical dimension in Judaism, established his own yeshiva. Here Sir Moses Montefiore, the great English philanthropist, came in 1846, having visited the czar in St. Petersburg on a mission to improve the condition of the Jews. Since the eighteenth century, Vilna was the seat of the world-renowned Romm Press, printers of the Talmud, the Bible, and rabbinical works.

Here Abraham Mapu, the creator of the modern Hebrew novel, lived, and also Kalman Schulman, whose Hebrew translation of Eugene Sue's *Les Mystères de Paris* became a best-seller. Here Judah Loeb Gordon, the nineteenth century's outstanding Hebrew poet and critic, was born. Here Isaac Meir Dick, the first popular Yiddish novelist, lived all his life, writing over 300 stories and novels, some of which, in weekly pamphlets published by the Romm Press, sold nearly 100,000 copies. Here Sholom Aleichem, I. L. Peretz, and Mendele Mocher Sforim, the founding fathers of Yiddish literature, came to pay homage to the capital of the realm of Yiddish. Hebrew and Yiddish poets enshrined Vilna in their writings.

Vilna was the cradle of the Jewish labor movement and of the Jewish Labor Bund. Here in 1902, the shoemaker, Hirsh Lekert, after a failed attempt to assassinate Vilna's governor general Von Wahl for his repressive policies, was hanged. Here the early societies of the Lovers of Zion flourished. Here in 1903, on a mission to czarist officials after the Kishenev pogrom, Theodor Herzl received a tumultuous welcome, being hailed in the streets as "the king of the Jews." Here Nahum Sokolow, president of the World Zionist Organization, and Vladimir Jabotinsky, founder of the Jewish Legion and of the Zionist-Revisionist movement, were welcomed when they came, each to further his particular Zionist cause. Vilna was centuries deep in Jewish history.

The history of Jews in Vilna was almost as old as Vilna itself, but few historical relics survived to testify to that antiquity. A Jewish community was believed to have existed in the days of Gedimin and Olgerd, but the extant records showed only the presence of individual Jews in that distant time. Jews more likely began to migrate in larger numbers to Vilna in the fifteenth century, in the reign of Władisław Jagiello, when he merged the Grand Duchy of Lithuania with the Polish kingdom, where Jews were already settled.

Jews had come to Vilna as merchants and traders and those who thought they could prosper stayed there. In 1440, so tradition has it, they already had a place where they prayed and studied. Later it came to be called *di alte kloyz* or *kloyz yoshen,* "the old prayerhouse." Nearly half a millennium later, in 1938, while sightseeing in the Jewish quarter, I saw an inscription "1440" over the doorway in that somewhat run-down synagogue with its pillars and vaulted roof. It was said to be the oldest Jewish building to have survived in Vilna, but it had obviously been reconstructed many times. Skeptics questioned the authenticity of the inscription, but in 1939 the Jewish community was already making plans to mark the *alte kloyz*'s 500th anniversary the following year.

From 1440 to 1793, when Vilna was ceded to czarist Russia in Poland's second partition, the Jews continuously struggled to maintain themselves economically and legally. Their history was marked by a recurrent pattern in which a period of Christian tolerance gave way to an eruption of animosity and violence. The anti-Semitism of the Vilna townspeople was sparked sometimes by the priests and the Jesuits, some-times by the guildsmen and merchants who resented the Jews' economic competition and their success. The Jews usually turned for protection to the king or to regional authorities, petitioning them to revalidate their rights to live and work and trade in peace in Vilna.

In 1527 Jews were forbidden to reside in Vilna, but in 1551, King Sigismund II Augustus reversed that decree and by 1568 a full-fledged Jewish community was already in existence, for, according to the rec-ords, the Jewish community was ordered to pay poll taxes to the royal treasury.

Sigismund II's death in 1572 brought an end to the rule of the Jagiellonian dynasty in Poland. Though the ensuing search for a succes-sor led far afield, it had direct consequences for the Vilna Jews. Various foreign princes competed for the Polish throne in a complex electoral campaign. Prince Henry of Valois, duke of Anjou and brother of the king of France, accepted the nomination at that time. Powerful members of the Polish gentry who belonged to the Orthodox Church objected, fearing that they would be persecuted under a French Catholic ruler. Those fears were not unwarranted, for at just that time—August 24, 1572—Henry's mother, Catherine de' Medici, had ordered the St. Bar-tholomew Massacre, in which, in a matter of a few days, 30,000 French Huguenots were murdered.

To put the gentry's fears to rest and to ensure Henry's election to the Polish throne, the Warsaw Confederation, representing all the parties to the electoral Diet, on May 3, 1573, adopted safeguards to ensure religious freedom for all non-Catholics, specifically citing the rights of

"Turks, Armenians, Tatars, Greeks, and Jews." And so, in that very year, non-Catholics—Calvinists, Uniates, as well as members of the Orthodox Church—began to build houses of worship throughout the Polish kingdom, seizing the opportunity given to them for the unhindered practice of their religion.

The Vilna Jews also took advantage of those guarantees. Having presumably outgrown the *alte kloyz,* they purchased a wooden building from a wealthy Pole on a street where many Jews lived and converted it into a synagogue. Nearby they built a bathhouse, a ritual bath (*mikveh*), and a slaughterhouse. They had already long had a cemetery on the far side of the Wilja. Within a few years, the street which led into the courtyard housing the synagogue came to be called ulica Żydowska—Jewish Street. Jews called it *yidishe gas.* It became the heart of the Jewish quarter in Vilna.

Sixty years later, in February 1633, shortly after a violent anti-Semitic outbreak, the Jews once again appealed to the king. This time they received a new charter confirming rights previously given them and granting new ones affecting work and trade. They were now permitted to engage in all crafts not under the jurisdiction of the exclusively Christian guilds, to operate retail and wholesale shops, and to sell a wide variety of goods.

The number of Jews in Vilna had meanwhile been growing and it's believed that there were some 2,000 at that time, about a fifth of Vilna's population. Perhaps because of the expansion of the Jewish community, the charter restricted the area where Jews were permitted to live to a small triangle consisting of only three streets: both sides of Żydowska; both sides of its continuation—Św. Mikołaja and ulica Jatkowa ("butcher-shop street")—but only on the side adjoining Żydowska; and ulica Niemiecka, which formed the third side of the triangle, where Jews were allowed to buy and build only such houses whose windows and entries did not open out on the street but faced rearward toward the Jewish streets.

The charter set a deadline of fifteen years for the Jews to relinquish their residential property outside that area and for Christians to move out of the Jewish district. But twelve years later, Christians still owned about one-third of the houses in the Jewish area and Jews still owned a considerable number of houses elsewhere in Vilna and lived in them. New regulations to restrict Jewish residence never managed to be enforced and eventually the question of a restricted quarter—or a ghetto—faded away. Never had there been a walled ghetto in Vilna's history or gates that were locked at night. The picturesque arches over two streets in Vilna's Jewish quarter were not, as has often been supposed, remnants of a ghetto wall. They were only architectural devices to brace the facing two- and three-story buildings on the narrow streets.

That same year, 1633, the king gave the Jews permission to build a masonry synagogue, stipulating that it should not be taller than other buildings in the vicinity and should not look like a church or a monastery. At that time, ecclesiastical regulations all through Europe specified that a synagogue could not be built higher than a church. To obey the law and yet create the necessary interior height, it was customary to dig a foundation deep enough for the synagogue's floor level to be well below that of the street. That's how the Vilna synagogue, later known as the Town Synagogue or the Great Synagogue, was built.

It was erected, at right angles adjoining the *alte kloyz,* presumably on the site of the wooden building that had served as a synagogue since 1573. That area later became known as the *shulhoyf* (synagogue courtyard), a warren of densely packed prayerhouses and places of religious study. The Great Synagogue had two entrances. One, at street level, consisted of a pair of iron gates which, when I was there, still bore the original inscription that they were donated by a tailors' society in 1640. The other entrance, a bit more imposing, was an elevated gabled portal with wrought-iron posts. The heavy iron door also had its original Hebrew inscription indicating it was a gift of a society of Psalm reciters in 1642. Between both entrances, recessed in an oval niche in the exterior wall, was a gracefully shaped stone basin, with iron embellishments and an attractive iron grille. Perhaps it had once been a decorative fountain, but in 1938 it was not functioning.

The synagogue's vestibule, which had originally been a pillory, led to a downward flight of steps, from which I caught my first glimpse of the synagogue's interior. It took my breath away, for I had never expected it to be so grand. Outside, the synagogue looked to be about three stories tall, but inside it soared to over five stories. Approximately seventy-five by seventy feet, this lofty rectangular shell was supported by four enormous Tuscan pillars, which divided the vaulting space into nine bays. The bimah—a platform holding the reading table on which the Torah scrolls are placed—stood between two pillars in the center of the synagogue. It was an elaborate elevated structure with eight small columns holding up a canopy. On the east wall facing the bimah was the intricately carved ark, which was reached by a pair of stairs—for ascending and descending—with iron balustrades. Rows of pews and their reading desks stretched the length and breadth of the synagogue. Behind grated windows high up on the wall was a women's gallery. In 1938, on the High Holy Days and other special occasions, the synagogue held about 5,000 worshippers.

To be sure, the synagogue that I saw in 1938 was not exactly like the one to which the tailors' and Psalm readers' societies had donated their gates and door in the 1640s or the same one Napoleon contemplated with awe, though surely the shell and its massive columns had remained intact through the centuries. Like the rest of the Jewish quarter, like Vilna's churches, and like much of the city, the Great Synagogue had been ravaged time and again in the course of three centuries by wars and fires. It was always being repaired or rebuilt. The paneled decorations that I saw, the sumptuous ark and bimah, the chandeliers, the pews and desks, the upstairs women's gallery were all later additions.

The Vilna Jews were not destined to enjoy either the expanded privileges they had won in 1633 or their new synagogue. Whatever hardships they continued to endure from the local townspeople faded before the disasters soon to be visited upon them—the massive influx of Jewish refugees from the massacres in the Ukraine in 1648–1649, followed by the Cossack and Russian invasion of Vilna in 1655. Most Jews then fled their homes and those who stayed were murdered. The Jewish quarter suffered grave losses in the great fire set by the Cossacks.

Finally, in March 1661, the Polish army recaptured Vilna and soon thereafter the Jews returned to rebuild their devastated homes and institutions. But the ruinous war had exacerbated endemic Polish anti-Semitism and the Jews faced renewed difficulties in trying to restore their economic positions. As the king's authority waned, tensions mounted between the royal government, which protected the Jews, and the municipalities, which defended the guilds and the town merchants.

The Jesuits, meanwhile, caught up in late Counter-Reformation fever, agitated unremittingly against the Jews. The students at the Jesuit academy, inflamed by their teachers' incitement, would attack the Jewish quarter, no doubt enjoying such a lively diversion from their theological studies in the serene precincts of the academy. The Jews used to refer to this student pastime as *shiler-geloyf*—student rampage. In March 1687, the Jesuit students spearheaded an assault on ulica Żydowska, breaking into homes and stores, killing and injuring many Jews, stealing and vandalizing Jewish property.

In the eighteenth century conditions did not improve. After the disasters of the Northern War and the consequent famine and plague, the Vilna Jews continued to be embroiled in disputes and litigation with the Vilna guilds, merchants, and municipal officials about their rights to do business and even their rights of residence. Finally, in 1783, the royal court ruled in favor of the Jews, confirming their rights of residence and rights to work and trade. But that victory was short-lived. Just a decade later Vilna was ceded to Russia in the second of the Polish partitions. Vilna's 3,600 Jews had now become subjects of the czars.

History had not given Vilna Jews cause to welcome Russian rule. On the other hand, they didn't have much affection for the townspeople among whom they lived. But they were devoted to Poland's royal government, which had, more often than not, protected them against the local authorities and the local population. It was natural, then, that when Thaddeus Kościuszko, a Polish general who had fought on the side of the Americans during the American Revolution, rallied the Poles in 1794 to rise up against the Russians and Prussians to regain their independence, the Vilna Jews supported his cause with money, supplies, and volunteers for his army. But Kościuszko was soon defeated. The uprising's failure hastened Poland's decline and a year later Poland was swallowed up by its neighbors in a third partition.

Meantime, since the seventeenth century, Vilna had become renowned among Jews as a place that attracted famous rabbinical scholars from Bohemia and the German lands farther west. By dint of that status and prestige, the Vilna Jewish community gradually assumed the leadership of all the communities then organized in the Council of the Land of Lithuania (*Vaad medinat lita*), an institution of Jewish self-government which oversaw the Jewish communities of the Grand Duchy of Lithuania within the Polish kingdom. (The *Vaad* ceased to function shortly before Poland was partitioned and thereafter Jewish communal institutions—Kahal and later the Kehillah—were subject to the state's jurisdiction.)

It was Elijah ben Solomon Zalmen (1720–1797), known as Elijah Gaon or simply as the Vilna Gaon, who above all gave Vilna its reputation as the fortress of rabbinic Judaism, the bastion for the study of Torah and especially *halakha,* Jewish law. Even in his own day, he became a legendary figure, the embodiment of intellect, rationality, and scholarship, described later as "the last great theologian of classical Rabbinism." His hardheadedness in intellectual matters reflected his toughness of will, which some called his obduracy.

He was not only a master of the Torah. He also studied Hebrew grammar, astronomy, geography, algebra, and geometry, and encouraged others to do the same and even to translate such worldly scientific books into Hebrew, for he believed that this knowledge would enhance one's understanding of the Talmud. At the age of twenty-five, some years after his marriage, he settled in Vilna. Though he lived a secluded life of study and never held any official position in the community, his reputation for learning and strict observance of Judaism spread rapidly and soon elevated him to the *de facto* spiritual leadership not just of the Jewish community in Vilna, but of all the Jewish communities of Lithuania and Russia. In 1800, in posthumous tribute to him, the Vilna Jewish community erected a synagogue on the site where the Gaon used to live. Called the Gaon's *kloyz,* "the Gaon's prayerhouse," it was the first building as one entered the *shulhoyf.* There, on October 13, 1938, the 141st anniversary of the Gaon's death was commemorated, as it was every year since his death. Talmudists, rabbinic scholars, and pious Jews assembled to hear learned talks and eulogies of the Gaon. His spirit was still alive when I was there.

The Gaon's fame was in no small measure attributable also to his relentless struggle against hasidism, which he feared would undermine the rabbinic foundations of Judaism and divide the Jewish people. Hasidism, a pietistic movement which originated among Jews in the Ukraine early in the eighteenth century, held that if a Jew worshipped God with sufficient enthusiasm and sincerity, he could attain the world to come, even if he didn't study Torah. Still more heretical was the hasidic reliance upon the charismatic and miracle-working *rebbe,* who functioned as intermediary between his followers and God. This movement spread with phenomenal success westward and southward into Poland and northward toward Russia, but it stumbled in Lithuania, where the Vilna Gaon saw to it that the standards for Talmudic study remained high and unbreached.

In the Gaon's lifetime, only two hasidic sects secured a foothold in Vilna. One consisted of the followers of the *rebbe* of Karlin, the first hasidic dynasty in Lithuania; the other belonged to the Lubavitcher, which had originated in White Russia. Even after the death of the Vilna Gaon, the hasidim did not make much headway in Vilna. More than 150 years later, in 1938, a bare handful of hasidic prayerhouses existed there, among them one belonging to the Koidonover sect, an offshoot of Karlin, and another to the Lubavitcher. In this regard, nothing much had changed: The hasidic sects in 1938 were, like their predecessors in 1772, marginal to Vilna's religious establishment.

The Vilna Gaon succeeded in keeping the heresy of hasidism at bay in Vilna. However, his advocacy of scientific knowledge created in Jewish Vilna a congenial climate not only for advanced rabbinical studies, but even more for the pursuit of secular studies, thus paving the way for the heresy of modernity. It was not long before the Haskalah, the movement to modernize the Jewish community through "enlightenment," that is, secular education, whose ideas and major texts were imported first from Moses Mendelssohn in Berlin and then from Jewish scholars in Galicia, became entrenched in Vilna. A whole generation of maskilim, "enlighteners"—Hebrew writers, scholars, and teachers— emerged in Vilna to propagate their goal of "light and education."

Matthias Strashun (1817–1885), for example, a native of Vilna, studied under a leading maskil and also in the yeshiva of Volozhin. His scholarly knowledge won him high regard in learned Jewish circles throughout Eastern Europe. The czarist authorities thought well of him, too—Strashun was appointed to the Vilna City Council and also invited to serve as an adviser to the Russian Imperial Bank. He was an ardent bibliophile and, having married into a wealthy family, he could afford to indulge his hobby. He accumulated a magnificent collection of about 7,000 volumes which he bequeathed to the Vilna Jewish community. That collection, known as the Strashun Library, became one of Jewish Vilna's famous landmarks. It was housed in a building in the *shulhoyf* adjoining the Great Synagogue.

Another maskil, Samuel Joseph Fuenn (1818–1890), a native of Vilna, was a wealthy businessman who devoted himself to Jewish communal, educational, and literary work. He was the founder of the first modern Jewish school in Vilna, the first Hebrew literary journal, and the first Hebrew weekly to appear in Russia. A scholar and a prolific writer in Hebrew and in Russian, he produced a history of Vilna in Hebrew.

Streets in Vilna's Jewish sections were named for those three—the Gaon, Strashun, and Fuenn—honoring the two traditions for which Vilna was justly famous, Talmudic learning and the Haskalah. They all represented that mentality which embodied the archetype of the *litvak,* the Lithuanian Jew.

It was natural that the Jews in the Lithuanian region should have developed characteristics which differentiated them from Jews elsewhere in the Polish kingdom. For instance, the distinctive dialect of their Yiddish speech immediately identified them, for they pronounced the diphthong *oy* as *ey* and they sibilated every *sh* into an *s.* Their food patterns, too, gave them a regional identity. Lithuanian Jews were notorious for peppering their gefilte fish instead of sugaring it, as the

Polish Jews did. Lithuanian Jews also fashioned a temperamental typol-
ogy, which the Vilna Jews embodied *par excellence.* The characteristics
of the *litvak* were reputed to be dryness and lack of emotionality,
coupled with mental quickness and a certain sharpness or pepperiness,
like their gefilte fish. It's quite likely that the attribution of these traits
to the Lithuanian Jews had its origin in Vilna's anti-hasidic history. In
Yiddish one says, *"a litvak hot a tseylem in kop"* ("a *litvak* has a crucifix
in his head")—that is, the *litvak* is something of a skeptic, even a bit
of a heretic. Perhaps the expression originated with the Polish Jews who
didn't think Lithuanian rationality was a virtue; perhaps it derived from
the hasidim who wanted to give the rationalists a bad name.

Under czarist rule, the Vilna Jews suffered the same civil and economic
disabilities which Jews everywhere in Russia had to endure. Nicholas
I (1825–1855) taxed the Jews exorbitantly and restricted their places of
residence. Driven by hatred of the Jews and a powerful ambition to
convert them, he subjected them to enormous pressure to abandon their
traditional garb and modernize the *heder* and yeshiva. In 1847 czarist
educational authorities established a rabbinical seminary in Vilna,
largely staffed by maskilim, to turn out Russian-speaking rabbis who
could represent the local Jewish communities in their relations with the
czarist regime.

Nicholas I's cruelest policy—the conscription law of 1827—was his
primary means of forcing the Jews to convert. Each Jewish community
had to provide a disproportionately large quota of recruits for the czar's
army to serve for a period of twenty-five years. Even crueler was the
policy of juvenile conscription, whereby children from the age of
twelve were forced to join preparatory army units where, under constant pressure to accept baptism, they stayed until they became eighteen.
Then they began to serve their twenty-five-year period. Kahal, the
executive arm of the Jewish community, was empowered to obtain the
recruits and its agents often did so by violent means, by kidnapping
children to fill the community's quota.

In a maneuver to help the young avoid conscription, yeshivot
sprouted everywhere and the enrolled students hoped that Kahal would
appreciate their Talmudic zeal. Such a yeshiva was established in Vilna
in 1831. It was called Ramayles' Yeshiva, after the courtyard and the
little lane off ulica Żydowska in which it was first housed. During the
height of the conscription panic, it had the largest enrollment of any
yeshiva in Vilna, some 200 students, most of them from other towns

and cities. Around the turn of the century the original building collapsed and shortly thereafter, thanks to a munificent bequest from a devout Jew, a massive three-story building was erected outside the Jewish quarter at the extravagant cost of 50,000 rubles. When I was in Vilna, it was still functioning and received a modest subsidy from the Kehillah.

During the 1840s, the Vilna maskilim, perhaps under the modernizing influences of German Jewry, but more likely because of the tensions between them and the traditionalists, formed their own congregation, Taharath Ha-Kodesh. It was called the Choir Synagogue, because one of its innovations was a boys' choir. Rumor had it that Kahal conscripted those choirboys for the czar's army, as the revenge of the traditionalists against the maskilic reformers. In time, Taharath Ha-Kodesh became the place where Vilna's upwardly mobile Jews attended services and the synagogue's officers wore top hats. In 1903 the congregation built an elaborate Moorish-style synagogue a few blocks away from the Jewish quarter.

Even under Nicholas I's harsh rule, the Jewish population of Vilna increased, partly because of a growth in births, but mostly because Jews banned from living in the surrounding villages flocked into Vilna. By the late 1830s the number of Jews in Vilna had grown to over 20,000, about half of the city's population.

In 1855 Alexander II succeeded to the throne and conditions improved gradually everywhere in Russia, and especially for the Jews. In Vilna, as elsewhere, Jews now enjoyed greater economic and educational opportunities. Still, the government persisted in its efforts to modernize traditional Jewish education. In 1873 the authorities shut down the government-sponsored rabbinical seminary in Vilna and turned it into a teachers' seminary, relocating it in a handsome three-story building quite a distance from the Jewish quarter, in a quiet dead-end square off Vilna's most elegant street. (The building was paid for out of monies collected from the Jews by the Ministry of Education and became the headquarters of the Vilna Kehillah after the First World War. Eventually it also became the Kehillah's property, because the courts ruled that it had originally been purchased with Jewish money.) The teachers' seminary soon became the seedbed of revolutionary conspiratorial activities among young Jews who had traveled the devious route from traditional Judaism, by way of the Haskalah, first to secularism, then to disbelief, and finally to radicalism. They had done away with God and were getting ready to do away with the czar.

In 1881, populist revolutionaries assassinated Alexander II. Alexander III, his son, succeeded him and it's widely believed that his advisers had instigated the wave of pogroms that swept the czarist empire, bringing havoc and desolation to the Jews. The pogroms were followed by years of repressive anti-Semitic policies intended to deny Jews the means of livelihood. The pogroms and those policies set in motion a mass migration between 1881 and 1914 when Jews in unprecedented numbers left Russia, among them Jews from Vilna as well.

Vilna was spared a pogrom, but its Jews suffered sporadic outbreaks of anti-Semitic violence on the part of the local townspeople as well as the economic hardships imposed by czarist policies. In 1894, after Alexander III's death, his son Nicholas II became czar and continued his father's harsh policies. Except for the interlude of political liberty in the wake of the short-lived revolution of 1905, the czarist authorities continued on their reactionary and anti-Semitic course until the First World War. Even so, the Jewish birthrate continued to rise and, despite the considerable emigration, the number of Jews in Vilna in 1897 increased to over 63,000, nearly half the city's population.

The First World War brought fresh hardships to the Vilna Jews. Thousands fled the city. Those who remained endured a succession of nine different occupations, as the war front rolled back and forth. Each occupier requisitioned Jewish property and conscripted Jews as forced laborers. Hunger was rampant everywhere. Nevertheless, following the Bolshevik Revolution and the civil war in Russia, with their accompanying terrible pogroms, thousands of Jewish refugees crowded into Vilna, straining the resources of the already overburdened Jewish community.

On April 21, 1919, two days after the Polish Legion had seized Vilna from the Bolsheviks, the Legionnaires began a rampage against the Jews, beating, torturing, killing them. Despite international protests, the pillaging and killing continued for months. In July President Wilson sent a Commission of Inquiry to Vilna headed by Henry Morgenthau, formerly United States ambassador to Turkey. But the inquiry proved fruitless and the violence continued until the Bolsheviks recaptured Vilna in July 1920. The Poles took back the city in October. Eventually the Allies accepted Poland's military *fait accompli* and recognized the incorporation of the whole Vilna district into the new Polish Republic.

Most Vilna Jews knew their history not so much from reading books as from visiting the two Jewish cemeteries, where their history was literally entombed. The Old Cemetery, as it was called, was just across the Wilja, about two miles from the Jewish quarter. Tradition has it that Jews used it as a burial ground as far back as 1487, but the first historical records begin in 1592. The Russian authorities closed that cemetery in 1830 for lack of space. But two years earlier the Jewish community had already bought land for a large cemetery in Zaczecze, which Jews called *zaretcha,* just across the Wilenka, east of Góra Zamkowa, an uphill three-mile walk from the Jewish quarter.

The Old Cemetery was a tangle of weeds and dried boughs, small crumbling gravestones on which inscriptions were scarcely legible. Its most famous monument was the mausoleum of the Vilna Gaon and, surrounding it, tombs of his relatives and other notable rabbis. Here also were buried the ashes of Count Valentine Potocki, better known as the *ger tsaddik* ("the righteous convert"), who had become a Jew and lived under the name of Abraham ben Abraham in Ilya, near Vilna. The Polish authorities discovered his identity, brought him to trial, but—so the story goes and it's never been fully authenticated—he refused to abjure his conversion to Judaism. He was burned at the stake at Góra Zam-kowa. A Vilna Jew managed to collect some of his ashes, which were then buried in the Old Cemetery. In 1938 pious Jews still used to visit his grave on fast days and the High Holy Days.

The new cemetery was even richer in necrological history. I first visited it in early September 1938 and found it beautiful with its long tree-lined walkways. Tombstones were crowded together, leaning against each other like infirm old people. Kalman Schulman was buried there, as were Matthias Strashun, Samuel Joseph Fuenn, Isaac Meir Dick, and the Romm family. There were several mass sepulchers of Jewish political victims, one consisting of individual graves of fourteen Bun-dists who had died in the 1905 revolution, with an impressive tall stone monument at the center. One monument moved me to tears—an enor-mous white sculpture of a mighty eagle, its wings spread, but with the right wing cut off. It was the monument to A. Weiter, a Bundist and Yiddish writer, one of the Jews murdered by the Polish Legionnaires when they captured Vilna in 1919.

In independent Poland, things went from bad to worse for the Jews, but now they had no king to succor them in their trouble. In the twenty years between the world wars, the successive Polish governments kept restricting the economic opportunities for the Jews. By the late 1930s, in Poland's intensifyingly anti-Semitic milieu, the government was on a course to force the Jews out of Poland by means of economic pressures. Yet everywhere in Poland, and in Vilna as well, the Jews stubbornly fought for their economic and political rights. At the same time, with pitifully few material resources other than their commitment and determination, the Jews continued to develop extensive networks of cultural, educational, and religious institutions to preserve their communal existence. They operated a wide range of Jewish schools, published daily newspapers and periodicals, supported a panoply of synagogues, yeshivot, and welfare institutions. In this period a new kind of Jewish culture emerged, characterized by the fertilizing interplay of opposites—the old and the new, the secular and the religious, Zionist and non-Zionist— where Hebrew and Yiddish competed with each other and also with a nascent Jewish literary culture in the Polish language. Both popular and high Jewish culture flourished. It was a feverish flowering in the shadow of death.

CHAPTER 3

—

Living from Day to Day

Early Saturday morning, August 27, 1938, a clear warm summer day, I arrived in Vilna. I had traveled all night by train from Warsaw, having slept through the journey in my second-class compartment. At the Vilna railway station the two YIVO staffers who'd been assigned to meet me recognized me by my American luggage. They took me directly to the home of one of YIVO's directors, Zelig Kalmanovich and his wife, Riva, where, it had been arranged beforehand, I would be put up until I found suitable lodging.

The Kalmanoviches received me warmly. The table was plentifully set for breakfast. I didn't know it then, but my hosts would become dearest to me of all the people I came to know in Vilna, whom I would love more than I had ever loved my own father and mother. Then I knew nothing about either of them, but I soon learned something of their history.

Kalman or Kalmanke, as his intimates called him—though I never dared such intimacy in the year I knew him—was then in his mid-fifties. He had a wide Slavic-looking face, straight grayish-brown hair over a very high forehead. He was a Yiddish scholar whose main field was philology, with history as his next interest. He was, as I discovered for myself, phenomenally learned in many abstruse fields. He had been raised in an observant home, but had left the yeshiva at fifteen, eager to pursue a general education. After graduating from the *gymnasium,* he studied Semitics, classics, and history at the universities of Berlin and Koenigsberg. Eventually he earned his doctorate at the University of St. Petersburg, though he never used his title.

In St. Petersburg, or Petrograd, as it was called in the days of the February 1917 revolution, he met Rebecca Luria, known as Riva, the younger daughter of a well-to-do lumber merchant of Bobruysk. They were married not very long after. The upheavals of the Bolsehvik Revolution and the ensuing civil war in Russia forced them to flee. For years they were on the move, living in Latvia, Berlin, and Lithuania, where their one son was born. During that time Kalman wrote and published scholarly papers and popular articles, earning a modest living as a Hebrew teacher and a translator of historical works into Yiddish. In 1929, on the invitation of the YIVO, they moved to Vilna, where Kalman became editor of *YIVO-Bleter*, YIVO's scholarly journal, and joined the YIVO's executive board.

He was a shy man with a gentle smile, happiest when at his desk at home or at the YIVO. In company he was often absentminded or outright bored, impatient with small talk. But when the conversation turned to matters of Jewish politics and history, the nature of Jewish existence, it engrossed him and he was eager to talk. His words and ideas then poured forth with volcanic energy. As he spoke, you felt as if his words opened up new worlds; they had the effect—on me and many others—of revelation. As a public speaker he was mesmerizing.

Riva, known by the affectionate diminutive Rivele, was an altogether different personality and I often wondered what their courtship had been like. She was a feminine woman of charm and grace, with an expressively pretty face, high cheekbones, and large limpid eyes. Her wavy brown hair was cut neck length and brushed back from her face. She must have been in her late forties. She loved to sing, dance, go to the theater, and be in company. Behind her gay and cheerful front, she was a worrier. Her occupation was to care for her husband and her son, and whoever else needed loving kindness. She was all maternal solicitude. I like to think that my presence helped to fill the terrible void caused by the departure in September of her only son, Sholem, to settle in Palestine. Though I was a poor substitute for her beloved son, caring for me somehow helped her to master her loss. I lived with the Kalmanoviches only four days, but as long as I lived in Vilna, I used to see them almost every day.

Both Kalmanoviches assumed responsibility for me, *in loco parentis.*

Kalman would worry if he thought I was going out with radicals, or was invited to some place that the police might check out or that hooligans might attack. He was patient with my ignorance of Jewish history and language, yet often, stirred by my questions, he'd become voluble, talk to me as if I were an equal. Those were very exciting conversations for me. Rivele, for her part, would supervise me in practical matters as in personal ones. She became familiar with my wardrobe and would advise me about what to wear when I was going out on a date and how to fix my hair. I didn't always heed Kalman's warnings, but I obeyed Rivele blindly. With her I shared the intimacies of my life, my joys and anxieties.

In the four days I stayed with the Kalmanoviches in their apartment on Kwaszelna Street, I felt enveloped in a warmth and protectiveness that I had seldom experienced before. At home, my mother's watchful supervision expressed itself in prohibitions, more for her good than mine, I used to think. With the Kalmanoviches, in contrast, I knew that their sole concern was for my well-being. They made me feel at home with them and with Vilna.

I came to Vilna when it was still summer, more than a week before the Aspirantur's academic year would start. I spent those days meeting people and exploring Vilna. Though my being American—my passport and even more my very Americanness—set me apart from the rest of Vilna's Jews, I soon felt comfortable in Vilna. They had a saying there: "If you were once in Vilna, then you belong to Vilna." That's what happened to me. My parents were Polish Jews, but I soon came to consider myself a Vilna *litvak,* at least by adoption.

Vilna, I learned, was Poland's second largest city, after Warsaw, not in population or its political or economic importance, but in acreage. Besides its numerous grass plots, parks, and public squares, the city contained within its limits extensive unsettled wooded tracts. Vilna was underpopulated for its acreage. One seldom saw the strolling masses of people that crowded the spacious and fashionable boulevards in Warsaw, where I had stopped for a few days on my way from Gydnia. Fewer people were to be seen in Vilna's streets, except for the constant military presence. A company of soldiers always seemed to be marching from one post to another. Perhaps it was just that year, when all Poland lived under the threat of war. Mostly the rhythm of Vilna's street life was relaxed and leisurely. Even the Jewish quarter lacked the frenetic energy and bustle of the Warsaw Jewish neighborhoods. It didn't take long before I realized that Vilna had few urgencies. A familiar Yiddish saying seemed particularly appropriate to Vilna: *kum ikh nit haynt, kum ikh morgn* ("If I don't show up today, I'll come tomorrow").

Despite its expanse, Vilna was a pedestrian's city. Everyone walked. Unlike Warsaw, Vilna had no streetcars or buses for public transport within the city. Before the First World War there'd been horse-drawn trolleys on tracks, but the German military occupying forces had ripped out the tracks. They were never replaced. There were interurban buses which coursed through the city on their way to the countryside and there were trains to take you to Warsaw or other more distant places.

In Vilna, if you didn't walk, you took a droshky, the common conveyance in town, not prohibitively expensive. It could be picked up at stands throughout the city. The droshky was a low-slung, four-wheeled, horse-drawn carriage, whose small wheels were fitted with rubber tires. The driver sat up front on a high seat. The cab, with two facing wooden seats each accommodating two passengers, was open in good weather, but had a folding top that could be raised in bad weather or when you wanted privacy. Because few drivers were Jewish, the first Polish words I learned were numbers, so I could engage in the obligatory ritual of bargaining over the price of the ride.

Unlike Warsaw, which had many automobiles on the streets (though few compared to New York, even in those days), Vilna didn't have much auto traffic. Buses traveled on a few of the main arteries and you'd see some cars and an occasional limousine in which a high government official was being driven about on his business. There were some taxis, but I don't remember ever riding in one, though I had used them in Warsaw. One saw bicycles and occasional motorcycles, but nothing comparable to the astonishing mass of bicycles I saw in Copenhagen in 1939.

Vilna was, after all, a provincial city, though its residents regarded it as veritable metropolis. It was a magnet for numerous youthful newcomers who had fled the stagnation of their hinterland small towns and villages. Young people flocked to Vilna—the great center of opportunity in their eyes—in search of work or education. One of them was a fellow student of mine in the Aspirantur. The whole year I knew him he lived in terror of Vilna's auto traffic, too scared to go near ulica Mickiewicz for fear he'd be run over by a bus. Occasionally you'd hear about an accident, though there were few. The saddest was when a half-blind woman, on her way to the doctor, was run over by a truck on ulica Wielka.

In the winter snows, horse-drawn sleighs replaced the droshkies. The drivers used to wear enormous greatcoats and the passengers were solicitously wrapped against the biting cold with heavy tattered blankets. The sleighhorses were wretched creatures, seldom covered with anything more than a thin layer of ice, but they were adorned with bells that tinkled all the way. For a New Yorker, whose habitual mode of transport had been the subway, the sleigh ride was magical. Vilna buried in snow was like an enchanted dream village. The sleigh ride, especially at night, under a moonlit, star-studded sky, evoked images of the Russian novels I had read in high school—wind-swept snow drifts, howling wolves, revolutionaries in flight from Siberian tryanny, lovers eloping.

The vehicles for moving and delivering also summoned up the past, but these were less romantic than the sleighs. Most of the trucks I saw in Vilna belonged to Poland's armed forces. A few businesses used small delivery trucks, but the standard conveyance for moving furniture, transferring goods, and delivering food products was a horse-drawn wagon, generally uncovered. Less bulky goods were moved in wheelbarrows and pushcarts.

According to a Vilna directory of 1938, barely more than half the city's streets were paved, and of these, only the largest and handsomest streets were paved with asphalt or concrete for a continuous flat surface. Most business thoroughfares were paved with flagstones and the rest of the streets, especially convoluted alleys and mean dead ends, were cobbled. The sidewalks were, for the most part, narrow, barely wide enough for two abreast. The gutters, particularly with cobbled streets, were very deep; you had to take a long stride when stepping off the sidewalk. No doubt this was to ensure drainage, especially during the snow season. The main streets were generally clean, kept so by street sweepers with besom brooms.

The unpaved streets were mostly in the outlying sections of Vilna, especially across the Wilja. The Green Bridge, a continuation of Wileńska Street, a main north-south artery, led over the river to a neighborhood called Śnipiszki, which the Jews called Shnipishok. The name became a byword in Yiddish for a run-down backwater. Ever since the seventeenth century Jews had lived there, but in time it became a place where only poor people lived. The city's power station was located there as well as Vilna's lumber and timber industry, with their numerous saw mills and lumberyards.

In the center of town, some of Vilna's ducal or princely palaces which had survived the succession of wars and fires now housed government offices and other public institutions, giving a touch of grandeur to the streets. The residential buildings in good neighborhoods, three or four stories high, had a massive look, some still displaying their eighteenth-century Classical Revival adornments. The windows were high, some arched, some with balconies. The tallest building in Vilna—all of seven stories high—was the headquarters of the railroad administration, on Wielka Pohulanka, not far from the Romanov Church. Newspaper kiosks, where you could also buy cigarettes and tobacco, could be found on the corners of busy thoroughfares.

The most elegant street in Vilna and one of its longest (a little over a mile) was ulica Adam Mickiewicz. An east-west boulevard, densely lined with plane trees, it stretched from Plac Katedralny (Cathedral Place) to the Zwierzyniecka Bridge, the second of Vilna's bridges over the Wilja. Ulica Mickiewicz boasted several impressive public buildings, including the County Court, the Appeals Court, and the City Court, imposing banks and insurance companies, chambers of commerce and industry, two hotels, apartment houses with ornate marquees, awninged shops, the Polish theater "Lutnia," a movie house, and elegant cafes. Sztral, with umbrella-covered tables on a large terrace, was one of the poshest cafes I'd ever seen. On a lovely day in May, perhaps for a special occasion that I no longer remember, a friend invited me to dine there. Afterward I learned that Sztral's used to turn Jews away and consequently most Jews now boycotted the place. I never went there again.

Across the street from Sztral's was a restaurant, Palais de Danse, which featured *thé dansants* at five on Saturdays and Sundays. Once, early in my Vilna stay, I was taken there by a young man employed in a Jewish-owned timber firm, who was, as my YIVO friends put it, one of Vilna's Jewish *goldene yugnt,* gilded youth. A string trio played waltzes and tangos, while couples spun around the small dance floor. We feasted on tea and pastries—Polish pastries were rich and luscious. I imagined that Paris must be like this. Never before had I been at a *thé dansant* and never thereafter.

On ulica Wielka, a north-south artery, you could find a couple of princely palaces; one served as a post office and the other was used by the University. Some buildings had historic markers—46 Wielka for

Adam Mickiewicz, who had lived there briefly, and 39 Wielka, the birthplace of Mark Antokolski (1843–1902), a Jewish sculptor who had been celebrated in czarist Russia and admired in Western Europe. Wielka was a busy street, a major shopping center for well-to-do people. Besides its stores and offices, it also had four movie theaters, three restaurants, and four cafes.

Intersecting Wielka was ulica Szklanna, "Glazier Street," which Jews called *glezer gas,* a narrow cobbled street with one of those picturesque buttressing arches. It had been mentioned in records as far back as 1619 and Jews were known to have lived there early in the eighteenth century. Its houses were two and three stories high, with steep roofs and short chimneys. In warm weather the casement windows were opened wide. I suppose that the residents could see and hear what was going on in the apartments across the street. The shops on the street were small and cramped.

Ulica Wileńska, another main thoroughfare, ran southward from the Green Bridge for about six blocks. One block was occupied by St. Catherine's Church of the Benedictine Nuns, another of Vilna's baroque churches, and by the adjoining Benedictine Convent. In the nearby square stood an ornate monument, a tall pillar topped by a bust of Stanisław Moniuszko (1819–1872), a composer noted for *Halka,* considered to be Poland's national opera. The rest of Wileńska was unexceptional—good solid buildings and lots of stores: haberdashers and dry goods, radios, toys, a florist, and a concentration of antique shops. Jews constituted one-half of all the people employed in trade and commerce in Vilna. Their shops were everywhere—on the finest streets with the finest goods and also in the meanest streets with the shabbiest merchandise.

Wileńska narrowed into ulica Niemiecka past St. Catherine's. "Niemiecka" is the Polish for "German" and the Jews called the street *daytche gas,* German Street. In the fourteenth century Gedimin was said to have brought Baltic German traders and artisans from Riga and settled them in this spot. Most buildings on the street dated back to the eighteenth and early nineteenth centuries, but the street had the look of a lively up-to-date thoroughfare. Niemiecka was primarily a shopping street, the center of Jewish retail trade, with stores for everything from sweets to pianos, from notions and trimmings to ironmongers, from children's clothing to liquor. Signs advertising the stores' merchandise in Yiddish as well as in Polish were more numerous and more colorful here than on the more elegant streets.

Back in the seventeenth century, Niemiecka had been the outer limit of the Jewish quarter, but the Jewish quarter had long since expanded, spreading southward beyond Niemiecka and spilling over beyond the confines of the triangle formed by Żydowska and Jatkowa. Nevertheless, even when I was there, Żydowska still remained the core of the Jewish quarter, for that was where the *shulhoyf* was, the crowded courtyard with the Great Synagogue, the Gaon's *kloyz,* the *kloyz yoshen,* the Strashun Library, and the dozens of other little prayerhouses. Nearly every building on the street boasted one or more prayerhouses.

Żydowska was not all piety and prayer. Across the street from the *shulhoyf* was the *durkhhoyf,* "the through-yard," so called because it led from Żydowska to Jatkowa. It was the center of the old-clothes trade, bustling and noisy, yet depressing in its poverty. At the corner of Żydowska and Niemiecka was Velfkeh's Restaurant, where droshky drivers stopped for a shot of vodka and where Yiddish Bohemia went for drinks, food, and fun. Levanda's vegetarian restaurant was in the same courtyard.

Access to buildings was usually through an inner courtyard. From the street one passed through an archway with a pair of wooden doors or iron gates, into the courtyard. In the yard I was often bewildered by the numerous doorways and stoops of the buildings which formed the three sides of the yard. In the older parts of the Jewish quarter the yards were cobbled, dirty, and run-down. Often you'd find ragged children playing there. I have a photograph of a yard on ulica Szklanna showing some primitive scaffolding bracing a crumbling wall. You never saw a tree or any greenery in the Jewish quarter.

Ulica Rudnicka, a southern extension of Wielka, cross-secting Niemiecka, was a densely populated street, almost entirely Jewish, the hub of the Jewish retail trade in shoes, haberdashery, and groceries. Some of its buildings still bore traces of their eighteenth-century baroque ornamentation. The Vilna Jewish Loan and Savings Bank, which had begun as an artisan's loan association, was located there, as were the Jewish Real-Gymnasium (science high school) and the Jewish Music Institute.

Ulica Zawalna ("za" + "wal" means "around the rampart") had once, as its name suggested, run along the old city ramparts, of whose original nine towers only Ostra Brama remained. For most of its length it was a handsome wide street lined with trees, whose buildings housed a number of public and private institutions. The Evangelical Church and its institutions were located there. Built in the 1830s in neo-Renaissance style, the church was set back from the street, behind a low wall and much shrubbery, as if it did not wish to flaunt its Lutheran presence in this Catholic city. Farther down was another impressive building— Taharath Ha-Kodesh, the Choir Synagogue of the well-to-do Jews. Across the street was the Jewish Hospital.

Zawalna was also a market street. At its southernmost end, toward the railroad station, was the city market, an enormous stone building with a glass-domed roof, an enclosure containing a few hundred booths, where Poles and Jews sold all sorts of goods—food and fabrics, leather and furs, building materials and musical instruments. Outside were more pushcarts and stalls where marketeers did business under the open sky.

At Zawalna's intersection with ulica Nowogródzka, not far from the Evangelical Church and the Choir Synagogue, one came upon the so-called Lumber Market, where you couldn't buy lumber, but could get fish, meat, and produce, and sometimes even old books. About one large square block, with a cobbled pavement, it was usually dense with marketeers and shoppers.

Rivele found a room for me in a brand-new building with a young couple whom she knew, Genia and Jacob Rudensky, and their five-month-old baby boy. Genia, pretty and plump, originally from a small town not far from Vilna, had boarded with the Kalmanoviches before she married Jacob. He worked for a Jewish lumbering firm and was doing well. They were still in their twenties, not much older than I. Their friends were like them, the men mostly in the lumber or plywood business, earning a decent salary, eager to enjoy life.

Their apartment was on ulica Makowa, a quiet side street, not yet built up, about a five minutes' walk from where the Kalmanoviches lived. I don't recall any buildings immediately adjacent to our house, but just across the way was an older apartment building, whose tenants included a Yiddish elementary school and a small grocery store. The street wasn't yet paved when I moved in, and the city administration somehow never got around to it in the course of the year. People used to complain about the dust in dry weather and the mud in wet weather.

Ours was a three-story building with about half a dozen tenants. Our apartment had three rooms and a kitchen. One entered into a short corridor, off which were the kitchen, a tiny room outfitted just with a bathtub and a hot-water heater, adjoining a cubicle with a separate entrance containing a toilet and sink. At the end of the corridor was my room and at a right angle to it was the door into the Rudenskys' dining/living room and their bedroom. My room had a large window overlooking the street, from which I could see the grocery store and the children going to and from the school. My room in Vilna, I wrote my mother, was larger than my room in the Bronx. It had ample space for a bed, a wardrobe, a table which doubled as a desk, and four chairs. My footlocker served as a tea table or overflow bookshelf. Genia put up lace curtains and draw drapes and provided me with a desk lamp. Rivele supplied me with towels and bed linen.

We didn't have hot running water, central heating, or a telephone. (I had a phone at the YIVO.) At times I relished my deprivations and prided myself on adjusting to Spartan conditions, feeling that my want of American conveniences enhanced my sense of living in a foreign world.

The conventional means of heating an apartment in Vilna was the brick or tile stove that served as a partition between rooms. If I remember correctly, it was about three feet wide and extended the entire height of the wall, with a small oven door about midway up. In our apartment, we had one oven on the wall between the dining room and my room, with the opening on my landlords' side. Generally pea coal was used for fuel, but at times we burned paper and wood. The heat of the bricks or tiles warmed both sides of the wall. During spells of frost, my room was so bitter cold that I'd go to bed swathed in woolens, wearing socks and gloves. I'd fortify myself with a shot of vodka, hoping it would keep me from freezing to death in my sleep. It was no use to complain about insufficent heat, because overheating the wall might set it afire. I remember reading a news story during a cold spell about just such an accident, which had tragic results.

Our kitchen had an iron, coal-burning range with four or five plates and removable lids. In cold weather it was kept going all day and banked up at night. (Our maid slept in the kitchen on bedding laid out on a wall bench.) An enormous kettle with hot water always stood on the stove, ready for tea. For a bath, you stoked the hot-water heater, I think, with wood. My rent included one bath a week. If I wanted another, I paid extra for the kindling. Every morning I washed in cold water. It was an exercise in stoicism.

The YIVO fellowship paid sixty zlotys a month, the equivalent of twelve dollars. A patron of the American branch of YIVO had agreed to supplement my stipend with an additional twelve dollars monthly, but he didn't do so regularly. My parents made up for it and I somehow managed to squeeze by on about 100–120 zlotys per month.

My monthly rent, which included tea for breakfast and supper and the weekly hot bath, cost thirty zlotys–six dollars. I had my main meal every day with the Rudenskys for another thirty zlotys, each meal costing about one zloty, twenty cents. It usually consisted of three courses—soup, meat or fish and accompaniments, and dessert. The first Friday-night meal I ate with the Rudenskys was more elaborate: gefilte fish, chicken noodle soup, chicken with carrots and potatoes, and applesauce. (For comparison: In those days in New York, a quarter would buy lunch at a Chinese restaurant—soup, egg roll, chow mein, and tea—or at the Automat—three vegetables, a roll, and coffee.)

For breakfast and supper, I'd have some bread or rolls, butter, cheese, tomatoes, sometimes sardines or cold cuts. In accounting to my mother, I wrote that the food for those meals cost me about twenty zlotys a month. That didn't leave me much for extras. My sweet tooth craved chocolate, but that raised a political problem as well as a financial one. The most delicious chocolate came from Wedel's, a Polish firm notorious for its support of Poland's most anti-Semitic party. I settled on Plutos, not nearly as good, but a Jewish firm.

Besides chocolate, I missed the variety of fruits and vegetables which we enjoyed in New York. Except in the summer, when Vilna had apricots and plums, the available fruits were usually only apples and sometimes pears. Oranges and grapefruits were exotic imports, beyond most people's means. On my birthday, a friend bought me a lavish gift: half a dozen oranges imported from Spain. Bananas were only for sick people or pregnant women. Well-to-do people would buy a pineapple, even more exotic than an orange, for Rosh ha-Shana, the Jewish New Year, as the first fruit of the year over which to make the blessing. Such fruits could be bought only in fancy-food shops on ulica Mickiewicz carrying imported luxury products.

Green vegetables were scarce and expensive. Besides, they didn't fit into the traditional Polish or Jewish cuisine. We ate mostly root vegetables—potatoes, carrots, beets, onions, and dried legumes. Milk wasn't pasteurized and had to be boiled. Coffee was terrible, made of chicory and who knows what else, and boiled. A percolator which you could get in New York for about two dollars was a prohibitive luxury in Vilna, costing nearly fifty zlotys. In my letters home I complained that I was getting fat on bread and potatoes. I used to daydream about going into the Automat and dropping a continuing supply of nickels into a slot for an unending supply of coffee. I thought about gorging myself on string beans and spinach, oranges and bananas, and ice-cold milk. But I found some comfort in the richly delicious Polish pastries.

My other expenses included three zlotys a month for the maid to clean my room, do my laundry, and a little marketing. An extra bath cost fifty groszy—about ten cents. Once in a while I went to the beauty parlor. A wash and set cost two zlotys. The Rudenskys and I split the cost—three zlotys a month—of the Yiddish newspaper, *Undzer Tog,* which was published six days a week, and delivered to our door. My American cigarettes had gone quickly, for I had handed them out with American magnanimity. Polish cigarettes, which were quite harsh, cost me about twelve zlotys a month, as did postage. An airmail stamp to the United States cost fifty-five groszy, about eleven cents. (A United States airmail stamp abroad cost only five cents.)

I didn't always have money left over for the movies. The nine movie houses showed mostly Hollywood films, which were very popular. Polish films were shown from time to time and once in a while a French movie. I can't recall any German films being shown that year I was in Vilna. The movies were the only place I could hear English spoken as it should be. They became my link to America and, when I needed it, a refuge from the Polish present. That year I saw Bette Davis in *Jezebel,* Greta Garbo and Robert Taylor in *Camille,* Tyrone Power and Loretta Young in *Suez,* Luise Rainer in *The Great Waltz,* Clark Gable and Myrna Loy in *Too Hot to Handle,* Claudette Colbert and Herbert Marshall in *Zaza,* and Merle Oberon and Laurence Olivier in *The Divorce of Lady X.*

Once the Aspirantur's academic year began, I settled into a daily routine. I'd get up about eight, shiver through my cold-water wash, dress, breakfast, and read the paper or write letters until 9:45. Then I'd walk to the YIVO. I generally did my own research in the morning or had some tutoring in Yiddish, with a customary break just before noon for a cup of tea. At two in the afternoon, I'd go home for dinner, then write letters, read, or even take a nap, if I'd been short of sleep. At 4:30 I returned to the YIVO and worked until about eight in the evening. If I wasn't invited out, I'd go home, prepare a light supper, talk to Genia and Jacob, listen to the radio with them, read, and, as always, write letters.

That daily routine was enlivened by visits with friends, occasional lectures, concerts, and theaters, invitations to dinners and parties, flirtations, and romances. My circle of friends was larger than it had been in New York, encompassing a wider social and intellectual range. For the Vilna Jews I seemed to be an exotic creature. What I was in fact was a short Jewish girl with nice eyes and trim ankles, at once serious, yet also cheerful and gay, afflicted with a sense of mission, energetic, yet also supercilious, self-confident, and even arrogant.

The celebration of minor and major Jewish festivals varied the quotidian routine, as did the changing seasons. But it was the hurtling, headlong course of European politics that shook us out of the accustomed grooves of our everyday pursuits. I had come to Vilna for its Jewish history and its thickly layered past, but each passing day the present became more compelling than the past, bringing new dangers of war and intimations of disaster. It was as though we were held in an ever-tightening vise from which we'd never escape. Nevertheless, though everyone worried about what might happen the next day, we all went about our usual routines, doing what we were expected to do, enjoying our little pleasures. I continued to study the past, though like everyone else, I lived from day to day, from crisis to crisis. As the seasons changed, so did the crises.

Vilna basked in end-of-summer warmth that August 1938. The city was still green, and everyone tried to take advantage of the balmy weather. People went swimming and boating on the Wilja, walked and picnicked in the nearby countryside. In mid-September autumn came, launching the school year with crisply cool and brilliantly sunny days, though the evenings now had a touch of chill. The trees took on crimson and russet hues. It was perfect weather for staying outdoors, walking and sightseeing. That wonderful autumn of 1938 coincided with the second Czech crisis. Hitler was making threats again. Once more the danger of war loomed and distracted us from our enjoyments.

We followed every detail of the unfolding events. That is to say, we followed every detail of the news available to us. The Czech crisis instructed me about the Polish media and government censorship. One would have thought that once Poland had been liberated from czarist rule and czarist censorship, its governing authorities would appreciate the freedom of the press. But Poland did not have a free press like in the United States. (Polish radio was directly under government control.) The government censor was omnipresent and no issue of a newspaper— left or right, pro-government or opposition—could be distributed without first being scrutinized and passed by the censor.

In November the government issued several decrees further limiting the freedom of the press. Newspapers became obligated to publish government releases of up to 1,250 lines. Editorials or articles critical of government actions or policies were subject to censorship. A newspaper would appear with a blank space where the offending piece had been slated to appear or the edition might be altogether banned. Even straightforward news reports were censored or outright suppressed if the authorities thought such coverage would reflect badly on Poland. Journalists and editors used to dilute the content of their stories so that they could pass the censor's black pencil. Under such heavy government censorship, publishers and editors learned to practice self-censorship.

Sometimes important events in Poland were not reported or were reported so sketchily that one had to depend on word of mouth to understand their full import. For instance: On Friday evening, September 9, at the start of the school year, Polish university students and other less educated hooligans launched a wave of attacks against Jews walking on Vilna's streets. *Undzer Tog*'s editor, Zalmen Reisen, had prepared an account of those assaults for his Sunday paper (the paper didn't appear on Saturday). But the censor ordered the edition confiscated. Reisen then wrote a second version which played down the violence, thus managing to get by the censor. Reisen himself told us about the episode at dinner at his house.

Even private letters written in Poland and sent abroad were censored, as I learned from my correspondents back home. One of my surviving letters, written late in August shortly after my arrival, had two lines blacked out by the censors. I have no idea what I had written, but I have not the least doubt that it was of no consequence.

The Yiddish and Polish press seemed provincial to me, habituated as I was to the *New York Times* and the New York *Herald Tribune*. *Undzer Tog* published a four-page tabloid-size paper from Sunday through Thursday. The Friday paper, the weekend issue, contained eight pages. The Polish papers didn't have many foreign correspondents and in those days liked to pick up stories from Germany, many of which proved to be unreliable. The Yiddish papers subscribed to the Jewish Telegraphic Agency and sometimes picked up stories from the HAVAS news agency and a Polish news agency. Yet however inadequate the news sources and however heavy the censor's hand, we devoured what news we could get. Not knowing Polish, I depended upon the Yiddish press and upon my friends' summaries of stories in the Polish press and of Polish radio broadcasts.

Every morning Jacob Rudensky and I would make a grab for *Undzer*

Tog. During the Czech crisis that paper and all the others used to print extras once or twice a day, usually consisting of just one sheet. These were available at kiosks on the street and from occasional hawking vendors. Every evening guests came to our house to listen to the news on the radio. One could pick up broadcasts from Germany, Sweden, even Russia. (The Polish press never published any political news from Russia.) One evening we got Berlin and heard Hitler orating, calling himself the preserver of peace. The hysterical roars of approval and the avalanche of applause with which the Germans responded to their leader upset me far more than his ranting talk.

The second Czech crisis began on September 12. Hitler, furious over the months of futile negotiations between the Czech government and the Nazi leader of the Sudeten Germans demanding autonomy, delivered a diatribe in Nuremberg at a Nazi Party rally. He violently attacked the Czech government and promised the Sudeten Germans that Germany would come to their defense. With the threat of a German invasion, the Czechs imposed martial law the next day in the troublesome border districts of Sudetenland and the Sudeten Nazi leader fled to Germany. Twice British prime minister Neville Chamberlain went, hat in hand and umbrella on arm, as a supplicant to appease Hitler and to find a peaceful solution. In a broadcast to the English people Chamberlain described himself as a man of peace, saying that the thought of armed conflict was a nightmare to him. But Hitler was not easily appeased and the tensions continued to mount. The Czechs and the French began to mobilize their reserves; the British started to mobilize their navy.

After two weeks of futile conferences, Hitler agreed to see Chamberlain on September 29, for a third meeting, held in Munich. Besides Hitler and Chamberlain, Mussolini and French premier Daladier were also present. Hitler then decided Czechoslovakia's fate and the others agreed to his conditions, thus setting in motion the beginning of its dismemberment.

The next day we heard a Czech broadcaster sum up the results of the Munich conference. He could hardly speak, choked as he was by sobs. I wrote home that weekend: "Who can tell how much longer the madman will wait before he asks for all of Czechoslovakia?" Yet I was relieved that Chamberlain had achieved "peace in our time." I wouldn't have to go home, at least not yet. Had I been in New York then, I wrote to a friend, I'd have bitterly condemned the Munich agreement and I would have preferred to see "the whole works blow up," as I put it somewhat apocalyptically. But sitting in Vilna, I saw it differently. "War would be terrible for Poland, a country so pitifully poor. It would be completely ravaged, torn apart by Germany and Russia. And the Jews would suffer more than anyone. No question but that there'd be fearful pogroms." Yet though I had been caught up in the fears and anxieties of my friends and, with them, had breathed a sigh of relief, I knew that the Munich peace was only makeshift.

On October 1, the day after the Munich agreement was signed, German troops marched into Sudetenland. That very day the Poles sent a note to the Czech government, an ultimatum demanding that within forty-eight hours the Czechs hand over the area of Teschen, a territory of about 850 square miles on the frontier near Upper Silesia, part of which had a preponderant Polish population. It was not Poland's finest hour. Poland, which itself had three times been partitioned by its neighbors, now turned on its neighbor. The mood in Poland changed. The pervasive fear of war gave way to boisterous jingoism as Poland decided to participate in cannibalizing Czechoslovakia.

Teschen transformed Vilna's atmosphere. Military units goose-stepped smartly around town—perhaps there'd been a partial mobilization—and their heels clicked resoundingly over the cobbled streets. Maps of the new area and proclamations were plastered all over the city. Thousands of Poles, as far away from the Czech border as Vilna, volunteered to enter Teschen and take it by force. On October 2, when the Poles officially occupied Teschen, church bells pealed all over Vilna and Te Deum services were held during the day. Vilna celebrated late into the night. Jews were afraid to venture out on the street. The vodka consumption reached new levels. Vilna consumed a total of 548,457 liters of vodka in 1938, at a cost of over five million zlotys—20 percent over the consumption in 1936.

In early October, the weather changed for the worse. The wind blew the withered leaves from the branches and the trees stood naked against the horizon. The clear blue skies turned gray and sodden. The rains began to fall. It was time to prepare for winter. In our house, as in most Vilna houses, we had the equivalent of storm windows, which everyone installed in October and removed in the spring. They were fitted inside on tracks about six inches away from the outer window and sealed with putty and plaster, creating a buffer of stale air against outside drafts.

But no buffer could protect us against the next calamity that came from abroad and directly affected the Jews in all of Poland, Vilna included. Back in March 1938, the Polish Sejm, fearing the Germans would expel Jews residing in Germany who were Polish nationals—estimated to be about 50,000—and return them to Poland, passed a decree intended to denaturalize these Polish Jews and prevent their return. The new regulation provided that Polish nationals who had lived abroad for more than five years had to get a special stamp from Polish consular officials by October 31; otherwise, they would be refused reentry to Poland. Learning of this development, the German Foreign Office anticipated the Poles. They instructed the Gestapo to round up those unwanted Jews. On October 26, some 17,000 were put on sealed trains and sent back to Poland. Some had family and friends in Poland who could help them, but many thousands who had been away from Poland for years had no one to turn to. Destitute, they were cast upon the mercy of the local Jewish communities all over Poland.

The Polish authorities were caught by surprise. But after the first trainloads had crossed the Polish frontier, the Polish government decided to prevent the reentry of the refugees, whom the Germans continued to expel forcibly. The trains coming from Frankfurt to Poznań were halted at the border, at a small town called Zbąszyn, lacking any facilities for the thousands who were unloaded there. November had just arrived and in Poland November heralded the arrival of winter. In a matter of days temporary shelters began to be put up in a no-man's-land on the German-Polish border at Zbąszyn—but not by the Polish authorities. They refused to do anything for these suffering people who were their nationals. Instead, the help came from Jews throughout Poland, having been initiated in Warsaw. On November 3, important communal leaders in Vilna formed a committee to raise funds for the refugees from Germany. Every day *Undzer Tog* printed front-page appeals for funds and back-page reports of the monies received.

The camp at Zbąszyn continued to absorb refugees, who lived under appalling conditions. It was not before the end of January 1939, after considerable international outcry, that the Polish and German governments reached an agreement on the fate of those Jewish Polish nationals, who were then permitted to return to Germany to liquidate their affairs by mid-June but were entitled to take out only 20 percent of their liquid capital. The Polish government had obligated itself to permit them to reenter.

Early in November a young couple from Berlin who had been in

Zbąszyn came to Vilna, Gerda and Saly—I no longer remember their last name. He was a photographer. The refugee committee had assigned them to Rivele Kalmanovich, who put them up in the same room where I had stayed. Later they managed to find a place of their own and some work. In the summer of 1939, when I was planning soon to go home, I asked Saly to take photographs of Vilna for me, since I had no camera of my own. After the war I gave those photographs to the YIVO Archives in New York. While working on this memoir, I managed to recover about a dozen of them, with my handwritten Yiddish identifications on the back.

Among the refugees stranded in Zbąszyn was a couple called Grynszpan who had lived in Hanover since 1914. Their son, then living in Paris with an uncle, became deranged by his parents' fate. He got a gun and on November 7 shot Ernst vom Rath, the third secretary in the German embassy in Paris. Two days later vom Rath died of his wounds. The Nazis called for revenge and on the night of November 9, with Hitler's tacit approval, they set fire to the synagogues and all other Jewish institutions throughout Germany. The smashed glass of Jewish storefronts and homes gave a name to that pogrom—*Kristallnacht,* the Night of Broken Glass. The next day the police arrested tens of thousands of Jewish men and put them in concentration camps. The Jews of Germany were fined one billion marks.

The sequence of events horrified the Western world. We had anticipated that the Jews in Germany would be deprived of their rights, discriminated against, harassed, but we hadn't foreseen so brutal and massive a pogrom, even in Hitler's Germany. "The Germans have outdone Czarist Russia as pogromists," I wrote home. "Kishenev will become a pale memory in the aftermath of the November pogrom." In Poland the rabbis designated November 23 as a fast day to mark that terrible event. That day the synagogues and prayerhouses in Vilna were crowded as the Jews prayed before the open ark.

One of my friends in the Aspirantur, Rachel Golinkin, whose parents and sister lived in Danzig, where her father was a rabbi, was in despair when she learned that the fires of *Kristallnacht* had spread to Danzig. (Though it had been a free city since the end of the First World War under the League of Nations, the Nazis were gaining power over the generally ineffective High Commissioner.) At last she received a letter after weeks of anxiety without word from home. Her family had gone into hiding during the pogrom. Her elderly father had become seriously ill. Weeks later, when they could safely return home, they began selling off their belongings, hoping to leave for America, where a son was trying to get them visas. "Our house," Rachel's mother wrote her, "has become a marketplace."

During the terrible days of *Kristallnacht,* winter arrived in Vilna with air so frigid that it cut into your skin like a knife and almost made you forget the bitterness of the political situation. Everyone took out their heavy underwear and bundled up. Well-to-do men wore greatcoats with big beaver collars and high fur hats that gave them the look of Cossacks. The marketeers and tradespeople wore sheepskin coats, usually hip length, and plushy hats with earflaps. Women wore fur coats or fur-trimmed coats and boots of leather or fur-trimmed heavy cloth. The poor wrapped themselves in shawls, old blankets, and rags.

In mid-December we were in the midst of a weeklong frost. The thermometer fell to −18 degrees centigrade. Waves of cruelly cold air blew in from Siberia. Still, the sky was brilliantly blue and the sunlight dazzlingly white. The Wilja and the Wilenka froze over. Numerous cases of frostbite were reported by the hospitals. Most children stayed home from school. When the frost abated, it began snowing and continued for a week, submerging Vilna in snow. The bare branches of the trees were sheathed in snow or ice.

Christmas in Vilna was a totally different experience from the cheerful commercial bustle of a New York Christmas. To begin with, the Poles in Vilna showed no evidence of extending their wishes for peace on earth and good will to men to include the Jews. Anti-Semitic groups distributed leaflets in the weeks before Christmas urging Poles not to do their Christmas shopping in Jewish-owned stores. Otherwise, Christmas in this Catholic city was unmistakably a religious festival. The only stores permitted to be open were Jewish-owned pharmacies. Everything else was shut down—all workplaces, retail stores, restaurants, cafes, movie theaters, nightclubs. Young Vilna, an organization of Yiddish writers, had applied for a permit to have a get-together on December 25 to celebrate the publication of a book by a member. The municipality denied permission.

New Year's Eve was called Sylvester, for St. Sylvester I, a pope during Constantine I's reign, whose feast day was December 31. Despite the religious cast to the New Year's celebration, Vilna's already elevated level of alcoholic consumption reached new highs. Jews knew they'd have to be extra cautious if they were out late. On that New Year's Day,

Roman Dmowski died. He was known as the "father of Polish anti-Semitism" and a founder of Poland's oldest anti-Semitic party. We didn't have much to cheer about, because we knew that his ideas and his party would continue to live on.

The first thaw in mid-January brought a deceptive hint of spring in the air. The ice in the rivers cracked. The massive runoffs of melting snow from the hills turned the little Wilenka into a torrential stream as it gushed into the Wilja, which, in turn, swelled on its way toward the sea. But the snow and cold soon returned to linger a few weeks more.

In mid-February a brief mild spell began to melt the snow, but when the cold returned, the melting snow turned the pavements into sheets of glass. The buses couldn't move out of their parking spaces or climb the hilly streets. Even spreading sand on uphill bus routes didn't help. Elsewhere, a droshky horse slipped on the ice, turning over the carriage and seriously injuring the driver.

During these winter months we became accustomed not only to our Jewish troubles but also to our anxieties and sorrows over the worsening political situation. The news continued to rivet us. *Undzer Tog* reported the fall of the Spanish Republic on its front pages all through the first two months of 1939. Franco's forces took Barcelona on January 26 and in a few weeks took all of Catalonia. On February 19, Poland rushed to recognize Franco as the legitimate ruler of Spain. England and France waited until February 28. Alternating on the first page with stories of Spain's imminent fall were accounts of the fruitless proceedings at the London Round Table Conference on Palestine, which Neville Chamberlain opened on February 5. Neither the Jews nor the Arabs were prepared to accept British proposals for a solution to their problems. After weeks of speechifying, the conference closed on March 17 without having reached a settlement. The British would not permit Palestine to become a haven for Europe's Jewish refugees.

That winter the Vilna municipality began a program of public education about air-raid defense. It was probably part of a national defense effort. In December the municipality, having set up a Department of Air Defense, sponsored public lectures for all building superintendents on defense measures against air attack. In January every building had to post large yellow-and-green posters, distributed by the city authorities, with instructions on how to proceed in case of an air raid. At the end of

February, teachers were compelled to attend evening courses on air-raid precautions. Then the municipality announced that citywide air-raid drills would be held on March 14, 15, and 16.

By that time, the thaw had set in; the ice was breaking up on the Wilja. The streets were muddy and dirty. To prepare for the drills, Vilna residents had to black out their windows—homes, businesses, institutions. Fines for noncompliance were high. There was a run on black paper and cardboard in the stationery stores. Those who couldn't afford blackout paper draped their windows with blankets and tablecloths. At home I had my window covered and I hung a dark-blue sweater over the shade of my desk lamp. It was preferable, I wrote to a friend, to going to bed at ten and staring into the dark. The YIVO blacked out several rooms, where we could assemble during a drill.

In the course of the three-day alert, we had five drills. We never knew when the sirens would be sounded or in what particular locality the low-flying planes would drop tear-gas bombs to give the drills verisimilitude. The first drill came on March 14 at 7 P.M., when I was still in the YIVO. A group of us piled into one room and talked for an hour, until the all-clear sounded and we could go home. The city was sunk in total darkness. Flashlights were permitted on the street, but could show only a blue light. On March 15, the drill came at 2:30 in the afternoon, as I was on my way home for dinner. The instructions were to head for the nearest doorway for cover and wait until the all-clear. I didn't get my dinner till nearly four, but the maid had kept it hot for me. That evening, listening to the news on the radio, we forgot the trivialities of our experiences in the air-raid drills. That day Czechoslovakia had ceased to exist.

Acting out a scenario drafted by Hitler, Slovakia seceded from Czechoslovakia and declared its independence. We all knew, even on that first day, that Slovakia was Hitler's puppet. Germany then annexed the rest of Czechoslovakia—Bohemia and Moravia—and turned it into a German protectorate. "It's too mournful and painful to discuss," I wrote to a friend. "Who knows who will be the next victim?" I'd hardly written the words before the next victim was swallowed up—Memel.

The Memel territory, called Memelland, was a district in Lithuania, formerly East Prussia, with a port city of the same name on the east coast of the Baltic Sea. After the First World War, Memel was administered by the French on behalf of the League of Nations, but in 1923 the Lithuanians seized it. Later, the Allies let them keep it. For over a decade the Lithuanian government, a virtual dictatorship, managed to restrain German nationalist restiveness in Memel, but after 1933 they could no longer do so, for the Germans in Memel were being manipulated by Hitler. In December 1938, in Memel's parliamentary elections, the German party won 87 percent of the vote. (We didn't know it then, but Hitler postponed taking Memel at that time because he had decided to deal first with Czechoslovakia. That accomplished, he was free to turn his attention to Memel.)

On March 20, Germany's foreign minister Ribbentrop told the Lithuanian foreign minister that the election results last December had demonstrated that Memel's population wanted to be reunited with Germany. He gave the Lithuanians forty-eight hours to cede the territory to Germany in exchange for various guarantees. The Lithuanians had no choice; the agreement was signed in forty-eight hours. Hitler happened to be on the battleship *Deutschland* in Baltic Sea waters, surely no coincidence. In the early morning hours of March 23, he was informed that the Lithuanians had agreed to evacuate Memelland and the *Deutschland* proceeded to Memel. There Hitler made a rousing speech of victory to the jubilant population.

By taking Czechoslovakia and Memel, Germany had extended pincerlike claws around Poland's frontiers. The Poles now felt the tightening German encirclement. The jingoism that had marked Poland's annexation of Teschen last October gave way to jitters. On the same day Germany took Memel, March 23, Poland began a secret partial mobilization—secret lest Germany consider it a provocation. Instead of publicly announcing which units were being called up and where they were to report, the army wrote to the reservists individually. The press was forbidden to mention the mobilization; the reservists were warned not to discuss their call-up. But of course people found out. It was obvious even from the cryptic warnings which the press printed that reservists had to inform the military authorities of any change of address immediately. Failure to do so would incur a fine of 1,000 zlotys or a month's imprisonment, or both.

On March 21, the day after Ribbentrop delivered Germany's ultimatum to Lithuania, the authorities in Vilna confiscated that day's edition of *Słowo,* a right-wing Polish daily, whose editor, Stanisław Mackiewicz, was noted for his conservative outspoken opposition to the government. The next day Mackiewicz was arrested. Zalmen Reisen's son, also a journalist, told me that Mackiewicz had attacked Poland's foreign minister, Colonel Józef Beck, as "a vassal of Hitler." Other papers wrote that Mackiewicz had incurred the government's displeasure by his "defeatism" and by questioning Poland's ability and will to defend itself. Under the November 1938 press decrees, "defeatist propaganda" was considered a criminal offense. To counter the gossip, authorities in Warsaw issued a statement that Mackiewicz was arrested because of his dangerous opinions on domestic matters. (This was one of those statements the papers were obligated to publish.) In any case, he was sentenced to one month in an isolation cell in Poland's notorious concentration camp for political prisoners, Bereza Kartuska, where many prisoners were Communists, companions Mackiewicz would not voluntarily have chosen. It was said that he agreed, on his release, to refrain from all journalistic and political activity for six months.

Polish jitters showed itself in an unparalleled drive undertaken by the government to raise public funds through a subscription loan to improve Poland's air defense. The campaign for the military aviation loan was launched at the end of March and concluded early in May. The authorities exerted intense pressure upon the Jews to contribute, forcing them, as it were, to demonstrate their loyalty to the government by their generous subscriptions. Every week, at public and private meetings, Jewish leaders pleaded with the Jewish community to give as generously as possible. Norms were set nationally for amounts people should give, according to their income and occupation. Every day *Undzer Tog* published, besides desperate appeals to contribute, the names of all subscribers to the loan and the amounts subscribed.

The anti-Semitic parties and their papers nonetheless attacked the Jewish community for not contributing sufficiently, alleging that the Jews controlled all of Poland's wealth. We heard stories about the pressures to which Jews in small towns were especially exposed. "The Jews have to give more money," the anti-Semitics charged, "because the Poles give their blood." When the subscription drive was over, Vilna had raised 3,900,000 zlotys, about $740,000. Of this amount, 2,000,000 zlotys, more than half, had come from Vilna's Jews, who comprised about 30 percent of the population.

In April spring arrived in Vilna. We removed the inside windows and opened the outer ones to the fresh spring air. The trees, shrubs, bushes, and flowerbeds in the parks, squares, and gardens showed buds, baby leaves, and tender shoots. Soon the grass began to grow and blossoms to appear. Vilna began to take on a green hue.

Meanwhile Poland was at the center of a flurry of new diplomatic developments in the wake of the German takeovers of Czechoslovakia and Memel. Months earlier Ribbentrop had demanded concessions from the Poles with regard to Danzig and the Polish Corridor. Both issues had impaired relations between Germany and Poland ever since the Treaty of Versailles. Under the treaty, Danzig had been made a free city under the supervision of a League of Nations High Commissioner and, to give Poland access to the sea, a strip of land had been carved out of German Pomerania, which became known as the Polish Corridor. Long before Hitler came to power, back in the 1920s, the Polish government realized that it could not rely too much on its relations with Danzig and began to construct Gdynia, at the tip of the Polish Corridor on the Baltic Sea, to serve as its own inviolable port city, its own guarantee of access to the sea.

Now the Germans were demanding the return of Danzig to Germany and the construction of an extraterritorial highway and railroad across the Polish Corridor. Poland rejected those demands and secured Britain's and France's backing for its firm stand. On March 31 Chamberlain announced in Parliament that, in the event of any threat to Poland's independence, Britain and France had agreed to lend Poland "all support in their power." A week later, that Anglo-French guarantee was expanded into a mutual-assistance pact.

Hitler's enraged response came on April 28, right after Poland had made public its partial mobilization. (England was then planning call-ups of its young men; Denmark had begun mobilizing one-year reservists.) Speaking in the Reichstag, Hitler denounced England, saying he would no longer be bound by the Anglo-German Naval Treaty of 1935. He then turned on Poland, denouncing its government for having failed to accede to his "reasonable" proposals concerning Danzig, for its partial mobilization, and finally for its pact with England. He declared the German-Polish nonaggression pact of 1934 as no longer in existence. An official German note to this effect was delivered to Warsaw the same day.

On May 5, speaking before the Sejm, Foreign Minister Beck responded to Hitler in a manner that must have made even Mackiewicz proud of him. Poland, said Beck, would not yield its rights in Danzig. Though peace is desirable, he went on, "we in Poland do not accept the concept of peace at any price. There is only one thing in the life of men, nations, and states that is without price, and that is honor."

This defense of Poland's national honor brought Beck the support of all parties and of the whole Polish people. The Jews, too, and their political spokesmen from right to left declared that they were ready to give their blood for Poland, that they would fight for its honor. Two days after Beck's speech I wrote home that "you hear people speak with great determination that they'll not give up Danzig." That determination exacerbated the war fears. A Polish army paper, *Polska Zbrojna,* published an article proposing that everyone lay in a two-week supply of food so that they wouldn't become dependent on the government in case of war. The article was widely reprinted throughout Poland and started a run on canned goods and dried legumes.

In June, after we had completed our academic year, I took a four-day trip to Warsaw. I was tired and depressed. The constant fear of war was no doubt a factor in my fatigue, but not the determining one. More oppressive than the fear of war was my sense of being suffocated in the Polish milieu. I had come to feel that I could no longer live in this stifling atmosphere. The relentless anti-Semitism from the outside exhausted one's emotional energy, but even more disheartening was the relentless poverty, from which there seemed to be no escape. All the avenues that seemed to lead to economic opportunity and a professional career for the young people I knew were only dead ends. Though I had come to feel at home in Vilna, I never felt it was my home. For all its charm and history, it was still a provincial town. Notwithstanding my preoccupation with Jewish history and my commitment to Yiddish, I longed for a more cosmopolitan society. I wanted to be back in my own familiar world, where I could be both a Jew and an American. By that time I missed New York: I was just homesick. In June, I made plans to leave on September 14.

Summer arrived and brought with it an exceptional heat wave. People went on vacation, mostly to modest resorts not far from Vilna. Others went swimming in the Wilja. The heat was punctuated by a series of violent rainstorms whose high winds and lightning knocked down fences and felled trees. It was as if nature sympathized with us, sharing in the accelerating tension between Germany and Poland over Danzig that hung in the political air. Jumpiness and jitters were still evident everywhere. The nations of Europe were mobilizing and even massing troops on their borders.

The Poles, who for years had shown their appreciation for Hitler's Germany, now expressed strong anti-German feelings. In the middle of July, I saw a Hollywood movie, *Confessions of a Nazi Spy,* with Edward G. Robinson as a G-man tracking a Nazi spy ring in the United States. The theater was filled and everyone, Jews and Poles, loved the film, vociferously applauding the Americans and booing the German spies. Just at that time, gas masks went on sale in Vilna. The authorities urged the public to buy them. An adult's gas mask cost seventeen zlotys; a child's mask was fifteen zlotys. If you didn't have the cash, you could buy on the installment plan—two zlotys per month.

On July 20, our Vilna *Tog* published extracts of an interview that Marshal Edward Rydz-Śmigly had given to an American paper. "Poland," he said, "will fight to the last man. We will fight for our independence. Whoever controls Danzig controls our economic independence."

Despite the political jitters, Vilna went ahead with its elaborate plans for the biennial northern trade fair, to open at the end of August. At the same time, the nationwide registration of skilled workers from the ages of seventeen to sixty, except for those in the military services, began in Vilna. The government was mobilizing not only its military forces, but also its civilians and their industrial resources in the event of war.

CHAPTER 4

────

The YIVO:
The Ministry of Yiddish

On Sunday, August 28, 1938, the day after I arrived in Vilna, I went with
Kalmanovich to see the YIVO, though our Aspirantur program was not
to begin for another week or so. (Sunday was a permitted working day
for Jews, a right which they had long struggled to win in place of the
obligatory Sunday rest day.) The YIVO was a fifteen-minute walk from
the Jewish quarter, in the center of a broad linden-lined and sparsely
settled street in a quiet area. Except for the playing field a block away
that belonged to Maccabi, the Jewish sports organization, there were no
other Jewish institutions and hardly any Jews in the neighborhood. The
YIVO occupied about a half acre of land, with a six-foot-high picket
fence enclosing the property on the street front. A discreet sign posted
at the picket-gate entrance gave only the address—Wiwulskiego 18—
and the Yiddish letters for YIVO just below.

Kalmanovich opened the gate for me. There, at the far end of a tree-
and shrub-lined paved walkway some seventy-five feet long, stood the
YIVO building. From the gate, we couldn't see it all, for it was partially
obstructed by the caretaker's house, about midway down on the left of
the walkway. On each side of the walkway a lawn with bright flowerbeds stretched to the end of the property, whose boundaries were
marked by clusters of trees. In New York I was familiar with all sorts
of Jewish organizations, from the dilapidated Mitlshul I had attended
to the dusty time-worn grandeur of the Jewish Division of the New

York Public Library, but I had never seen a Jewish institution in so verdant a setting.

Once we passed the caretaker's house, the face of the whole building became visible. To my big-city eyes its wooden facade gave it the look of a large country house. At first sight it seemed disproportionately broad for its two stories, with the third story and its five dormer windows tucked under the gabled roof. The dark gray exterior was brightened by vertical strips of white-painted wood and by the two rows of large white wood-framed windows.

We entered an enormous vestibule. I gasped with astonished pleasure at its uncluttered spaciousness. This was not at all like the interior of a provincial country house. Two square pillars stood at the center of the otherwise bare vestibule. The whole place shimmered with the sheen of its highly polished wood floor. Wall vitrines on each side of the vestibule displayed YIVO publications. Just beyond the pillars, and dramatically framed by them, was a double staircase leading up. On the first landing, which we faced as we came into the vestibule, hung a huge colored map of the world, with markers indicating the location of YIVO's farflung branches. On each side of the double staircase were single staircases going down to the basement. Corridors off the vestibule led to the library stacks, archives, exhibit rooms, and a public reading room. This was plainly an institutional building that prided itself on understatement.

Kalmanovich showed me around the building, which, besides the basement with its storage space and central-heating apparatus, had twenty-four rooms. He introduced me to the staff, which then consisted of fourteen clerical and professional employees. On the main floor, an impressive bibliographical center was housed in a high-ceilinged room with shelves all the way up to the top, layered with neat piles of folders as far as the eye could see. It contained over 220,000 registered items. We took a look into the library stacks, containing some 40,000 books, including rare books. The Press Archives, a separate room, held about 10,000 volumes of Jewish newspapers from many countries and in many languages. Other rooms contained massive archival collections of manuscripts and autographs, of leaflets, pamphlets, and Jewish communal records, some dating back to Vilna's early Jewish history.

Kalmanovich told me about some of the YIVO's special collections gathered by YIVO committees—folklore materials, Yiddish linguistic and terminological materials, and an archive of over 300 autobiographies of young Jews in Eastern Europe, which served as the basis for sociopsychological research. We looked into the Theater Museum with its permanent exhibit. Artifacts of the Yiddish theater—playbills, posters, and programs, manuscripts and working scripts of Yiddish plays—were collected and displayed here. The public reading room had about six or eight reading tables, each seating four persons. I was impressed that each seat had its own built-in tubular fluorescent lamp—something you didn't have in the main reading rooms of the New York Public Library.

Upstairs on the second floor were individual study rooms for the research fellows of the Aspirantur, a large conference room, and the offices of YIVO's executives. Kalmanovich showed me the room I was to share with another *aspirant*. Large and sunny, it had two facing desks, bookshelves, desk lamps, and an interoffice telephone. On the top floor we saw a large exhibit hall and several work rooms.

This YIVO building was utterly unlike the institutions of the Yiddish world I knew in New York, most of which were housed in cramped, dingy, and dilapidated quarters. Everything about the YIVO—its location, its landscaped setting, its modern design, the gleaming immaculateness of the place—delivered a message. I interpreted it to mean that the YIVO had class, was no moldering institution, but a place from which distinction and excellence would issue. Even more: The YIVO was no seedy relic of the past; it belonged to the future.

Soon I came to realize that the look of this building signified even more. The founders of the YIVO were determined to raise the status of Yiddish and its culture not just among Jews, but also—perhaps especially—in the worldwide scholarly community. Even if YIVO's founders did not often articulate that goal, they wanted to redress the wrongs done to Yiddish, which from its earliest days had always been treated with contempt as the vernacular of the common people, decried as a corrupt "jargon" of German, denied its standing as a pedigreed language with its own grammar and syntax. For generations Jews who wanted to achieve success in the world shunned Yiddish, as if it were the impediment to their advancement. Even at best, Yiddish was regarded as a vehicle for a folk culture, never as a medium for high intellectual endeavor. The YIVO aimed to change both the image and the reality. The very look of its building was intended to show that an institution associated with Yiddish could be sophisticated and polished.

The YIVO was created at a meeting of Yiddishist intellectuals in Vilna on March 24, 1925. There the participants discussed a proposal to establish a Yiddish academic institute. The idea had been developed in

Berlin by émigré Jewish scholars. In the years immediately after the Great War, Berlin was a place where all sorts of new ideas about Jewish national renewal were afloat, ideas soon to be realized there and elsewhere. Thus, in 1919, the Akademie für die Wissenschaft des Judentums was established in Berlin to promote Jewish scholarship along the lines of the nineteenth century's Science of Judaism and to encourage the development of a new generation of Jewish scholars. A year later, Franz Rosenzweig, Martin Buber, and an extraordinary galaxy of Jewish scholars opened the Freies Jüdisches Lehrhaus in Frankfurt as a center for adult Jewish education. In Jerusalem, meanwhile, the Hebrew University was coming into being, shaped by the model of German scholarship which German Jews had brought to Palestine. By an ironic coincidence of history the Hebrew University was formally inaugurated on April 1, 1925, just a week after the meeting in Vilna that decided to establish the YIVO.

The idea for a Yiddish academic institute might seem to have been merely a copy-cat adaptation of those scholarly innovations. But in fact it represented something new—the coming of age of the culture of Yiddish, whose advocates were now ready to stake out a place for it in the territory of modern Jewish scholarship. The Jewish intellectuals who proposed the creation of a Yiddish academic institute were responding to the profound social changes which had been wrought in the Jewish community during the last fifty years and which, in the wake of the Great War and the Russian revolutions, had transformed the Jews and their institutions in Eastern Europe. The old triple order of status, Judaic learning, and money which had ruled traditional Jewish society no longer exercised the same unchallenged authority it had once wielded.

The working class everywhere was asserting itself, demanding its economic and political rights, articulating its cultural needs. The Jewish working class was no exception. The lowest stratum in the Jewish world, it was composed in Eastern Europe almost entirely of Yiddish speakers. These were the hewers of wood and the carriers of water, the little people without learning, money, or status. Now it was their turn to play a greater role in Jewish politics and to push their way up in the cultural hierarchy of Jewish society. In Poland their political interests were represented mainly by the Bund, while their cultural needs found expression in Yiddish and its expanding organizations.

Yiddish culture, as it had developed in the late nineteenth century, offered a secular alternative to the culture of traditional Judaism. It had produced a brilliant literature and a lively prolific journalism that flourished in Eastern Europe and its immigrant outposts, especially in the United States. The literary culture, in turn, had given rise, in the early decades of the twentieth century, to a secular Yiddish school system in Poland, Lithuania, and the United States. It was inevitable that those who regarded Yiddish as a Jewish national language and a vehicle of Jewish continuity should want to create an institution of higher learning in Yiddish, comparable in excellence and vitality to the literary culture.

The Yiddishist leaders in Vilna who met on March 24, 1925, to consider the Berlin proposal were more finely attuned than the émigré intellectuals in Berlin to the social realities of the Yiddish-speaking community in Poland. They knew that Vilna would provide the most suitable habitat for a Yiddish academic institute because of the density of its Yiddish speakers, the presence of a Yiddish educational substructure, and the support of a prestigious Yiddish-speaking elite. But even in Vilna reservations were voiced about the Berlin proposal.

Max Weinreich, then an instructor at the Yiddish Teachers' Seminary and already a noted Yiddish philologist, was enthusiastic about the proposal, but wanted to give it a somewhat different emphasis. He argued that an academic institute was elitist, an unaffordable luxury, since it did not address the educational and cultural needs of the Yiddish-speaking community. He was very much aware that the emergent lower-class population of Yiddish speakers still needed to be primed, educationally speaking. Weinreich supported the view that the new institution should concentrate on independent research, but such research, he held, had to serve the interests of the whole Jewish community. This could be accomplished only through ties with the Yiddish educational establishment. Furthermore, the new institute would also have to undertake to train a cadre of young Jewish scholars to carry on the pursuit of modern Jewish studies.

Weinreich's views prevailed and the new institution immediately came into existence, in Vilna, with the very name he had proposed— *yidisher visnshaftlekher institut*—"Jewish" or "Yiddish Research Institute." Its acronym "YIVO" was to become the new institution's most familiar tag. In English its name appeared as "Yiddish Scientific Institute," the word "scientific" being used in the German academic sense of critical scholarship.

Now, as I reflect on the history of the YIVO in the light of my own experience in Vilna, I'm convinced that notwithstanding the special and particular circumstances which made it possible to establish the YIVO in Vilna, it could not have come into being, even there, without Max Weinreich and his extraordinary willpower. To be sure, he couldn't have done it single-handedly, but he was its true enabler. His determination was a powerful engine that propelled him forward relentlessly, and he had energy to spare to move others along with him. He could create worlds if he decided to do so.

He was just about forty-four when I first met him, of medium height, with brown hair already graying, combed back off his high forehead. His most distinctive physical features were an irresistible smile, often like a boyish grin, which accompanied his humor, and his penetrating eyes, which though always behind thick glasses, saw everything, even deep inside you. Yet he was nearly blind in one eye. Back in 1931, he was one of a group of journalists whom a stone-throwing student mob attacked during an anti-Semitic riot in Vilna. One of those stones hit him in the eye.

I knew little about him before I came to Vilna, except that his field was Yiddish linguistics, and that he was also interested in psychoanalysis, that he'd known Freud and had persuaded him to become a member of YIVO's honorary board. (Einstein was also an honorary board member.) Weinreich had recently written an important book, which I had not yet read, *Der veg tsu undzer yugnt* (*The Way to Our Youth*), a sociopsychological study of Jewish youth in Poland based on those 300 autobiographical essays which the YIVO had collected and which Kalmanovich had pointed out to me on my first visit. The Aspirantur was his creation and he served as its academic adviser.

A distinct Germanic cast defined Weinreich's intellectual and managerial style. He came by it naturally. He had been born in a small town in Courland, a region in Latvia where German culture prevailed. German had been his mother tongue and, given his family's aspirations, it was predictable that he would eventually earn his doctorate at a German university. Academic credentials always impressed him, though in the YIVO he learned to respect the gift for scholarship exhibited by several of YIVO's self-taught *aspirantn*. He prized discipline in all matters and he highly rated the virtues of accuracy and precision. Once he patiently explained to me that when copying a text for citation, one had to do so exactly as it was with all its mistakes in spelling, punctuation, and grammar. He was also, as long as I knew him, a workaholic who couldn't grasp the concept of leisure and a perfectionist who was never satisfied with his own or other people's work.

Had he been merely an East European variant of a Teutonic pedant, Weinreich wouldn't have appealed at all to me, nor could he have evoked the loyalty and love he enjoyed from the staff and the *aspirantn,* and from many in Vilna's Jewish community. He was a passionate out-and-out secular Jew. Yiddish was at the center of his Jewishness. His communal concerns focused on the millions of Yiddish-speaking Jews who comprised his constituency, as it were. Not his family, but a childhood friend had introduced him to Yiddish when he was only about eleven. A few years later he was caught up in the revolutionary ferment of his time and became a Bundist.

In 1912, at the age of eighteen, he enrolled in the University of St. Petersburg. Meanwhile, he had become so proficient in Yiddish that he worked as a correspondent for a Bundist Yiddish paper in Vilna. After the Bolshevik Revolution of November 1917, he moved to Vilna and continued his journalistic career. When the First World War ended, he went to Germany to complete his studies at the University of Marburg. There he earned his doctorate with a dissertation on the history of Yiddish linguistic studies, thus combining his love for Yiddish with his academic talents and predilections.

He returned to Vilna in 1923 and there married Regina Szabad, the daughter of one of Vilna's most distinguished families. The Yiddish Teachers' Seminary, then the top Yiddish educational agency in Vilna, invited him to teach Yiddish and its literature. At the same time, he continued his journalistic career as a regular correspondent for the New York *Jewish Daily Forward.* He wrote under several pen names, to keep his journalism distinct from his scholarship, though the journalism enabled him to support his family in a comfortable middle-class style. At the time of the YIVO's founding, he was about thirty years old, already an influence in Vilna's cultural life.

Among those present at that meeting in Vilna on March 24, 1925, was Zalmen Reisen, who seconded Weinreich's views. Reisen, born in 1887, had already made a name for himself as a writer and scholar, having published a Yiddish textbook and a Yiddish grammar; he was influential in the movement to standardize Yiddish grammar and spelling. His *leksikon fun der yidisher literatur un prese (Lexicon of Yiddish Literature and Press)*, a biographical dictionary of all Yiddish writers and journalists in modern times, had appeared in 1914.

Reisen had moved to Vilna from his native White Russia in 1915, and in 1919, shortly after Piłsudski's Polish Legionnaires captured Vilna for Poland and slaughtered its Jews, he became editor of *Undzer Tog,* the Yiddish daily I used to read. During his tenure as editor, he made it as aggressive a defender of Jewish interests and of Yiddish as the Polish censor would tolerate.

Once the YIVO was established, Reisen joined Weinreich on YIVO's executive committee. He was the most enthusiastic Yiddishist I ever met. He used to argue that Jews should use Yiddish in their public activities as well as in the privacy of their homes and it was said that he had influenced Jewish doctors in Vilna to speak Yiddish to their patients. Reisen's prodigious energy had enabled him to expand his original one-volume biographical lexicon to a monumental four volumes, published between 1926 and 1929. For years that lexicon was a standard reference work. When I first met him, he was in constant pursuit of biographical material for a new edition of his masterwork. His pockets used to bulge with scraps of paper bearing fugitive bits of information about one or another writer. He was generous with these materials and shared many with me for my own research.

In 1929, as I already mentioned, the YIVO board invited Kalmanovich to Vilna to join the staff as one of YIVO's three executives and editor of its publications. Each of them—Weinreich, Reisen, Kalmanovich—had different political views, but as far as I could see, those differences never intruded on their warm personal relations or affected the primary interests that bound them together—their love of Yiddish and their total commitment to the YIVO.

Though Weinreich was no longer an active Bundist when I first met him, he still remained loyal to that party and voted its ticket. Reisen, it was said, had Trotskyite sympathies, though I don't remember ever hearing him say anything that would have given me a clue to such political views. Kalmanovich, for his part, had never been on the left. When I knew him, he had become an advocate of territorialism, a movement which had originated in Eastern Europe as an alternative to Zionism. The territorialists proposed that Jews who didn't want to settle in Palestine might nevertheless want to establish an autonomous society of their own on a territory large enough to sustain them economically and culturally. Kalmanovich identified himself with the Freeland League, a territorialist organization founded in 1935, which aimed to find such a territory, and even conducted some negotiations with Australian authorities for a place called Kimberley, a tract of about 140,000 square miles in northwestern Australia.

The Yiddishists who created the YIVO in 1925 had deep faith in its future. That faith not only overcame the objections of skeptics, but even enabled the founders to surmount the financial obstacles of the time. Poland in 1925 was not the most promising place for an institution of higher Yiddish learning. The government was in political crisis. Poland's economic situation then hovered at the edge of disaster. The bottom had dropped out of world prices for those exports on which Poland's economy depended. Polish banks were failing. Inflation and unemployment impoverished the population and paralyzed the government. The zloty kept falling; by early 1926 it had dropped to half its former value.

No matter: The YIVO operated on faith. Without financial resources, it exploited its intellectual and scholarly resources, drawing upon a whole generation of university-trained Jewish scholars in a wide variety of disciplines. Right off, the YIVO established four research sections, as had been envisaged in the original Berlin plan. The History Section was headed by Elias Tcherikower. Born in the Ukraine, then living in Berlin, and soon to move to Paris, he had already made a name for himself as a historian of Russian Jewry and a documenter of the Ukrainian pogroms during the Russian civil war. Jacob Lestchinsky, who headed the Economics and Statistics Section, had come from Russia, but was then living in Berlin. After Hitler came to power, he moved to Warsaw and then, in 1938, to New York. He had established himself as a leading demographer, having founded a Yiddish journal devoted to studies of Jewish demography and statistics. Max Weinreich, in Vilna, headed the section for linguistics, literature, and folklore. Leibush Lehrer, my Mitlshul teacher in New York, headed the Psychology and Education Section.

The YIVO succeeded in attracting to its research sections a wide variety of established scholars and also drew into its orbit the younger generation of scholars eager to become part of an institution whose academic standards were high and whose social policy appealed to them. They all comprised a diaspora of Jewish scholars. Many lived in Poland, others were among the émigrés in Berlin, some had settled in the United States, and still others were scattered elsewhere around the globe. Though they had published their scholarly works in a medley of Western languages, for most of them Yiddish was their mother tongue. Even those who knew little or no Yiddish were attracted to YIVO's desire to enlist scholarship in the service of the Jewish community. They rallied to the YIVO because it gave them a common national purpose, provided them with an institutional address, and promised them a wider readership and following than they could otherwise ever have had.

The YIVO headquarters was at first located in a room in Max Weinreich's apartment and then in rented space. Its founders began a twofold operation—to shape the YIVO's research programs and to send emissaries abroad to raise money. At the start, a series of pamphlets called *The Organization of Jewish Scholarship* began to appear, reporting on YIVO's institutional progress and its research plans.

Early on the YIVO's founders realized that they needed to develop a support structure for their institution not only to strengthen its financial base, but even more to strengthen its social underpinnings. To do so, they began to create a network of *zamlers,* "collectors," which stretched across all Poland, into Lithuania, Rumania, and more distant places. The idea was to enlist the Jewish man-in-the-street in the YIVO's activities and to make him a partner in its scholarly work. It was no token association or mere busywork that the YIVO solicited from these *zamlers.* YIVO's research programs needed documentary and archival materials that had never before been collected systematically. Linguists wanted the written and oral evidence of Yiddish dialects, regional diction, and pronunciation. They were in search of Yiddish nomenclature, Yiddish terms for trades, occupations, sports, sciences, classifications of nature. Folklorists wanted Yiddish folklore—jokes, songs, stories, sayings. In 1931, the YIVO published a brochure called *What Exactly Is Ethnography?,* which became something of a best-seller. It introduced thousands of *zamlers* to the study of folklore and instructed them in the methods of collecting its materials. The economists needed a wide variety of economic and statistical data not available from government records and they hoped to obtain these from a network of field informants.

This method of gathering data had its own history, having been used a half century earlier with great success by the historian Simon Dubnow. (He, too, along with Freud and Einstein, was a member of YIVO's honorary board.) In the last decade of the nineteenth century, Dubnow enlisted an army of foot soldiers—Jewish university students as well as the common folk—to collect documentary sources for the history of the

Jews in Russia. That way Jewish scholars tried to compensate for the lack of Jewish government chancelleries and Jewish official records, for the lack of Jewish universities and academies.

The YIVO network of *zamlers* crisscrossed Poland and created a dense web of moral support for its work. It generated enthusiasm among people who would not likely be the consumers of YIVO's research studies, but who looked upon the YIVO as a kind of national university. With scarcely more than the traditional elementary education of the *heder,* and sometimes not even that, they considered it an honor to be able to do something for so prestigious an educational institution. By 1929 some 500 circles of *zamlers* had come into being throughout Poland. In addition, the YIVO's Folklore Commission kept in touch with hundreds of individual correspondents.

In its first five years, the YIVO published three volumes of *Filologishe shriftn (Studies in Philology)*, one volume of studies in economics and statistics, one in history, and one bibliographical annual. In 1931, the YIVO launched its monthly scholarly journal *YIVO-Bleter.* The first issue carried a lead article by Simon Dubnow, about a previously unknown manuscript of 1816 documenting the struggle between the maskilim and the hasidim.

As the YIVO's undertakings multiplied, its staff increased. The library kept growing and the documentary collections expanded. The Institute needed more space. In 1927, the YIVO board proposed that the YIVO erect a building of its own. Eventually a suitable site was found on Wiwulskiego Street. In the presence of nearly a thousand people, the cornerstone for the new building was laid on a cool Friday afternoon, October 25, 1929. It was during the very week the New York Stock Exchange began its spectacular collapse that ended in the great crash of the stock market.

The ensuing Great Depression in America sent devastating economic tremors across the ocean to Europe, even as far as Vilna. The young institution went through a severe financial crisis. But in 1932, Zalmen Reisen went on a fund-raising tour to Argentina, with the slogan: "Raise a roof over the YIVO." He succeeded in bringing back enough money for the building to be completed. Early in 1933, the YIVO moved into its own home.

Meanwhile, in accordance with Weinreich's early ideas about the potential role of the YIVO in raising the level of the Yiddish school system and its teaching staff, the YIVO had formed close ties with the Central Yiddish School Organization, known by its Yiddish acronym

CYSHO. Founded in 1921, the CYSHO was the umbrella organization for the secular Yiddish schools in Poland, most of which were affiliated with the Bund. At its peak in 1929, the CYSHO school network consisted of 114 elementary schools, 46 kindergartens, 52 evening schools, and 3 secondary schools, with about 850 teachers and about 24,000 pupils, the Yiddish Teachers' Seminary in Vilna, and a magnificent children's sanatorium, named after one of the Bund's founders, Vladimir Medem. In the 1930s, the Polish authorities began a campaign of political harassment against those schools, closing them on one pretext or another, arresting teachers, depriving them of their licenses. By the late 1930s the overall pupil enrollment had dropped to about 17,000.

The Yiddish secular schools attracted only a small proportion of the children of school age, perhaps about 10 percent of all children in Jewish schools and about 5 percent of all Jewish children of school age. Nearly all of the children who attended the Yiddish schools were children of the working class or of the poor. Most Jewish children attended either the public schools or the Jewish religious-school network. The Tarbut schools, the secular Hebrew school system organized by the Zionists in competition with the CYSHO, soon attracted about twice as many pupils as the Yiddish schools, drawing their children mainly from the middle class.

Yet whatever the limitations of the CYSHO school system, it was important to the YIVO that CYSHO acknowledged YIVO's leadership and accepted its tutelage. Under CYSHO sponsorship, the YIVO offered enrichment courses for CYSHO teachers, held at the YIVO during the winter vacations. Most important, the CYSHO adopted YIVO's standardized spelling rules for use in all its institutions and in its instruction.

The YIVO also influenced editors and publishers of Yiddish newspapers and journals, some of whom agreed to abide by the YIVO's standardized spelling rules. To do so, they manufactured new typefaces for the diacritical marks which the YIVO's orthography required.

In less than a decade, the YIVO became widely known throughout the Yiddish-speaking and Yiddish-writing world for its strict standards to preserve the purity of the Yiddish language. To be sure, there were critics and mockers, poking fun at the YIVO's attempt, as they saw it, to purge Yiddish of its Germanisms and put the language in a straitjacket, but for the most part the YIVO had attained the reputation as the guardian of Yiddish. In about a decade, it had truly become an academy. In the realm of Yiddish, the YIVO had emerged as the Ministry of Yiddish.

In mid-August 1935, the YIVO celebrated its tenth anniversary with a grand conference in Vilna. It coincided with one of the darkest periods in Jewish history, in all European history. Hitler was firmly entrenched in Germany. The political outlook in Poland was not encouraging. Piłsudski had died just three months before. As an anti-anti-Semite, he had managed to restrain the use of anti-Semitism as a political weapon in Poland. Without his powerful presence in the government, Poland's political parties would be more likely to flex their anti-Semitic muscle, intensify their anti-Semitic propaganda, and introduce legislation to deprive Jews of their political rights and deny them the opportunities to earn their livelihood.

At just that time, when Jews clearly had more urgent problems to attend to, the YIVO announced the establishment of its newest division—the Aspirantur, to train young people for independent scholarship. Dubnow, addressing the conference, justified the YIVO's continuing expansion and its vitality, even—and especially—in those terrible times. He compared the YIVO's situation to that of people living along earthquake faults. Just because they live there, he said, they don't stop studying seismology.

The Aspirantur could be seen as a parallel to the *zamlers* network. Both represented systematic attempts by the YIVO's leadership to create a normal pyramidal structure in the Yiddish-speaking community. The *zamlers* program was intended to extend and reinforce the YIVO's base in the Jewish community. The Aspirantur was intended to develop the top. Its task was to train a cadre of scholars fluent in Yiddish, proficient in the methods of research, and knowledgeable about the Jewish past and present.

In September 1938, the fourth annual Aspirantur began its academic year with sixteen research fellows. About half had already put in a year or more in the Aspirantur. Most had university training. Fourteen were from Poland, one from Latvia, and I from New York. Six were women. At twenty-three, I was the youngest; the oldest was probably around thirty-five.

When I first arrived, my new colleagues were curious to meet me— this American-born young woman who had come from New York to study in Vilna. An epidemic of English afflicted them. Everybody began reading English books with words they didn't understand. They kept coming to my office or calling on the phone for help. Weinreich soon heard about this rage to learn English. Never one to inhibit the study of language, he decided to channel their linguistic curiosity into a systematic course: I was to give a class in English once a week for those who wanted it. Otherwise, so he instructed everyone, they were not to intrude on my time. The class lasted just a few weeks. It petered out once they got to know me and I them.

Most of my colleagues were poor. Though by American standards I, too, was poor, by their standards, most of them considered me rich. For I had been raised in a milieu of sufficiency, if not of plentifulness. I'd never known hunger; my family always had a roof over our heads. Compared to the poverty in which my colleagues had been raised and with which most of them still had to contend, I really wasn't poor, even if I didn't have any money.

Besides the matter of rich and poor, I differed from them because I had been born and raised in America, innocent of the experience of war. When I was two years old, the United States entered the Great War and sent its soldiers to fight in France. We at home had never experienced the terrors of war. I remember only, when I was a little over two years old, the scary excitement of the kaiser's effigy strung high over the street, to celebrate our entry into the war. But that war discomposed the lives of my friends and colleagues in the Aspirantur, turning their existence upside down and inside out, even the youngest among them. Their families were dislocated. They fled first from the armies of czarist Russia and then from the armies of Kaiser Wilhelm's Germany. Whole families uprooted themselves, on the move for months in search of bread. They suffered hunger, even famine. The war deprived older children of their education; they lost years they later had to make up. Some never recovered their childhoods. Nothing like that had happened in my life.

Besides that difference in our experiences, my American passport constituted an ever-present difference between me and them. Whenever I chose to do so, I could run away to the safety of the United States, finding refuge in my American home far from the war that we all felt would surely come. They had no choice but to stay.

Even so, despite our different pasts and the expectation of our different fates, I was on good terms with all the *aspirantn* and became close friends with some.

The senior member, in status rather than age, was Ber Schlossberg, with whom I shared an office. Born in Vilna, he was only five years older than I, but already carried himself with middle-aged maturity and worry, a slight figure of a man, already balding, gentle and soft-spoken.

He had earned a master's degree in Germanics from the University of Vilna with a study in Yiddish linguistics. Technically speaking, Schlossberg was no longer an *aspirant,* but a staff assistant, earning the munificent sum of eighty zlotys per month, twenty zlotys more than our stipends. He was married to a lovely young woman who gave piano lessons and together—they did not yet have a child the year I was there—they managed to maintain a frugal household.

Besides doing his own research on the abstruse subject of Eastern Yiddish in the sixteenth century, he shared the pedagogic responsibility for the YIVO's newest venture—the Pro-aspirantur, designed to train candidates for the Aspirantur. He was assigned also to tutor me in Yiddish for two one-hour sessions a week. Besides all that, he edited manuscripts and read proof for the YIVO's publications.

Schlossberg was utterly devoted to the YIVO, especially to Weinreich. He was always at work when I arrived in the morning, no matter how early, and when I left, no matter how late, he was usually still there. He was the first independent scholar produced by the Aspirantur and Weinreich's particular pride.

The only other philologist in our group was Shmuel Friedland, who came from Dvinsk (Daugavpils), Latvia, just for the spring semester. It was his first time in Vilna. About twenty-seven, tall, blond, Nordicly handsome, he spoke a good Yiddish and also Russian, German, Lettish. He even knew some English. He'd done his graduate studies at the University of Prague and was working on the language of the *Maasebukh,* a Yiddish compilation, first published in 1602, of some 250 stories and fables derived from Talmudic and Midrashic sources. He must have come from a well-to-do family, for he was always well dressed and had more ready cash than most of us.

There were two folklorists. Shmuel-Zeinvel Pipe (pronounced Pippeh) was probably the most original personality among us. Of medium height, with light brown curly hair, a high forehead, and laughing eyes, he had a lovely face, all friendliness. His humor was as integral to him as his eyes and ears. It was often hilarious, never mean or cruel. It was fun to be in his company, even though we ribbed him for his Galician accent.

He was born in 1907 in Sanok, a Galician town whose Jews made up nearly half its inhabitants, and he'd lived there all his life. He had attended first a Polish elementary school and then a Hebrew one, and had no other education. His father had been a tailor and so was he. All his life he collected things—as a child, buttons and other such objects which children cherished and exchanged with one another. When the YIVO issued its call to *zamlers* to gather folklore materials in accordance with its specifications, Pipe became an ardent collector. The material he sent to Vilna was of such high quality that he soon became an active correspondent of YIVO's Folklore Commission and came to the attention of the YIVO's leading folklore scholar, Judah Leib Cahan.

Cahan, a native of Vilna, but then living in New York, headed up YIVO's folklore program and had been corresponding with Pipe. When Cahan came to Vilna in 1930 to supervise some aspects of YIVO's folklore activities, he financed Pipe's trip from Sanok to Vilna so that they could meet. Cahan then arranged for Pipe to take a short course in folklore methodology. The next five years, living in Sanok, Pipe continued to earn his living at his tailoring, but he'd now become a folklorist. With YIVO's help, he began to read systematically in the field. In 1935, when the Aspirantur was founded, the YIVO invited him to join, even though he had no academic degree. With his ferocious energy, he applied himself to his education and did not limit himself to folklore. Before I arrived, he'd already produced some notable studies in his field.

In 1937 Cahan died and the YIVO then undertook to publish his literary remains. That became Pipe's major project, together with the other folklorist, his colleague Nechama Epstein. They were to assemble, edit, annotate, and prepare for publication those works of Cahan's which had appeared in periodicals or which were still unpublished.

The first thing I noted about Nechama Epstein was that she was an unattractive woman. I thought she was about forty, but now, studying a couple of photographs I have of our group, I realize she was probably younger. She was short, with a squarish build, a squarish face, and straight black bobbed hair, unbecomingly held in place with barrettes. Her strongest asset was her sense of humor. It was evident to all of us that she was in love with Pipe, while he was fond of her. They were always together, yet we didn't quite figure out their relationship. They got married soon after I left Vilna.

Nechama had come to Vilna in the mid-twenties. Perhaps she had had some academic training, most likely teacher training. She'd been variously a teacher in Polish and Yiddish schools, a lecturer (she was an excellent public speaker), a poet, and a translator from Polish into Yiddish. Most of all she loved literature. Like Pipe, she met Cahan in 1930 and was persuaded by him to turn her talents to the study of Jewish folklore, particularly to Jewish humor and Yiddish jokes. She was very diligent in her work, organized and systematic, and had mastered the theoretical literature in the field.

My closest friend in the Aspirantur was Chana Piszczacer Mann, ten years older than I, and a little taller than my five-foot-nothing. She had an expressive face with a Slavic look—wide cheeks, a short upturned nose, straight straw-colored hair parted in the middle and combed behind her ears. Everyone called her Chantche, a diminutive of her name. She had a girlish quality, though she was the mother of a six-year-old daughter. I loved her for her charm, her penetrating judgments of people's character, and her tragic family history.

She'd met her husband when they were both students of the Yiddish Teachers' Seminary in Vilna. After their graduation in 1927, they taught in the Bundist Yiddish schools, but were harassed by the authorities for their politics. In 1934 the Education Ministry took away their teaching licenses. Chantche's husband managed to get work at the Bundist Medem Sanatorium, just outside Warsaw, a year-round institution for poor children and also a summer camp. She was accepted in the Aspirantur when it first opened in 1935 and came to live in Vilna with her little daughter Esther. The separation was difficult, though her husband used to visit several times a year and she and Esther spent the summers at the Medem Sanatorium. They were always short of money. Still, Chantche kept her good humor and lived with the unwarranted hope that things would get better. Like Schlossberg, she was extraordinarily devoted to the YIVO and especially to Weinreich.

Her project in the Aspirantur was in the field of child development: She kept a detailed record of Esther's physical, mental, and emotional growth. Under Weinreich's supervision, she became familiar with the professional literature and corresponded with child psychologists all over the world, especially with those keeping day-to-day records of child development. The year I was there she was concentrating on the role of play in a child's life.

We had only one *aspirant* in the field of education. His name was Elihu Teitlebaum; we called him Elya. Five years older then I and not much taller, he looked like a cherub, with apple-red cheeks and a baby smile. He taught singing in the Yiddish schools, conducted the choir at the Choir Synagogue, conducted the Maccabi orchestra and from time to time other institutional choral or instrumental groups. He already had achieved a reputation in Vilna as a composer. He'd set a number of Yiddish poems to music and arranged many songs for voice with piano accompaniment and for choral groups, many of which were played at local concerts. As part of his Aspirantur study—on teaching singing in the elementary school—he was preparing a collection of Yiddish children's folk songs with his own music.

In literature there were two of us. My project on the Yiddish press in nineteenth-century England was the least interesting of any of the Aspirantur topics and without much social value. Still, everyone was kind to me, even when I presented my oral reports. Esther Schindelman, the other *aspirant* in literature, was far more competent than I. She had been born in Rovno; her mother, if I remember correctly, was a dentist. Esther was then thirty years old, in her second year in the Aspirantur. She was not attractive as a woman or as a person, chattering incessantly about boyfriends of whom we never had any evidence and who—so we agreed when we gossiped about her—were probably figments of her overheated sexual fantasies. Though she had no success in her social life, she had better luck academically.

She had earned a master's degree in literature from the University of Vilna and had impressive references from her professors, among them, Manfred Kridl, one of Poland's leading literary scholars. She'd been engaged in a study of Polish themes in Yiddish literature, but had just had her subject changed. At the start of our academic year, the Yiddish novelist and dramatist Isaac Meir Weissenberg died. He'd begun his career as a disciple of the Yiddish classicist Isaac Leib Peretz. The YIVO decided it would be fitting for Esther to do a study of his work. It was ironic, because she was the least interested of any of us in Yiddish. Her spoken and written Yiddish was poorer than mine. Her linguistic passion was for Esperanto; she was an officer of a local Esperanto society and even wrote articles in Esperanto. Her commitment to Esperanto as the future universal language was her way of running away from her Jewishness.

The field of history had four *aspirantn,* yet none had what I would now call historical imagination. Rachel Golinkin, daughter of the Danzig rabbi, was a nondescriptly pretty young woman of twenty-six, quiet and unassuming. I think that she was not as poor as the others in our group. We used to poke fun good-naturedly at her demure rabbinic ways and call her the *"rebbetzin."* She had studied history at the University of Vilna. In the Aspirantur she worked on documents in YIVO's Archives of the Vilna Kahal for the period 1808–1845. Chana Smuczkewicz, also twenty-six, was much prettier, apple-cheeked, dark-haired, dark-eyed, animated, and liked to laugh as much as I did. She'd grown up in a small town near Vilna, and at nineteen began study at the

University of Vilna. She was studying Jewish guilds in Vilna in the first half of the nineteenth century.

Pinhas Tikoczinski, about twenty-seven, came from Bialystok, a medium-sized industrial city between Vilna and Warsaw. Tall, rather good-looking and sophisticated, a persuasive speaker, he was then entering his third year in the Aspirantur. He, too, had studied history at the University of Vilna and was working on a paper about East European Jews during the Great War. More exciting—to him as well as to us—was his debut as a fund-raiser for the YIVO. That seemed to suit his moody, often stormy, temperament better than poring over documents. In the spring he went on tour, visiting small Jewish communities, speaking on behalf of the YIVO, making contacts, raising money. We all took pride in his success. Proudest was Weinreich, for he had nurtured this homegrown product.

Chaim Munitz wasn't a historian at all, but an artist. Originally from Brasław, a small town not far from Vilna, he'd studied at the Yiddish Teachers' Seminary and for a while at an art school. He was tiny—about my height, thin to the point of emaciation, with a beautifully expressive face, dark eyes, and a rich head of dark wavy hair off his high forehead. He was a person of fine sensibility and was known to write poetry. He lived at the edge of penury. Sometimes he had work drawing maps or retouching and at the YIVO he did whatever artwork or design was wanted. His Aspirantur project, in the field of social history, suited his visual and graphic talents. He was preparing a lexicon of Jewish clothing in the first half of the nineteenth century.

In February 1939, at twenty-eight, Munitz decided to get married. The *aspirantn* were invited to the wedding. We were his family. His mother was dead, and his father, seriously ill in Brasław, was being cared for there by Munitz's only sister. The bride, a seamstress, was as small, thin, and dark as he, and just as poor. She had only her parents, who lived in an old-age home, which was where the wedding ceremony, canopy and all, was held. We tried to be cheerful, but it didn't seem to us a happy occasion. We didn't approve of his bride, thinking she wasn't good enough for him. Still, we bought them a tea service for six as a wedding present.

The three *aspirantn* in sociology weren't exactly sociologists, yet their research projects were livelier and of greater consequence than those of the historians. David Ornstein, who came from a tiny town in eastern Galicia, had not completed his law studies at the university in Lwów (Lemberg)—why I don't know. It's likely that he had run out of money.

He was a sweet, nice-looking, tallish young man with country-pink cheeks and dark hair. He lived in utter terror of the perils of Vilna, the big city. I could never understand why, since he'd lived in Lwów, a livelier and more populous place than Vilna. He was always in mortal fear of being run over by a bus or attacked by a hoodlum. Most of us thought him tiresome.

He'd already been a year in the Aspirantur, working on an ambitious project conceived by Weinreich, on the socioeconomic background and aspirations of Jewish male and female apprentices, youngsters from Vilna's poorest population. The YIVO distributed questionnaires among them, offering as an incentive small cash prizes for the best replies. The response rate turned out to be quite high and the question-naires contained a wealth of personal, financial, and social data, as well as insights into their future expectations.

Daniel Lerner, who had been studying history and philosophy off and on for years at the University of Vilna, had been an *aspirant* for several years. He was thirty-two, short and ugly, with a dynamic and com-manding personality that compensated for his physical unattractiveness. A Bundist, he was always aggressive and adversarial in his opinions and viewed everything through the prism of class differences. He wanted to introduce me to Bundist politics in Vilna, much to Kalmanovich's dismay, who was afraid I might get arrested. He was also vice-chairman of the Jewish Students Union, though that year he was not attending courses at the University. I think he preferred to be involved in the livelier milieu of politics than in the more reclusive and reflective life of a scholar. His Aspirantur project was a sociological study of a small Jewish town, which he hoped eventually to use also as his master's essay at the University.

About Shlomo Berezin, our third sociologist, I remember little. He was a shy, handsome young man from a village in eastern Poland. He had attended a university, probably the one in Vilna. The year before I came he'd heard Marian Anderson sing in Vilna and was much taken with Negro spirituals and blues. He would ask questions about Negroes in America and wanted me to sing whatever spirituals and blues I knew. ("St. James Infirmary Blues" was my favorite.)

His Aspirantur project was more ambitious than Ornstein's. It was a study of Jewish-owned light industry in Vilna, based on field visits and questionnaires about each enterprise, its physical facilities, its workers (family and hired help), their wages, industrial costs, the mechanics of production, the product's sale and distribution, and, of course, the enterprise's profitability. Shlomo had a small staff of investigators whom he had trained. Not all the shop or mill proprietors chosen for the study were entirely cooperative. Even those who agreed to participate withheld information or gave doctored figures. But the YIVO's good reputation in town helped to reduce their anxieties. People tended to look at the YIVO as a defender of Jewish interests, even if it was a scholarly institution, and many proprietors were willing to go along with the YIVO study.

We had one economist in the Aspirantur. A native of Vilna, Jacob Rivkind had a master's degree in economics and statistics from the University of Vilna. He was about thirty, married, tall, handsome, with a distinctly Jewish look. For some years he'd had a good position with a Polish statistical bureau in Warsaw, but was fired when the company "Aryanized" its staff. The YIVO Aspirantur was a last resort for him. His inability to get a proper job crushed his professional pride. His own situation confirmed his general pessimism about Jewish chances for a prosperous future in Poland. He'd already begun to stoop; his posture reflected his despair over the future.

Rivkind headed up the most ambitious of all Aspirantur projects—a study of the budgets of about 300 Jewish families in Vilna, selected as a representative sample. The study of family budgets was then a widely used method in Poland to estimate national income, though professional economists considered it a crude and inaccurate measure. Polish government statisticians were apparently unfamiliar with the concept of gross national product. Rivkind's study was designed to gather more reliable data than the government figures on Jewish income, its sources and amounts, and on its expenditure.

He trained a small corps of interviewers to visit his selected households and win their cooperation. Their first task was to compile data on each household, the demographic characteristics of its members, and the sources of their income. Then they had to persuade a responsible member of the household to agree to keep a record of the family's income and expenditures for a period of, I think, three months. Each participating household was instructed in how to keep these records and given little notebooks in which to enter their figures. All of us, but especially Weinreich and Rivkind himself, had great expectations for this study, which promised to provide an extraordinary body of data to document the socioeconomic conditions of the Jews in Vilna.

Though we didn't have any connection with the students in the Pro-aspirantur, I knew two of them. One was the Yiddish poet Abraham Sutzkever, then twenty-six years old. He had already achieved a reputation as a serious poet. He'd been encouraged, so I assumed, by

Weinreich, to study early Yiddish. I suppose that Sutzkever thought this knowledge would enrich his poetic vocabulary and style. He eventually wrote a lovely cycle of poems using archaic Yiddish syntax and diction.

All of us in the Aspirantur knew Elihu Yonas, who was everyone's darling. He was then about nineteen, a nice-looking young man, with a delicious sense of humor. He'd grown up an orphan, had never gone to school at all. He had taught himself to read and write Yiddish and Polish. As an adolescent he'd worked at a job that taxed his physical strength—carrying impossibly heavy loads in a glove factory. Given his history, it was to be expected that he became a Bundist at an early age. Whatever free time he had he devoted to his duties as a leader of a SKIF group, the Bundist youth organization.

The strenuous demands of his job made him seriously ill. It was said he almost died. While he was recovering in the hospital, some kind soul arranged to get him a job that involved less physical effort—as receptionist at the YIVO and occasional errand boy. He was thrilled to work at the YIVO and to be so close to learning and to scholars. He was paid forty zlotys a month, an amount that seemed like riches to him. Then, when he learned about the Pro-aspirantur, he applied. It was the greatest pride of his young life when he was accepted. He hoped that with this education, he would be able to make something of himself.

That's who we were—a mixed bag of young people, sharing many interests and concerns. We had become a family and most of us enjoyed each other's company. From time to time, mostly during our report sessions, we'd make parties—tea and cookies—where we'd talk and sing Yiddish songs for hours. When I had some money, I'd invite some of my colleagues to my room for tea, drinks, and refreshments. Often we'd go in small groups to the movies or the Yiddish theater. Elya Teitlebaum, who soon learned of my addiction to music, used to take me to concerts. A couple of the other young men tried to make passes at me, but they were not the ones I was attracted to.

We were young Jews in search of a future. Being Jewish was a given, and for all of us, except me, it meant being severely limited in opportunities for a career and even for a decent livelihood. But everyone, with the possible exception of Esther Schindelman, accepted that as the cost of being Jewish. No one ever considered any other alternative. Being Jewish was as intimate and essential a part of us as our arms and legs.

The YIVO bound us together in a way that no large impersonal institution could have. All of us loved the YIVO. Some were prepared to dedicate themselves to it. For others—in the Aspirantur, on the staff, and among YIVO's scholars and supporters, notably Max Weinreich himself—the YIVO had become a religion, a kind of surrogate Judaism.

My own feelings during the year were volatile, wildly unstable. At times I used to feel exalted, believing that the YIVO was engaged in a sacred mission for which I was prepared to make personal sacrifices. I thought that by developing an intellectual elite in the realm of Yiddish, the YIVO had become a guarantor of Jewish continuity in the modern secular world. In my optimistic phase, I was convinced that Vilna was precisely the place to do this. Here about 2,000 children attended Yiddish schools. We had Yiddish newspapers to inform us about what was happening in the world. Shop signs were in Yiddish. People at work conducted their businesses in Yiddish; you could get a receipt in Yiddish for your transactions. At the Jewish banks, you could write a check in Yiddish. Trade unions and craft guilds managed their affairs in Yiddish. Doctors talked to their patients in Yiddish. Political parties competed with one another in Yiddish and posted Yiddish placards on the streets. Young poets wrote their verses in Yiddish and composers set Yiddish songs to music. Nature-study hikes had Yiddish-speaking guides and Maccabi boxing matches had Yiddish-speaking referees. Even the Jewish underworld, the pickpockets and the horse thieves, plied their trades in Yiddish.

Other times I succumbed to dark moods. I'd express skepticism that we in the Aspirantur were competent to carry the banner of scholarship. I was discouraged about the scholarly caliber of the *aspirantn* whom the YIVO had recruited. I sometimes thought that if the stipend were larger, the YIVO might attract more committed and talented young scholars. Except for Schlossberg, Pipe, and Rivkind, few of us were truly committed scholars. Schindelman didn't give a damn about Yiddish literature. We were a motley crowd of unlicensed lawyers, unemployed teachers, half-baked intellectuals. We were declassed, without a future. The Aspirantur had become our temporary sanctuary while we—I included myself—tried to stave off the future. Sometimes Weinreich could see I was depressed and we'd talk. A session with him would restore my faith, but not for long.

But my bleakest thoughts centered on the viability of Yiddish as a self-sufficient, even autonomous, culture in Poland. It seemed to me that the relentless anti-Semitism I witnessed in Vilna and read about in the paper and the desperate poverty I saw every day were the strongest factors in preserving Yiddish. If Poland would someday make peace with its Jewish citizens and allow them to integrate into the larger society, then Yiddish probably wouldn't have much of a future. But if Poland continued to pursue its present course, so I thought, the Jews wouldn't have much of a future of any kind, with or without Yiddish. I had come to see that an enclave of Yiddish without a political or economic base could not survive. Midway during my year in Vilna, I wrote to one of my teachers in New York: "The YIVO has created an illusion, at least in Vilna, that there's a Jewish people which earns its daily bread in Yiddish and takes pleasure in using its own language for matters of mind and spirit. I know that it's only an illusion because the headlines in the daily papers belie it everyday."

My pessimism was confirmed in my conversations with Kalmanovich. He was contempuous of Yiddishism as an ideology that proposed a solution to the anomalies of Jewish existence. "It's bankrupt," he would say. "What kind of movement can it be whose program is to read a Yiddish book and to go to the Yiddish theater once in a while?" He mocked it as a movement whose appeal could be only to people with a literary bent. Besides, Yiddishism had as its unarticulated premise the acceptance of bilingualism. Jews had to know the language of the country. "They need to buy bread and repair their shoes and work; they need to do it in the language of the country in which they live," he would argue. Then he would conclude triumphantly, with his sweet shy smile: "The only solution is for Jews to have their own territory, where they can live a normal life."

Kalmanovich never persuaded me as to the merits of territorialism, but his logic was irrefutable. I applied it not only to the realities of Vilna, but also to New York. I wrote to a friend there, referring to our Yiddishist organization, the Sholem Aleichem Yugnt Gezelshaft: "Every day it grows clearer to me that you can't build an organization just on the basis of Yiddish culture. Yiddish literature alone cannot generate a passion for being Jewish. Why should it interest young American Jews, if they're not interested in literature to begin with?"

I would never have predicted that in Vilna, the citadel of Yiddish, I would come to realize that Yiddish was an insufficient basis on which to maintain one's Jewish identity, that it could not ensure Jewish continuity. Reluctantly and unwelcomingly I accepted that conclusion. It didn't mean that I wanted things to be that way. It didn't mean that I loved Yiddish any the less. Sometimes I felt I was watching the end of a world I had come to love.

CHAPTER 5

In the Realm of Yiddish:
On the Periphery

Long before I left New York for Vilna, I had been assured that I'd get along in Vilna without having to learn Polish, that Yiddish would tide me over even in practical matters. Besides, I thought of my journey exclusively in Jewish terms, as a pilgrimage to an autonomous Yiddish realm that happened to be located in Poland. Poland itself had nothing to recommend it to me: I saw it only as a locus of anti-Semitism.

When I was still in high school, devouring the novels, stories, and dramas of the great Russian writers, discovering the literature of other cultures in the fiction of Thomas Mann, Knut Hamsun, Romain Rolland, and Ignazio Silone, I had already concluded that Polish literature had little to attract me. The only work of Polish literature that I'd ever heard about and actually read was Henryk Sienkiewicz's *Quo Vadis*. It didn't make me want to read more, even though Sienkiewicz had won the Nobel Prize for literature before I was born. Altogether the Poles had few entries in the arts and sciences. Besides Copernicus, Chopin, and Ignace Paderewski, the only Poles we'd ever heard about were anti-Semitic hooligans.

With that attitude of cultural superiority, it never occurred to me that not knowing Polish could be a liability. I didn't consider myself illiterate, because, besides English and Yiddish, I also knew German and some French. To be sure, once in Vilna, I soon picked up a kind of pidgin Polish—"hello" and "goodbye," "excuse me," "please," and "thank you," "yes" and "no," "good" and "bad," "how much" and "too much," numbers for shopping and bargaining. I learned the words on warning signs: "danger," "stop," "no smoking." Still I managed to get along that whole year in Vilna without properly knowing Polish.

All year I worked and played almost exclusively in Yiddish, for I was, after all, in the Jerusalem of Lithuania, the capital of Yiddishland. At the time it never occurred to me that there was anything anomalous about the near-universal presence of Yiddish in Vilna. I took it for granted and attributed it to two fundamental factors. The first was solidly statistical and a sufficient explanation—the dense presence of Jews in Vilna, some 30 percent of the whole, and nearly all of them Yiddish speakers. Even the small number of Polish or Russian speakers surely knew some Yiddish. The second factor was an imponderable, though I considered it to be just as solid and tangible as the statistic to account for the presence of Yiddish. I attributed the preeminent place of Yiddish in Vilna to the indomitable will of a people to survive, to the tenacity of the Jews to keep their language and their culture. I had evidence of that every day at the YIVO, when I talked to Max Weinreich and Zalmen Reisen. But after several months in Vilna I came to realize that willpower was only part of the story.

Yiddish lived in Vilna for reasons which had less to do with Jewish idealism and Yiddishist ideology and more with extrinsic factors like Vilna's geography and history. Situated at Poland's outermost eastern borders, Vilna stood at the crossroads of Poland, Lithuania, and White Russia, a geographical circumstance which shaped its history and culture. Measured in the space of kilometers and in the perspective of the distant past, Vilna was closer to Kaunas than it was to Warsaw, nearer to Minsk than to Cracow. Having been the ancient capital of Lithuania, Vilna differed from Warsaw, Cracow, and other cities which had since time immemorial been part of Poland and where Polish had been the only language ever spoken. In Vilna the Polish language could make no such claim to longevity or exclusivity.

Vilna's geography also accounted for the ethnic mix of its population. Besides its Polish and Yiddish speakers, Vilna had, even as late as 1933, many residents who still reported Lithuanian as their native tongue and others who claimed White Russian, a linguistic hybrid of Polish and Russian. In addition, Vilna still had many Russian speakers, a heritage of the czarist past—only twenty years gone, when Russian was the official language and when its culture had been imposed upon the population by the Russian authorities. Even German speakers, remnants of the Baltic Germans, were still to be found in Vilna. It was inevitable in that multinational and multilingual society that the Jews, too, should have their own language.

In independent Poland, the ethnic minorities—all of them also religious minorities (except for the Lithuanians, who were Catholic)—accounted for about one-third of Poland's population. About one million Germans (mostly Protestants) lived in the westernmost regions of Poland, over four million Ukrainians (Orthodox Church) in the southeastern border areas, and about one million White Russians (also Orthodox Church) and 300,000 Lithuanians in the northeastern border regions. Only the Jewish minority, just over three million people, was spread throughout Poland, mainly in urban places.

From the day it declared itself an independent state, Poland treated its minorities as afflictions. In 1918 the Poles celebrated their independence with pogroms against the Jews and acts of violence against the Germans, Lithuanians, and Ukrainians. Not unreasonably, then, the Great Powers at the Paris Peace Conference made Poland's independence conditional upon its guarantees to safeguard the rights of those minorities. Poland ratified the Polish Minorities Treaty in January 1920, with considerable reluctance, obligating itself to protect the civil, political, religious, and cultural rights of its minorities. One of the twelve articles spelling out those rights guaranteed that no restriction was to be imposed on the free use "of any language in private intercourse, in commerce, in religion, in the press, or in publications of any kind, or at public meetings."

As for education, Poland committed itself to providing "adequate facilities" in towns and districts where non–Polish speakers were "a considerable proportion," so that the children could be educated in their own language within the public educational system. The treaty furthermore assured the minorities of an equitable share of public funds from national or municipal budgets for educational, religious, or charitable purposes. But, alas, those guarantees were seldom honored. The archives of the League of Nations contain hundreds of petitions filed by all of Poland's minorities, claiming violations of their rights. Even the German minority in Poland, protected also by a second treaty, the Agreement on Upper Silesia, saw their extensive prewar schools dwindle under relentless Polonizing pressures and the lack of public funds. None of the other minorities succeeded in developing an adequate school system in its own language with the benefit of public funds. In 1934, the Polish government denounced the Minorities Treaty and declared that it would no longer be bound by it.

Most Jews were unwilling to entrust their children to the Polonizing and—so they suspected and feared—the Christianizing influences of the public schools and they therefore undertook to create their own school systems. Since they did not get the promised public funds, they had to rely on their own limited resources, which were further pinched by the divisions within the Jewish community.

Each different, and often warring, religious and ideological schism established its own school system. The most extensive was the network of traditional religious schools, the *heder* on the primary level and the yeshiva as the secondary school. In postwar Poland the *heder* was somewhat modernized, with obligatory supplementary instruction in Polish and arithmetic. A postwar innovation was the Beth Jacob network of religious schools just for girls, with Yiddish as the language of instruction and Polish required for the general subjects. In the late 1920s a new kind of religious-Zionist school, called Yavneh, was introduced, with Hebrew supplanting Yiddish. The secular Jewish schools, for their part, were split between the Yiddishist Bundists and the Hebraist Zionists. Within the Zionist movement, the schools were divided ideologically— right (Tarbut), in which Hebrew and Polish were the languages of instruction, and the left-wing Zionists, who favored the combination of Hebrew and Yiddish.

In the early 1930s about 60 percent of all Jewish children of school age throughout Poland attended Jewish elementary schools. In Vilna the proportion was even higher. In these schools—religious and secular— children were taught not only the basics of reading, writing, arithmetic, and geography, but also Jewish subjects, *their* languages, culture, history. Theirs was an education in commitment to Judaism or to one of its modern surrogates—Yiddish or Zion.

For about a week at the end of October, I sat in on classes in the Yiddish school across the street from my house. It was named in honor of Sophia Markova Gurevitch, who had been a pioneer in the field of progressive Jewish education. A seven-grade elementary school, unaffiliated with any school system, it was noted for the breadth and depth of its curriculum and the excellence of its teachers. The school's premises consisted of about ten good-sized rooms in the apartment house at Makowa 5. It employed a principal and six teachers, one of them Max

Weinreich's wife, Regina. (The Weinreich's younger son, Gabriel, was a pupil there.) The course of study consisted of Yiddish, Jewish history, Polish and Polish history (both subjects conducted entirely in Polish), Hebrew, geography, nature study, music and singing, arts and crafts.

Unlike the other Yiddish secular schools, whose pupils were almost all impoverished, the 250 children in this school were about evenly divided between the privileged and underprivileged. This school attracted children of Vilna's Jewish intelligentsia because of its experimental educational programs and because those parents preferred the school's leftist orientation to that of the Zionist or religious schools. A teacher told me about a little girl who sat in class like a lump on a log, day in, day out. She didn't understand Yiddish, but her well-to-do parents had transferred her here from a Polish-speaking school. The child dutifully copied everything on the blackboard into her notebook without understanding very much. She had a tutor at home who then helped her with her lessons. When I told Max Weinreich about this child, he said it showed that Yiddish was taking hold even among well-to-do Jews. In any case, it was clear that in a few months that child would know Yiddish.

Yet even with Yiddish or Hebrew as the language of instruction, the pupils who attended the Jewish schools in the 1930s learned more Polish than their parents ever knew. In my ignorance of Polish, I was not alone among Vilna Jews.

Yiddish was the single language of communication for Vilna's *proste yidn,* "common Jews." We'd call them "plain folk." They were the Jews who'd never had any secular education. They were poor and most of them were pious. They were the peddlers and shopkeepers, the workers, artisans, and apprentices, housewives and domestics, butchers and bakers, porters and wagoners, beggars and pickpockets, and the old people.

If they would have needed Polish, they would surely have learned it. East European Jews were usually bilingual, sufficiently fluent in the language of the land, when they needed to know it for their economic existence. But in Vilna that was hardly the case, except among professionals. Jews and Poles seldom inhabited a common space. They hardly ever worked together; they didn't meet socially. Yiddish writers didn't associate with Polish writers. Trade unions and craft guilds were segregated into Polish ones and Jewish ones. Why, then, should the Jews have needed to know Polish?

In May 1939 *Undzer Tog* published a story that dramatized this situation. It seems that a new regulation had been introduced as part of the government's ongoing efforts to regulate the industrial crafts in Poland—their numbers, criteria for membership, conditions of work, and taxes paid to the state. This new statute required that all craft guilds keep their books in Polish and conduct their meetings in Polish.

The Jewish furriers guild was chosen by the Vilna authorities as the first to be inducted into the new regulation. At a specially convened meeting, spokesmen for Vilna's municipality and its Industrial Division came to explain the new statute. The guild members, they said, had no option but to adopt it. The guild officers responded that they had always kept their books in Polish, but that they conducted their meetings in Yiddish because 90 percent of their members barely understood Polish and couldn't speak it at all. But the authorities threatened to dissolve the guild, unless it approved the statute. The officers hastily called a recess to confer. Faced with an ultimatum, they accepted the new regulation, but asked for permission to use a translator. The authorities assented and the meeting proceeded. The chairman and the city authorities spoke in Polish and their words were translated, sentence by painful sentence, into Yiddish.

The middle-class Jews of Vilna, with more secular education than the *proste yidn,* were bilingual, even though their Polish was sometimes corrupted with a Yiddish accent and Yiddish syntax. Well-to-do Jews, with some university training, were often trilingual and, more likely than not, spoke Russian and Polish more correctly than non-Jewish native speakers. As a class they were likely to regard Russian, a residue of their past, as the language of a culture that was superior to Polish and preferable to Yiddish. They spoke Russian at home, taking pleasure in reading and quoting Pushkin, Krylov, and Lermontov.

The Polish speakers among Jews, more numerous and more influential in Vilna's civic life than the small enclaves of Russian speakers, probably didn't amount to more than a few thousand, perhaps 10 percent of all Vilna Jews. They consisted mainly of doctors, lawyers, engineers, and leading businessmen. Each year their numbers grew with the accretion of young Jews who had completed their schooling at Polish-speaking *gymnasia* and of those who had gone on to the university. In the late 1930s, Jewish enrollment at the University of Vilna was down to about 400 students, less than 20 percent of all registered students. Most of those 400 Jewish university students came from homes where Yiddish was a familiar tongue, even if, like Esther Schindelman, my colleague in the

Aspirantur, they didn't speak it well or didn't want to speak it at all. All of them hoped to make professional careers for themselves. With those ambitions, they began to crack the hitherto intact solidity of Vilna's Yiddish-speaking population.

Not knowing Polish, I didn't get to meet many of those Polish-speaking university-educated Jews. That didn't bother me, for I had somehow come to believe that they weren't my kind of people and didn't live in my kind of world. I had met a Polish-speaking young man who was a Zionist and a young woman who was moderately observant, not at all like the people one saw in the *shulhoyf*. The other Polish speakers whom I met, yet barely knew, I labeled as "assimilated," even "assimilationist," that is, advocates of assimilation. Those were a Yiddishist's pejorative words, darkly intimating that to speak Polish instead of Yiddish was a public act of betrayal, an abandonment of one's people. It took me a while to realize that this was an unfair judgment.

The distrust which the plain Jews and the ideological Yiddishists had for the Polish speakers was largely a heritage of the past. A hundred years ago czarist authorities had relentlessly pressed the Jews to "assimilate," that is, to give up their traditional schools, their traditional garb, their language. In the czarist grand design "assimilation" would lead to conversion, the ultimate step which, so the czar's elite believed, would eliminate the existence of Jews as Jews. In independent Poland, too, the authorities tried to assimilate the Jews, to Polonize them. Yet, despite the strong ties of the Polish state to the Catholic Church, the Poles had no plans to convert the Jews.

In 1938 the world was different from what it had been in 1895. Though traditional Jews were still trying to resist the seductions of the modern world, the rest of the Jews were adapting to it. This was unmistakably evident in Poland, which emerged as a nation-state only in the twentieth century. Most Jews felt that they had a lot of catching up to do. Except for the ultra-Orthodox who wanted to preserve the past as it had existed a hundred years before, Jews wanted to break out of the economic and intellectual confines of the ghetto and enjoy the benefits of modern society. The more educated and the successful among them were also in search of ways to reconcile their dual identity as Jews and as Poles.

Now, in retrospect, I think my sentimental vision of Vilna blurred my perception of its social realities. I looked at Jewish Vilna as a living relic of the past rather than as a society in the process of change, however slow that change. Why should I have asked more of my counterparts in Vilna than I asked of myself? English was my first language and its literature my first love; Yiddish was my second language, as it was theirs. Why shouldn't they have been attracted to Polish and its literature? In New York, I hoped to make some kind of professional future for myself as a teacher, writer, or scholar in English. Why shouldn't those young Polish Jews want to become doctors and lawyers, statisticians and critics, in their country, in their language?

The comparison was not entirely apt, because on every possible occasion the Poles—individuals and government—did their best to make Jews feel that Poland was not their country, that there could be no future for them in Poland, no matter how well they spoke Polish or how deeply attached they were to its culture. A colleague at the YIVO, who had completed his master's degree at the University of Vilna and whose Polish—so I was told—was excellent, once said to me that he would not speak Polish "to spite *them*," that he would "not give *them* the pleasure of hearing him speak *their* language." He despaired of his professional future in Poland, but other Jewish Polish speakers had not yet given up on the possibility of making a life for themselves in Poland.

They were undergoing a process called "acculturation," a term not in use in those days. Now we make the distinction between acculturation and assimilation, between the desire to adapt and thereby survive and the will to self-destruct. That distinction was harder to make in Poland than in an open society like the United States, for it didn't seem likely that the Poles would ever allow the Jews the choice of acculturating without paying the price of totally assimilating, that is, disappearing.

One of those ambitious Polish-speaking young Jews became a friend of mine. He himself did not put much stock in his own future in Vilna. Michael Rubinstein was a doctor, the only Jew on the staff of the University's hospital. His father was a leading figure in Vilna. Michael had a firm sense of Jewish identity which was shaped not only by his parents, but by the anti-Jewish milieu in which he worked. Every day he felt on his own skin his colleagues' anti-Semitism; at every occasion for advancement, he saw himself being bypassed just because he was a Jew. Still, Polish was the language which he spoke at home, with his friends, and at work. Michael's English was better than his Yiddish and we usually spoke English to each other for he had sought out my company just for that reason, wanting to practice his English, since he hoped soon to emigrate to the United States.

I had met him on English-speaking ground, as it were. One evening, some three weeks after I had arrived in Vilna, I was invited to a restaurant frequented by Yiddish literary and theater people to meet some Yiddish writers. While we were sitting there, a middle-aged woman came into the restaurant, imperiously inquiring for "the American girl." When she located me, she introduced herself, in excellent English, as Mrs. Taybe Kaplan-Kaplansky. The name was familiar to me, for I had already met her husband, David, at a YIVO reception at the opening of the Aspirantur and learned that he was one of Vilna's wealthiest men and a prominent figure in the Jewish community. She told me right off that she had just returned from London where she had taken a three-month course at a polytechnical institute and that as soon as she had heard an American had come to Vilna, she'd gone in search of me. Straightaway she invited me to her salon for English speakers. They assembled at her home once a month at an English high tea to practice their skills in conversational English.

She was a thin woman in her late forties, medium height, well dressed in an understated way, with an air of aristocratic assurance, yet with a spinsterish personality. Born in Vilna into a prestigious family, Taybe was something of a Vilna anomaly in that her Yiddish was not good. I don't remember all of her history, but Russian had been her mother tongue. From early childhood, she had always exhibited a talent for the study of languages. She had attended the university in St. Petersburg, where she met her husband.

David Kaplan-Kaplansky came from a well-to-do family in Bialystok. His father had been an observant Jew. His mother, a native of Riga, spoke German all her life, for it was the language in which she had been raised. During his student days in St. Petersburg, David broke with his parents' traditions. He plunged into Jewish politics and became a Yiddishist. He was associated with the founding of the Folkspartei, a party committed to Simon Dubnow's theory of Jewish national autonomy, which advocated Yiddish as the official Jewish language. In 1918 he moved to Vilna and there he married Taybe. A dedicated Yiddishist, he insisted that she learn Yiddish. It wasn't hard for her, because of her gift for languages. Besides, she must have known some Yiddish from her childhood days. Still I don't recall that Yiddish ever interested her. Besides her English, she knew French, Italian, and German, and, of course, Russian and Polish.

Several weeks after that encounter in the restaurant, I attended the English-speaking salon in her palatial home on ulica Szopena (Chopin), a lovely, wide, tree-lined street. It was the only residence I knew in

Vilna with central heating and surely the most elegant I was ever in. We met in an enormous parlor. Its three full-length curtained french windows were hung with dark velvet drapes. I think the windows opened on a garden, but I no longer remember. The floor was covered with several Oriental rugs. Several large family portraits gave the room an aura of aristocracy and of family distinction. A huge fireplace, with screen and andirons and a mantelpiece with many adornments, occupied the center of one wall, but I don't recall that it was ever used. A giant silver samovar on a sideboard dominated another wall. In a far corner stood a grand piano. In the center of the room stood a circle of open armchairs and a graceful loveseat, upholstered in a dark red silky fabric. That was the setting for the English circle—an English high tea done in Russian style. A uniformed maid—not the usual Polish peasant woman—served tea in fine china cups, setting small mahogany tables before us to hold the delicate little sandwiches and pastries.

The people who attended are dimmer in my mind than the furnishings of the room. There may have been about eight of them, mostly middle-aged women, with a couple of elderly men, all native Russian or Polish speakers; the youngest was Michael, five years older than I. Several women taught English in private secondary schools. All were delighted with this rare opportunity to put their academic English to the test with a real native American.

The English salon amused me. I wrote home that being there made me feel as if I were living in the middle of a Russian novel, where the upper classes addressed each other in artificial French dialogue. The English conversations were even more contrived, stilted, unconnected to any reality. The desiccated ladies at the salon discoursed on English novelists and poets, showing off their literary knowledge, gushing about Galsworthy and Longfellow, competing with one another for my approval of their literary tastes and judgments.

After the first two meetings, the English-speaking teas bored me, even as a comic subject to write home about. I found excuses not to go, appeasing Taybe with mountains of English reading material, which my family and New York friends supplied me—the book review and magazine sections of the *New York Times,* issues of *The New Yorker, The New Republic,* and *Partisan Review.*

Just as marginal as the Polish speakers were to me, so were Vilna's observant Jews. Observance of Judaism had never been part of my world. Under the influence of my Mitlshul teacher Leibush Lehrer, I came to understand that Judaism was not all a matter of ritual and personal faith, but had a strong national component. Still, with all the brashness of a village atheist, I rejected its religious content. Nevertheless, as a student of Jewish history and a tourist in the Jerusalem of Lithuania, I wanted to see something of Vilna's religious life.

Even before I had set foot in Poland I knew that the Vilna of the Vilna Gaon—where everyone studied Talmud and observed all the minutiae of Jewish law—no longer existed. Vilna had not been exempt from the onslaught of secularism which affected Jewish communities everywhere. Since the late nineteenth century, Vilna had been at the center of turbulent radical and national movements within the Jewish community which had sapped the vigor of traditional Judaism and continued, year by year, decade by decade, to seduce into their ranks new generations of Jews eager to shake off the dust of the past. The relentless process of secularization took many forms, but surely the secularization of the Jewish schools accelerated the secularization of their pupils. In premodern Jewish society, which had flourished as recently as only thirty years earlier in that part of Eastern Europe, Jewish children spent their childhood studying Jewish religious texts. Now most Jewish schools taught children subjects which, besides their abc's, devout Jews regarded as trivial pursuits—singing and drawing, nature study and gymnastics.

The young people growing up in the thirties were no longer as devout as their parents and grandparents had been. Their education had abetted that falling off. They preferred to dedicate themselves to education for a professional future, like the Polish speakers, or to Zionism, hoping someday to emigrate, or to join a leftist political movement which would make life more tolerable for them in Poland. Even young Jews with little education and with lower expectations preferred to go to the movies rather than to read Psalms or study Talmud—which they weren't competent to do anyway.

The graying of traditional Judaism was obvious even to a sightseer. Wandering around the *shulhoyf* and the surrounding streets of the old ghetto, I would look into a few of the smaller prayerhouses, the *kloyzn,* as they were called. It was said that there were 103 in Vilna, besides the Great Synagogue and the Choir Synagogue. Some had been organized by trades and served as self-help organizations, maintaining loan funds for their needy members. The gravediggers, who had formed a society in 1667, still had their own shul. So did the bookbinders, glaziers, housepainters, shoemakers, white-bread and black-bread bakers, wagoners, and tinsmiths. There must have been dozens in the *shulhoyf* alone and in the nearby streets, housed on the second and third floors of dilapidated buildings. Some had fallen into disuse by 1938 or were so sparsely attended that the Jews who lived in the neighborhood wanted to turn them back into living quarters for young couples who otherwise couldn't find an affordable place to live.

Each *kloyz* was supported by its own congregants, but usually depended upon one well-to-do member to provide the money for its upkeep—rent, lighting, heat, and the services of a *shamos,* a caretaker of the premises. Some *kloyzn,* like the Gaon's *kloyz* or the *kloyz yoshen,* were well kept and well attended for daily prayers. Behind their modest exteriors were unexpectedly spacious quarters, some with short pillars supporting a low-vaulted ceiling, some with rococo ornamentation on the ark. Other *kloyzn* were gloomy, dark, dusty, with occasional shafts of sunlight stealing through a high overhead window. One was closed in the winter, because its members couldn't afford to heat the premises. All had sets of the Talmud and other works for religious study, sometimes in glass-enclosed bookshelves, sometimes just lying on dusty wooden study tables.

Yiddish was the language of the *kloyz* and every other place where pious Jews met. On my tour through these *kloyzn,* I'd see a few elderly men, poorly clothed, studying or just chatting idly among themselves. Right away I felt comfortable talking to them. They were as curious about me as I was about them. They wanted to know about Jews in New York and there was always someone who'd ask if I knew his relatives in Brooklyn. I learned that not all of the *kloyzn* could muster a *minyan,* the required minimum of ten men, for communal prayer during the week. On the Sabbaths they were better attended and most of them filled up during the High Holy Days.

Decades later, while wandering around the small synagogues in Safed, I was reminded of those run-down prayerhouses in Vilna. Like Vilna, Safed was once a center of Kabbala and *halakha.* There Joseph Caro had written the *Shulkhan Aruch,* the codification of Jewish law. Safed, too, like Vilna once, had a warren of small old prayerhouses, where great rabbis and scholars once used to pray and study. The beggars around the synagogues in Safed all spoke Yiddish, summoning up the ghosts of a disappeared past. In the twilight cats scampered through Safed's dirty alleyways, as once cats had darted through the dark alleyways of Vilna.

Just a month after I had come to Vilna, the High Holy Days arrived, beginning with the two-day observance of Rosh ha-Shana, the Jewish New Year, and ending on Yom Kippur, the Day of Atonement, the most solemn observance in the Jewish calendar. The YIVO was to be closed for those days. I was then still settling in, not yet accustomed to the routines of work and play and hadn't had time to think how I would spend the holidays. At home in New York, the Jewish New Year was just time off from work and school and a festive meal at home. In Vilna I wanted to experience the holiday in a way that would put me in touch with the past, with tradition. But I had no notion of how to do this, nor did I know anyone who could guide me.

The Jewish New Year arrived late Sunday afternoon, September 26, 1938, the eve of Rosh ha-Shana. Jewish shopkeepers all over Vilna began to close their stores, shuttering the windows and securing them with horizontal iron bars. Practically the whole city's business and trade had come to a dead halt. A hush fell all over town. Suddenly the streets looked unfamiliar. Their vacancy made Vilna look like a deserted town. The next morning Vilna's Jews, dressed in their holiday best, filled the vacancy, as they poured through the empty streets on their way to shul. There was exuberance in the air. Vilna's 105 synagogues and prayer-houses, most of which had sold seats for the High Holy Days, were filled to overflowing.

I wanted very much to attend a synagogue service, but I was timid, being unfamiliar with the ritual. What would I do there? Never in my life had I been at a synagogue service, though I had gone sightseeing at Temple Emanu-El, which, because of its cavernous space and organ music, my friends and I used to call the Jewish Cathedral. Finally I decided to join the throngs milling around the *shulhoyf.* I watched the people, observed their dress, eavesdropped on their conversations, as they greeted one another and exchanged good wishes for the New Year.

The only person I knew in Vilna who was at all connected with a synagogue was Elya Teitlebaum, who conducted the choir at Taharath Ha-Kodesh, the Choir Synagogue, but it was too late to get in touch with him. Finally, mastering my anxiety, I tried to push my way into the women's gallery of the Great Synagogue, but was turned away because I didn't have a ticket. I then decided to try the Choir Synagogue. There, so I thought, I'd feel more comfortable, it would remind me of Temple Emanu-El.

The Choir Synagogue was where Vilna's well-to-do Jews, the lawyers, doctors, and businessmen, went to pray. Here, too, I discovered, there was a separate entrance to the women's gallery. So it was really not at all like Temple Emanu-El. Still, even without a ticket, I managed to get in. It was elegant and dignified in design and architecture, with a high vaulted ceiling, an imposing Moorish-style ark, and a choir loft high over it.

The women were, by Vilna standards, a fashionable lot and you could see them casting an appraising look at every newcomer. I was given a prayerbook. I could make out many of its Hebrew words, but the whole of it was beyond me, for I had not the faintest notion of what the service was all about. I would have been more at home at a mass in the Vilna Cathedral. My Latin was superior to my Hebrew and years of listening to Bach's B Minor Mass had made me familiar with the liturgy. (Some twenty or more years later, when I began to attend synagogue services, I discovered that the "Sanctus" of the mass had been cribbed from the *kedusha,* the blessing for the sanctification of God's name, an integral part of the Jewish liturgy.)

After floundering around in the prayerbook, I gave up and just listened to the cantor's rich tenor voice. The boys' choir which my friend Elya conducted sounded lovely, its cadences more Jewish than the music at Temple Emanu-El. The Choir Synagogue, being a traditional shul, did not have an organ. I rather enjoyed the singing for a while, but since I didn't follow the service, I became bored. No synagogue service, I thought then, could ever be as moving as a Bach mass. When I saw some women leaving, I left too.

I never went to services again in Vilna, though I often talked to Kalmanovich about my longings for a religious experience, which I wanted to be expressed through music. My father had, unwittingly, pointed me in that direction, when we used to listen to the recordings of great cantors singing portions of the Sabbath and High Holy Day services. But Kalmanovich used to dismiss my notions as excessively romantic. He repeatedly cautioned me that what I searched for no longer existed.

For the rest of the year, my observance of the Jewish festivals was much as it would have been in New York—largely culinary. But in one instance of religious observance Vilna did not disappoint me—the preparations for Passover. It was like all the accounts one had read in the Yiddish stories of the *shtetl*. Vilna began to clean house: to wash, launder, dust, brush, sweep, scrub, scour, and otherwise remove—along with the *chometz,* the leavened food—the dust, dirt, grime, soot, mud, and slime accumulated during the year. Bedding was aired on the windows and balconies; laundry was everywhere hung out to dry. Gallons of dirty soapy water formed rivulets in the streets and alleys. I'd never witnessed such a frenzy of spring cleaning, but, as I noted in a letter home, it was much needed in most parts of town. On the first Passover eve, I was invited to a traditional seder, but it was not at all what I was looking for. The men were bunched at one end of the table, where the host and his children read the Haggadah. The women, clustered at the foot of the table, paid little attention to the reading, preferring to gossip instead, while the servants looked after the guests.

The High Holy Days, paradoxically, provided me also with an occasion to witness the aggressiveness of the secularists in Vilna. When Daniel Lerner, the most outspoken Bundist in the Aspirantur, learned I had been to the synagogue on Rosh ha-Shana, he insisted that I go with him on Kol Nidrei eve, the first and most solemn part of the Yom Kippur service, to a local meeting of the Bund's youth division, *Zukunft* ("The Future"). That meeting, too, followed tradition—the tradition of the Jewish left, one I was surprised to discover still being practiced. Back in the 1880s and 1890s, Jewish socialists and anarchists used to mark the solemn fast day with a "Yom Kippur ball" or some other iconoclastic activity that mocked Jewish religious observances. I had thought such practices had died out. In New York no one had to demonstrate any more against religious observance, because in the 1930s such observance had reached an all-time low anyway.

When we entered the hall that Kol Nidrei eve, the place was abuzz. A goodly crowd—perhaps 200 or so boys and girls in their teens, all wearing their red neckerchiefs—cheerfully milled about. The guest speaker, Joseph Brumberg, a Bundist from Warsaw, an elected member of Warsaw's City Council, and assistant director of the Medem Sanatorium, delivered an old-fashioned firebrand exhortation against religion. The young people applauded him heartily. The meeting closed with the singing of the Bund anthem. It struck me that the aggressive stance of the "anti-clericalists" was somewhat anachronistic, that they hadn't yet realized they had already won their battle. I left the meeting as disappointed and discontented as I had been on leaving the synagogue on Rosh ha-Shana.

On Yom Kippur day, my friends and I went for a walk along the Wilja and the Wilenka and in the park around Góra Zamkowa. It was a sunny crisp day. We were not alone in our outing. Hordes—so it seemed to me—of young Jews were there, all in a gay and festive mood. This had apparently become a counter-tradition of the secularists—to enjoy the High Holy Days with a stroll along the banks of Vilna's rivers, far from the Jewish quarter. It reminded me of Crotona Park in the East Bronx during the High Holy Days. If the weather was good, secular Jews who never stepped into a synagogue congregated there to enjoy their leisure.

Even before the High Holy Days I'd learned something about the extent of nonobservance among Vilna Jews. I'd been invited to supper at the Weinreichs. They lived in a fine building on Wielka Pohulanka, a hilly street. Their apartment was much larger than that of the Kalmanoviches and more richly furnished. I was especially impressed by Max Weinreich's splendid study with its enormous library. From their windows you had a panoramic view of the Vilna landscape.

His wife, Regina, was a tall, handsome woman, fair-skinned, with stunning long red hair, which she wore tied in a loose bun at the back of her neck. A teacher at the Sophia Markova Gurevitch school, she had an unmistakably schoolmarmish personality, all business, no nonsense, and always spoke her mind. She dressed that way, too, in plain, dark, and unadorned clothes, never in any pretty feminine things. The Weinreichs had two sons brimming with energy and playfulness—the older boy, Uriel, about thirteen; the younger one, Gabriel, just over ten.

Supper was a casual meal. While Regina was putting food on the table—bread, butter, cheese, tomatoes, herring—Max Weinreich asked if she had any *shinke.* She said there was none left. He then suggested that we go down to the store to buy some. I was agreeable, but I asked him what *shinke* was. "Ham," he said. I gasped and then I blushed. Weinreich was amused by my befuddlement.

Why had I been so shocked to learn that the Weinreichs ate ham at home and offered it to their guests? I myself wasn't a kashrut observer. While in high school, I had already ventured outside my mother's kitchen into forbidden territory and had treated myself to forbidden foods with much the same sense of daring as when I had smoked my first cigarette. Nor should I have been surprised that Jews in Vilna were not all that different from Jews in New York when it came to kashrut. Nevertheless, the incongruity of ham in Jewish Vilna had unsettled me.

In my romantic view of Vilna as the Jerusalem of Lithuania, Jews didn't eat ham within the precincts of their own homes.

Looking back at that *shinke* incident, I believe that my piety for the past concealed a more visceral reaction, the residue of my mother's influence. In our house we never had unkosher meat, because of my mother's abhorrence for pork, ham, bacon—that's how she had been raised. During my childhood, she used to tell a story time and again about how, on her second steamship journey to America, she had mistakenly eaten a pork chop, thinking it was veal. When she found out otherwise, she became violently sick.

In Vilna of 1938 the upholders of the Gaon's tradition were embattled, even if they did not yet consider themselves beleaguered. They knew that they were confronting powerful enemies in secularism, Jewish nationalism, and radicalism. They saw that Jews were less concerned about having a share in the world to come and preferred to reap their rewards in the present world. Still, the observant Jews remained a force to be reckoned with, in numbers and influence. In 1938, the Kehillah, the central Jewish communal organization, which supported Vilna Jewry's religious, educational, and welfare institutions, spent nearly 90,000 zlotys to maintain Vilna's rabbinic establishment. That included six members of the rabbinate, a number of learned rabbis and preachers, widows of deceased rabbis, and also the cantor and choir of the Great Synagogue. In comparison, the Kehillah's subsidy for the Yiddish secular schools amounted to only 70,000 zlotys, even though the majority of the Kehillah's elected board were secular Jews and were presumably representative of their constituencies.

The rabbis tried to exercise their authority mostly, as far as I could tell, in the enforcement of kashrut, but there was no way to measure their effectiveness. Nor could one know how many Jews bought non-kosher meat. In 1938, the Kehillah spent nearly 60,000 zlotys to maintain and supervise the practice of *shehitah,* the Jewish method of killing animals and poultry permitted to be used for food. Yet even on ulica Jatkowa, Butcher Street, in the heart of the old ghetto, nonkosher butchers sold their meat next door to kosher butchers. No one knew what proportion of their customers were non-Jews, though it was obvious that well-to-do Jews were more likely to buy forbidden foods than others. Except for the poor and pious Jews who lived in stiflingly close quarters in the old ghetto, Jews were no longer able to look into their neighbors' pots to see what was cooking. Even if Vilna was still a provincial town, it already belonged to the modern world and the old social sanctions no longer operated as effectively as they had fifty years ago.

Once, during the year I was there, the Vilna rabbinate tried to flex its muscle with regard to the sale of kosher meat. It happened just after the Polish Sejm had passed a bill that would limit and eventually altogether prohibit the right of *shehitah.* A conference of all the rabbis of Poland had decreed that the Polish Jews should protest by abstaining from any meat at all for a period of sixteen days.

On the first Sabbath of the protest, March 18, 1939, the rabbi of the Great Synagogue preached a sermon against the nonobservance of kashrut, but that apparently did not suffice. On Sunday, March 26, the rabbis decided to issue a *herem,* a proscription against those who violate Jewish law, in this instance against unnamed butchers who were charged with selling forbidden meat (*trefa*) as kosher. The proceedings were held at the Great Synagogue at five in the afternoon. An hour before, the place was already packed to the rafters. *Undzer Tog* estimated that some 6,000 people packed the shul. When the members of the Rabbinical Council arrived, they had to push their way through the throng with great difficulty to reach the bimah.

The rabbi of the synagogue opened with a short sermon on the sacred importance of kashrut. Then the members of the Rabbinical Council lit black candles which they held throughout the brief ceremony. This was followed by responsive readings from Psalms. The cantors then intoned the *herem* curse in Yiddish: "Cursed is he who leads a blind man on to a wrong path," which the rabbi repeated. The entire congregation responded with a thunderous "Amen." The candles were extinguished and the shofar was sounded. Though the names of the excommunicated persons had not been invoked, it was said that everyone knew who they were. An official communiqué of the *herem* was issued by the rabbinate the next day.

In the old days everyone in the community would have ostracized the persons who'd been anathematized. In modern times such bans no longer had any force. The *herem* of March 1939 changed nothing with regard to the sale and distribution of kosher and nonkosher meat. To me the *herem* was not just a historical curiosity; it was an ugly ritual, a desperate last stand by the rabbis to halt the relentless sweep of modernity over Vilna. Cynical people said that the rabbis had been put up to it by the kosher butchers who believed they were losing trade to the *trefa* butchers.

Sometimes the conflict between tradition and modernity had its comic moments. At a Kehillah board meeting in March 1939 to vote on the allocation for religious affairs, the one member representing the Agudah—an ultra-Orthodox anti-Zionist party—voted with the three Bund members against the entire religious allocation. The Bundists always voted against the religious allocation as a matter of principle, though they knew their opposition was futile. The Agudahnik, by voting no, wanted to express his displeasure because one member of the rabbinate, which the Kehillah supported, belonged to Mizrachi, the Religious Zionist Party.

You could see the conflict between the worlds of tradition and modernity played out every day in a kind of dumb show in the reading room of the Strashun Library. I had gone there not just for sightseeing, but to look for material on the Yiddish press in England. Since this great library had no proper catalogue, it took several visits for me to locate, to my surprise and pleasure, three issues of a short-lived Yiddish periodical published in London in 1874, of which I had found no trace in New York.

The Strashun Library was open all week and also on Saturday afternoons. On Saturdays you could read the books you had reserved beforehand. The use of pencil or pen was strictly forbidden. Because the library was rich in Talmudic and rabbinic works, it was used by pious Jews for advanced study. But the wealth of its holdings in other areas of Judaica also attracted secular scholars and university students. Consequently, on any day you could see, seated at the two long tables in the reading room, venerable long-bearded men, wearing hats, studying Talmudic texts, elbow to elbow with bareheaded young men and even young women, bare-armed sometimes on warm days, studying their texts. The old men would sometimes mutter and grumble about what the world had come to. The young people would titter.

How far modern times had encroached on traditional life was evident in Vilna's Jewish sporting life. On March 11, 1939, which was a Saturday, Maccabi, the Jewish sports organization, launched its first boxing event with eight pairs of boxers taking part in a series of short bouts. What would the Vilna Gaon have thought about that?

Even Yiddish, the language of Jewish secularism, had to catch up with these modern times. The YIVO's Terminological Commission needed authentic Yiddish words—not mere borrowings from Polish, Russian, or German—to transmit the Jew's experiences with sports and nature. The rich Yiddish vocabulary of the *talmid khokhem,* the learned Jew, which reflected the distinctive culture of Judaism, was giving way to a vocabulary of modernity.

CHAPTER 6

In the Realm of Yiddish:
At the Center

There was always something going on in Vilna—a world-famous Zionist leader came to speak; a Yiddish school put on its annual children's show; a visiting poet from Warsaw was feted with a public poetry reading; the Jewish Symphonic Orchestra had a concert; a Yiddish theatrical troupe came for a short run; a Jewish scholar from Lodz delivered a lecture. These programs, conducted in Yiddish, usually drew a full house. My greatest astonishment, at least in the early months of my stay in Vilna, was that the audiences were mostly young people. In New York, during the 1930s, a Yiddish lecture, even the Yiddish theater, drew mainly older people, balding, graying, our parents and grandparents. We of the Sholem Aleichem Yugnt Gezelshaft were the exceptions. On those occasions we felt the special obligation that rested on us, for we represented—in our own eyes and, even more so, in the eyes of our elders—the hope for the future of Yiddish in America.

In Vilna, things were just the reverse. Cultural and political events drew a young and lively audience. To be sure, there were older people as well, but it was exciting for me to be with a young generation of Yiddish speakers. I felt at the center of things. Here, I didn't bear the burden of responsibility for the future of Yiddish. In Vilna, the world of traditional Judaism, as I saw it in the *kloyzn,* was in the hands of the old, but the secular culture of Yiddish belonged to the young.

A few weeks after I had arrived in Vilna I was introduced to a group whose very name epitomized the connection between Yiddish and youth. Called *yung vilne,* Young Vilna, it was an association of writers and artists, of which I had already heard back in New York. In mid-September, someone called Shmerke Kaczerginski telephoned me at the YIVO and introduced himself as a member of Young Vilna. He'd been told by a mutual friend in New York to look me up. He invited me to join him and his friends that Saturday evening at a place where Vilna's Yiddish Bohemia congregated. When he came to pick me up, I was taken aback by his appearance. He was barely taller than I and, though I later learned that he was then thirty years old, he looked like a teenager. Behind his big round black-rimmed glasses you could see that he was slightly cross-eyed. He had a high forehead and a snubbed nose. He was shabbily dressed, but that didn't inhibit his boisterous sociability.

He took me to a place called Velfkeh's ("Wolfie's"), named for its owner, Wolf Ussian. It was, I learned, one of Vilna's famous institutions. Here Vilna's Yiddish writers, actors, and intellectuals came to eat and drink, to entertain their out-of-town guests, to celebrate festive occasions, and sometimes just to enjoy themselves. In a short time I, too, began to go there frequently. Located in the very heart of the Jewish quarter, on ulica Żydowska (*yidishe gas*), corner of ulica Niemecka (*daytche gas*), Velfkeh's was unprepossessing on the outside and even more so on the inside. A large Yiddish sign on the street directed you into the courtyard to the restaurant where you could get breakfast, dinner, and supper.

You always saw knots of people outside Velfkeh's, for Vilna's droshky drivers used to stop off there for a drink. As I remember it, Velfkeh's, like Caesar's Gaul, was divided into three parts. You came into a saloon, sawdust on the floor, with a bar-buffet and a bartender. A group of burly men always congregated at the bar, drinking, talking, guffawing, swearing. Besides being a watering place for the droshky drivers, Velfkeh's bar was a hangout also for Vilna's Jewish toughs.

You walked through this entry-room into a second somewhat larger space, with about six tables, where you would sometimes see middle-class families who had come to mark a special occasion with a meal out. Passing through this room, you came into a place that was at least twice as wide as it was deep, like a banquet hall. I remember it as utterly plain, without attractive lighting or ornamentation. It was furnished with several long tables and benches and a few smaller tables and chairs. The floor was bare with space for dancing; a radio provided the music. The kitchen was someplace off this room. Here you could be served beer, wine, vodka, or just tea, if you preferred. You could eat chopped liver and cracklings, gefilte fish, boiled beef, cholent, and roast goose. On Hanukkah we came for potato pancakes and on Shevuot for cheese blintzes.

Velfkeh took pleasure in his literary-bohemian clientele, even if they didn't always have money to spend. Their presence gave his place a certain cachet in Vilna's Yiddishist circles. Besides, the bohemians were sometimes accompanied by a patron of the arts who picked up the tab. The Yiddish journalists of Vilna, being better paid than the writers and actors, would often dine and drink at Cafe Prater, about a block away and classier, but they, too, liked the easygoing atmosphere of Velfkeh's.

When Shmerke and I arrived at Velfkeh's that September evening, we met his friends. The company included several pretty girls and at least two other writers of the Young Vilna group, of whom I remember only Peretz Miransky, a handsome melancholy-looking young man who wrote fables in verse. The conversation was gay, but not what I had hoped for—a hubbub of literary talk, a brightness of ideas. We sang Yiddish songs and danced to the music of the radio. My letter home mentioned tea as the only refreshment we had. Everyone smoked and they cadged my American cigarettes. About midnight, the party broke up.

Thereafter Shmerke visited me often and uninvited. I used to complain that I would find him on my doorstep like a daily delivery of milk. He wanted to show me Vilna in his free time, but I soon found out during our walks that he didn't know enough Jewish history, or Polish history, to answer my questions about the landmarks we saw. Instead I learned about his life. He'd been orphaned very young, during the Great War, I think. He was raised in the orphanage of the Town Talmud Torah, Vilna's charity school for the poorest Jewish children in town. After he completed the Talmud Torah, probably when he was about thirteen, he became apprenticed to a lithographer. He chose printing as his trade, because he had fallen in love with the printed word, with books and writing. After work, he used to attend night school. As soon as he began to earn money, he moved out of the orphanage and rented a room for himself. When I met him, he was still working in a printing shop, but he was still very poor.

Genial and good-natured, he was also rough and tough, ready with his fists. He'd grown up in a harsh and brutal world where he learned to protect himself. He was known to have taken on anti-Semites spoiling for a fight. Today we'd call him street smart. He was reputed to be—or to have been—a dedicated Communist. Kalmanovich knew his history and warned me that Shmerke had been arrested a couple of times for writing or publishing pieces the authorities considered subversive. Thereafter, he had been under police surveillance, but that was probably no longer the case when I was there. At the time, though neither Kalmanovich or I knew it, Stalin had ordered the Communist Party in Poland to be liquidated, following the pattern of the purges within the Soviet Union. Shmerke surely was aware of what was happening and no doubt trod carefully between the proscriptions of the Polish authorities and the party's repressions. In any case, I don't recall that we ever talked politics. He wouldn't have trusted me.

Shmerke's literary output was small. He had written some stories and journalistic pieces. His occasional verses were like folk songs, some sentimental, others bristling with leftist militancy. Some had been set to music and were sung in Vilna. He was all sociability and gregariousness. His greatest talent was organizing things—meetings, art exhibits, excursions, parties. He kept Young Vilna together as a group, socially and institutionally.

Young Vilna became known in the Yiddish literary world on October 11, 1929, when Zalmen Reisen devoted a whole page in the Friday edition of *Undzer Tog* to the poems and stories of its writers, under a heading: "The Triumphal Entry of Young Vilna into Yiddish Literature." They were a coterie of writers and artists who had organized themselves a year or two earlier as Young Vilna to give one another moral support and help in getting published. They were then still beginners: The writers among them had not yet been published, the artists had not yet exhibited. Children of Vilna's Jewish poverty, products of the Great War's dislocations, they were all committed to the left. Moshe Kulbak, a Yiddish poet and novelist, who'd lived in Vilna before the war and then from 1923 to 1928, had been their literary and political mentor. In 1928 he left Poland to settle in the Soviet Union.

Young Vilna issued no literary credo or manifesto. Nor did its members formulate a particular literary agenda for the group. They did not advocate any specific style or school of writing. They were just a group of young writers and artists of like artistic and political sensibility. Aspiring writers who had not yet been published would apply to read their work at a meeting of Young Vilna, hoping to be accepted and thereby legitimated as writers. From time to time the group issued a modest little journal called *yung vilne*. Its leftism was reflected not only in its contents, but also in its orthography, using the Soviet style of spelling the Hebrew words in Yiddish phonetically.

Within days of my first meeting with Shmerke, I met other writers associated with Young Vilna and began to read what they wrote. In about ten days, I had already reached a firm literary judgment. I wrote home: "I've met quite a number of the writers associated with Young Vilna. But only Chaim Grade and Abraham Sutzkever are serious writers." At that time, only five of the original eleven members of Young Vilna were still around. Grade (pronounced "grad-eh") and Sutzkever had not been among them, but had been admitted later, in the early 1930s.

Zalmen Reisen had introduced me to Sutzkever at an exhibit of a Young Vilna artist. A tall, thin, pale young man of twenty-five, fair-haired, with a long narrow face, bespectacled, Sutzkever looked like a shy provincial youth. But he wasn't so much shy as quiet, reserved, standing apart from the more gregarious and boisterous members of Young Vilna. That aloofness was part of his nature; it befitted, so I thought, the Olympian persona he was cultivating as a poet.

Sutzkever had been born in 1913 in Smorgon, a town in White Russia not too far from Vilna, where Jews had been the majority of the population in those days. In 1915, during the Great War, when the German army began advancing into Russia, his family fled to Siberia. In 1920, they came west and settled in Vilna. His father died shortly thereafter. Sutzkever attended a Hebrew-Polish secondary school. When I met him, he worked as a retoucher. (I never saw a photograph in Vilna that hadn't been retouched.) He was also a student in the YIVO's Pro-aspirantur, exploring early Yiddish literature and language. He had learned Russian, so he told people, to read Pushkin in the original and he audited a couple of courses on Polish literature at the University of Vilna given by Professor Manfred Kridl, the eminent Polish literary scholar.

Sutzkever lived with his widowed mother in Śnipiszki. Once, on a brisk autumn Saturday afternoon, he took me to meet her. I remember our long walk over the Green Bridge to his house, all the while engrossed in an earnest conversation about future hopes for art and poetry and society. Later, at his house, his girlfriend joined us, a pretty, very pink-cheeked girl, whom he later married. Sutzkever, so it seemed to me then, hedged his political bets. He flirted with the Freeland League, the Territorialist society to which Kalmanovich was committed. I remember hearing him speak at a Freeland meeting in January 1939. Other times, he leaned leftward.

His first poem was published in *Undzer Tog* in 1934. He was attracted to the Introspectivist Yiddish poets in the United States and sent his poems to Aaron Glanz-Leyeles, a foremost poet of this school, who took Sutzkever under his wing. After I got to know Sutzkever, I noticed how often he used to drop Glanz-Leyeles's name in conversation, as though he constantly had to validate his position as a comer in Yiddish literature. In 1937, Sutzkever's first book of verse, titled *lider* (*Poems*), was issued by the Library of the Yiddish Pen Club in Warsaw. He gave me an inscribed copy in November 1938.

His was a honed and disciplined lyric voice. In contrast to the folk or "natural" lyricism of other writers of Young Vilna, Sutzkever was producing verse of formal technical complexity and poetic sophistication, pliant and polished. He was not so much a modernist as an aesthete, an even more unlikely breed to emerge out of Vilna's Jewish poverty. He was captivated by words and by form. He used to visit me with some frequency because he wanted to learn something of English poetry. I would read English and American poems to him, translate, and analyze them. He was interested mainly in rhythm and rhyme, the sound and form of poetry. I believe that he was self-consciously in search of new and unfamiliar poetic modes that he might experiment with. That's why he studied early Yiddish diction, Polish prosody, and Pushkin.

In those days, he had little content to breathe into his words or to fill the forms he created. To me, his poetry lacked the substance of experience to give it depth, maturity. Though I admired the precision of his diction and the grace of his poetic line, I thought his work had an effete, even a deracinated, quality. Yet despite my reservations, I was sure that he would emerge as a first-rate poet.

Chaim Grade was unlike Abraham Sutzkever in every respect—in appearance and temperament, in his personal history, and in the kind of poetry he wrote. Short and squarish, his squat build made you think— especially when he was angry—of a bull. But on closer observation you could see that his was not sinewy brawn, but flabby fat. He had a roundish baby face and wore glasses. At twenty-eight, he was already balding, with a receding hairline that made his high forehead look even higher. He had a rich strong voice, with which he could hold an audience rapt as he recited his own verse.

Born in Vilna in 1910, Chaim was a child of his father's old age; Chaim's mother, Velle, a rabbi's daughter, was his second wife. When Chaim was a young child, his father, a learned Jew and a maskil, who had eked out a living as a Hebrew teacher, died, leaving his widow utterly without resources to support herself and her son. During the Great War, Chaim was boarded in a home for poor children. But his mother wanted him to become a *talmid khokhem,* a man learned in Judaism, and after he finished his elementary schooling, Chaim spent about ten years of his youth as a yeshiva-*bokher,* studying in a number of yeshivas in and near Vilna. His mother, meanwhile, living in a wretched cellar hovel behind a smithy on ulica Jatkowa, in the heart of Vilna's Jewish poverty, supported herself and her son by selling fruit on the street.

In the yeshiva, Chaim was soon confronted by the irreconcilability of the world of tradition with modernity. He was caught reading forbidden secular books and punished for his transgression. Finally, in 1932, when he was twenty-two, after years of inner conflict, driven by his ambition to become a poet, Chaim decided for the modern world.

He returned to Vilna and lived with his mother in the wretched hovel. Now he was free to read secular books. He devoted himself especially to reading philosophy and to writing poetry. In his first year back home he began to publish in *Undzer Tog.* Thereafter his poetry appeared not only in Vilna, but also in the major Yiddish literary journals in Warsaw and in New York. In 1936 his first book of poems was published by Vilna's major Yiddish publisher, B. Kletzkin. It was called *yo* (*Yes*). Though the title poem spiritedly affirmed the poet's presence in the world, the pervasive tone of the other poems was gloom-ridden. Like most first books of verse, these poems described the intimacy of Grade's life—the memory of his father, the bitterness of his mother's life, his friends, his fears and passions.

In addition, the collection included a cycle of poems called "Ezekiel," in which Grade spoke in a prophetic national voice. Those densely Jewish poems drew upon Jewish historical experience for their content, upon traditional Jewish sources for their ideas. His poetic voice resonated with the vigor of biblical diction and the poems brimmed with the dramatic passion which would soon become a hallmark of his verse. His Yiddish, unlike that of other Young Vilna writers, was thickly layered with a Hebraic-Aramaic vocabulary, a poetic distillation of the language of the *talmid khokhem. Yo* sold out and a second edition appeared in 1937. Thereafter, Grade became the first and only member of Young Vilna who managed to support himself, however marginally, by writing poetry.

He married an attractive young woman, a registered nurse, who was ambitious to succeed in her field. The daughter of a rabbi, she, like Chaim, had turned her back on traditional Judaism. She and her brother, to the despair of their father, had become Zionists. Shortly after Chaim married, his mother Velle, now freed of her responsibility for her son, remarried and at last left the cheerless cellar hovel to move into her husband's home.

Chaim Grade's life and writing were shaped by two dominant influences—his mother and the yeshiva. The lead poem in *yo,* called "My Mother," evoked the weariness of her life as a street peddler. Even after she remarried, she continued to sell fruit on the street and she continued to inhabit her son's conscience and consciousness. Chaim once told me that he was afraid that his ability to write would peter out or waste away. For till then, he said, the vitality and power which animated his work derived from his mother who sold apples on the street and from the world in which she lived. Now that he'd separated himself from that world, he feared he'd lose the source of his creativity.

Chaim had separated himself far more decisively from the yeshiva, the other formative influence upon his life and work, yet he remained obsessed by the particular yeshiva where he spent his late teen years. It was the *musar-* yeshiva of Nowogrodek (which Jews used to call Navaredok), a town about 150 kilometers south of Vilna. Before I met Chaim, I'd never heard of *musar* as a religious movement. Then, from him and from Kalmanovich, I learned about it. Its emphasis on self-mortification was chilling; it was an ascetic mode I had never before associated with the observance of Judaism.

Musar in Hebrew means both edification and chastisement. As a movement, *musar* originated in Vilna in the mid-nineteenth century and then spread throughout the Lithuanian area of Russian Poland, but it never made headway anywhere else in Eastern Europe. It must have appealed to the *litvak* mentality and became the *litvak*'s alternative to hasidism. *Musar* aimed to restore ethical integrity in daily life and to reinvigorate the observance of Judaism through moral reflection and self-improvement. Students in the *musar-* yeshiva devoted as much time to the study of ethical literature as to the study of Talmud. Spiritual wrestling was the core of the curriculum. The students had to practice a regimen of spiritual exercises whose purpose was to inoculate them against sin and secularism. They would deliberately behave eccentrically so as to humble and humiliate themselves, for instance, wear a coat inside out or go without shoes. They would do so in their own yeshiva circle, and also in public, so that the townspeople could mock and despise them.

Self-mortification, the *musarnikes* believed, could bring about a state of moral restoration. Man's evil urge had to be repressed. Navaredok was known as a maximalist yeshiva because it demanded of its students not only the exercise of self-discipline, but self-denial and self-flagellation. The id and the ego, lust and vanity, man's instinctual passions, had to be totally extirpated.

Grade's experiences in the *musar-* yeshiva gave him the subject matter for his second book, *Musarnikes,* which was published in February 1939. Seventy-four pages long, it consisted of a single narrative poem, composed in eight chapters, about life in the Navaredok yeshiva. Its cast of characters included the *rosh yeshiva,* the head of the yeshiva, and a varied group of its students, including Chaim himself, each wrestling with the world, with his own lusts, vanities, and ambitions, struggling against disbelief and impiety. Grade's talent for the drama of confrontation, even in old-fashioned rhymed anapests, created spellbinding tension. *Musarnikes* more than fulfilled the promise of his first book. It won him immediate recognition and a prestigious monetary award from a major Yiddish cultural organization based in New York. Critics compared him to Chaim Nachman Bialik, the greatest modern Hebrew poet, who was often characterized as a "national poet."

After *Musarnikes* appeared, Young Vilna organized a big literary evening to celebrate Chaim's success. The large hall was packed. Zalman Reisen was one of several speakers to talk about Grade's work. Many of his poems were read. At the end, he spoke. His words about the obligations of the writer to his people—not just to his readership—had a grandeur about them and there was grandeur also in the reach of his ambition. He wanted to be a poet of the Jewish people, not a poet who happened to be Jewish and wrote in Yiddish.

The literary award and the program in his honor had exhilarated him, but the next day he was overwhelmed by melancholy. He came to see me at home, during dinnertime, needing addresses of New Yorkers to whom to send copies of *Musarnikes.* That business took about five minutes. But he stayed for three hours. I was on pins and needles; I had to be in the YIVO. Yet I didn't have the courage to tell him so. He, for his part, was oblivious to everything but his own needs. He talked about himself and read some of his new poems. After a while, I forgot my anxiety about being late. Then he began to recite some of his old poems—all with the mournful chant of the *musar-*yeshiva-*bokher.* Still not ready to leave, he began to sing several poems by H. Leivick, an exquisitely lyrical poet and then one of the great figures in American Yiddish literature. I knew him through his son Daniel, who belonged to the Sholem Aleichem Yugnt Gezelshaft. "When you go back to America," Chaim said, "tell Leivick that I sang his poems—not with the music composed for them. That's worthless. Tell him, I sang them with my own melody. Tell him they were all poems that everyone else has long forgotten."

Chaim's emotions raged tempestuously within him, buffeting him from one extreme to another. In the year I knew him, I could see his moods change from day to day, ricocheting from high to low. One day he might be intolerable in his overweening pride and self-confidence, secure in his gifts and his superiority to his colleagues in Young Vilna. The next day he might be consumed with self-pity, depressed about himself, unsure of his creative ability, in despair about the world around him. Once he said to me: "I'm as sad as my poems, and you know that I'm even sadder." Then, wryly, he added: "Even if I'm not an emaciated fellow with a frail body and sunken eyes." He constantly needed—or wanted—reassurance about his place in Yiddish literature. I used to tell him that his readers and admirers believed more in him than he did in himself. He didn't have the political optimism of Young Vilna's leftists to buoy his spirits, having long resisted their efforts to enlist him on their political side.

Chaim could explode at the slightest affront or what he thought was an affront. He could be brutally direct, brusque, yet he was always an exciting person to be with because of the intense feeling with which he addressed the world. He had no craft in personal relations; his personality was too volcanic for him to dissemble. Perhaps that's why he disliked Sutzkever's cultivation of a literary persona. He'd poke fun at him for being a poseur. When I'd meet Chaim on the street, he'd greet me—knowing that I might have seen Sutzkever at the YIVO—with a mocking inquiry: "Have you seen Pushkin lately?" And he'd drawl Pushkin's name with a broad flourish.

He was driven by precisely those passions which Navaredok had tried to eradicate—lust and greed for everything the world could offer, vanity and pride, rage and envy. He was still at war with himself. Though he no longer went to shul and no longer studied the religious texts, he was still in many private ways a child of tradition. In those days, he was pursued by guilt for not having fulfilled his mother's ambitions for him and for having chosen to write poetry, an occupation for which her world had little regard.

I had met Chaim Grade through David Kaplan-Kaplansky, the man whose wife Taybe had a passion for English. A dedicated Yiddishist since his days in St. Petersburg, Kaplansky was at the center of every cultural and educational undertaking in Vilna. His interest, his engagement, and his money made it possible to publish Yiddish poetry, to organize a Jewish symphony orchestra, and to mount a Jewish art exhibit. He was a patron of the arts and one of Vilna's most influential figures. In his early fifties in 1938, he was a fine figure of a man, tall and handsome. He wore glasses, but behind them you could see his eyes twinkling with humor and good nature. He had dark hair, beginning to recede off the high forehead. His most distinctive features were a bushy dark mustache and a well-trimmed Vandyke beard. He was an elegant dresser and had elegant manners.

I had no idea where his money came from. He never seemed to work or to attend to any business matters, other than his philanthropic activities. In Bialystok, his birthplace, his family had once owned a big iron firm and his father had prepared him for a business career by sending him to the St. Petersburg Polytechnicum, where he was graduated with distinction. Perhaps he still had an income from the family business; more likely he owned property in Vilna. He was a member of Vilna's Kehillah and on the board of every important Yiddish educational and cultural institution—the YIVO, the Jewish Arts Society of Vilna, Vilna's Central Education Committee, among others. He owned a magnificent private library, collected the paintings of Jewish artists, was lavishly hospitable in his luxurious house, and was always ready to stand treat at Velfkeh's.

Though he was a man of substance and a pillar of Vilna's upper-class Jewish society, Kaplansky was not usually to be found in the company of his contemporaries and social equals. Early in our acquaintance, I saw that he preferred to consort with the bohemians of Young Vilna and with the Jewish university students, even when it didn't become him to do so. I'd been invited one evening to dinner at the Kaplanskys, with other guests. After dinner, we all went to a concert of a Jewish choral group where we met many friends. Daniel Lerner, my colleague in the

Aspirantur, who was the vice-chairman of the Jewish university students' union, invited me to a dance the university students were having after the concert. Kaplansky decided to join us; Taybe went home by herself. That evening, which lasted till 3 A.M., cost Kaplansky almost sixty zlotys, an amount equal to my entire monthly YIVO stipend.

Kaplansky wanted to be with the young bohemians because of his lecherous proclivities, which were the talk of the town. The reputation, as I soon learned for myself, was well-founded. At a party at Velfkeh's one evening, which included David and Taybe Kaplansky, I had the bad luck to be seated between them. She, on my right, kept addressing me in English. He, on my left, was trying to explore my anatomy under the table. Either she didn't care or never noticed my extreme discomfort as I tried to keep his hands off my knees without making a public scandal. But she must have known about his goatish pursuits; she may also have known, as I learned by sharing experiences with other young women, that those pursuits usually ended up as wild-goose chases.

After I persuaded David Kaplansky to adopt a hands-off policy, we got along well and I was a frequent guest at his house, even if I neglected the meetings of Taybe's English-speaking circle. One evening I went with them to the opening of a Yiddish musical revue. The players, a local group of young actors, called themselves "Balaganeyden"—a punning contraction of two words, *balagan* (pandemonium) and *gan-eyden* (the Garden of Eden, paradise). The "balagan" part of their name was appropriate for their production, a series of skits and song-and-dance routines. After the show, Kaplansky collected a crowd of people, including the actors and some of Young Vilna, and we all went to Velkfeh's. I had more fun there than at the theater. The Balaganeyden troupe played in Vilna until the end of November. On their last night before they set off to tour in Poland, Kaplansky threw a big farewell party for them at Velfkeh's.

Vilna had not had a resident Yiddish theater for many years. The Vilna Troupe, once the most illustrious name in the history of Yiddish theater, had had a brief tenure in Vilna. It had originated there as an amateur theatrical group in 1916 during the wartime occupation of the kaiser's army. The next year the Vilna Troupe moved to Warsaw, where the players felt they would have wider scope for their talents. They all aspired to high art in the Yiddish theater, euphemistically referred to as *dos besere yidishe teyater*, "the better Yiddish theater," to contrast to the prevailing style of playing to the gallery with tawdry melodramas and trashy revues. The Vilna Troupe soon won its reputation for distinguished achievement with its marvelous ensemble work (the company disdained the star system) and its dedication to serious drama. It produced plays of high literary caliber—classics of Yiddish literature and translations of new or classic plays from other languages. It achieved its greatest success with its production in 1921 of S. Anski's *The Dybbuk,* with which it toured Western Europe and the United States. Soon thereafter, the company broke up, as its members scattered to all parts of the world.

In Vilna, meanwhile, for the next two decades, amateur and not-quite-professional dramatic circles and acting groups came and went. A Jewish Dramatic Studio operated for a while in Vilna, but had little to show for its efforts. In the late 1930s a Vilna-based Yiddish marionette company, called *Maydim,* enjoyed a modest success, mostly as entertainment for children. I didn't see their show, because marionettes, even Yiddish-speaking ones, didn't interest me.

About four or five visiting companies came to play in Vilna during the year I was there, all but one from Warsaw. They'd stay for a couple of weeks or longer, depending on the box-office response. At the end of January I went with my friends of the Aspirantur to see a Yiddish comedy called *Meylekh-freylekh* (*Kingly-jingly*), brought from Warsaw by a company called New Theater. In a letter home, I described it as an unpretentious comedy, made explosively funny by a marvelous comic actor, Władysław Godik.

Yiddish theater as high culture enjoyed a short run in Vilna in January, with performances of *Der shturem*—Shakespeare's *The Tempest.* It had been brought to Vilna by the *Folks- un yugnt-teyater* (People's and Youth Theater), based in Warsaw. The company's administrative director was Mordecai Mazo, who had been the founder of the Vilna Troupe, and had, since its demise, made a distinguished career in the Yiddish theater in Poland. The company's artistic director was Clara Segalovich, who enjoyed a great reputation as a serious artist of the Yiddish stage. Her company was the true successor to the Vilna Troupe in its devotion to quality drama and ensemble acting.

Der shturem was put on in the auditorium of Vilna's Conservatory, a lovely hall with a small stage, originally designed for piano recitals and lectures. It was painfully inadequate for this production. I later learned from the actors that they couldn't use half their sets, which had been designed originally for a large theater in Lodz where they opened

the show. Even so, *The Tempest* in Yiddish was a magnificent achievement. Despite the cramped space, everything worked. The sets and the
lighting were superb. The Yiddish blank-verse translation by Aaron
Zeitlin, a Hebrew and Yiddish poet and dramatist, then living in Warsaw, was stunning. Since Zeitlin's English had not been up to the
demands of Shakespeare, I was told that he had relied heavily upon
August Wilhelm von Schlegel's German translation.

Prospero was masterfully played by Abraham Morewski, a native of
Vilna and one of the great actors of the time. Born in 1886, he had
studied acting in czarist Russia and become enamored of Shakespeare.
He knew the plays inside out and had himself done some Shakespeare
translations. He'd even dabbled in what he called Shakespeareology,
having written a study in Yiddish on Shakespeare's Shylock. Morewski
had played with the Vilna Troupe in the early days; later he made a
name for himself, especially in the role of Shylock, and was featured
in several German films produced in Berlin in the twenties.

He was an imposing figure, majestic, tall, broad-shouldered, often
to be seen on Vilna streets flourishing his voluminous black cape. His
big resonant voice boomed out on the street as he conversed with his
cronies or hangers-on. Vilna was proud of him and in 1937, to mark
the thirtieth anniversary of Morewski's career on the stage, the Society
of Friends of the Yiddish Theater published a new edition of his study
on Shylock and Shakespeare. He was known to have a terrible temper,
would publicly revile Jewish audiences for their low tastes, because even
in Vilna, he found, they'd sooner buy tickets for popular revues than
for Shakespeare. We often saw him at Velfkeh's, larger than life, eating
and drinking as if he were playing Henry VIII.

Morewski almost outshone the rest of the cast in *The Tempest,* but
they were all good. I was particularly enchanted with Esther Golden-
berg, the beautiful woman who played Ariel. She, too, had once been
associated with the Vilna Troupe. She floated about the stage with the
fluid grace of a ballerina. Caliban, played by Moses Lipman, also impressed me. I left the theater elated, thrilled that Yiddish actors could
rise to the demands of *The Tempest* and bring it off. Afterward we went
to Velfkeh's, where I was introduced to some of the actors.

In May 1939, two American Yiddish actors came to play in Vilna,
with a cast they had assembled in Poland. The leading man was Pesach
Burstein, then almost forty, who had made a name for himself as a star
on New York's Second Avenue stage, with his singing, whistling, and
dancing routines. When I read the ad in *Undzer Tog* for their run, I

was astonished to discover that his leading lady was Lillian Lux, who'd been at the Sholem Aleichem Mitlshul with me. Since she'd been a child, she had wanted to go on the stage. When Maurice Schwartz needed two children for the first scene in Sholem Asch's *Kiddush ha-Shem,* he got them from our Mitlshul; one was Lillian. When I told all this to Zalmen Reisen, he said we must go to the theater. His Yiddishistic enthusiasm carried him away. "Imagine," he said, "two New York girls—each finding her own Yiddish satisfactions in Vilna." It boggled his mind. One might have thought we were a high-wire sister act in the Jerusalem of Lithuania.

Reisen, his wife, and I went to see *Der gasn-zinger (The Street Singer),* one of three or four shows which Burstein put on in the four weeks or so he played in Vilna, performing only on weekends. This authorless show was a fatuous melodrama, spiced up with a murder and a prison scene, and featuring Burstein's song-dance-and-whistle routines. Between acts we went backstage to see Lillian. She almost fainted with shock, then gathered her energies to shriek over and over again: "My God, my God, my God, can you believe it!"

How well they did at the box office I never knew, but I suppose it was worth their while. No wonder Morewski went about in a rage, declaiming against *shund*—trash.

Early in December 1938, I went to hear what was billed as a "word-concert." It was a reading of Yiddish poetry, by Hertz Grossbard. Tall and thin, with a long face, Grossbard exuded an air of thoughtful melancholy. He, too, had once been associated with the Vilna Troupe and then had gone off to play in Germany. In the 1930s he returned to Poland and the world of Yiddish and soon made a career as an elegant interpreter of contemporary Yiddish literature, mainly poetry. His Yiddish diction was exquisitely beautiful, his reading expressive, every sound and gesture disciplined.

That December evening he began reading from his standard repertoire—fables by Eliezer Steinbarg, bubbly and comically inventive poems by A. Lutzky. Then he read several poems by Moshe Nadir, a Yiddish poet and a committed Communist living in New York. Those were poems I disliked. Grossbard was trying to ingratiate himself, I thought, with his leftish audience. He closed with Chaim Grade's *geveyn fun doyres* ("Lament of Generations"), which Grade had read some weeks earlier with greater intensity.

Grossbard's elegant Yiddish diction and his preference for understatement made Max Weinreich an admirer and even a friend. A few days after hearing Grossbard read, I heard him again at the Weinreichs. They were giving a party in honor of Dr. Paul Ariste, a non-Jewish Yiddish-speaking linguist and folklorist from Tallinn, who was in Vilna for a series of lectures at the YIVO. Grossbard was invited to the party and, to everyone's delight, performed for the company, reading some of the lighter poems in his repertoire.

In New York I was an addicted concertgoer. I used to sit in the upper reaches of Carnegie Hall to hear Toscanini conduct the New York Philharmonic and I would buy standing-room tickets at the Metropolitan Opera almost every time Lauritz Melchior and Kirsten Flagstad sang in *Tristan und Isolde*. Vilna, I knew, was not New York. Still I was surprised that Vilna had so little a musical life. To be sure, Jasha Heifetz had been born there, but he hadn't stayed long. Whatever music was played in Vilna was largely the product of Jewish talent and enterprise.

From time to time, touring instrumentalists and singers came to perform in Vilna. The most satisfying concert I attended the whole year I was there was a recital on January 23, 1939, by Nikolay Andreyevich Orlov, a Russian pianist, then living in the West, of whom I had never heard before or after. A wonderful interpreter of Chopin, he made familiar pieces sound freshly exciting. As for that famous funeral march which we used to parody in college, Orlov's fingers restored it as a work of tragic grandeur.

The year I was in Vilna was actually a big year musically. For the first time in its history Jewish Vilna had an orchestra of its own. Before that, there'd been only school and institutional bands which hadn't lasted long. The Maccabi sports organization had a marching band, conducted by my friend Elya Teitlebaum, which performed on special occasions— for instance, on the evening honoring Chaim Grade for the literary award he received.

The Jewish Symphony Orchestra was composed—as was to be expected—almost entirely of amateurs. It was created by the efforts of the Society for Jewish Arts in Vilna (*Di yidishe kunst-gezelshaft in Vilne*), which had been established in 1921 and whose objective was to promote the arts in Vilna, Jewish arts particularly. The Society had fathered a Jewish Institute of Music in 1925, through which some 500 students were said to have passed, but only 30 had completed the course of study. Besides programs to train young people in the arts, the Society arranged concerts, art exhibits, dramatic performances, stimulated public interest in the arts, and provided support for cultural projects or subsidies for artists. But its financial and artistic resources were limited.

The inaugural concert of the Jewish Symphony Orchestra on Sunday, November 27, 1938, was a gala event. I went with Elya Teitlebaum. It was held at the City Hall auditorium, whose stage just managed to accommodate the orchestra, composed of about fifty to sixty players. The conductor, making no big claims for his ensemble, offered as the program's major work Beethoven's First Symphony. The orchestra didn't sound bad at all; the debut performance actually had an exciting quality, probably because both the performers and the audience were keyed up for the occasion.

At its second concert in January, the orchestra played Schubert's Unfinished Symphony and at its last concert of the season, February 26, 1939, a violinist whose name I immediately erased from my mind played Mendelssohn's Concerto in E Minor so badly I could hardly sit still in my seat. Afterward the orchestra repaired the damage with a decent performance of Mozart's Haffner Symphony.

Vilna had a good choral group, named for its conductor Jacob Gerstein, which performed with some frequency. The singers were, of course, all amateurs. At a concert I heard in February, Yiddish folk songs, some of them in arrangements by Teitlebaum, made up half the program. The classical repertoire was represented by excerpts from Handel's Samson oratorio and Borodin's Prince Igor, along with songs by Schubert and Mendelssohn. The program closed with three Yiddish labor songs, which were the most familiar numbers on the program to the audience.

Despite Vilna's lack of artistic resources, an ambitious cultural entrepreneur decided to produce *Aida* in Yiddish, an undertaking that struck me as absurd as it was foolhardy. The ads promised a mammoth production—two orchestras (the Jewish Symphony and the Maccabi), chorus and ballet, a hundred people on the stage at one time. On opening night the lights failed during the second intermission, a fitting judgment, in my opinion, on the proceedings. I seized the opportunity to leave. Hundreds of patrons more patient than I waited for well over an hour until repairs were made and the performance resumed. The show, I heard, finished about two in the morning.

The state of the fine arts in Jewish Vilna, as in all Vilna for that matter, was even more dismal than that of music. Not since 1863, when Mark

Antokolski left Vilna to study in St. Petersburg, had Vilna had a serious artist. In September 1938 I went to an exhibit of a Young Vilna artist. The charcoal drawings that I saw had little individuality, most of them reflecting the combined influences of Käthe Kollwitz and socialist realism.

Where would artists with originality have come from? I knew that the development of the arts of drawing, painting, and architecture had been inhibited by the biblical injunction against making graven images. Unlike music, which for centuries had been integrated into religious worship, the plastic arts had hardly any place in Jewish life, except for the ornamentation one might find in the synagogue. Furthermore, what could one have expected, when Poland itself had such a weak artistic tradition? In Vilna, when people talked about the fine arts or music, they usually meant folk art and folk music. The nationalist movements that had swept Eastern Europe in the late nineteenth century sparked interest in national cultural roots and everywhere national groups began digging up their native arts and crafts. The Jews had done that too and in Vilna the An-ski Museum, in the Kehillah building, consisted of historical ethnographic exhibits. Once, after a concert of folk music, I tried to persuade my friends that, however lovely the performance, the folk songs themselves were not artistically comparable to the art songs of Schubert or Brahms.

Vilna had no resources for training and developing artists and art appreciation, nor did the Jews there have a sufficient tradition to build on. If young people wanted to paint or sculpt, they had to do what their predecessors in Eastern Europe had done for generations past—leave home for Paris or Rome, where they could study art and live among artists. Nor did Vilna have the facilities, except perhaps through the elementary schools, to foster the appreciation of, and develop the taste for, the fine arts. Vilna had no institution to do for high culture what the YIVO was doing for high scholarship. Only literature had a venerable tradition among the Vilna Jews as a form of art or entertainment, for Yiddish and Hebrew literature had a history of several generations of creative activity, in Vilna particularly. That's why it could produce talented newcomers like Chaim Grade and Abraham Sutzkever.

The kind of Yiddish cultural life I was looking for didn't exist. I had thought that Vilna might become a center for a modern secular Yiddish culture, where the finest achievements of Western art and civilization could become blended with the world of Yiddish. It was a naive expectation. Just as I realized that Yiddish flourished in Vilna for the wrong reasons, because of Polish anti-Semitism and Polish economic backwardness, so I came to realize that Vilna was too weak and poor to sustain the ideal culture I was searching for. Kalmanovich was right. Such a culture could be created only under conditions of autonomy and freedom.

CHAPTER 7

Rich and Poor,
Right and Left

On my first day in Vilna, Saturday, August 27, 1938, after I had break-fasted with the Kalmanoviches and washed up from my overnight train ride from Warsaw, Rivele took me visiting. We boarded a bus for a twenty-minute ride through the countryside to Niemesz, a village about six kilometers away. We were going to spend the day with Mrs. Stefania Szabad in her country house.

Szabad was one of the most prestigious names in Vilna and I knew something about Stefania's late husband, Dr. Zemach Szabad, because the YIVO's Aspirantur had been named to memorialize him after his death in 1935. Born in Vilna in 1864, Szabad had attended Ramayles' Yeshiva as a youngster, but the world of the enlightenment attracted him more than the yeshiva. He went to Moscow to study medicine and eventually returned to Vilna where he set up his medical practice. In time he emerged as an influential figure in the city and a communal leader. During the difficult years of the Great War, he was one of the key notables who tried to protect the Vilna Jews against the depredations of the successive occupying powers. He had been the head of the Kehillah and had served many years as a member of Vilna's City Council. In 1928 he was elected to the Polish Senate and served one term.

About Stefania Szabad I knew little, except for her widowhood and motherhood. She had a son, Jascha, and a daughter, Regina, married to Max Weinreich. On the short bus trip, Rivele filled me in briefly about where we were going. The house at Niemesz was not just a summer home, but was also operated as a modest truck farm, producing vegetables for the local markets. The Szabads had a larger farm at Leoniszki, at the outer rim of Vilna, which was run by Jascha, who had studied agronomy in Berlin.

We arrived at a large wooden house, surrounded by trees. Waiting on the wide porch to greet us stood Stefania Szabad, a woman then about sixty. Though she was of medium height, her erect carriage and self-assured bearing made her look taller, stately. Broad-shouldered, with her gray-white hair tied in a bun, she was dressed in a plain white blouse and a full ankle-length skirt. She wore heavy shoes that day, not boots, which—so she later told me—she usually wore on working days at the farm. You knew right away you were in the presence of a commanding personality.

As we walked up the porch, Stefania introduced herself to me, immediately offered us a cool drink, and presented me to her guests. The Weinreichs were there and others whom I can no longer recall. Minutes later Stefania began questioning me about America, particularly about the foods Americans ate. "They eat lettuce, I hear," she said. I confirmed that it was true. Though she grew lettuce on the farm, she was still skeptical. "Let's see if you're a real American," she challenged me. She soon brought out a large plate filled with freshly washed lettuce. "Eat," she commanded. In awe of this formidable woman, I timidly protested, saying I wasn't hungry. But she'd put me to the test. Everyone watched me, as I set to, attacking the lettuce as if I were a knight defending a holy truth. I speared the greens on my fork, chewing, crunching, fiercely determined to prove that I was a true-blue American. I realized I must look comical, but I was too intimidated to dare to mock Stefania Szabad's peremptory command. Between swallows I ventured to suggest that we never ate such huge quantities of lettuce; besides, it was usually served with salad dressing to make it tastier. But to no avail.

Meanwhile, during my ordeal, Stefania Szabad expounded on her philosophy, justifying her commitment to Tolstoyan ideas. She wanted to live a simple existence, to return to nature, to experience life without the artificialities and encumbrances of modern civilization. All people, she held, were equal and to prove it, she worked together with the peasant women who came to help her in planting and harvesting the vegetables. Furthermore, she was persuaded that the peasants' way of life was good enough also for the bourgeoisie. The lecture had been for my benefit. The others had heard it many times, but continued to humor her in her then already anachronistic notions.

On this, my first day in Vilna, it seemed to me that some mysterious force had transported me into another time and place. Instead of having arrived in contemporary Poland, I felt I had been retrojected into nineteenth-century Russia as a visitor to a provincial country house of the landed gentry. Stefania Szabad belonged in a Turgenev novel.

In the course of the year I learned more about her history. She had been born in 1879 into one of Vilna's most illustrious families and was a descendant of the great rabbi and Talmudist Akiva Eger. Though she took pride in her ancestry, she had never evinced any interest in traditional Judaism. She had studied at a Russian university and in her youth had been caught up in the revolutionary movement. That was when and where she acquired her Tolstoyan populism. Fifteen years younger than her husband, she'd been headstrong and flamboyant. According to gossip, she had run away from her husband with a Russian officer, but that affair hadn't lasted long and Zemach Szabad took her back. When I met her, this strong-minded, willful woman had grown into a domineering matriarchal figure.

After I had completed the ordeal by lettuce and validated my American credentials, Max Weinreich rescued me from Stefania Szabad and the company. He volunteered to show me around the farm. I had never seen anything like it before. One summer, when I was about five, my parents took me to a dairy farm in the Catskills and we watched the cows being milked. I met the farmer's children who showed me a vegetable patch they tended. But never had I seen such extensive vegetable beds as Stefania Szabad had—rows upon rows of cucumbers, tomatoes, lettuce, green peas, string beans, carrots, cabbages, beets, potatoes, onions. The radishes spread like a wild growth. Pails and baskets of all sizes were scattered everywhere, for the picking season was then at its height. I saw no machines of any kind. Everything was done by hand.

We stopped among the green-pea vines and Max Weinreich showed me how to pick pea pods, split them open, and eat the peas. Growing up as a city child, I'd never known that peas grew on vines and were edible raw. I found them more appetizing than lettuce, though not exactly an epicurean delight. All the while, we were getting acquainted. Then Stefania summoned us to the midday meal. At the table I understood why Max Weinreich had so purposefully nourished himself on raw peas. The meal consisted of one dish—a huge steaming bowl of string beans, supplemented with bread and tea. Stefania Szabad explained: "If the peasants can subsist on beans for a whole week, so can we."

After dinner, she decreed that I must rest. I'd been talking a lot, answering everyone's questions about America. She installed me in a lovely little guest bedroom, gave me some notepaper, and instructed me to write home. In that letter describing my first day in Vilna, I closed: "I hope this is not a dream from which I'll suddenly awake." Stefania Szabad and Max Weinreich added postscripts, assuring my parents that I was in good hands. Later we played a game of croquet on the lawn. At about sunset, Rivele and I returned to Vilna.

The Weinreichs had invited me to dinner at their house the next day. Stefania Szabad was there, too. She insisted on taking me back to her Vilna residence after dinner. She lived on ulica Styczniowa, just off Mickiewicz, in the finest part of Vilna, in a spacious apartment with a garden at the rear. It was elegantly furnished, with a servant to care for its management. There I saw little evidence of the peasant life.

Stefania Szabad provided me with my first lesson in the sociology of Jewish life in Vilna. If Vilna Jews would have had a pedigreed aristocracy, Stefania Szabad would have qualified as grand duchess. She enjoyed the distinction of a great family name and the prestige which accrued to her from her late husband's position both as a physician and as one of Vilna's leading citizens. She owned property and considerable farmland, not commonly held by Jews in Vilna or elsewhere in Poland. *Noblesse oblige* was her watchword. In her relations with her servants and with the peasants who worked on her farms, in helping those who turned to her, she was always aware of the responsibilities of her position. In her private and public life she conducted herself as if she were indeed a grand duchess and she fulfilled the obligations of her social position.

The Jews in Vilna lived in an unevenly stratified society, which the statisticians commonly represented as a pyramid. At the top, the upper class, constituting a thin layer, was composed of people like Stefania Szabad and the Kaplan-Kaplanskys. They were property owners, entrepreneurs, top professionals, persons with inherited wealth.

The Jewish middle class was much larger and more diverse, occupying a wide swath just below. Its upper reaches were inhabited by people like the Weinreichs and the Reisens. At its bottom were people like my friends in the Aspirantur—Ber Schlossberg, the YIVO staff assistant, and Jacob Rivkind, the statistician—who, together with their working wives, eked out a bare living. Yet though they were chronically short of money, they were middle class by occupation and their standard of living. The middle segment of Vilna's Jewish middle class was the most substantial, consisting of self-employed artisans and established merchants.

The lower class, the most populous class of all, occupied the bottom half of the pyramid and consisted of workers, small shopkeepers, peddlers—the deserving and hard-working poor. It included also the old, the sick, the destitute, those who couldn't make ends meet, beggars, and the underworld.

The standards of living and the levels of income of all classes, from top to bottom, fell far below the comparable standards in the United States. We Americans lived better than our class equivalents in Vilna. The American poor, at least as I knew them in New York, were better off than the Vilna poor. One had only to take into account our plumbing and sanitary conveniences, which helped people stay cleaner and healthier. A few of my New York friends' parents lived as well as Stefania Szabad did in her city house, though they did not have her social standing. My Mitlshul friends who had just married and were starting their own households lived close to the margin, but not nearly so precariously as my young friends in the Aspirantur.

According to the statistics of family consumption which Rivkind had accumulated in his study of family budgets, a four-person working-class family in Vilna spent 265 zlotys per month, averaging about 67 zlotys per person. That was about half of what I spent just to keep myself afloat. I could never have managed on that money, if I would have stayed on for an extended period of time. And I didn't need to maintain a household, or replenish broken dishes or a damaged pot. I didn't need to buy clothes. I was spared the expenses of medical care. I had no small children to provide for. Besides, because of my unique status, I was socially in demand and was invited out a lot for meals and treated to the theater and other entertainments. How others managed on those scant incomes, I could never fathom.

Poverty in Vilna was everywhere within sight and reach, but I never grew accustomed to it. Whenever I came face to face with the squalid and unremitting poverty of Jewish Vilna, I flinched, finding it more oppressive than the anti-Semitism which also enveloped the Vilna Jews. At home, during the Great Depression, poverty was widespread, but in the New York I knew, I seldom saw people as pitiably poor as those in Vilna, or people who displayed their poverty so publicly, so obtrusively, and—so it seemed to me—so shamelessly. Though I had courage enough to take personal risks and I had learned to steel myself to confront unpleasant truths, my defenses crumbled before the distress I saw everywhere, and especially when I saw how poverty afflicted the little children and the old people. It didn't take long before the ugly realities of poverty among the Jews in Vilna shattered my sentimental notions about the viability of the realm of Yiddish. Everything I loved in Vilna rested upon a rotten crumbling foundation.

In my early days in Vilna, while I was sightseeing in the heart of its Jewish quarter with a companion, I encountered an aspect of poverty that utterly unnerved me. As we were walking through the dirty serpentine streets of the old ghetto area, we were accosted by a swarm of beggars. They besieged us on every side. Ragged children chased after us, screaming for a grosz—the Polish equivalent of a penny (100 groszy equaled one zloty). The beggars were unwashed, foul-smelling, a rough lot. They were dressed in layers of tatters that had once been clothing. Some didn't have shoes, but had swaddled their feet in strips of rags. Traveling in packs, they conducted themselves as though begging were an established occupation and it was their legitimate business to beg and ours to give alms. At first they pleaded, whined, and wheedled. When we didn't readily respond, they became abusive and began to curse volubly in pungent Yiddish idioms.

That grotesque encounter suddenly seemed familiar to me, as if I had once experienced it. Then I remembered I had read it in *Fishke der krumer,* a novel by Mendele Mocher Sforim, whose characters included a vagrant rascally band of beggars. Mendele had cruelly depicted the demoralization which poverty had wrought among the Jews in the old czarist Pale of Settlement. I used to think that his ugly portrait had been exaggerated, but now I understood he had written with brutal frankness. Just a few years earlier, I learned, Vilna merchants had formed a Committee to Support the Poor and Combat Beggary, hoping to protect themselves and their customers from the aggressions of the organized beggars. But nothing came of their efforts; the merchants were powerless against the beggars and the rampant poverty which spawned them.

As I became more experienced in coping with Vilna's street life, I would prepare myself with a handful of ready groszy if I expected to be in the neighborhoods the beggar bands worked. Some of my friends, especially those who needed that small change themselves, were not so easily intimidated. Once, when I was walking with Nechama Epstein and Shmuel Pipe, the beggars advanced on us. Pipe was tough in his humorous way. "Come the first of the month," he shouted at them. "That's when I take care of my obligations."

But the combative beggars were only a small part of Vilna's ubiquitous beggars. Most of them were not threatening, often just sitting on the sidewalk, sometimes wandering about. Men and women, they were old and infirm, crippled, sometimes crazy. Whenever I could, I'd drop some coins in their tin cups or old caps. But alms never made any perceptible dent in Vilna's poverty.

The most dismal public place of poverty I knew in Vilna was the *durkhhoyf,* the "through-yard," the hub of Vilna's old-clothes and secondhand trade. One could enter either at ulica Żydowska 9, across the street from the *shulhoyf,* or at ulica Jatkowa 10. (These streets formed part of the original triangle constituting the ghetto early in the seventeenth century.) The courtyards of the two back-to-back buildings adjoined, forming a through passageway. Its width varied from about twelve to twenty-four feet, depending on how far the buildings on each side protruded. The courtyard was dotted with some half dozen stairways and stoops through which one entered the several buildings, which housed also two prayerhouses. The courts had been paved haphazardly, and the traffic of centuries had eroded the cobblestones and the grout that had held them in place. Now the yards were pockmarked with patches of dusty sand. A narrow gravelly path that turned muddy in bad weather wound through the yards.

The *durkhhoyf* was not used much as a shortcut between the two streets. Its fame or, more aptly, its notoriety derived from its being the site of the most wretched marketplace in all Vilna. Some vendors had tiny shops which were literally holes in the wall. Others displayed their merchandise near a stoop or against a patch of wall. They sold old clothes, broken-down furniture, pots and pans, whose bottoms had been repaired, salvaged from the junk heap. Once I saw a pair of torn shabby shoes that the vendor boasted he had recovered from someone's garbage. The air in the *durkhhoyf* was close, musty and fetid with the odor of old clothes, the stink of refuse, and the rank odor emanating from the building's moldering walls. People came here to trade in one another's castoffs, to exchange each other's misery.

Vendors and peddlers also operated in nearby courtyards. In one, bundles of kindling and pails of pea coal were sold; in another, all kinds of old iron—chains, locks, discarded tools, mostly rusted. Coal dust and wood splinters littered the cobbled yards and kept them perpetually black and dusty. On any corner and in every courtyard you could see fruit and vegetable peddlers, elderly women like Chaim Grade's mother, selling their stale and shoddy goods. They were especially piteous in the winter cold, their old sweaters and threadbare shawls insufficient against the weather. Some had firepots—small earthen vessels filled with small coals—over which they hovered, trying to keep their hands and feet warm.

The Lumber Market at Nowogródzka and Zawalna, where you couldn't get lumber, was near my house. Most of the vendors weren't Jews, but Polish peasants. Women outnumbered men as marketeers. They looked older than they probably were, weatherbeaten by their outdoor occupation and aged by a hard life. They wore long skirts or dresses and were bundled in big shabby sweaters and shawls. Their stockings were dark cotton and their shoes were heavy, dark, and laced. Only their babushkas provided color at the marketplace.

Except for a few unwalled sheds for shelter and one shack, the marketplace was open to the weather. Nearly everything was exposed to sun, wind, rain, or cold. A handful of vendors had their own covered pushcarts. Here and there you saw long rough-hewn wooden tables on which goods for sale were displayed and occasionally long benches on which people or produce rested. The marketeers brought their products in large baskets or sacks—apples, pears, potatoes, cabbages, beets, onions, carrots, eggs, chickens. In the summer months there was more variety— plums, apricots, tomatoes, radishes, cauliflower, eggplant, squash. The fish dealers had round water-filled tin tubs with live pike and carp. Boxes and crates were everywhere, used as stands or as seats. As the day wore on, the square began to empty out, for the marketeers stayed until they sold all their goods. In the winter the women warmed themselves at their firepots. After dark you could see the reddish lights dotting the marketplace.

The market was a crowded and noisy place, as the vendors hawked their goods and shoppers pushed their way around, bargaining, arguing, quarreling. Yiddish was heard everywhere and many Polish peasants knew enough Yiddish to conduct their business in it. The market fascinated me as a relic of a past long extinct in my world. Notwithstanding its bustle and liveliness, it exuded sadness. Its poverty was not as repugnant as that at the *durkhhoyf,* but its goods were inferior, the produce of poor quality, overripe or underripe, shabby. I was benumbed by the primitiveness and backwardness, depressed that Vilna had not yet been brought into the modern world. Historic relics were one thing; human misery another.

Years later, on my first visit to Jerusalem, wandering around the crowded downtown shopping center, I came upon Machne Yehuda, a market near Jaffa Street. The stalls and carts were dense, the crowd was hard to penetrate, the products were not of the best quality. Buyers and sellers were speaking Yiddish, arguing, bargaining. For a moment I thought I was on Zawalna. For a moment I imagined that Vilna still existed.

Max Weinreich had suggested to Jacob Rivkind, who headed the study of Jewish family budgets, that he take me along with him when he visited one of his respondent families. Rivkind decided to take me to the family of a man purported to be a horsethief. I don't remember now where they lived, except that it was not in the old ghetto, but someplace away from the center of town. We went about five in the afternoon; it was getting dark.

The courtyard in the small building was filthy. We found the door, knocked, and then stepped down two or three steps into what seemed to me to be utter darkness and treacherous underfooting. It was like entering a cave. Gradually one could make out some shapes in an enclosure perhaps six by nine feet. There seemed to be no firm flooring; it had probably crumbled under the accumulation of mud and filth. At the far end, I could make out some half dozen adults and children huddled on what appeared to be a bed or a heap of old mattresses. Nearby stood a small kerosene lamp on a box or a table. It was cold, yet the air was malodorous. Rivkind asked a few questions, checked out the entries in the little books, and we left.

I felt nauseous, but I was ashamed of my queasiness. These people lived like animals, in the very bowels of poverty, passively enduring an unendurable life. I must have wanted to blot the scene from my mind, because I wrote home only that I had visited extremely poor people who lived in a vile hovel. Perhaps, at the time, I was afraid my mother would worry too much about the places I visited. A few years later, when I was back in New York, I spent long hours reading the many volumes of Charles Booth's *Life and Labour of the People in London* for some research. All the while the degrading poverty I had seen in that vile hovel in Vilna haunted my memory.

Most of all it hurt to see the children of poverty—hungry, cold, sick, drooping, unsmiling, without childish playfulness. Given their parents' plight, many must have been unloved. Their lives were comfortless. Some had already become beggars and others were destined to live like the horsethief.

One day in mid-November I had an opportunity to glimpse into their plight, when I went with my landlady, Genia, and her little boy to a baby clinic. The clinic was a place for the indigent, but Genia thought that its medical care had to be extra good, since it was maintained by the Vilna municipality and supported by the Rockefeller Foundation. That's why she went there rather than to a clinic more suitable to her financial means. This was a small building, modern and clean. Genia was excited about what to me was an ordinary drinking-water fountain built into the wall. She'd never seen one before. While we were waiting to see the doctor, the baby dropped his pacifier on the floor. I went to wash it at the fountain. It turned out there was no running water.

Genia and her baby looked out of place among the other mothers and their children. Hers was the only happy and healthy-looking child there. I'd never seen such babies in my life—ashen, skinny, withered, sad-eyed, cheerless, cranky, coughing, wailing, unbelievably filthy. Children were swaddled in old dirty rags. One tot, with frail spindly legs, wore a pair of oversized coarse woolen stockings whose feet were full of holes.

Most of the mothers were Polish women, servants or janitresses. Some held babies about six months old, but they were already visibly pregnant. I was surprised that we met quite a few Jewish mothers. One didn't have shoes, wearing soft slippers over heavy woolen socks. Few had proper coats—the winter frosts hadn't yet arrived, but it was already quite chilly. One Jewish woman cradled a little girl not yet two years old in her arms. The child was beautiful, with large gypsy eyes, but utterly unresponsive, lethargic. I began talking with the mother, who poured out her troubles. It seemed that, since birth, the child kept getting sick. The mother told me she'd had three other children, all of whom had died. Crying all the while, she said she had lost twenty pounds in the weeks since the child's latest bout of illness. All she wanted in life, the mother wept, was *khotch eyn hemd, khotch eyn kind*—just one shirt, just one child.

In February I went with friends to see a dramatic performance put on by the pupils of the Frug-Kuperstein CYSHO school. The 600 children who attended that school were the poorest in Vilna. After the performance, we observed them going home with their parents. They wore what I thought were rags. It was likely, my friends told me, that they'd have nothing to eat when they got home. Before the performance, one of the teachers told us a pitiful story of a little girl who had a part in the play. The child was an orphan who lived with her grandmother. Just a few days before the performance, the grandmother handed her over to the city authorities, explaining she didn't have the means to support the child. The teachers found the girl in the custody of the police and managed to rescue her.

Poor children didn't have shoes and so they didn't go to school. In March 1939, the Kehillah, in its allocation to the religious institutions, included an amount of 5,150 zlotys for shoes for the children in the Town Talmud Torah and for other shoeless schoolchildren. A few days later, *Undzer Tog* published several of the letters which sixty-six children of a religious school had written to thank the Kehillah for the shoes. They said that they hadn't been able to attend school during the winter months because they didn't have shoes.

The Kehillah and all of Vilna's welfare and health organizations tried to relieve the hardships of poverty. The Kehillah appropriated money for the old-age home, for the Town Talmud Torah and its orphanage, for the Jewish Hospital. They allocated funds to buy kindling and coal for the poor. They gave grants of money to individual families. Every year they provided matzo for Passover to the poor. But they couldn't stem the tide of impoverishment that was overtaking the Jewish community. Nor could the multitude of Vilna's loan societies cope with the applications that kept mounting. Even the relief funds from the American Jewish Joint Distribution Committee were inadequate to the needs. Yet those needs would have been even more insurmountable without the infusion of money from private gifts—remittances from family members in America. No one knew exactly how much money came to Jewish Vilna from that source, but those funds enabled many families to hold out against starvation.

Every day the Jews in Vilna grew poorer. Their pauperization was accelerated by the government's anti-Jewish policies, which were intended to improve the economic opportunities of the Poles by depriving the Jews of theirs. All Poland was poor, Poles and Jews. Poland's anti-Semites blamed the Jews for the poverty of the Poles, but the real explanation for Poland's unhappy circumstances lay in the feebleness of its economy. It could not generate jobs or capital; it could not support its population. Unemployment in 1938 stood officially at about 10 percent, but that figure did not reflect the true extent of unemployment in the overpopulated rural areas.

Poland suffered from economic stagnation and industrial backwardness. Since its founding, Poland existed in a state of perpetual economic crisis, exacerbated by the effects of the Great War and the worldwide economic depression. According to the statistics, the economy of interwar Poland showed few significant improvements in industrial production as compared to production in 1913, in the same geographical areas which had then been under czarist rule. Coal, iron, and steel production in 1938 had sunk well below the levels of czarist times.

Despite its rich natural resources, Poland remained underdeveloped, unequipped to compete industrially with the Western world. Its index of national production was one of the lowest in Europe. Poland's lack of the most elementary and necessary mechanized tools for its agriculture and industry was both cause and consequence of its backwardness, preventing the development of the country's resources. That, in turn, deterred entrepreneurs and foreign investors. Poland's industrial backwardness accounted for the paucity of consumer goods, from foodstuffs and basic household goods to luxury items. Most disastrously, it affected the country's capacity to provide adequate military defenses, even though Poland faced fearsome enemies on its eastern and western borders. In the late 1930s, the government began to invest capital in the modernization of its military industry and its armed forces. Consequently, even fewer of Poland's meager financial resources were available to develop private industry and to raise the level of education.

In 1931, despite more than a decade of compulsory education, over 30 percent of the Polish population was illiterate. In rural areas, the illiteracy rate was even higher, with the highest proportion to be found in the eastern border regions, including the Vilna area. Yet, contrary to the trend in the Western world, illiteracy in Poland kept increasing at an alarming rate, according to a government study conducted in 1938. Large numbers of children left elementary school after attending for only two or three years. The educational backwardness of the Polish population was further exacerbated by widespread and chronic alcoholism, thus further contributing to low productivity.

Since I had read Max Weber on the Protestant ethic and the spirit of capitalism, I attributed Poland's economic backwardness in part also to the pervasive influence of the Catholic Church. In a letter to a friend, I paraphrased Henry Adams: "In Vilna the force of the Virgin is more familiar than that of the dynamo."

The Jews, in contrast, were likely to be more energetic in finding work, more enterprising in developing new areas of trade and industry, more innovative in finding new methods of production. They also had a lower proportion of illiterates than the Poles. Their literacy increased dramatically as the Jews, in contrast to the Poles, flocked to the schools. Their long history of having been excluded from various trades and professions made them value literacy. It also encouraged them to cultivate versatility and adaptability as they searched for a livelihood. That was true wherever Jews lived and it was true also in Vilna.

Vilna had never been an industrial city. In czarist times it had filled an economically significant role as a center of cross-country trade and commerce, serving as a passageway for imports and exports in and out of the Russian empire by way of the Baltic ports. But after Vilna became part of independent Poland, it lost its geographical advantage and became instead a geographical dead end. To the north, the Lithuanian border had been closed since 1919, because of the conflict over Vilna. (Only in early 1939 did the Poles and the Lithuanians establish diplomatic relations and open the border for normal traffic.) The border with the Soviet Union was closed to travel and trade.

Industrially, Vilna was outclassed even by Bialystok, whose population was less than half of Vilna's but which had long been a center of the textile industry in the eastern part of Poland. Still, over 43 percent of Vilna's gainfully occupied Jews were engaged in industry, as compared to 33 percent in trade and commerce. The Kehillah and Jewish communal leaders were committed to "productivizing" the Jews, that is, encouraging young people to get the proper education and training so that they could take up a useful trade, rather than join the ranks of the impoverished shopkeepers and peddlers. The Kehillah subsidized various courses in vocational training. In October 1938, ORT, an organization dating back to czarist times whose object was to provide vocational training for Jews, opened the first technical school in Vilna. On October 12, 1938, some 300 people, everybody of consequence in Jewish Vilna, attended a banquet in honor of the occasion. Daniel Lerner had invited me to go with him.

Though Vilna did not have any heavy industry to speak of, it did have light industry. Some two-thirds of its industrial enterprises, large and small, were owned and operated by Jews. They provided employment for Jewish workers in factories and livelihoods for artisans at all levels—master craftsmen, journeymen, apprentices. Only a few factories, even by Polish standards, were considered large. One was Elektrit, producing radios for the national and export market. Another was

Rochlin's plywood factory, established in 1936 and employing about 280 workers in its Vilna branch and several hundred more in two nearby branches. Jews operated sawmills, pioneered in the local oil and rubber industries, and dominated the extensive fur and leather-goods industries. But most of the city's industrial plants consisted of small shops.

The mechanization of industry and the use of power were expensive in Poland and especially in so underdeveloped a city as Vilna. Capital for industrial development was scarce, while labor was cheap. As a result, most artisans produced handmade goods that could compete in quality and price with factory-produced goods. A case in point was the manufacture of leather gloves, one of the oldest industries pioneered by Vilna Jews back in the nineteenth century. After the Great War, the number of shops producing leather gloves had declined precipitously. When I was there, about thirty shops making leather gloves were in operation—half of them were one-man enterprises; only one employed as many as ten workers.

The fierce competition between factories and artisans for markets intensified cost cutting. As an unexpected consequence, cottage industries increased, as people worked at home and produced goods from materials supplied by an outside employer. These home workers competed most directly with independent artisans and the result was to drive many artisans out of business altogether. Cottage workers were the lowest paid in the industrial sector and the most marginal. They were not unionized.

Jewish workers in Vilna had their own unions—leather workers, printers, hairdressers, teachers, dental technicians, and bookkeepers. Artisans were organized in guilds: photographers, butchers and sausage makers, tailors, bakers, house and sign painters, engravers, jewelers, watchmakers, metalworkers, furriers, leather workers, hairdressers, carpenters, turners, cabinetmakers.

One of my colleagues in the Aspirantur, Shlomo Berezin, engaged in a study of Jews in Vilna's light industry, took me to see a workshop that made hard candies and chocolate. It was located in a densely populated street in the Jewish quarter. The courtyard which we entered was like a maze, with entrances to several buildings and odd structures like cottages adjoining them. But, Shlomo told me, they were hovels. The courtyard hummed with activity, people coming and going in all directions, paths crisscrossing the courtyard. Finally, we located our building.

The workshop consisted of a four-room apartment with a kitchen. The first room, more like a foyer, served as a shipping office. In the next room the candy was wrapped and boxed. In the other two rooms and the kitchen the candy was made. The premises were, I thought, unusually clean. The owner employed eight workers. But he, his wife, and their daughter worked just as hard. The enterprise's net profit, so he told us, was some 400 zlotys per month, the wages a highly skilled worker in a large factory might earn. The owner probably understated his income, but not by much. He was not a rich man.

The Industrial Revolution had not yet arrived here. There was almost no machinery. When I remarked on this, the owner said he had a machine to mix chocolate, but it didn't pay to use it. Power cost too much; hand labor was cheaper. Besides, then you didn't have to worry about the machine's breaking down. He couldn't afford modern equipment for such a marginal enterprise.

We were invited to watch the manufacture of fruit-flavored hard candies. It was a slow and tedious process, all done by hand. First, the workers boiled sugar and milk in large cauldrons over an open fire on the kitchen stove. Then they added fruit syrup, bringing the mixture once again to a boil. The cauldrons were then carried into one of the workrooms and the boiling-hot mixture was poured onto tin tables with two-inch-high wooden enclosures around them, to prevent the viscous mass from overflowing.

When the liquid thickened into a dough-like texture, the workers kneaded it with their bare hands, though it was still painfully hot. A gelatinous coloring was then added and the tacky mass was kneaded again. Then, while it was still hot, two workers began to stretch it, as if it were a length of rubber. This was to increase its volume and thickness. Then a worker with a pair of ordinary scissors cut the stretched substance into strips, which then were passed through a hand-operated metal roller with shapes of fruit etched on it. The jellied strips came through the roller perforated in fruit forms—an apple, cherry, pear. When the strips cooled and dried, they were shaken into a strainer and the fruit forms came apart at the perforations. The leftover bits were tossed into the next cauldron of boiling water and sugar. The whole process took not quite two hours. For months thereafter, I never touched a piece of hard candy. The image of the two men stretching the sticky dough turned my stomach.

Notwithstanding the talent that Jews had for business and no matter how much ingenuity they exercised in trying to make a living, Poland provided them with little economic opportunity. Even worse, the government had in the late 1930s, after Piłsudski's death, embarked on a systematic program to drive the Jews out of the Polish economy altogether. One way they did this was to deprive them of access to enterprises which the government regulated or for which it issued licenses. Another way was to raise legalistic obstacles for Jewish entrepreneurs and artisans. These policies pauperized the Jews throughout Poland.

The lack of work and the poverty that pursued and overtook them brought many Jews to the edge of despair, to hopelessness and apathy. I used to hear talk about a rise in the number of suicides, though I don't recall that any of my friends knew firsthand of such instances. David Ornstein, my colleague in the Aspirantur, engaged in a study of Jewish apprentices in Vilna, would sometimes show me their questionnaires. Those youngsters lived in the depths of Vilna's poverty and had little expectation for a viable future. Their responses summoned up before me the image of the character *Bontche shvayg,* Bontche the Silent, in one of I. L. Peretz's most devastating stories. Bontche was one of the downtrodden of the earth, a suffering creature who all his life never complained of his poverty and hardships, never asked anything of his fellowman. After Bontche died, he went to heaven. His moral record was presented before the Heavenly Judge. In recompense for his earthly deprivations, Bontche was offered his heart's desire. Alas, his only wish was to have a fresh roll with butter every morning. Peretz told the story with a controlled, yet savage, irony.

The apprentices, too, had minimal expectations. One questionnaire stuck in my mind. Not that that apprentice demanded more of society than the others, but somehow he communicated his sense of desperation. His ambition was to emigrate to Australia, to get as far away from Vilna as he could. If he couldn't go to Australia or to the United States, he'd be ready to go even to South America. *Abi emigrirn*—as long as I emigrate. The subtext resonated very clearly: as long as I leave this godforsaken place that can give me no future. That poignant phrase, *abi emigrirn,* kept reverberating in my memory. This youngster wanted to escape his imprisonment, flee from this country that offered him no hope of a decent livelihood, no likelihood of political security as a Jew, and little chance for a future life of comfort or even personal joy.

Abi emigrirn was a modest request. Yet most of the Jews who wanted to leave Poland found that emigration was an unrealizable goal. Some people I knew were trying to get to the United States with one kind of papers or another, but in those years, the immigration quota for Poland was too small to accommodate the multitudes who wanted in.

Furthermore, after *Kristallnacht* in November 1938, the German Jews took priority over the Polish Jews. As for Palestine, the chances of getting a certificate were just as remote as getting a U.S. visa. Just when Jews needed a safe haven most, Britain was capitulating to Arab demands to restrict Jewish immigration to a mere trickle.

Since emigration was not a realistic option for most of Poland's Jews, their only recourse was to defend their rights by means of political action. The Jewish parties followed the prevailing pattern of political organization in Eastern Europe—representing ideological positions or class interests. Sometimes the two converged, as in the case of workers' or peasants' parties. Some parties represented the interests of their constituents on a narrowly circumscribed occupational basis—retailers, merchants, industrialists, artisans, property owners, groups which in the United States would have been organized into lobbies or public-pressure associations.

The Jews in Poland developed a politics of opposition, as every Jewish party offered resistance to the anti-Jewish policies of the national government in Warsaw and the municipal authorities throughout Poland. That adversarial posture was not exclusive to the Jews. All Poland's national minorities—Ukrainians, White Russians, Lithuanians, Germans—stood in opposition. During the late 1920s, they all, including the Jews, formed a National Minorities Bloc to consolidate that opposition and elected a number of their people to the Sejm, Poland's parliamentary assembly, and to the Senate. Dr. Szabad was one of the Jewish deputies elected on that ticket.

Poland's system of proportional representation encouraged the proliferation of parties. In the 1920s, over ninety political parties were registered in Poland and about one-third of them managed to elect one or more of their candidates to the Sejm. The multiplication of parties increased factionalism and fragmentation, exacerbating class differences and intensifying the antagonism between the national minorities and the Polish majority. It also aggravated the divisions within the Jewish community.

Still, regardless of their ideological differences, the Jewish parties united in defense of Jewish interests, but they were outnumbered, never able to muster enough votes or support to defeat the anti-Jewish policies of the Polish majority. The Poles, for their part, never accepted the responsibility of safeguarding the rights of the minorities. That was evident in national politics and in local politics. It was evident in the operations of Vilna's City Council, about which I read in *Undzer Tog* and which were often the topic of dinner-table talk.

In 1938, the City Council had twelve Jewish councilmen, less than 20 percent of the whole body, though the Jews were almost twice that in the population. Polish authorities had effectively gerrymandered the districts to reduce the Jewish presence in the governance of the city. The twelve councilmen were elected from ten different Jewish electoral lists, representing divergent economic and ideological interests. Two were elected from the retailers' list and one each from the merchants', artisans', and industrialists' lists; two represented the General Zionists and one each the Labor Zionists, the Mizrachi, the Revisionists, the Bund, and the Democrats (an outgrowth of the Folkist Party). But despite the splintery politics within the Jewish community, those twelve Jewish councilmen voted together in matters affecting the common Jewish interest.

The elections to the Kehillah produced an even more diverse board of councilmen. In the Kehillah, the Bund had five councilmen, the General Zionists four, the Agudah three. The Revisionists, retailers, and artisans each had two; the other groups one each. The ideological differences were sharpest during the Kehillah's debates over the allocation of funds, since there never was enough money to meet the communal and institutional needs. That was when the Agudah voted against the Mizrachi, the Bund against the Zionists, the Hebraists against the Yiddishists, and nearly everyone against the Revisionists.

The year I was in Vilna the mainstream Zionists were at war with the Revisionists, a right-wing militarist group that had seceded from the World Zionist Organization in 1935 because it refused to give up its independent political activities and would not submit to the discipline of the larger body. In the summer of 1938, the Revisionist movement's charismatic leader, Vladimir Jabotinsky, launched a campaign against the Zionist policy of *havlagah*, "self-restraint," nonretaliation against Arab anti-Jewish violence in Palestine. This factional quarrel among the Zionists was played out also in Poland, surfacing from time to time in Vilna. One heard stories or read accounts of Revisionist assaults on Labor Zionists and vice versa. Once the principal of a Tarbut school was beaten up by a gang of young Revisionists, presumably for having criticized them at a meeting of the Tarbut's Educational Council.

On May 8, 1939, Jabotinsky came to speak in Vilna, his subject "The Three Imperatives of the Hour." The day of his lecture, the Labor Zionists flooded Vilna with Yiddish flyers, parodying Jabotinsky's topic. His "three imperatives," the flyer mocked, were (1) Jabotinsky is the "fuehrer" of the Jewish people; (2) he threatens England and the Arabs with his wooden sword; (3) he wants to evacuate all the Jews from Poland, which is just what the anti-Semites want.

That night Jabotinsky spoke in the Cinema Mars, a large movie house on ulica Ostrabramska. The theater was filled with an audience of about 2,000. The hall was decorated with Revisionist banners and posters and members of Betar, the Revisionist youth movement, dressed in their military uniforms, marched in as an honor guard. Later, they were deployed around the hall to keep order. The audience was mostly Revisionists and, as was their effect when they turned out in numbers, they created a bullying presence in the hall. Besides them, there were people like me, who had come to hear this famous man, though they didn't agree with his politics. The several Zionist parties had their scouts present. When Jabotinsky attacked their parties and policies, they hissed and hooted. But the Betar troops were good at keeping order and intimidated them into silence.

I'd been warned that Jabotinsky was no longer the spellbinder he had once been. Then nearing sixty and graying, he was not a prepossessing figure of a man, with his medium height, stocky build, and dark-rimmed glasses. He wore an ordinary business suit, contrasting with the military dress of his entourage. But when he began to speak, he was mesmerizing. He spoke for two hours. His Yiddish was Russian accented, his diction bold, sharp, and rich. The audience responded to his every inflection, to his ironies and his rages.

His three imperatives were nothing more than the staples of revisionism. First he reaffirmed his—and his party's—fundamental view that the Jews could acquire their homeland in Palestine only by military means, by battle and conquest. Second, he launched into a bitter tirade against the Zionist leadership, specifically, the Jewish Agency for Palestine, and its policy of *havlagah,* accusing them of cowardice and betrayal. Third, he bitterly denounced the European Jews for passivity, for their "insane indifference," as he put it, to their terrible predicament. He wasn't afraid to point the finger at his own audience and likened the Jews of Vilna then, in 1939, to the Jews of Berlin in 1933. Later, he said he was not persuaded that a world war would break out, but if it did, he wanted the Jews to have their own army—not just an army of Palestinian Jews, but one recruited from Jews everywhere in Europe. He closed with a melodramatic flourish and then, for the first time that evening, I saw him as a pathetic and comical figure. He pounded his breast with his fists and shouted: "Here are lodged the sufferings of the Jewish people!" He received a standing ovation.

Nine days later, on May 17, 1939, the British released their latest White Paper on Palestine; its contents were published the next day on the front page of *Undzer Tog*. The White Paper crushed Jewish hopes. It restricted Jewish immigration to a total of 75,000 over the next five years. Thereafter, Jews could enter Palestine only with Arab consent. Even in Vilna, where the Revisionists were not a dominant party, one heard people say that the British White Paper vindicated Jabotinsky's policies. It demonstrated the futility of diplomacy.

Just three weeks after, on June 9, Zerubavel, one of Jabotinsky's numerous antagonists in the Zionist movement, came to Vilna to speak on "The Jewish Answer to the White Paper." Zerubavel was his party name. Born Jacob Vitkin, he had been a leading figure in the Labor Zionist movement in Russia at the beginning of the century. In czarist times, Zerubavel had helped to organize a self-defense group in his hometown to protect the Jews against pogromists. In 1920, when the Labor Zionist movement split over the issue of affiliating with the Third (Communist) International, Zerubavel became the head of the extreme left faction. For years thereafter, the British refused to admit him to Palestine, but finally relented in 1935. Now he had returned to Poland on a fund-raising and lecture tour for his party. At that time, the Left Labor Zionist movement was slavishly pro-Soviet, distinguishable from the Communists only in its commitment to the Jewish settlement in Palestine.

Like Jabotinsky, Zerubavel was reputed to be an eloquent orator, and I decided to hear him too. He spoke at the Conservatory, a hall not as large as the Cinema Mars, but it was packed. Left Labor Zionist banners, posters, and slogans decorated the hall, but this meeting lacked military elan. In fact, the organizers were unprepared for the Revisionists, who tried to break up the meeting. Early on, when Zerubavel began to speak, the lights went out. People said the Revisionists were behind it. But the lights came on again and the meeting got under way. Afterward I heard that the Revisionists had tried, but failed, to set off a stink bomb. They had also attempted to release some pigeons with blue-and-white ribbons within the hall, but somehow that didn't come off either.

Zerubavel, then in his early fifties, was an impressive-looking man, with a big grayish-white beard. He cultivated the prophetic look to go with his name and he spoke in prophetic accents. He, too, held his audience for well over two hours, though he was frequently interrupted by boos and catcalls from the Revisionists and from other Zionists who didn't approve of his far left views. In my letter home, I remarked that he didn't offer any solution to Palestine's problems, but he criticized everybody in the predictable rhetoric of the left. He condemned British imperialism and attacked the policies of Chaim Weizmann's General Zionists and David Ben-Gurion's Mapai (Labor Zionists). When he denounced the Revisionists for adventurism and terrorism, they responded with a torrent of hooting and hissing that threatened to disrupt the meeting. But after a while they quieted down, because the rest of the audience outshouted them. Then Zerubavel, making sure that he left no party unscathed, attacked the Bund for its opposition to Zionism.

The Bund in those days, notwithstanding its anti-Zionism, was the most popular political party among Vilna Jews. It showed its strength at the polls and in the trade unions. In the election for the City Council on May 21, 1939, the Bund emerged as the strongest Jewish party in town, receiving more votes than all the other Jewish parties combined.

City councilmen were elected under a system of proportional representation, which gave the voters multiple choices on the ballot. The results, released a week after the election and published in *Undzer Tog*, showed that 68,579 voters cast 289,987 ballots for candidates on six different lists. In this election, the economic-interest groups did not run candidates, why I don't remember. There were only three Jewish lists: (1) the Bund and its affiliated trade unions, (2) the Jewish National Bloc, comprising all the Zionist parties, except (3) the Labor Zionists, who went it alone. The three Polish lists were (1) the Polish Socialist Party (PPS) and its affiliates, (2) the National Democrats (Endecja), a virulent anti-Semitic party, and (3) OZON, an acronym for a party called "The Camp of National Unity," whose unity seemed to be largely based on its anti-Semitic policies. The Polish political spectrum consisted of two colors—pink and black. There was no center.

The Bund received 43,359 votes, just a little more than the combined vote for the other two Jewish lists. The Jewish National Bloc had 30,008 votes; the Labor Zionists, 13,220. The vote worked out, in terms of council seats, to ten seats for the Bund, five for the Jewish National Bloc, and two for the Labor Zionists. The Bund had won a significant victory over its Jewish rivals, but in the long run, it didn't matter, even if the Jewish councilmen stood united. The Jewish deputies, even with the support of the PPS—which they didn't often have in those days—were outnumbered. The Endecja and the OZON together received more than half of all the ballots cast—156,896. The Endecja won twenty-seven seats, the OZON nineteen, and the PPS only seven.

The Bund's strength at the polls might be attributed to the fact that Vilna had more poor Jews than prosperous ones and a larger Jewish working class than a middle class. But in fact many middle-class Jews supported the Bund. Some might have been the Vilna equivalents of what we in the YCL used to call the Park Avenue pinks, people like Stefania Szabad, who, in nostalgia for her youth, flirted with the left in the midst of her affluence. But middle-class Jews supported the Bund, not for its socialist principles, but because it concretely addressed the problems of the Jews in Poland, undistracted by the issue of Palestine. Besides, the middle class had been radicalized by the intensifying anti-Jewish policies of the government. They believed, then, that the only option still open to them was to take a belligerently adversarial posture.

The Poles in Vilna, as elsewhere in the country, associated the Jews with the left. Czeslaw Milosz remembers that in his circle May Day was called the "Jewish holiday." The Jewish association with the left had originated back in the times of the czars, when only, but not always, the radical movements opposed the anti-Semitic repressions of the czarist regime. Jews had no choice then but to oppose the *status quo*. In those days, it was an article of faith among Poland's anti-Semites that the Jews were subversives, Communists, intent on overthrowing the Polish government. Like most anti-Semitic charges, it contained a kernel of truth, yet it was grossly false. Though a high proportion of Communists were Jews, most Jews were not Communists or Communist fellow travelers. The Socialist Bund was fiercely anti-Communist. It had rejected Communist proposals made a few years earlier for "united-front" activities.

In the late 1930s the Polish Communist Party operated quasi-legally, camouflaging its true identity under a succession of front organizations and publishing papers with constantly changing mastheads. The party was under constant police surveillance. The government had enacted a number of statutes which, in vaguely defined terms, penalized anti-state conspiracy and subversion. Article 97 of the Criminal Code was the most commonly invoked of these statutes, under which persons suspected of Communist activity were arrested and tried. *Undzer Tog* reported on several such trials in Vilna during the year I was there. One case involved only White Russians, but the defendants in two others were Jews. One such case came to trial in November 1938. Six young Jews were charged with membership in a Communist youth organization. One had had four Communist leaflets on him when he was arrested. All six were found guilty; one received a two-year sentence, the others got three years. They were sent to the concentration camp at Bereza Kartuska to serve their prison terms.

In contrast to the Communists, the Bund, like the PPS, with which it was often politically allied, was a legal political party in Poland and a universally recognized part of the Polish political scene. Its candidates ran for public office and were often elected. Bundists sat on city councils and Kehillah boards in dozens of Polish cities. The party published a daily Yiddish newspaper in Warsaw and countless other periodicals. It headed a large and effective Jewish trade-union movement. Still, the Polish authorities, nationally and locally, hounded the Bund, its leaders, its activists, and its subsidiary institutions, more than they ever harassed the PPS. The Bund was doubly vulnerable—because it was left and because it was Jewish.

In April 1939 the Bund and the PPS in Vilna applied to the municipality for a permit to have a May Day parade. In response, the municipality issued a statement forbidding any parade or public demonstration. The two parties then applied for a permit for an indoor meeting. On April 28, the city authorities gave permission, but rescinded it a day later, without explanation. That arbitrary behavior was common. Late in May, after the City Council election, the Bund applied for permission to hold a dinner meeting to celebrate its electoral victory. At first the authorities refused; then, a week later, relented.

The cruelest instance of the government's harassment of the Bund was its never-explained and, to me, quite bizarre refusal to permit a CYSHO school exhibit in Warsaw. To be sure, I knew that the CYSHO schools and especially their teachers had long been persecuted by the government. I knew from the experiences of my friend Chantshe Piszczacer Mann and her husband, whose teaching licenses had been revoked only because they were Bundists. But the closing of the Warsaw CYSHO exhibit served no political purpose; it was nothing more than an irrational show of anti-Semitism.

Every other year, the CYSHO headquarters in Warsaw would organize an exhibition on a single theme in which the pupils of the schools all over Poland took part. Each school chose, or was assigned, an aspect of the exhibit's theme and each class, according to its abilities, would be involved—research, drawing, building, writing. In 1936, the subject of the exhibition was Sholem Aleichem, to mark the twentieth anniversary of his death. In 1938, the schools prepared for an exhibition that would depict the history and accomplishments of the Jews in Poland. It was scheduled to open on Sunday, April 2, 1939.

For months the children worked on their projects. In Vilna, they used to come in droves to the YIVO library after school to research their projects. That completed, they began to construct their models and displays, their maps and graphs. Everything was then shipped—from Vilna and elsewhere in Poland—to CYSHO headquarters in Warsaw, where the entire exhibition was designed and assembled. By early 1939, it had all gone according to schedule and, at last, on Friday, March 31, when the exhibition was in place, a government commission came to inspect it. They appeared to be quite amiable and, on leaving, said that several of the exhibited displays would have to be removed.

The verdict appeared satisfactory, for the CYSHO staff presumed that apart from those few offending items, the exhibit passed the political test. Everything was set for opening on Sunday, April 2. Everywhere in Poland, CYSHO schools began to organize outings to Warsaw. On Saturday, while the teachers were putting a few finishing touches on some of the exhibits, a new crew of inspectors arrived to announce that the government denied permission to show the exhibition. They padlocked the door, leaving a police guard behind to make sure that their ban would be obeyed. No explanation for the interdiction was ever given, despite countless interventions. For weeks, while the CYSHO and its lawyers tried to get the injunction rescinded, the exhibition stayed in place and nothing was dismantled. But the padlocks and the police guard remained.

In mid-June 1939, when I took a four-day holiday to Warsaw, Max Weinreich and David Kaplan-Kaplansky together managed to get me permission from the authorities to see the banned exhibition. At CYSHO headquarters in Warsaw, a young teacher was assigned to serve as my guide. She told me that no more than twenty people had been allowed to see the exhibition since its arbitrary cancellation. At the building where the exhibition was housed, a couple of Polish policemen were on duty; they checked our papers and let us in.

We came into a large room and faced an enormous map of Poland, which took up the entire wall. The map itself was black, but it was covered with hundreds of tiny colored electric bulbs. Places where Jews had settled in the thirteenth century were marked with red bulbs, the fourteenth century with green, the fifteenth with blue. Panels on both sides of the map listed the towns and cities and the dates of the first Jewish settlements.

In the center of the room was a huge sculpture of a pyramid, symbolizing four generations of Vilna's Jewish history. One side depicted education, and showed a *heder,* a rabbinical seminary, evening classes for working people, and a CYSHO school. We went from room to room—all in all, about seven or eight, each with a different theme, such as economic life, history, geography, social movements, culture, schools. One showed models of the development of weaving and textiles in Lodz and Bialystok, maps and figures showing the proportion of Jews in various industries, trade, and agriculture. In another we saw reproductions of the early statutes which gave Jews the right to settle and work in Poland. Elsewhere were models of small-town marketplaces, of the Vilna Kehillah. Finally, I saw a room devoted to Jewish participation in the struggle for Polish independence since the time of the partitions. On display was a model of Piłsudski's secret press, during his socialist period, on which a Yiddish socialist paper had been published.

You didn't need any legal or legalistic explanations to understand why the Polish authorities had closed the exhibit. At just that time, the government and the anti-Semitic parties at its helm were clamoring to drive the Jews out of Poland, charging that they were alien to the country. This CYSHO exhibition graphically documented just the opposite. It showed the deep roots that Jews had struck in Poland and how abundantly they had contributed to Poland's industrial development and cultural endeavors. It was a message that Poland did not wish to have delivered.

CHAPTER 8

━━━

Them and Us

When I was in New York, reading the *Times* and the Yiddish newspapers about anti-Semitism in Poland, I concluded that it wasn't so much an ideology or a racist philosophy as it was raw and ungovernable hatred, different from what was happening in Germany. There anti-Semitism, whether it took the form of law or mob violence, was noticeably orchestrated from above, unleashed by the authorities when it served their purpose. In Poland, anti-Semitism erupted spontaneously, volcanically, so it seemed to me. When its rage was spent, it subsided. I had read about pogroms in Poland in 1935 and 1936, and in 1937, as my friends and I prepared the issues of our Yiddish journal *Shrift,* we would track the incidents of anti-Jewish violence in Poland. Before I left for Vilna, I thought I understood the nature of Polish anti-Semitism, and I expected to see it in operation firsthand. What I had not foreseen was that Polish anti-Semitism was changing, that the Poles, taking a leaf from Hitler's Germany, would try to discipline their rage against the Jews and channel it into a more enduring form, into public policy.

Once I arrived in Vilna, it didn't take long before I came face to face with the overt and persistent anti-Semitism to which the Vilna Jews were exposed day in, day out, year in, year out. Each day *Undzer Tog* introduced me to another aspect of anti-Semitism. Each day my friends told me of new developments in politics or in the country's economic life, in which one could discern the unfriendly hand of the government.

The random violence of anti-Semitic hoodlumism was the most familiar and commonplace kind of anti-Semitism, something every Vilna Jew took for granted as a part of life. About a week after I had arrived, I read in *Undzer Tog* about attacks on Jews on the street that had taken place the previous Friday and Saturday nights. Small packs of Polish students had beaten up Jews as they were leaving movie theaters or walking home from an evening out. The Poles also smashed windows in some Jewish houses. In a few instances, the paper reported, the victims had to be taken to the hospital by ambulance.

The Jews had a word for this violence—hooliganism. The Polish word *chuligan* was obviously derived from English. It had entered Yiddish in the same guttural form. Hooliganism, as it was practiced in Vilna, had its own anatomy and in a month, I could dissect its components in a letter to my family. Hooligans, I explained, were always male, usually young, whose boisterousness was often fortified by vodka. Their attacks were unpremeditated and unorganized, more likely—though not necessarily—to occur after dark. A hooligan might go at a Jew he just happened to pass on the street. Perhaps he didn't like the Jew's appearance. Sometimes a small band of hooligans would set upon one or more Jews. The hooligan attacked with bare hands or a stick. He might slap the Jew's face, punch his back, pummel him, knock him down, kick him. If the Jewish victim wore glasses, the hooligan enjoyed knocking them off and grinding them into the ground with his heel. Hooligans had no intent to rob. Their purpose was purely expressive— to vent their rage. In one respect, hooliganism had a chivalric quality, as Max Weinreich put it: "Thank God, they never attack women or children."

As disturbing as the unprovoked assaults upon Jewish males was the reluctance of the police to arrest and prosecute the hooligans and the disinclination of the judges to try and punish them. The police might book a hooligan, if he was caught at the scene or subsequently identified by his victim, but then they'd let him off on one pretext or another. Or, when his case did come before a judge, he'd likely be released with a mild warning, especially if the physical injury to his victim had been slight. Sometimes, in cases of mass attacks or where the victims sustained serious injuries, hooligans were given prison sentences. At the end of September, the District Court of Vilna gave a leader of the Endecja youth organization three months in prison for leading a hooligan foray against a number of Jews. In instances when the Jewish victim of a hooligan attack fought back and injured his assailant, the Jew was likely to be arrested and charged with disturbing the peace, even if he himself had been badly wounded. That, Shmerke Kaczerginsky told me, had once been his own experience.

Having become knowledgeable about hooliganism, even if I myself or my immediate circle of friends and acquaintances had not been victims, I was able to enlighten my New York friends on how my Vilna friends coped with it. After an evening at Velfkeh's, for instance, young men, especially those escorting a girlfriend home, would take the safest route. That meant avoiding the main thoroughfares, using the quieter side streets instead, even if it was a longer way around. Once, when I was being taken home by way of a main street, we noticed a group of Poles coming toward us, talking and laughing loudly, probably somewhat tipsy. We crossed the street, walking slowly to avoid any sign of fear, trying to be quiet. I was afraid to breathe. On another occasion, going home at night, my companion spotted what we assumed to be a gang of rowdies at the far end of the street. He grabbed my arm, spun me around, and we dashed into a side street.

Anything could precipitate hooliganism. In the second half of November a Polish newspaper reported that several hundred Jewish refugees from Germany were due to arrive in Vilna on November 26. That was when Polish Jews, having been expelled from Germany and dumped over the border, were languishing in the makeshift shelters at Zbąszyn. An anti-Semitic youth organization had made plans to protest their arrival and perhaps let some blood flow. About 100 of them turned up at the railroad station to greet the train from Warsaw. While waiting, they distributed a leaflet demanding the expulsion of the refugees. Meantime, the police, having been advised of possible trouble, were at hand. But no refugees arrived that day. It must have been a false rumor and the crowd dispersed in disappointment.

Late in February 1939, an Endecja-affiliated student group held a meeting to protest anti-Polish demonstrations which the Germans had whipped up in Danzig. Afterward, the students marched down ulicas Wielka and Mickiewicz, to display their Polish patriotism. Since no Germans were at hand to beat up, the students broke a window in Katz's ice cream parlor on Mickiewicz, the only Jewish store that was open. The other Jewish shopkeepers, having heard that the students were marching their way, speedily pulled down their shutters and closed up.

One incident turned out, fortunately, to be only funny. It occurred on Saturday night, March 4, 1939, during a week of academic festivities, at the Palais de Danse, a restaurant and nightclub on ulica Mickiewicz, where I had once gone with a date to a *thé dansant*. After midnight, about sixty students, in varying states of inebriety, marched into the premises and stationed themselves on the dance floor. The musicians froze; the frightened patrons retreated to their tables. One student, quite far gone, started a harangue against "non-Aryans." By that time, the proprietor had gathered his wits and told the band leader to play several loud flourishes. That drowned out the orator. The patrons, taking courage, began to laugh, ridiculing the students, who then about-faced and marched out, somewhat unsteadily. It could have been a scene from a Rossini comic opera. A day later, the proprietor of Palais de Danse sent a letter to *Undzer Tog,* apologizing to his "respected patrons, whatever their nationality," for the untoward incident. He assured them of his desire for their continued patronage.

The most zealous practitioners of hooliganism and the most reliable source of supply for hooligans were the students at the University of Vilna. Universities in every country of Europe were reputed to be, besides centers of learning, arenas of anti-Semitic agitation and violence. Poland was no exception among countries, Vilna no exception among university cities. In Poland, where the universities were government run, a *numerus clausus* was everywhere in operation. In 1923, Jewish students had constituted about 24 percent of the university enrollment in Poland; in 1933, they were down to 17 percent and had fallen to 8 percent in 1938.

But a *numerus clausus* did not satisfy the Endecja and the Obóz Naradowo-Radykalny (National Radical Camp)—ONR, a breakaway from the Endecja, which outdid it in aggressive anti-Semitism. They clamored for a *numerus nullus,* a university altogether without Jews. Early in September, I was handed a leaflet which a couple of students were distributing on the street. One of my YIVO colleagues translated it for me. It summed up the Endecja program:

A Struggle for a Great Poland, a Poland of Social Justice
1. Numerus nullus
2. Only Polish Catholics in Polish schools
3. No Jews in Polish schools
4. Not a single Jew in Polish society

To hasten the removal of Jews from the universities, the Endecja and the ONR had been agitating for the segregation of the Jewish students.

They proposed to seat them on "ghetto benches" in the rear of the classrooms or lecture halls. The idea spread all over Poland. Jewish students, with the courage to attend classes, preferred to stand during the lectures. At first, some professors refused to enforce ghetto-bench seating, but the Polish students then retaliated—with violence. One professor's classroom, at the University of Lwów, was bombed in November 1938. It was a shocking incident, even at a time when I thought nothing could shock me anymore.

At the end of the previous semester, in May 1938, some thirty student organizations had presented a memorandum to the rector of the University of Vilna, urging him to halt the University's admission of "students of Jewish nationality, Jewish religion, or Jewish origin." I suppose the rector didn't comply with the students' request, but on October 14, so I read in *Undzer Tog,* he informed the Jewish students at the University that ghetto-bench seating would be enforced. During my year in Vilna, no one I knew was taking courses at the University and so I never knew what was happening inside. If I asked Daniel Lerner, who might have known something, he'd just express his devoutly felt hope that the rector and the anti-Semitic students would roast in hell.

Jewish students were not the only victims of the anti-Semitic university students. Every year, the whole Vilna Jewish community awaited violence from them, particularly on November 10. I first learned about this anticipated unpleasantness in an enigmatic reference in *Undzer Tog.* My friends at the YIVO explained that November 10 was the anniversary of the death of Stanisław Waclawski, a Polish student who had died in the aftermath of a university student rampage against the Jews in 1931. The riot had started when Polish medical students at the university began to beat up Jewish students, claiming they had not provided their fair share of cadavers for the laboratory.

With fervor reminiscent of the Jesuit students' *shiler-geloyf* in seventeenth-century Vilna, the students overran the city's business district and the Jewish quarter, beating up Jews, breaking shop windows. One contingent advanced in the opposite direction toward the Kehillah headquarters, where they hurled stones at the windows, while a meeting was in progress inside. On the way they encountered a group of Jewish journalists returning from a press conference with the provincial governor. Max Weinreich was among them. The students showered them with stones. One stone hit Weinreich in the eye and the injury rendered that eye nearly sightless for the rest of his life.

Minutes after the students had begun their rampage, the Jews responded in kind. Jewish university students and Jewish working people whose turf had been invaded fought back with fists, sticks, and stones. In the end, it turned out that sixteen Jewish and four Gentile students had been seriously injured. One of them, Stanisław Waclawski, died a few days later of his injuries. Three Jewish students were charged with responsibility for Waclawski's death. None of the Polish students was tried for disturbing the peace, inflicting bodily harm on innocent people, damaging Jewish property, or blinding Max Weinreich. The court found one of the Jewish students guilty and sentenced him to two years' imprisonment. The judge declared solemnly that the Jews had been the aggressors. It was to be expected, he said, that the Jews should harbor vindictive feelings toward non-Jews because "the Jews have been inspired with deep and strong hatred against Christians, particularly against the Christians of Poland, since the time of the Inquisition when Jews were burned."

Every year thereafter, Vilna University students commemorated Waclawski's death, usually with another anti-Semitic rampage. In one year an ONR leaflet exhorted its readers: "On the anniversary of Waclawski's death, Jewish blood must flow." But in 1938, the Vilna Jews breathed a sigh of relief when the day passed without incident.

Another form of anti-Semitism I encountered in Vilna was the anti-Jewish boycott, which combined raw hatred with ideology. On Friday, September 2, 1938, barely a week after my arrival, after I was settled in my room on ulica Makowa, I was going out to buy writing paper, envelopes, and some supplies for my desk at the YIVO. (I was to start my studies there on the following Sunday.) Rivele had told me that I'd find a nice stationery store on ulica Wielka.

As I came near the store, I saw two young men picketing, distributing leaflets, shouting. About a dozen or more people, children and adults, stood about, some watching, others having come to buy but hesitant now about going in. I took a couple of fliers. It was easy to figure out one of them: "Don't buy from Jews." Without a moment's hesitation, I went toward the store's entrance. One of the young men barred my way, shouting words I didn't comprehend, though I had no doubt about their meaning. I pushed him away and screamed in English: "Don't touch me. I'll go wherever I want."

I didn't know the rules of Polish picketing, that the pickets stopped only those who they thought were Gentiles. Jews were not prevented from buying in a Jewish store, though the pickets insulted and abused them as they went in and out. For good measure, the pickets would also abuse Jews who just happened to be walking by on the street. The picket must have taken me for a Gentile, perhaps because the cut of my clothes made me look different. In any case, taken aback by my speaking English, he let me pass. Perhaps, by then, he had figured out that I was, after all, a Jew.

Inside I found a few customers, all eager to answer my questions about what was going on. For years now, at the opening of each new school year, the Endecja, Poland's venerable anti-Semitic political party, had organized a nationwide boycott of Jewish-owned stores—stationery, books, school supplies. The proprietor told me that one of the leaflets I held listed the names and addresses of Gentile-owned stationery stores to be patronized instead of the Jewish stores, and that those Polish shopkeepers paid the organizers of the boycott to be listed.

That was my first direct encounter with real live anti-Semites. Though I was raised in a household that divided the world between Them and Us, I never knew any of Them at firsthand. No child in school or on the street had ever called me a Christ-killer or a dirty Jew. Nor do I remember ever seeing anti-Semitic pickets or marchers, though I had read about them. The only person I had ever seen who was an anti-Semite was Otto Koischwitz, the German professor at Hunter College, who supported Hitler.

Now, for the first time in my life, I was myself a target of the anti-Semites. It made the blood rise to my face and set my pulse beating faster. It enraged me to look at them. I don't know if I would have had the courage to do so, but I thought I would hit that picket or swing my handbag at him, if he would have laid a hand on me. When I left the store later with my purchases, I gave the picket the most withering look of contempt I could manage and swore loudly in English: "Lousy Polish scum." I must have been relying on my Americanness to protect me from the humiliation of being a Jew in Poland.

The next day, visiting the Reisens, I described my experience. Zalmen Reisen told me that while I was being harassed on ulica Wielka, leaders of the Kehillah had met with Vilna provincial authorities to express their anxiety about the safety of Jews during the back-to-school boycott of Jewish stores. They wanted the police to take necessary precautions against a repetition of last year's violence. The Jewish leaders were assured that the Public Safety Department would take strong measures to keep order on the streets.

For a couple of weeks thereafter, I saw pickets in front of many Jewish stores in various streets of the city. The boycott had spread to Jewish dry-goods, lingerie, fabrics, and clothing stores. Picketing, like hooliganism, had its specific procedures. The pickets were mostly young men and women, university or even *gymnasium* students, usually members of the Endecja's youth organization. They distributed leaflets as they marched up and down in front of the store; they interfered bodily with Poles who wanted to patronize the Jewish stores. From time to time, they would dash into the store they were picketing, disarrange merchandise on the shelves, sweep goods off the counter, flaunting their hoodlumism. Jewish shopkeepers used to appeal to the police for protection against that aggressive picketing and vandalism, but the customary answer was that as long as the pickets didn't disturb the public peace, they were within their rights.

The back-to-school boycott lasted a couple of weeks. A new boycott was launched the week before Christmas, at the height of the Christmas gift-shopping season. This time, at least in Vilna, the Endecja's "Buy Polish" campaign enjoyed the cooperation of the local OZON and ZMB, its youth organization. On the street I was handed an OZON leaflet. It proclaimed that Polish economic power could be strengthened by buying only from Polish shopkeepers. Another leaflet urged the Poles to support the boycott as their "most sacred national duty." That week before Christmas, bitter frost gripped Vilna, but it failed to daunt the pickets. Passing by in a droshky, I saw them in front of Jewish stores on ulicas Wielka, Wileńska, and Mickiewicz. Some wore student uniforms with ZMB armbands. Only fanatics, I thought, would be willing to endure that cutting wind and frost for their cause.

The idea of patronizing only Polish stores and boycotting Jewish ones had been introduced in Warsaw back in 1912 by Roman Dmowski, a founder of the Endecja in 1897, who remained its leader until his death on January 1, 1939. In 1912, after the Endecja candidate in Warsaw was defeated in the election to the Fourth Duma, Dmowski wanted to punish the Jews for their part in that defeat. The Endecja's paper then began to carry a slogan over its masthead: "Everyone to His Own and for His Own." In practice it meant: "Buy Polish—Don't Buy from Jews." Thenceforth the anti-Jewish economic boycott became a staple of Endecja policy.

In independent Poland Endecja's influence grew. By the late 1930s, the "don't-buy-Jewish" boycott had developed into a nationwide movement, even winning the support of many municipal officials. In February 1938, the Warsaw City Council enacted a decree which required all merchants to display signs carrying their full names at the entrances of their businesses, a measure long advocated by the Endecja. That made it easier to identify Jewish businesses in order to boycott them.

But picketing Jewish retail stores was just the opening gambit in the Endecja's grand strategy to drive Jews altogether out of Poland's economic life. Dmowski's party called for "the de-Judaizing of Poland" and for "propaganda on behalf of Polish commerce and handicraft." Gentile merchants' and artisans' associations pressured city governments to keep Jews from participating in trade fairs, to deny them licenses to practice certain trades, to limit their number in various occupations. Many trade and professional associations, having learned from the Germans, began to introduce an "Aryan" paragraph into their bylaws to exclude Jews from membership and from practicing their trade or profession. The most prestigious body to do so was the Association of Physicians of the Polish Republic, which adopted the "Aryan" paragraph in 1937 and subsequently disbanded several chapters which had refused to go along with that policy.

A few public groups and municipalities resisted the pressure by the Endecja and other extremist anti-Semitic organizations. But in the year I was in Vilna one could see, simply by reading the newspapers, that popular prejudice was little by little becoming incorporated into government policy. On September 8, I read in *Undzer Tog* that the government-run Vilna Radio was being "Aryanized." Jewish actors, singers, and musicians who used to perform on radio had been told that their services would no longer be needed. Some six weeks later, the Polish Broadcasting Company, the government's national network, dismissed nearly all the Jewish musicians it employed. In January 1939, one of the Sejm deputies demanded that Jews be removed altogether from the film industry. Shortly thereafter, the papers reported that Jewish owners of movie houses in Warsaw were informed that their licenses would not be renewed.

For centuries Jews in Poland had played a major role in the production, distribution, and sale of liquor and tobacco. Jewish entrepreneurs used to lease the rights to do business from the owners of the estates that raised the crops and Jews developed the industries which manufactured the products. Early in the 1920s, after the Polish government nationalized the tobacco and liquor industries, entrepreneurs and retailers had to apply to the government for licenses to do business. Because Jews had had long years of experience in those industries, they naturally obtained a large proportion of licenses. Consequently, the Endecja directed much of its anti-Jewish agitation against the Jewish presence in those industries and organized the competing Gentile merchants to pressure the authorities to issue licenses exclusively to Gentiles.

Early in February 1939, the Budget Committee of the Sejm adopted a resolution along the lines advocated by the Endecja. It called upon the government to revise its methods of licensing the monopoly concessions and to issue such licenses only to Gentiles. (One of the Sejm's Jewish deputies protested that such a procedure would violate the constitutional rights of Poland's Jewish citizens.) Soon thereafter, the papers reported that the authorities were informing Jewish businessmen in the tobacco and liquor trades in a number of cities that their licenses were to be withdrawn. They were given several months in which to liquidate their businesses. In mid-August, when gas masks had gone on sale in Vilna and the fear of war was everywhere, the Vilna Bureau of Customs and Excise conducted its anti-Jewish business as usual, announcing that it would withdraw from Jews all licenses to sell liquor in restaurants and liquor stores. The Jewish proprietors were given one year's time to liquidate their businesses.

The increasing penetration of anti-Semitism into the policies and operations of the government reflected a struggle behind the scenes among Piłsudski's heirs, between those who had remained true to his political views—including his opposition to anti-Semitism—and those who were prepared to accommodate to the Endecja and the pressures of popular anti-Semitism. That power struggle and its public developments initiated me into the mysteries of Polish politics.

On September 13, 1938, the president of the Polish Republic, Ignacy Mościcki, with the approval of Marshal Rydz-Śmigly, who held the post of minister of defense but was in fact the head of state, dissolved the Sejm and the Senate and called for new elections to be held—November 6 for the Sejm and November 13 for the Senate. This maneuver surprised and mystified everyone. Nobody I knew could explain with any assurance what was behind this drastic and sensational move.

Under the Polish Constitution of 1935, the president appointed the prime minister and all the members of his cabinet, the people who constituted the government. They could be removed from office only by the president or by a joint legislative decision of the Sejm and Senate.

The Constitution of 1935, which had been drafted to ensure Piłsudski's control of the government, inordinately strengthened the position of the president for it also gave the president the authority to forestall any parliamentary effort to remove a cabinet officer. All he had to do was to suspend or dissolve both houses.

Mościcki's invocation of this powerful constitutional weapon suggested a number of possible political scenarios. People began to weave their wishful fantasies or dark terrors into theories about what it all might mean. Many believed that the president's action had averted a coup and that he must have wanted to install a new and democratically elected Parliament. But no one was clear as to who had been behind the attempted seizure of the government, from which the country had been so providentially rescued. Writing home, I reported some of the rumors I had heard. The one my friends hoped was true, which had been published in *Undzer Tog* and no doubt taken from the Polish press, was that Mościcki had stopped Dmowski's Endecja from taking over the government. The government censors had not suppressed the story, and so we assumed it had some truth. That explanation put a liberal face on the president's action. It made sense then, in mid-September, to think that the government would want to strengthen national solidarity in the midst of the Czech crisis, at a time of growing tension and fear of war. It made sense then to believe that the government was prepared to appease the liberal opposition parties and the dissidents within its own party.

But that hypothesis collapsed after the Munich conference. It didn't fit at all into the turn of events, after Poland's seizure of Teschen during the dismemberment of Czechoslovakia, which I described earlier. In October my friends realized that the election would not democratize the Polish government. As we later understood the behind-the-scenes intrigues and maneuverings that had preceded the Sejm's dissolution, we realized that Mościcki's intent had not been to liberalize the government, but the opposite—to entrench its right-wing elements.

Poland's governance was an arcane subject, but I found lots of people ready to instruct me. Every morning, on arriving at the YIVO, I'd discuss the latest political developments with Ber Schlossberg, with whom I shared an office. All my friends, rich or poor, right or left, passionately cared about what was happening on the Polish political scene. It was, after all, a matter of their life or death.

The first political lesson I learned was about the existence of a party, amidst the profusion of Poland's ideological parties, that represented the people running the government, a party of chiefs without Indians, as it were. The most recent party on the Polish political scene, it had been founded in February 1937 with the name Obóz Zjedniczenia Narodowego, "Camp of National Unity," known by its acronym OZON. It had been formed at the initiative of General Rydz-Śmigly, who was trying to fill Piłsudski's shoes as dictator of Poland. He wanted a government-front party to consolidate his position and he had entrusted this task to a right-wing associate, who enlisted other right-wingers in shaping the new party's ideology and goals. The OZON platform turned out to be a call for the Polonization of every aspect of the country's life, a thinly disguised attack on the presence of Jews in Poland. This party, which had been intended to rally the whole country to the "Camp of National Unity," had signaled that it would exclude the Jews from the national consensus.

The enunciated OZON policies sharpened the divisions among Piłsudski's successors. In October 1937 some of them seceded from the OZON to form the Democratic Club and they condemned the OZON for its chauvinism and nationalism, for abandoning Piłsudski's heritage, and for moving closer to his lifelong opponents, the Endecja. (Stanisław Mackiewicz, Vilna's conservative maverick editor and OZON opponent, used to say that it must have heartened Dmowski to see his opponents implementing his program.)

Before then, I hadn't realized how vigorously Piłsudski in his lifetime had opposed the Endecja. I had thought of him only as a militarist and an authoritarian, but my Bundist friends informed me there had been another side to him. In his youth, when Poland was under czarist rule, Piłsudski had been a member of the PPS, then illegal and operating underground. Later in his political career, after Poland's independence, though Piłsudski was no longer associated with the PPS, the left continued to regard him as a friend and even supported him in his coup to return to power in 1926. The Jews, too, regarded Piłsudski as a friend, because all his life he had resisted the intrusion of anti-Semitic policies in the government.

The struggle between the liberals and the reactionaries continued to plague the OZON and manifested itself in the Sejm. Matters came to a head in the summer of 1938, when the Sejm voted to appoint as its marshal Walery Sławek, Piłsudski's faithful friend from their earliest days in the PPS and one of Mościcki's opponents. At that point Mościcki, fearful that the government could no longer count on the support of a parliamentary majority, decided to dissolve the Sejm and obtained Rydz-Śmigly's support to do so.

The opposition parties—including the Peasant Party, PPS, and the

Bund—boycotted the November elections, refusing to nominate candidates on the ground that the electoral procedures were stacked against them. Nevertheless, two-thirds of the electorate turned out to vote. That good showing was explained, in part, by the popular support the government enjoyed because it had seized Teschen during the Czech crisis. The OZON won 161 of the 208 seats in the Sejm. The government had triumphed.

In a letter home, I tried to explain this baffling situation. How come people voted, even though their parties didn't run any candidates? "The pressure on the voters has been terrific, particularly on the Jews," I wrote. That pressure operated in various ways. To begin with, public prosecutors announced that propaganda to boycott the election would be treated as a criminal act, liable to a prison term. The parties were then hard pressed to explain to their constituencies why they should boycott the election. Though the left was skilled in the use of Aesopian language, in this matter they needed to use greater clarity than they were permitted. Given the heavy censorship of the press, it would be hard for the average reader to figure out why the opposition parties refused to run candidates.

Meantime, the government exerted pressure at every level to bring people to the polls. They enlisted Cardinal Hlond to declare that it was a patriotic obligation to vote. People were afraid that they might be penalized in some way if they did not vote. As for the Jews, they had been warned of unpleasant consequences if they'd claim later on that the government was not of their choice or to their liking. Consequently, leading Jewish businessmen publicly supported one or another candidate. The Agudah and the centrist Zionists ran their lists of candidates and won five seats in the Sejm and one in the Senate. On the day of the election, I wrote home, transmitting my friends' premonitions: "Everyone feels that things will go from bad to worse."

On Friday, November 11, just five days after the Sejm election and two days after the fires of *Kristallnacht* in Germany, I happened to be on ulica Wileńska, where a couple of young men were distributing a leaflet. Issued by OZON, it had a long text which I couldn't fathom at all. In the afternoon, I brought it back to the YIVO and showed it to Zalmen Reisen. It was an ugly anti-Semitic tract. The OZON had surpassed the Endecja in its anti-Semitic fulminations. I asked Reisen if it foreshadowed things to come in Poland. He shrugged his shoulders in an uncharacteristically weary gesture. The following Sunday he published a Yiddish translation of the text in *Undzer Tog:*

. . . there is still much to be done. Till now, Jews continue to feed parasitically on our national organism. Till now, 90 per cent of fluid capital and 58 per cent of immovable property are still in Jewish hands. Till now, the process of demoralizing Polish souls with the doctrine of Marxism continues. Till now, we are still in the toils of Freemasonry.

The struggle against the deluge of Żydo-komuna [Jew-communism] and Masonry must go on ceaselessly until victory. The first stage of this struggle is to lock the Jews in a ghetto, isolate them from their destructive work. First of all, we must remove Jews from the neighborhoods adjoining churches and army barracks. Wherever Christian institutions or military forces are located, Jews must not be present. We therefore call on all Poles to strengthen the boycott activities in those neighborhoods.

Not a single grosz in Jewish hands! Poles, awake to action!

It didn't take long before the newly elected Sejm showed its anti-Jewish colors. On December 3, an independent deputy, known as an ultra-anti-Semite, introduced a measure to abolish the practice of *shehitah,* the Jewish ritual method of slaughtering animals and poultry for food. Since 1935, *shehitah* had been severely curtailed in Poland and the quantity of kosher meat available for consumption had been limited by a government quota.

A staple of anti-Semitic propaganda in Europe since the mid-nineteenth century, anti-*shehitah* agitation was usually camouflaged as concern for a humane method of animal slaughter. In Poland anti-*shehitah* agitation had first surfaced in 1928, but only after Piłsudski's death did it make headway. In July 1935, the Endecja launched a new campaign to abolish *shehitah.* Six months later, in February 1936, a bill was introduced in the Sejm requiring animals to be stunned before slaughter, in effect prohibiting Jewish ritual slaughter. At that point, it had become evident that the anti-*shehitah* move was promoted not only by ideological anti-Semites, but also by Gentile butchers and meat slaughterers intent on driving the Jews out of the meat trade.

Despite the energetic opposition of the entire Jewish community, the Sejm favored that bill. In March 1936, the minister of agriculture, who was responsible for Poland's meat production, advised the Sejm that passage of the anti-*shehitah* bill, as drafted, would expose Poland to serious charges of failing to provide for the religious needs of its national minorities. He proposed to get around that by including a clause which would permit a specified quota of meat to be ritually slaughtered for consumption, whose sale would be licensed by the government. That version of the bill passed the Sejm and the Senate in March 1936 and went into effect on January 1, 1937.

Two months later, the minister of agriculture reported that 50 percent of the meat trade had already been taken out of Jewish hands and he anticipated that, before long, most of Poland's meat trade would be in Gentile hands. Thereafter, the government set monthly quotas for the amount of meat permitted to be ritually slaughtered and, as the months passed, frequently reduced the quota. Every time the Jews protested, the Sejm deputies responded with a threat to abolish *shehitah* altogether.

That threat was finally realized with the introduction of the anti-*shehitah* bill on December 3, 1938. Within the week, the bill passed its first reading in the Sejm. It provided for a three-year period, to begin January 1, 1940, during which the amount of ritually slaughtered meat would be progressively reduced until December 31, 1942, when *shehitah* would be altogether abolished. After its first reading, the bill went to the Sejm's Administrative Committee for further consideration. It was reported out favorably on February 28, 1939.

Every day *Undzer Tog* featured the news about the Sejm proceedings and about the efforts of the Jewish community to resist the passage of the bill. But the Jewish deputies in the Sejm, even with the support of the Ukrainian deputies, were too negligible a number to exercise any political or moral influence over the Polish deputies. Nevertheless, they formed a united committee to try to oppose passage of the bill.

Meanwhile, on March 7, a conference of 300 rabbis from all Poland met in Warsaw to consider means of preventing the prohibition of *shehitah*. They proposed gathering two million signatures on a petition which they would present to the government. Two days later, the rabbis adopted a resolution which affirmed *shehitah* as a fundamental principle of Judaism and declared that its prohibition would violate the Polish Constitution and its guarantees to protect religious and national minorities. The rabbis appealed to the government to continue Poland's tradition of religious tolerance. In an attempt to exercise whatever clout they could muster, the rabbis proclaimed a sixteen-day meatless period, to begin on March 14.

On Monday, March 13, 1939, the lead front-page story in *Undzer Tog* reported on the decision taken at the rabbinical conference in Warsaw, which the Vilna Kehillah and the Vilna Rabbinical Council had ratified—that is, that the Jewish community was to abstain from all meat from March 14 to March 30. The prohibition affected beef, lamb, veal, poultry, and all kinds of delicatessen. Jewish butcher shops and delicatessens were ordered to be closed; Jewish-owned restaurants were forbidden to serve meat. The Kehillah also issued a warning to fish dealers not to raise their prices. If they did so, the Kehillah and the Rabbinical Council would prohibit the consumption of fish as well. To make sure of adequate supplies, the Kehillah advised fish dealers to bring in a substantially larger stock of fish than they usually bought.

The same day, the radio carried statements by government spokesmen who tried to minimize the possible effects of the Jewish meat boycott on Polish agriculture and the meat industry. They warned the peasants not to lower their prices and, above all, not to deal with Jewish cattle merchants.

On March 15, after the first meatless day in Vilna, I wrote a long letter home about the strike and about the other overwhelming events of those two days. For besides the meat strike, we were going through our first air-raid drills and that very day we learned that Germany had gobbled up Czechoslovakia. Still, the meat strike was our most immediate crisis, directly affecting every Jew in Vilna. In the long run, if there was to be a long run, it was a deadly serious matter for the Jews in Poland.

Though the ritual aspects of *shehitah* concerned me little, even if my mother ate only kosher meat, I understood the economic and political implications of its ban. In my letter, I tried earnestly to explain to my anti-religious father that "even though the rabbis called the strike, even though the issue at hand is a matter of ritual observance, religious freedom is at stake, and even more, the very right of the Jews to live in Poland. I hope the strike works, but . . . ," and I trailed off into inexpressible hopelessness.

All the Jewish butcher shops in Vilna were closed, except for a few selling nonkosher meat to non-Jews. The restaurants agreed not to serve meat. Jews who patronized non–Jewish-owned restaurants were offered meatless menus. Already on the first day of the strike, the price of cheese, eggs, and fish had risen. A few days later, the price of fish had soared: Carp, which used to sell below two zlotys a kilo, was now selling for over three zlotys.

The Yiddish newspapers began to publish recipes for dairy meals, sometimes giving the caloric equivalents of meat. They included cucumber soup, pea soup with croutons, vegetarian borscht, fried herring, rice patties, cheese blintzes, applesauce. For the Sabbath, the paper printed a recipe for a dairy cholent. (Cholent was the traditional Sabbath dish, which consisted of pieces of meat with potatoes, barley, beans, and onions, slow-baked in an oven from Friday afternoon to the Sabbath midday meal.) My landlady, our neighbors, and all the housewives in Vilna talked incessantly about what to prepare for dinner. It was hard for them because Vilna didn't offer much of a variety of vegetables, and canned fish, which was imported, was even more expensive than fresh fish.

After a week of meatless days, I wrote home that the Vilna Jews were abiding by the rabbis' injunction and refraining from all meat. People said that even Jews who ate nonkosher meat were observing the meatless days. At lavish wedding parties, the guests had to make do with a meatless feast. The only hopeful sign, I wrote, was that the government was losing considerable income as a consequence of the strike. Perhaps, I concluded, that would make them reconsider the question.

I was too naive. On March 22, just eight days after the Jews of Poland had stopped eating meat, the Sejm adopted the anti-*shehitah* bill and sent it on to the Senate. They did so against the advice of the ministers of agriculture, religion, and public education, who had warned them that the bill contravened the constitutional guarantee of freedom of religion and that its passage could embarrass the government and even create a government crisis. On that day I happened to be wearing a gray suit and a black blouse. At the YIVO, Jacob Rivkind, always depressed about Polish anti-Semitism, commented: "You're dressed in the colors of our Jewish destiny: gray today and black tomorrow."

In accordance with an earlier rabbinic decision, March 22 was decreed a fast day for the Jews of Poland. In Vilna and elsewhere, Jewish stores closed and Jews halted their work.

The Senate never voted on the anti-*shehitah* bill. Not long afterward, Poland had to face other problems.

Meanwhile, during this very period when the Vilna Jews had to cope with the anti-*shehitah* bill and the meatless days, they were confronted with a new affliction, this one local. Early in January, the Magistrat, the city government's municipal board, in an effort to cut its costs for the coming fiscal year, decided to eliminate the subsidies which the city provided to the Jewish schools. At that time, about 3,500 children attended eleven Yiddish, Hebrew, and religious schools in Vilna. (Probably four or five times as many attended the public schools.) The most recent subsidy, for 1938–1939, had been about 60,000 zlotys, half the amount which the schools had received in 1933. Since then, the city had steadily been cutting its support. Now the Magistrat proposed to eliminate it entirely, except for a sum of 9,000 zlotys to tide the schools over for the rest of the school year.

The motion to eliminate the subsidy had been put forward by board members who represented the Endecja and the OZON and was approved unanimously, except for the one Jewish board member. The Magistrat justified its decision by declaring that the Jewish children were entitled to attend the public schools. On January 20, in my letter home about what had happened, I betrayed my sense of the futility of Jewish political resistance to the government's anti-Semitism. I couldn't imagine how the schools could henceforth operate. I couldn't foresee any decent life for the Jews in Vilna, or any place in Poland, for that matter.

The mean-spiritedness of the Magistrat became even more evident at the end of January, when the Budget Committee, considering the proposed budgets of the city's Social Welfare, Cultural Affairs, and Education departments, eliminated the allocation for lunches for children in the Jewish schools.

On January 31, the city budget, as adopted by the Magistrat, came before the City Council. The Jewish members tried to restore the subsidy for the Jewish schools, but, except for them and for two OZON councilmen who abstained, the majority of the council upheld the cut. The twelve Jewish councilmen then walked out in protest. Every day *Undzer Tog* ran long articles on how the municipal budget was becoming de-Judaized.

On February 20, the Kehillah board addressed itself to its new budgetary responsibilities to maintain fully the Jewish schools. At the conclusion of the board's session on February 23, the Kehillah adopted a series of resolutions, expressing the community's protest against the anti-Jewish policies of the government in Warsaw and against the withdrawal of the municipal subsidy to the Jewish schools.

In the next few days, the municipal authorities demonstrated the depths to which their mean-spiritedness could descend. Without serving any notice, they sent bailiffs into the Jewish schools, equipped with itemized lists of the furniture which the city had lent the schools years ago. The bailiffs had instructions to remove the furniture from the premises. On March 23, the city's bailiffs barged into the Town Talmud Torah to recover its old furniture. The school principal pleaded with them to wait until the end of the school year, but they refused. The bailiffs removed the following items: twelve desks, fourteen chairs, eight dining tables, seven bookcases, one clock, three benches, three map stands, two blackboards, and other items. Soon thereafter, the city also cut off the Town Talmud Torah's free supply of water, heat, and lighting.

The Jews of Vilna rallied, as they did after each misfortune that befell them. Vilna's Jewish business community took the lead in replacing the furniture or donating money to buy replacements. For several weeks, *Undzer Tog* published lists of the donors and contributors and the Jewish schools managed somehow to complete the school year.

Over the rumble of anti-Semitism to which even I was becoming accustomed—the hooliganism, the boycotts, the ghetto benches, the violence, even the anti-*shehitah* bill—we began to hear a steady howling from the Sejm in December, which had convened after the election. They were shrieking: "Expel the Jews from Poland!" Every day that slogan was seconded in the right-wing press and even by high government spokesmen. Sometimes they called for "evacuation" rather than "expulsion." More circumspect government officials spoke of "organizing the emigration of the Jews from Poland by legal means."

Back in 1936, the Polish government tried to place on the international agenda their alleged problem of overpopulation and their wish to be rid of the Jews. They argued that they needed colonies as a means of resettling their "excess" population. Poland even initiated talks with France to explore the suitability of Madagascar as a place of settlement for Jewish emigrants from Poland. The French supplied information about Madagascar's climate and resources, but quickly distanced themselves from the idea which had prompted Poland's inquiry.

In January 1937, Poland's minister of foreign affairs, Józef Beck, speaking in the Sejm on behalf of the government, said that since Poland had room for no more than half a million Jews, the other three million would have to leave the country. A year later, on February 21, 1938, General Stanisław Skwarczyński, head of the OZON, in a nationwide radio address, said: "We see the solution of the Jewish problem by means of a radical reduction of the number of Jews in Poland. This can be achieved by carrying out their planned emigration."

Just about the time of *Kristallnacht,* in November 1938, Foreign Minister Beck put pressure upon several leading Jews known for their accommodationist posture to launch a "constructive program of Jewish emigration." Under duress, they formed a "Committee for Jewish Colonization" and went abroad, hat in hand, first to the Intergovernmental Refugee Committee in January 1939 and later to the British government, begging for help in dealing with the "natural emigration needs" of the Polish Jews. My friends disparaged these "court Jews," saying they should have refused to accept such a task.

In December 1938, Skwarczyński returned to the subject of Jewish emigration, during the first session of the OZON-controlled Sejm. He warned the Jews that Poland was serious about demanding their emigration. To drive his point home, he called for restrictions upon the number of Jews in trade and in the professions, for so long as they would remain in Poland. The next day, during the continuing Sejm discussion, Vice-Premier Eugeniusz Kwiatkowski called on the government to expedite Jewish mass emigration from Poland and to get rid of the "surplus" Jews in Poland's economic and cultural life.

That December I wrote home that "the jackals are barking in the Sejm, including those who were elected with Jewish votes. They are demanding emigration. Not over a period of years, not even in two or three years, but right now. The debate in the Sejm has encouraged the hooligans. These days the streets are especially unsafe and young men try to avoid going home late from the movies or visiting."

Every day *Undzer Tog* featured on its first page reports of the continuing debate in the Sejm on the "Jewish Question." The Sejm debate had brought to the surface the smoldering mass of anti-Jewish hatred which had been kept in check for years by Piłsudski's attempts at responsible government. Now the Sejm spoke openly of how to get rid of the Jews—to exclude them from Poland's economic life, to exclude them from Poland's cultural and educational life, to drive them out of the country altogether. On December 21, Skwarczyński and 116 of his party colleagues in the Sejm submitted an interpellation to the government, asking it "to take immediate, energetic, and multilateral actions to achieve the broadest possible reduction of the number of Jews in Poland by the use of all available means."

The Sejm's obsession with the Jews set off persistent rumors of worse to come. It was widely rumored that the OZON deputies were planning to submit a bill which would strip the Jews of all civil rights. Some people said that it would apply to the whole Jewish population; others held that it would affect "only" those hundreds of thousands of Jews who had come to Poland from Russia and had been naturalized after 1926. And indeed, in January 1939, two OZON deputies submitted proposals, independent of their party's legislative efforts, to that effect. Those bills would have stripped the Jews of their Polish citizenship and declared them to be only temporary residents. The bills further provided that the costs involved in the compulsory emigration of the Polish Jews were to be paid entirely by the Jews themselves and that Jewish property confiscated by the state could be used as an "emigration fund." But the two deputies could not get sufficient support among their party to get discussion on their proposals.

On January 23, in reply to the interpellation from the 117 OZON deputies, Premier Felicjan Sławoj-Składkowski explained that the government was working tirelessly to develop a viable and comprehensive plan for Jewish emigration, that it would use its influence to obtain outlets for emigration by international action, and that it would appeal to Jews abroad for financial assistance in organizing that emigration. In the meantime, he urged the deputies to strive to achieve the complete Polonization of the country's economic, social, and cultural life by peaceful means.

The premier's reply did not satisfy the more aggressive anti-Semites, who argued that the government was engaging in talk instead of action. In this vein, the debate on the fate of the Polish Jews continued in the Sejm through the month of February. In the middle of the month, Colonel Zygmunt Wenda, vice-speaker of the Sejm and OZON chief of staff, declared Jews must emigrate from Poland and, so long as they remain in the country, must accept restrictions as to their place in the country's economic and cultural life. I wrote home on February 22, reporting on what I read in the papers and about what my friends had told me: "Every day in the Sejm they scream about driving out the Jews, first from trade and industry, then from the universities, and finally from the country. But without Jewish initiative and enterprise, they'll never be able to modernize Poland. Polish industry is still in the stage of feudal production."

During the months of this debate, I realized how much my being an American separated me from my friends, from people I had come to love. With them I had experienced the anxieties and exposure to hooliganism, the violence of the boycotts, the meatless days. But whenever I chose to do so, I could pack my things and go home to the safety of the United States. But what would become of them? My being an American became an unspoken barrier between us. My fate would not be their fate. I often felt a sense of guilt about the security of my passport.

In the spring—perhaps as early as March, after the demise of Czechoslovakia, or perhaps in April, when Foreign Minister Beck was negotiating with the French and English to win their support for Poland against

Germany's threats about the Polish Corridor—it was rumored, so Zalmen Reisen told me, that Beck had advised the government to call a halt to its anti-Jewish policies. The Sejm's anti-Semitic course would prejudice the conduct of his foreign policy. According to a story that appeared in *Undzer Tog* in May, Premier Składkowski had advised the deputies not to embarrass the government by pushing anti-Semitic measures. Since the Senate, then in session, never took up for its consideration the anti-*shehitah* bill, we speculated that their failure to do so was not to be attributed either to philo-Semitism or to sloth, but rather to caution and calculation. Perhaps they were afraid that the adoption of the anti-*shehitah* bill would embroil the country in a constitutional crisis or, even worse, alienate Poland's Western allies.

On June 11, 1939, *Undzer Tog* cited an article in the Polish press which argued that now was the time to call a halt to anti-Semitic and racist propaganda in the interests of national unity and national morale. But even that modest wish for a moderation of anti-Semitism was not popular. On July 23, *Gazeta Polska,* the semi-official government paper, rejected the idea that Poland's difficult position vis-à-vis Germany should lead it to adopt a reconciliatory attitude toward the Jews. Poland's "internal Jewish problem," the paper declared, had nothing to do with Poland's external relations with Hitler's Germany.

By that time I was weary of Poland. I wanted to go home, even though my heart ached for all the people I knew.

CHAPTER 9

—————

Flight

On June 20, 1939, the YIVO marked the end of the Aspirantur's fourth year with a convocation. At other times, it would have been a festive occasion, but at that time our private joys and personal accomplishments mattered little. The threat of war darkened our days. We lived in the shadow of the storm that had been gathering all year. Every day we awoke to premonitions of disaster. Every night we lay down to sleep and to dream the dark dreams of our fears. A year ago, when I had first come to Vilna, Hitler stood ready to explode the tinderbox over Sudentenland. Now the tinderbox was closer, as Germany's shrill and unceasing clamor over Danzig and the Polish Corridor deafened our ears. Just the day before the YIVO's convocation, Josef Goebbels, Germany's minister of propaganda, declared that no power could bar Danzig's return to the Third Reich, that Danzig was German territory.

The Polish Parliament had adjourned three days earlier. We were consoled that it had failed to act upon the anti-*shehitah* bill, but when the Parliament voted to give President Mościcki emergency powers and the right to issue special decrees, we realized that Poland was readying itself for the catastrophe to come.

Nevertheless, though we faced each new day with anxiety, we all went about our business as usual, as we had done all through the year.

We assembled to mark the end of our academic year in the YIVO's auditorium. Max Weinreich reported on the past year's accomplishments, citing each of us and our research projects. Jacob Rivkind delivered an address on the methodological aspects of his study of Vilna Jewish family budgets. The reception that followed was an occasion for leave-taking. Several of my colleagues were going home and it was unlikely we'd ever meet again. Others would be returning to continue their studies for yet another year.

For months I had vacillated about my plans for the coming year. Should I stay one more year, as Max Weinreich insistently had urged me to do, or should I go home to confront my uncertain future in New York? I thought that one year's experience in the Aspirantur might help me get a job in a Yiddish-speaking institution in New York and might even stand me in good stead for a scholarly career, but two years wouldn't give me any extra advantage. Besides, by now, I had grown weary of the hopelessness that enveloped the Jews in Vilna like a shroud. Even though I was an outsider, I had felt constricted by the tightening vise of poverty and anti-Semitism in which the Jews of Vilna were held. I wanted to escape from it. New York drew me like a magnet back to my English-speaking American world, where I felt I really belonged, no matter how well I had fitted into Vilna's Jewish society.

Rivele had been baffled by my indecisiveness all through the spring. She and Kalmanovich, thinking about my future and even more about my safety, were determined that I should leave Vilna that summer and return to America. By early June I realized that I did indeed want to go home, though I was ashamed to admit it, ashamed that I longed for the comforts of New York. Even harder to deal with was the guilt I felt about leaving behind the people I loved to face the danger of war, while I would be safe on the far side of the Atlantic. Most of all, I was afraid to tell Max Weinreich of my decision. He would think me faint of heart, an irresolute partisan of Yiddish and the YIVO.

As I expected, Weinreich was disappointed in me when I told him of my decision to go home, but the Kalmanoviches and the Reisens were relieved. Rivele said that at last I had returned to my senses. I arranged to work with Weinreich through July and early August and then take some time off before I would sail home from Gdynia on September 14 on the return ticket supplied by the YIVO in New York. In preparation for my departure, Rivele began working on a beautiful tablecloth for her sister in New York. Stefania Szabad took time off from picking cucumbers on her farm to knit several sweaters for her grandson Theodore, Jascha's only child, then in the United States with his divorced mother.

At the start of the summer, when my landlady and her baby left for the country, I moved back to the Kalmanoviches. Rivele was glad to have me then, for Kalman had left on a trip to Paris, to see his Territorialist friends and deliver some lectures and then to visit their son in Palestine. Though she, too, longed to see her son, they couldn't afford two fares.

Besides the routine of the YIVO's English-language correspondence, Weinreich and I worked to prepare for an upcoming lecture series by John Dollard, a psychoanalytic sociologist, then a research associate at Yale's Institute of Human Relations. Dollard was a friend of Weinreich's. They had first met at Yale University in 1932, as Rockefeller Foundation Fellows in a two-year International Seminar on the Impact of Culture on Personality. In 1937, Dollard published his seminal work *Caste and Class in a Southern Town*. Weinreich thought the *aspirantn* would benefit by hearing about his research on the sociopsychological problems of minority groups.

Weinreich also asked me to help him with a scholarly paper he was preparing in English for the Fifth International Linguistic Congress that would meet in Brussels at the end of August. In it he proposed a schematization of the history of Yiddish, its periodization and geographical course from Western Europe eastward. I translated the first draft into English and then we worked together, as he enlarged and embellished the paper, while I struggled to find the appropriate vocabulary for a field about which I knew nothing.

Meanwhile, after Kalmanovich returned from Palestine and Zalmen Reisen from his vacation, they approached me officially—Weinreich was afraid that, if he asked, I'd turn him down—to stay on until the end of September, when Dollard would have concluded his lectures. Because Dollard didn't know Yiddish or Polish, and the students' English was inadequate, I was needed to back up Weinreich as a translator. Reluctantly I agreed and rescheduled my departure to September 29, on a later Polish liner sailing from Gdynia.

On August 17, Max and Regina Weinreich, together with their older son, Uriel, left Vilna for Copenhagen. Their younger son, Gabriel, stayed behind in the care of his grandmother, Stefania Szabad. In Copenhagen Weinreich planned to visit Dr. Joseph Davidsohn, a sociologist, whom he had first met at the Rockefeller Foundation seminar at Yale in 1932, and with whom he had become good friends. From Copenhagen, Max and Uriel were to go to Brussels.

Most of my Vilna friends were then away. I had arranged with Rachel Golinkin, the Aspirantur's *"rebbetzin,"* and her sister who had come from Danzig to spend a week with them at Kolonja Magistracka, a riverside village about six kilometers from Vilna, where I had visited earlier on weekends. The beach was tiny, the place devoid of interest, but I needed a rest before plunging back into the new tasks that John Dollard's visit would bring. On Monday morning, August 21, I took my small suitcase and boarded the bus for Kolonja Magistracka.

On Wednesday, August 23, a fair day, with a clear blue sky and a strong sun, we set off in the morning for the beach. We returned in the early evening to find several urgent messages from Rivele. Our place didn't have a telephone, but Rivele had telephoned repeatedly to a nearby boardinghouse, where we sometimes ate. The messages added up to a peremptory command: I was to pack my suitcase and return to Vilna immediately. A registered letter had come for me from the American embassy, warning that if I intended to leave Poland, I should do so right away.

We went to the boardinghouse to find out what had happened. They had a radio there and everyone had already heard the news. That day, to the world's astonishment, Hitler's Germany and Stalin's Russia announced that they had signed a nonaggression pact. None of us had foreseen this bizarre contract between these deadly enemies. Yet when I first heard about it, I was struck by a sense of inevitability. The scenario was clear. First they'd divide Poland between themselves and then all of Europe. War was now a looming reality, perhaps a matter of days.

The boardinghouse was full of hubbub, of goings rather than comings. We decided to return to Vilna the next morning. We talked long into the night, mostly about whether all this would affect the Golinkins' immigration to the United States. Their younger brother Noah, already in New York, was trying to get them the necessary papers. Their older brother Elia, whom I had met in Warsaw in June, was trying to expedite matters from the Polish side.

Early Thursday, August 24, we set out for Vilna. No transportation was to be had. The army had requisitioned anything that moved—buses, taxis, the few private cars, trucks, droshkies, horses and wagons. Lugging our suitcases, we walked the six kilometers to Vilna. There panic reigned in the streets. The army's mobilization of its reservists, previously conducted with circumspection, was now evident everywhere and especially at the railroad station. We saw husbands and wives, parents and sons, saying goodbye, crying. Long lines of agitated housewives wound around the streets, in front of grocery stores. They had begun to stock up on food before war would bring shortages.

When I arrived home at the Kalmanoviches, Rivele kissed and hugged me. Kalmanovich had gone to the YIVO. They had hardly slept last night for worry. She gave me the letter from the American embassy, mimeographed, dated "Warsaw, Poland, August 22, 1939." It was one of the few souvenirs I brought back from Vilna. This is what it said:

> 1. In view of the recent developments in the international situation, of which you are undoubtedly acquainted through the press and otherwise, it is suggested that you give immediately serious consideration as to whether in case an emergency arises, you would remain in Poland or depart. In case you should have the intention to depart from Poland in such circumstances, it is further suggested that as transportation and other facilities might be interrupted or made difficult, arrangements for a planned departure should not be delayed too long.
>
> 2. American citizens in Poland are expected at all times to comply fully with Polish law and regulations, including the measures promulgated recently for the defense of the country, such as anti-air, gas defense, and similar measures.
>
> 3. American citizens should study carefully all requirements of this nature with a view to being thoroughly familiar with them in case any emergency arises.

Though most of the events of that day and the days that followed are blurred in my memory, like the tear-stained writing of a love letter, my first conversation with Rivele became fixed in my memory. She was all business. I was to leave right away. There was an afternoon train to Warsaw. There I could consult with the American consul and check out the steamship company as to whether I could still sail from Gdynia. She and Kalman had worked everything out for me. Perhaps, she said, I should go to Copenhagen where the Weinreichs were and where the Polish liners took on passengers for New York. Meanwhile, she had already pulled my footlocker out from under the bed. She'd help me pack.

The thought of fleeing so precipitously, in such a cowardly manner, was intolerable to me. I wanted to leave on my own terms; I could not stand the idea of running away. Nor could I then, at that moment of danger, conceive of leaving the Kalmanoviches. I made a passionate avowal that I would remain with them. I was young and strong, I could work, I could help them. I would share their fate. My love for Rivele and for Kalmanovich overwhelmed me. I was ready—so I thought then—to give my life for them.

But Rivele responded harshly to me. "What do you know of war? You can't begin to imagine what it'll be like. You won't be a help to us. You'll only be a burden, another mouth to feed, another person to care for. Go home to New York. Thank God you have time to go." She hurt me. I felt her rejection like a knife. I went into my room, weeping. Yet I realized she wanted to protect me from the hardships she had known when she'd been about my age, during the years of the Great War. Rivele and Kalman were both on familiar terms with war, revolution, and deprivation.

My determination buckled. I said I'd go—but only temporarily. I'd go to Warsaw just to see the American consul, just to get some reliable information, and then I'd come back and decide what to do. Rivele said I was foolish, this was no time for coming and going. She wanted me to take the first train, that afternoon. I argued I couldn't go without taking leave of friends who were in town. At the end, I agreed to take the train at eleven o'clock that night, with all my belongings. I began to pack and Rivele helped me.

Kalmanovich came home for dinner. He had already arranged for the YIVO to advance me money to see me as far as Gdynia and, if need be, Copenhagen. The money would eventually be repaid by the New York YIVO. He had telephoned Menahem Linder in the YIVO office in Warsaw and asked him and his wife to put me up, in case I'd have to stay over. Linder, just a few years older than I, was an economist who had been an *aspirant* two years earlier and was now on the YIVO staff in Warsaw. I'd met him and his wife in June, when I had visited Warsaw. Kalmanovich also gave me Dr. Davidsohn's address and phone number in Copenhagen.

After dinner, I went to the YIVO to say my goodbyes to the staff, gather whatever belongings I had there, and pick up the money. I scarcely remember how I made my farewells. I was in the grip of warring emotions—desolated by being separated from Rivele and Kalman, consumed by guilt for being an American, ashamed of running away like a coward. I spoke encouraging words; we'd see each other again; I assured them—on what authority I don't know—that everything would turn out well.

For the last time I stood in the YIVO's gleaming vestibule with the map of the world on the first landing. I looked around as if I wanted to fix it in my mind forever. Then I opened the door and went out, down along the tree- and shrub-lined walkway to the gate at the street. I was in tears. Just a year ago, almost to the day, I had had my first glimpse of this building.

Back at the Kalmanoviches, I tried to make little jokes, to discipline my grief, but I couldn't control the tears. We went to the railroad station, only about two blocks away, to pick up my ticket and check my baggage through to Warsaw. I don't remember how we got my footlocker and one suitcase there; perhaps Rivele found someone with a hand truck. The latest "extras" were on the street. Hitler was escalating his demands on Poland. Beck was conferring with foreign diplomats. Roosevelt appealed to Hitler.

Later that evening friends came to say goodbye. I tried to restrain the tears, repeating phrases of hope, in which I myself had little confidence, insisting that we'd see each other again, that I'd return. Then it was time to leave. Rivele, Kalman, and several friends accompanied me to the station. I carried a small suitcase and my indispensable typewriter. We wisecracked and we wept, clinging to each other in a last embrace. They left and I was alone. I cried myself into fitful sleep as the train sped toward Warsaw. Weeping, which had seldom been my mode, now became the only way I could express my feelings.

Early Friday, August 25, I arrived in Warsaw and checked my hand luggage in the station. I picked up a couple of Yiddish newspapers, read the headlines, but found no relief there. Unlike Vilna, droshkies and taxis were available; Warsaw apparently had more resources. Warsaw was usually full of bustle and that morning things didn't seem much different from what I had seen last June, except that everywhere you saw men in uniform.

Right away I got to see the consul. He seemed well informed and was even more categorical than Rivele in telling me to leave right away. This time, he said, war was really in the cards. American consulates all over Europe were advising Americans abroad to leave Europe immediately. The State Department was making contingency plans to evacuate Americans, once Hitler invaded Poland. It was only a matter of days. It was rumored, he added, that Russia had demanded, as the price for the nonaggression treaty with Germany, a piece of Poland. Poland would be partitioned between them. It was now the most dangerous place in Europe.

The visit to the consul had the effect of making me feel more like an American. In Vilna I felt like a Vilna Jew, belonging to the Kalmanoviches, even if Rivele had denied me that status. Now emotional distance, in addition to the mileage, had come between me and Vilna. Did the fear of war, whose imminence a voice of authority had confirmed, finally register? When I walked out of the consul's office, I was ready to flee to the safety which my American passport guaranteed. The consul had given me practical advice—the same advice Rivele had given. By now Gdynia was surely closed to commercial traffic. He had heard that Polish civilian shipping—passenger and merchant vessels— had been ordered to stay in West European ports. In Gdynia Polish ships might be seized by the Germans. I should go to Copenhagen to board my ship. But how would I get there? He advised me to take the train, via Berlin. When I asked him if it was safe, he assured me that with an American passport, I'd be absolutely safe. "Just go before war breaks out."

From the consulate I called Menahem Linder, told him of my plans, and arranged to see him later. At the Orbis Travel Agency I made my reservation on the S.S. *Piłsudski,* sister ship of the *Batory,* on which I had sailed from New York. The *Piłsudski* had been scheduled to sail from Gdynia on September 4. I hoped it would sail from Copenhagen on September 5.

At the railroad station, I couldn't get a seat on a train to Copenhagen before the next day, Saturday evening, August 26. "Via Berlin," I now realized, meant changing trains and stations in Berlin. I would have to get from the Schlesischer Bahnhof, the Silesian Station, where trains from the east arrived, to the Stättner Station, where trains to the north departed. Disquieted, I bought the ticket and shipped my footlocker and suitcase straight to Copenhagen. I took my small suitcase and typewriter out of the baggage checkroom and went to the Linders. All Friday afternoon and Saturday morning I kept trying to telephone Vilna, but I couldn't get through—the trunk lines were busy. Finally I wrote to Rivele, hoping the letter would reach her.

I remember my stay in Warsaw only as a series of single images, like slides of unrelated scenes. When I was with the Linders, we discussed the latest events. Hitler was making new threats against Poland and inciting the Nazis in Danzig to create new incidents. Mościcki had offered to negotiate. Beck continued to meet with foreign envoys. The pope appealed for peace. Roosevelt asked Hitler to desist from attacking Poland.

How I spent Saturday I don't remember, but in a letter to my family—written two days later from Copenhagen—I described taking a walk in Warsaw. In the public parks, we saw people digging trenches. What for? Were they preparing shelters? In front of many stores—not just groceries—we saw long queues. The papers reported that several grocers had been arrested for selling food at speculation prices and had been sent to the concentration camp at Bereza Kartuska. The more important news in the papers that day was that Hitler had summoned Sir Neville Henderson, the British ambassador, and was angered to hear from Henderson that Britain would stand by its promises to Poland. Later that day, we picked up some "extras." England and Poland had finally signed their treaty, thus formalizing the mutual guarantees to which they had committed themselves last April.

Saturday night, August 26, the Linders saw me off on the train to Berlin. At the station we saw scenes of hysterical separation, as the reservists took leave of their wives and relatives. Ours was a more muted farewell. Now I was impatient to leave. Since I had come to Warsaw, I never once thought of returning to Vilna, though my thoughts constantly returned to Rivele and Kalman. Feelings of guilt afflicted me for having left them and I was ashamed by the instability of my emotions. Yet even while I was castigating myself, I looked forward to the adventure of my journey into the capital of Nazi Germany.

Three other passengers, all Poles, traveled in the second-class compartment with me—a uniformed nurse and two Polish officers. No one spoke. I didn't speak the language, but they didn't talk among themselves either. Each one was preoccupied; it didn't take much imagination to project their anxieties and fears. I had some magazines—*Partisan Review,* I think, and perhaps a *New Yorker,* which had come in the mail before I left Vilna. I turned the pages, unable to concentrate, dozing off and on.

At Poznań, near the Polish-German border, the three Poles got off. Four Germans took their place—an elderly couple, a tearful young woman saying goodbye to her Polish husband, and a rather handsome middle-aged man. He saw the magazines in my lap and began speaking to me in serviceable English. He was a third secretary, or something like that, in the German consulate in Poznań. We talked for a long time. He was in high spirits. The Germans were recalling their diplomatic staff from Poland, he told me. I don't suppose it crossed his mind that I was Jewish. To him, I was an American and he exhorted me to bring back his message—the message of Hitler's Germany—to my countrymen.

The message was simple and crude as German propaganda. War was coming and the Germans were glad about it. He advised me to get out of Europe as fast as possible. "Tell your fellow Americans," he said, "Danzig is only an excuse. Germany wants much more." When I asked him how he felt about the pact with Communist Russia, the archenemy of his country, he replied that it was a gift for Germany. "We Germans now have security on the eastern front."

For a few hours I dozed off and on. As the sun rose, I watched the German landscape. It was easy to distinguish Germany from Poland just by looking at the farmland. From Vilna to Warsaw, I had seen unkempt farmlands, straggly fields, the wheat still unharvested. In Germany, the land was bare, but you could see the contours of the various crop fields laid out neatly. All the fields had been harvested. Hitler had planned well: The early harvest was surely no lucky accident. We passed endless trains of boxcars moving eastward—toward Poland—crammed with soldiers and horses. It was ominous.

Sunday morning, August 27, our train pulled into the Schlesischer Bahnhof. Just before the train entered the depot, we saw soldiers stationed on a rise facing us, with cannons directed at the tracks. The station was aswarm with people, civilians and military. I told the German consular official that I needed a taxi to get to the Stättner Station, that I was desperate to catch the train to Copenhagen. He responded to my feminine helplessness with courtliness and German efficiency. He got me a taxi; it seemed to me that he commandeered one. Once again I was on my way, tense, yet filled with excitement. I was in the heart of enemy territory, witnessing a pageant of Nazi war frenzy. The taxi driver had to inch his cab through the traffic. We were afloat in a sea of soldiers, waves of Nazi flags, and the trappings of war. The air was heavy with jubilation: cheers, shouts, rousing songs. The German will to fight and to conquer Poland deafened the air.

We made it to the Stättner Station. The train was still there, though I had come late. German punctuality had been undermined by the exigency of war. On the platform and in all the crowded cars I heard English spoken in American and British accents. People were sharing rumors—the train which arrived from Warsaw was the last to leave Poland; this train would be the last to leave for Denmark. (Neither rumor was true. My trunk arrived in Copenhagen on the third train after ours.)

A tall German sporting a swastika pin in his lapel made room for me in the compartment. He, too, spoke English. When I said I'd like to see a newspaper, he left the train and brought back three German papers. One was the *Völkische Beobachter,* the official Nazi Party paper. The headlines in all three papers howled about Poland's aggressiveness against peace-loving Germany. I asked the tall and courteous German if he really believed that Poland would attack Germany. He seemed genuinely not to fathom how I could think otherwise. He had not the slightest doubt about Poland's belligerence and he earnestly tried to persuade me of it. It was like listening to a very polite lunatic.

Barely two and a half days ago, a mere sixty hours earlier, I had left Vilna with a broken heart. Yet with every cycle of new sights and new experiences, Vilna receded from my consciousness. Not that the Kalmanoviches were out of my mind. I thought of them constantly, but they had become memories, rather than present realities. Every few hours I came face to face with utterly new experiences, all in constant motion, changing like a rapid sequence of kaleidoscopic images. My feelings couldn't keep pace with the events I was witnessing. The grief that had possessed me in Vilna had given way to a state of excitement. Aware that I was at the center of great events, I realized that my own fears and hopes were trivial, even to me.

The train finally moved. It was a slow journey toward Copenhagen. Perhaps German troop movements impeded us. At Rostock, the German passengers got off the train. We were now mostly Americans and Britishers. Very soon thereafter we arrived at Warnemunde, on the Baltic shore, the last stop in Germany. Several railroad cars were uncoupled from the locomotive and moved onto an enormous ferry that plied the waters between Germany and Denmark. We docked at Gedser, on Danish soil, to general relief and muted rejoicing that we were safely out of Hitler's Germany. I could feel my body's tenseness slackening. While our train was being hooked up to another locomotive, Danish border officials checked our passports. Toward evening we arrived in Copenhagen.

The hundreds of disembarking passengers turned into a seething mass of hysterical Americans. Many were panicky about this European unpleasantness which had interrupted their vacations in Germany, Russia, Rumania, Bulgaria, Hungary, and Poland. Like me, they had been advised to leave and to do so fast. They were frantic about getting passage home, about money. An American Express representative at the station said most hotels were all filled up, but he could get us rooms at the Palace, an expensive hotel. It was in the Town Hall Square, in the very center of things, not far from the station. Though it was well beyond my means, I figured I could manage for one night. I checked in and then cabled home and to Vilna, to the Kalmanoviches, to tell them of my safe arrival. When I called the Davidsohns, no one answered. I had no idea where the Weinreichs might be or if indeed they were still in Copenhagen.

Tired, but keyed up, I was too restless to stay in my hotel room. I walked around the lively Town Hall Square. High up on a building there—perhaps it was the *Berlingske Tidende*'s headquarters—was an electric billboard continuously flashing the latest headlines. Crowds of people stood around, following the news. I bought a couple of papers— the *Manchester Guardian* and a Danish paper, I think. I could make out the printed Danish, though I couldn't understand spoken Danish at all. I went into a cafe to eat and read the papers. Hitler was demanding that the British and French break off the treaty they had just signed with Poland. Italy announced its neutrality. Other countries were prepared for war. Germany introduced food rationing.

Then, at loose ends, I went to the movies to see *Three Smart Girls Grow Up,* with Deanna Durbin. The very frivolousness of the film turned my thoughts back to Vilna. Just three days ago I had been there, yet now I felt as if I had traversed half the world and a sea of time. I went back to the hotel, thinking about Rivele and Kalman, about the sufferings the coming war would bring to them and to all the people I had left behind. Once again I cried myself to sleep, this time in the luxury of the Palace Hotel.

Monday morning, August 28, I reached Dr. Davidsohn. His English was good. He told me that Max and Uriel were in Copenhagen, that Regina had flown back to Vilna to be with her younger son. She'd left August 23, the day they learned about the German-Soviet pact. Davidsohn gave me Weinreich's telephone number and patiently spelled out the address of their pension. When I called there, the Weinreichs had already gone out for the day. But rooms were available. The place was just a couple of blocks away from the Palace, on the other side of Tivoli Gardens, on a quiet street, not quite a pension, but a place that let rooms. It was clean, comfortable, and much cheaper than the Palace. I checked in and left a note for Max Weinreich. Then I went to the American consulate.

The consul didn't seem very well informed. When I told him of my journey from Warsaw, he called in two vice-consuls to listen to my story. Nor did they know anything about transportation back to the

States. They did volunteer that they could advance money to stranded Americans, if need be. Then, at the office of the Gdynia America Line, near the harbor, I learned that the S.S. *Piłsudski* was somewhere in English waters, but no one knew, or would say, what its course was likely to be. When I asked whether it might sail to New York directly from England, the clerk shrugged his shoulders. I thought I might get some money from the consul to fly to London, in that case. The American Express office was jammed with Americans. Some were going on to Oslo. They said it was the safest place in the world.

The rest of the day I wandered around Copenhagen. I felt as though I were suspended in time and place, for there was nothing I could do to alter my situation. Besides, I was in an altogether volatile emotional state. I relished the sights and smells of the city, marveled at the richly stocked shops and department stores, and gorged myself on Danish food and coffee. In the late afternoon, I bought the morning's London *Times,* which had come by air, and went to yet another cafe to read the paper. Hitler and French Premier Daladier had exchanged messages; Daladier stated that Hitler refused to negotiate with the Poles. Italy's foreign minister Ciano conferred with the British ambassador to Italy; the Vatican ordered the churches to pray for peace. Mobilizations and war preparations were going on in Germany, Poland, and France.

Later that evening, Max and Uriel Weinreich came back to their rooms. We had a warm reunion, though Max Weinreich was not given to the display of affection and was uncomfortable with the flow of tears. We talked late into the night, sharing each other's experiences. He'd heard from Regina; everyone in Vilna was well, but apprehensive. We speculated about what would happen to the world and to us.

Tuesday, August 29, was another day in limbo, but now I was not alone. We had lunch with two Czech refugees, Max Weinreich's friends, Professor Roman Jakobson, a philologist, and his wife, Svátava. Then in his mid-forties, Jakobson had already made a name for himself as a pioneer in modern linguistics. Nevertheless, though he knew many languages, including Yiddish and English, he would not speak English, afraid of being ungrammatical. His wife, however, chattered in English without inhibition or syntax. Mostly we communicated in German; with Weinreich, Jakobson spoke Russian.

Reading the papers was our constant occupation. We bought papers twice a day and, when there were "extras," more frequently. We followed every diplomatic move by each of the major nations. That day the papers reported that Hitler was conferring with British Ambassador

Henderson again and would send a message to Chamberlain; France was reported to have closed its frontier with Germany; the German-Polish border was also closed. That evening, to give Weinreich some time for himself, I took Uriel to Tivoli Gardens, where we rode on the roller coaster and saw a ballet with music by Offenbach.

On Wednesday, August 30, my luggage arrived from Warsaw. Meanwhile, in response to my cable, my family had sent me some money via American Express. There was still no news of the S.S. *Piłsudski* and its sailing. Once again I went sightseeing with Uriel, while Weinreich worked, at what I don't know, but it was likely some scholarly project to occupy his time usefully and discipline his anxieties. The three of us lunched together and read the papers. Hitler had sent a message to Chamberlain; von Ribbentrop was conferring with the Italian ambassador; Chamberlain pledged to the House of Commons that Britain would resist German force in Poland; Germany assured Denmark and Lithuania that it would respect their neutrality. For myself, I followed the news about shipping in the hope of getting home.

That evening we dined with the Jakobsons along the Gammel Strand, at the canal where fishwives sold fresh fish, herring, and eels wriggling in pails. Then we visited the Davidsohns. Dr. Joseph Davidsohn, a native Dane, held a high post in the Danish Ministry of Social Welfare. His Russian-born wife, Fania, was a biologist. Several Danish professors were also there. Conversation proceeded slowly across the language barriers. Someone said something in Danish; Dr. Davidsohn translated it for me into English; I repeated it to Weinreich in Yiddish; he told it to Jakobson in Russian, who passed it on to his wife in Czech.

On Thursday, August 31, we were invited to lunch by a Dane who had a house on the sea. During the day we listened to the radio for news. Negotiations were still going on to persuade Hitler to settle his claims peacefully with the Poles. When we returned to town, we bought our usual quota of papers. The British were still continuing to press Hitler to negotiate with Poland; Mościcki conferred with Beck and Rydz-Śmigly; Britain promised to respect Danish neutrality; in New York, Cardinal Spellman prayed for peace.

Friday, September 1, we awoke to the news that the Germans had already invaded Poland. The newspapers which had been printed the night before were outdated. At 4 A.M. the Germans had opened fire on the Polish post office in Danzig and other places in the Polish Corridor. At 5:40 A.M. Hitler had delivered a radio address to his armed forces, declaring that Poland had refused his offer for a peaceful settlement. The

Germans in Poland, he claimed, were being persecuted and terrorized. A few hours later Hitler addressed the Reichstag deputies, telling them that Germany had "counterattacked." He never used the word "war" that day, but he had just launched what would become the Second World War.

The fears we had lived with for the past year had finally materialized. I gave in to feelings of fatalism and helplessness. The British and the French wouldn't do anything. America was too far away. Americans wouldn't think that this would be their war. No one would help the Jews, once Hitler took Poland. The course of history had taken a wild trajectory and lurched crazily out of control.

Still, I managed to rouse myself on my own behalf—getting passage home. At the Gdynia America Line I learned that all sailings had been canceled. Only one Norwegian line would honor my Polish steamship ticket but its earliest available booking was September 27 from Oslo. A Swedish ship sailing from Stockholm on September 17 had space, but I decided I'd be better off with the American Scantic Line and to get a refund for the Polish ticket in New York. In normal times, the American Scantic Line operated a fleet of freighters, each with accommodations for about twelve passengers. Now each ship would carry about 200, Americans only, who would rough it on cots in the hold and cafeteria-style meals. The *ScanYork* was scheduled to sail on Tuesday, September 5. I put down a ten-dollar deposit and cabled my closest friend's father for money, explaining I'd pay it back from the refund I'd get in New York. I expected the money to arrive on Monday, in time for me to complete my travel arrangements.

For the time being, Max and Uriel planned to stay in Copenhagen. Before Regina had flown back to Vilna, they had all decided on that strategy, believing that women and children would be safer than men, even under a German occupation. That was the European tradition of chivalry, which even Polish hooligans had respected. To remain in Copenhagen, Weinreich would need a permit; with Davidsohn's help, he expected to get it. We talked about his coming to New York. He worried about the fate of the YIVO in Vilna under the Russians or the Germans. In New York, I suggested, he could do more for the YIVO than anywhere else.

On Saturday, September 2, we saw the Jakobsons off to Oslo via Sweden. He'd been offered a lectureship at the University of Oslo. Afterward, Uriel and I walked around Copenhagen, sightseeing, but mostly we watched the news flashing from the *Berlingske Tidende* building. Every hour or so we bought a new "extra." Poland was appealing for aid from the Great Powers; Britain and France asked Germany to halt its aggressive action; Italy proclaimed its neutrality; heavy fighting was reported in Poland. That day I wrote home, informing them that I hoped to sail on the *Scan York,* scheduled to arrive in New York on September 17. "There's no point writing about the news," I went on. "Before the ink is dry on the paper, the news is stale." Still I wrote them that we had heard, via Paris, that Vilna and other cities near the Russian border had been bombed: "I'm afraid the Russians, not the Germans, will take that part of Poland. They're not any better; they're just as evil."

Sunday, September 3, at 11:15 A.M., Prime Minister Chamberlain made a radio broadcast declaring that his long struggle to win peace had failed, that Britain was already at war. "It is evil things that we shall be fighting against, brute force, bad faith, injustice, oppression, and persecution." An hour later, he spoke before the House of Commons: "We are fighting to save the whole world from the pestilence of Nazi tyranny." The French issued their declaration of war at 5:00 P.M. the same day.

Monday, September 4, I went to the American Express office to await the arrival of my money from New York. I was not alone; dozens of anxious Americans were there. But no money came that day. We'd forgotten it was Labor Day in the United States; all banks were closed. The money arrived the next day, too late for me to sail on the *Scan York,* though my footlocker was on it. That Monday, we thought that Denmark, too, might be drawn into the war. Esbjerg, on the west coast of Jutland, was bombed. All Denmark assumed the Germans had done it, but Germany denied responsibility. Two days later, we learned that British bombers had made a mistake. The Danes breathed a little easier, sent a note of protest to the British, and gave the Esbjerg victims a state funeral.

After the *Scan York*'s departure, no definite schedule of sailings was available. I knew I couldn't leave before September 11 and probably not even then. On September 6, I received a card from the Kalmanoviches, dated August 28. Kalman wrote that everyone was well and that they were hoping for peace. I read it over and over again, crying without restraint. Then I wrote them that I expected to sail for home soon. I was careful not to say anything more than that I loved them and hoped that they would be well. One didn't know how strict the Polish censor would be, now that Poland was actually at war.

Weinreich and I decided we had had enough of sightseeing, of exploring Danish castles and climbing spiral staircases. Our thoughts were usually elsewhere. We decided to settle down for the duration, though mine was to be a short one. Uriel was enrolled in school. Max worked on some research project. I signed up at the University for an English-language course on Hamlet and its Danish origins. In the evening, we often dined with the Davidsohns. I remember going to the movies and seeing Bette Davis in *Dark Victory*. I cried my heart out, thinking of Rivele and Kalman and Vilna as I wept. One day followed the other in the usual routine. We still bought newspapers, but there was less news now. We stopped getting British newspapers. The warring countries had all imposed varying degrees of censorship. We tried to get news of Poland, particularly of Vilna.

Every day I'd stop off at the American Scantic Line to find out about a sailing. Finally, on September 11, I was told I had a reservation on the S.S. *Donald McKay*, sailing Saturday, September 16. There was talk of having a German pilot take the ship through the minefields the Germans had laid in the North Sea.

Meanwhile, Weinreich had briefed me on his affairs, which he wanted me to discuss with the YIVO people in New York—he needed money and papers to come to the United States. And he wanted to arrange contact with his wife and son in Vilna.

On September 16, the day I left Copenhagen, Warsaw was already encircled by the Germans, but was still fighting, with the gallantry the Poles had always summoned up in their unequal and losing battles. All sorts of rumors were afloat that the Lithuanians were about to "liberate" Vilna from Poland.

Max and Uriel took me down to the pier. It was a sunny clear day, but we were draped in gloom. We embraced and kissed each other. Visitors were not permitted to board the ship. I asked them not to stand on the pier, waiting until the boat sailed. They said they'd stay just long enough to see me wave from the deck, after I'd located my cot in the hold, now our sleeping quarters.

I stowed away my belongings and returned to the deck. I saw them both standing below, alone and forlorn. I waved goodbye. They waved back, shouted goodbye, turned, and walked away. I stood at the rail, watching them disappear in the distance. I was choked with tears.

Some Americans were standing next to me, saying goodbye to their friends on the pier. One of the Americans shouted: "Don't be afraid." A thickset middle-aged woman replied with fervor in her voice: "Wir Deutschen haben keine Furcht"—"We Germans have no fear." I burst into tears and stepped away from the rail. I went aft to the ship's stern. No one was there. I sat down on a coil of rope, my head on my knees, and sobbed uncontrollably. Then I felt a light touch on my shoulder as if someone were soothing me. I looked up. There was a grinning burly American sailor, wearing a high knitted cap. His extended arm held out a package of Wrigley's Spearmint chewing gum. He said: "Come on, it can't be that bad."

I knew then that I was on my way home, to the good-naturedness and innocence that was America. On Thursday, September 28, 1939, the S.S. *Donald McKay* docked in Boston and landed its passengers.

PART II

CHAPTER 10

New York 1939–1942: War Watch

In September 1940 the American branch of the YIVO began to operate as the YIVO's headquarters for the duration of the war. The Vilna YIVO as I had known it no longer existed, though we heard that its physical facilities had remained intact. The city of Vilna had become the capital of the Lithuanian Soviet Socialist Republic by authority of the Red Army. It was being Sovietized and so were all its institutions, including the YIVO. As commissar over the YIVO the authorities had appointed Moshe Lerer, whom I had known when he worked in the Vilna YIVO Archives. He was then reputed to be a troublemaker. Kalmanovich, who had never concealed his dislike for communism and Communists, had been dismissed, along with other staff members. Under Lerer's guidance—according to the Communist press—the reorganized Vilna YIVO would offer instruction in Marxism to teachers in the Yiddish schools. More disquieting were newspaper reports of large-scale roundups of "reactionary stool pigeons, prison wardens, provocateurs, and spies." I feared for the Kalmanoviches and my Bundist friends.

Meanwhile, Max Weinreich and his son Uriel had come to New York from Copenhagen in March 1940. He had proposed that the American YIVO take over the chief functions of the Vilna YIVO for the time being. After lengthy deliberations about their financial resources, the board agreed to Weinreich's plan and appointed him to a newly created post as YIVO's research director. Early in August, he asked me to become his secretary. I was then living in Albany, where I'd been working for about a half year at a tedious civil service job. When he offered me the job, Weinreich explained that he didn't want me just to be a secretarial assistant. For that he could have hired someone with better skills than mine in Yiddish shorthand and typing. He wanted me because I represented continuity between the YIVO in Vilna and New York, because I understood the YIVO's mission and the spirit that had animated it in Vilna. I would be paid the same salary I was earning in Albany—$900 a year, a sum on which one could then live, unlike the stipend I had had in Vilna. We were to start work right after Labor Day. I didn't need to be persuaded to accept. I would have rejoiced to leave Albany for any job in New York, but this particular job was what I had been in training for all my life. I had served my apprenticeship in Vilna. Now I would become a journeyman, working for wages with a master—not just any master, but the Master of Vilna. It was the best thing that had happened to me since my return from Vilna a year ago.

Those twelve months had been the bleakest period of my life, when I felt so assaulted and battered by history that my personal life had all but collapsed. In that time most of Europe had become engulfed in war. Poland had been carved up between Hitler's Germany and Stalin's Russia. After the Red Army entered Vilna on September 19, 1939, Soviet commissars arrested hundreds of people, among them Zalmen Reisen and his son Saul. For more than a year, the YIVO people in New York kept appealing on their behalf, first to the Lithuanian delegation in the United States and to the American consul in Lithuania, then to Molotov and other U.S. and Soviet officials, but no one ever received any information about the Reisens' whereabouts or the charges against them.

My attention was riveted on the fate of the Jews in German-occupied Poland. The newspapers gave accounts of German atrocities against Poles and Jews, detailing incidents of violence and military-style executions. The *Times* didn't supply much news about the Jews, but the Yiddish press printed every scrap of information, even rumors about escaping refugees and expelled diplomats brought out of Poland and the Baltic countries. All sources, English and Yiddish, confirmed that Jewish blood was flowing in German-occupied Poland. Entire Jewish communities were reported to have been uprooted from their towns and cities on a few hours' notice and driven onto the highways. The Germans were everywhere taking Jewish hostages and demanding the accumulated wealth of the whole community as the price for their release. The most terrifying reports came from small towns where the Germans rounded up the local Jews and confined them in synagogues, which they then set afire. The morning news became the stuff of my nightmares.

In city after city, town after town, the German occupiers began to segregate the Jews from the Polish population, compelling them to wear yellow armbands with the Star of David. There were rumors of ghettos. Rivele's dark words about war never ceased to haunt me. I was weighed down with the burden of guilt for having left my friends behind, mourning the loss of my private universe. The only one of my Vilna friends to have escaped was Michael Rubinstein, the English-speaking doctor, who had reached New York before me in the summer of 1939, but his company was not sufficient comfort for the despair that overtook me.

Most Americans then did not want the United States to become involved in the European conflict, though they didn't like the Nazis or approve of their actions. They favored strict neutrality and kept an embargo on the sale and export of all arms and munitions to belligerents. But right after the German invasion of Poland, President Roosevelt, while vowing to keep the United States out of war, succeeded in getting Congress to lift that embargo and to put the sale and export of arms to belligerent powers on a cash-and-carry basis. It was too late to help Poland, but the United States could now sell arms to Britain and France.

Predictably the pro-Nazis, the anti-Semites, and the isolationists railed and ranted against aid to Britain and France. Predictably the Communists fought American intervention in Europe, even if they didn't yet have a coherent line. They were still in shock over the Nazi-Soviet pact and the Soviet invasion of Poland, which they tried to justify to their own ranks, some of whom were quitting the party. Even the Socialist opposition to lifting the embargo was predictable, given their penchant for pacifism and their doctrinaire anathemization of war as an instrument of imperialism. In May 1938, Norman Thomas, head of the Socialist Party, had founded an anti-interventionist pressure group called the Keep America Out of War Congress, which often gave a platform to right-wing isolationists. Predictably the Jews were the most enthusiastic in their response to the lifting of the embargo. Ever since Hitler had come to power in 1933, American Jews had vociferously condemned the Nazi regime. After the demise of Poland, they wanted America to give the utmost help to Britain and France so that *they* might stop Hitler. For holding such views American Jews were vilified by the isolationists and the anti-Semites as warmongers.

But in November 1939 the argument about intervention seemed academic, for the fighting in Europe had stopped. In the West the French army was nestled in its Maginot fortifications, while the English sat tight on their island. People talked about the "phony war." Only the Russians disturbed the quiet when they invaded Finland at the end of November. Though the Finns resisted, they finally capitulated in March, forced to give the Russians even more territory and bases than they had refused them in November.

On April 9, 1940, the "phony war" came to an end. German forces swooped into Denmark and Norway. The Norwegians resisted, but even with the help of an Anglo-French expeditionary force, they could not drive the Germans out. The English and French withdrew on May 3 and the Germans occupied all Norway. A week later, without the least warning, German armed forces invaded Belgium, the Netherlands, and Luxembourg. That day, May 10, Chamberlain's government fell and Winston Churchill was asked to form a new British government. We cheered, for we knew that Churchhill would at last bring to Britain the moral energy and political determination to fight—and defeat—the Germans.

In Albany, the radio was my constant companion, even at the office, as my colleagues and I followed the rush of catastrophic events. On May 14, Holland capitulated. A few days later the Germans invaded France and by May 19 German Panzer divisions had smashed through the Maginot line. On May 26, Belgium capitulated. France was on the verge of military collapse. Some 250,000 British expeditionary forces and about 140,000 French troops had to be withdrawn from the French coast. In that extraordinary evacuation from the beaches of Dunkirk, which lasted nine days, almost 400,000 men were rescued by a makeshift flotilla of some thousand ships, which the Royal Air Force shielded from the fire of German planes. The deliverance from Dunkirk was a victory of sorts, but clearly the British and French had suffered a disastrous military defeat.

No one had expected France to fall so fast. The shock finally made many Americans realize that Hitler's Germany now threatened Britain's existence and even imperiled America's security. People began speaking up about America's obligation to help Britain, as the first step in our own defense. William Allen White, the influential editor of the Emporia (Kansas) *Gazette,* had already formed an interventionist pressure group, the Committee to Defend America by Aiding the Allies. The New York *Herald Tribune* wanted the United States to declare war on Germany. The *New Republic,* which had followed the then fashionably left noninterventionist line, now frantically editorialized that "there is not a second to be lost" in gearing up America's defenses and in helping Britain. In June both parties sponsored legislation in Congress to inaugurate compulsory military service. The *New York Times,* which had opposed conscription before, now reversed itself. The War Department shipped over 40 million dollars' worth of surplus and outdated arms to Britain to replace their losses at Dunkirk. Now the war was no longer a "Jewish war," as the anti-Semitic isolationists charged. Now it threatened to swallow up the Western world.

The shadow of the war hovered like a minatory presence. The young men I knew expected that sooner or later the United States would enter the war and that they would be drafted into the army. They didn't relish the idea, but they felt it was their obligation, *their* war. Two of my friends in Albany decided not to wait until Congress would pass the draft bill. They quit their civil service jobs that summer and went to Canada to enlist.

At the end of June, the fighting in Europe once again came to a halt. News of the presidential political conventions filled the papers. The Republicans nominated Wendell L. Willkie, a former Democrat who supported Roosevelt's foreign policy, but opposed the New Deal reforms.

The Democrats nominated Roosevelt for an unprecedented third term. The debate between the isolationists and the interventionists heated up. On the Jewish left, a sharp split had developed between Socialist Party loyalists, Norman Thomas's followers, and a cluster of Jewish socialist groups, including the influential newspaper *Forverts,* which accused the Socialist Party of having abandoned socialism for isolationism.

In July the German air force began its bombing raids over England. Everybody believed that Germany was preparing to invade Britain. Early in August, the Germans launched a massive air offensive against Britain's airfields and industrial cities. In September, they began their merciless bombing of London. The British retaliated with raids on Berlin and Germany's industrial cities.

That Labor Day weekend, just before I began working at the YIVO, was a turning point in the battle between the interventionists and the isolationists. On Friday, September 3, President Roosevelt announced that the United States had concluded an agreement with Britain to transfer fifty overage destroyers in exchange for a ninety-nine-year lease of naval and air bases in Newfoundland, Bermuda, and the British West Indies. The next day, the America First Committee came into existence. It would soon become the leading anti-interventionist pressure group in the country, rallying isolationist sentiment against Roosevelt's foreign policy. That same weekend, the American Communists mustered their then declining ranks for an Emergency Peace Mobilization in Chicago. Out of that meeting they created another Communist front, an anti-interventionist pressure group which they called the American Peace Mobilization, but which everyone else called the Russia First Committee.

About a week later, despite vigorous isolationist opposition, Congress passed the Selective Training and Service Act, by a nearly 2 to 1 vote in the Senate and a smaller margin in the House. It provided for the registration of all men twenty-one to thirty-six and for training 1,200,000 troops and 800,000 reserves for a one-year period. A month later, 16,400,000 men were registered. The draft lottery began on October 29. A number of my friends were among the first to be called up and soon were inducted at Fort Dix, New Jersey, for their basic training.

The air war over Britain dominated the foreign news; the draft and the presidential election campaign were our national preoccupations. Intervention was the campaign's chief political issue. The Republicans accused Roosevelt of wanting to lead the country into war. The isolationists charged that the Jews supported Roosevelt in the hope that he would launch a war of revenge against Hitler. The Yiddish papers lambasted the Socialists for running Norman Thomas against Roosevelt and playing into the hands of the Republicans. When all the ballots were tallied on November 5, Roosevelt had won with some 27 million votes to Willkie's 22 million.

In those days, the YIVO was located in lower Manhattan, at 425 Lafayette Street, around the corner from Cooper Union, in the north wing of a long, low-storied, red-bricked building. Its center section was occupied by the offices of the HIAS (Hebrew Immigrant Aid Society), which used the south wing as a temporary shelter for new immigrants. The building had been erected in the mid-nineteenth century to house the Astor Library, the first free reference library in New York, named after John Jacob Astor, whose will had provided for it. (The Astor

Library, later consolidated with the Lenox and Tilden private libraries, became the New York Public Library.) Whatever grandeur the Astor Library may have had in its prime had long since faded. The run-down exterior and the drab interior were like all the seedy habitats of the Jewish organizations I had known in New York. (In the late 1960s, the building was renovated to become Joseph Papp's Public Theater.)

The YIVO occupied the north wing's whole second floor, except for the offices of the monthly Yiddish journal *Di tsukunft* and the Central Yiddish Culture Organization, publisher and distributor of Yiddish books. The offices adjoined each other, their windows facing on a dreary inner courtyard. The rest of the large space, separated by a wooden partition, was occupied by the stacks of the YIVO's modest library and a reading room, whose tall windows faced the street. Windowless offices for Weinreich and me were carved out of the perimeter of that space.

Weinreich had laid out a formidable program for the reorganized YIVO. He wanted to step up the activities of its research sections; enlarge the library; publish, besides the *YIVO-Bleter,* a news bulletin and a linguistic journal; inaugurate an Aspirantur; extend YIVO's constituency beyond its immigrant base; and develop contacts with the non-Jewish academic world. We didn't have much money to work with and I didn't think we had enough manpower, even with people like my former teachers Jacob Shatzky and Leibush Lehrer.

What I hadn't counted on were the extraordinary human resources which the European war had put within our reach. New York in 1940 had become a haven for Jewish talent in flight. Scholars, writers, lawyers, communal leaders, and intellectuals from Eastern Europe congregated around the YIVO. Most were refugees from a list of countries that kept expanding as Hitler's anti-Semitism spread over Europe like the Black Death. Some had become practiced in refugeehood, having fled from the pogroms and the civil war in Russia in 1917, then from Germany in 1933, Austria in 1938, Czechoslovakia in 1939, and Holland, Belgium, and France in 1940. Others had left their native Lithuania, Poland, and Rumania before the war. Those remarkable East European Jews, many of whom had lived for a decade or so in Western Europe, enriched modern Jewish scholarship in the United States for several decades.

Among them was Raphael Mahler, tall, good-looking, a Left Labor Zionist and a Marxist, who wrote Jewish history with a class-conscious perspective. A friend and colleague of Emanuel Ringelblum, the Warsaw Jewish historian, he had been affiliated with Ringelblum's *Yung historiker krayz* (Young Historians Circle). In New York he worked closely with the YIVO as lecturer and contributor to the *YIVO-Bleter*. In 1942 the YIVO published a book of his, a Marxist interpretation of the struggle between the Haskalah and hasidism in Galicia in the nineteenth century. Despite his doctrinaire views, he had an engaging personality and a ready wit. He'd like to clinch an argument by saying: "This is not just a truth. It's also a fact."

Another recent immigrant was Jacob Lestchinsky, a pioneer in the field of Jewish statistics, economics, and demography, the head of the YIVO's research section in economics and statistics, under whom Menahem Linder, my friend in Warsaw, had worked. Lestchinsky was about twenty years older than most of his refugee colleagues. His energy and prolific scholarly output aroused their envy.

Yudel Mark, one of YIVO's insiders, had come from Lithuania. A linguist and grammarian, he earned his livelihood as a Yiddish teacher. He was a tall, strikingly handsome man in his early forties. His courtly manner and somewhat effeminate voice belied his priapic nature. He spoke the most exquisite cadenced Yiddish I'd ever heard. Though he held heretical views about some of the YIVO's standard spelling rules, which Weinreich regarded as immutable and infallible, Weinreich nonetheless invited him to edit the YIVO's new journal *Yidishe shprakh,* devoted to the problems of standard Yiddish. The first issue appeared in January 1941.

In the summer of 1940, a contingent of East European Jews who had been living in Paris and had fled through Vichy France to Lisbon arrived in New York. Among them were Elias Tcherikower, head of YIVO's History Section, and his wife Rebecca, whom everyone called Riva. In Vilna I had heard a lot about Tcherikower and one of the few souvenirs I had brought home was an enormous tome published in Vilna in 1939 which he had conceived and edited—the third volume of the YIVO's Studies in History, over 800 pages of research studies, memoirs, and documents about the prehistory of socialism among Jews. Tcherikower was a man who had lived at the crossroads of history all his life. A disciple of Dubnow, he had been the prime mover in 1919 in Kiev in establishing an extraordinary archive of eyewitness accounts of the pogroms in the Ukraine during the Russian Revolution and civil war. (The archive had its own history, having traveled from Kiev to Berlin to Paris and eventually to New York.)

When I first met the Tcherikowers in 1940, he was not yet sixty, a small sprightly man with cropped graying hair, dark bushy eyebrows, the disposition of a merry child, and—as I soon learned—a limitless capacity for loving friendship. Riva, three years younger, had an unmistakable gift for motherliness, though they had no children. She had strong likes and dislikes: If she liked you, you became the beneficiary of her maternal affection. Soon I became a frequent guest in their home, almost part of their household. They didn't heal the ache in my heart for the Kalmanoviches, but they were the next-best substitute.

The largest single accretion of refugees to our community, about 200 or so, came from Poland on emergency visas which the State Department issued to them as political refugees. Because they were prominent Labor Zionists and Bundists in Poland, they were wanted by both the German security police and the Soviet security police. The idea for their rescue had originated with the Jewish Labor Committee, whose officers had turned for help to David Dubinsky, head of the International Ladies' Garment Workers' Union, then a powerful union on the American labor scene. Dubinsky, in turn, brought the proposal to William Green, head of the American Federation of Labor. Both managed to persuade Secretary of State Cordell Hull to authorize the issuance of several hundred emergency visas to those whose names the Jewish Labor Committee had provided.

These political refugees traveled a long and hazardous route to reach the United States. They had started out on foot from Warsaw shortly after the German invasion. As they moved eastward, they soon found themselves under Soviet rule. Some traveled disguised to elude the NKVD, the Soviet security police; nearly all had false identity papers. Sometimes the police picked up their tracks, sometimes informers sniffed them out and betrayed them. That was what had happened to the Bund's top leaders in Poland, Henryk Erlich and Victor Alter, each arrested in separate incidents in October 1939. For a long time no one knew what had become of them, but later they were reported to have been seen in a labor camp somewhere in Siberia. The refugees who successfully eluded the Soviet secret police continued their journey eastward. Some found visas waiting for them in Moscow at the American embassy. Then they embarked on the weeks-long grueling trip on the Trans-Siberian Railroad across the Urals to Vladivostok. From there they traveled to Japan. Some received their American visas in Kobe or Tokyo. Then they left for San Francisco.

Several of these political refugees came to work for the YIVO and became my friends. The suspenseful stories they told about their adventures—their escapes from police traps and their mishaps, the searches for incriminating documents, the police interrogations, and their conspiratorial adventures in getting and making forged papers—used to hold me enthralled. Years later I married Szymon Dawidowicz, one of those storytellers. Our romance no doubt had its origins in those stories, for, like Desdemona and Othello, I loved him for the dangers he had passed and he loved me that I did pity them. In Warsaw he had been business and production manager of a Bundist newspaper. At the YIVO he took charge of the production end of YIVO's publications. Before long, Weinreich trusted him to edit Yiddish manuscripts.

The most intriguing of the political refugees I met in those days was Shmuel Zygielbaum, whom everyone called Arthur, his Bundist party name. He had no connection at all with the YIVO, but worked next door, having become the business manager of *Di tsukunft* early in 1941. Even before he appeared on our premises at 425 Lafayette Street, his history was as thrilling to us as any adventure story. A leading Bundist City Council member in Lodz before the war, Zygielbaum had fled from Lodz in September 1939 to Warsaw. There, after the German occupation, he was co-opted to the Warsaw Judenrat (Jewish Council), created on German orders. When, in November, the Germans announced they would establish a ghetto in a few days, panic spread through the Jewish community. An enormous crowd gathered in front of the Judenrat building. In a fiery speech Zygielbaum exhorted them to resist the Germans.

The Germans abandoned their plan for a ghetto then, but they put a price on Zygielbaum's head. He went into hiding and two months later, the Socialist underground managed to smuggle him out of Poland. When he came to work in our midst, I was at first awed by his history of heroism, yet once I got to know him a little, he didn't seem to fit the heroic mold. Slender, of medium height, with an attractive face—a high wide forehead, finely contoured bones, a small mustache—he was a dapper man who enjoyed frivolous pursuits. In our close quarters, his reputation as a skirt-chaser spread quickly from office to office. None of us ever got to know what he was like in his serious moments. He stayed about a year in New York. In the spring of 1942 he went to London, to represent the underground Bund in the Polish National Council of the Polish Government-in-Exile in London.

The stream of refugees also brought my friend Rachel Golinkin and her sister, with whom I'd spent my last days in Vilna, and their elderly parents. They moved to Worcester, Massachusetts, where their father had obtained a rabbinical post. Rachel came once or twice to New York and stayed in my house. Later, when they were settled in Worcester, I visited them. Roman Jakobson and his wife reached New York early in 1941, having escaped from Norway after the German invasion. We had a reunion and he reminded me that in Copenhagen I had given him his first ten-dollar bill just before he left for Norway.

Late in January 1941, Regina Weinreich and her younger son Gabriel arrived in New York from Vilna, having come by way of the Soviet Union and Japan. Weinreich had used every high-ranking contact, including his old connections at the Rockefeller Foundation, to get visas for his wife and son. Regina, to whom I'd never been close, reported little, at least to me, about the people in Vilna I cared about, whom she had left in December 1940, or about conditions in Vilna, except to say that life was hard, that people managed and helped each other. I attributed her reticence to political caution, lest her words harm those whom she left behind. Years later, after Max's death, when I came to know her better, I became aware of the anguish she had concealed beneath her brisk matter-of-factness and the deep feelings of guilt that never ceased to afflict her for having left behind her mother, Stefania Szabad.

The East European refugees made it possible to expand the YIVO's research program and fill the pages of the *YIVO-Bleter*. They became the faculty for the Aspirantur, which Weinreich launched on short notice on November 31, 1940. In those days graduate students were harder to get than professors. Since October 29, young men were being called up for military service. For about three years, the Aspirantur struggled along with a small complement of students. For the first two years, I, too, was a research fellow, dabbling in my research on the Yiddish press in nineteenth-century England, in whatever free time I had. Each year we lost about half of our male students to the army or to defense jobs. In 1943, if I remember rightly, we gave up the effort, offering instead an array of courses to which people could come and go, without long-range commitment.

The depression that had possessed me on my return from Vilna had long since dissipated, though I had not yet entirely exorcised my guilt feelings for having fled to safety. Once again I took pleasure in waking up in the morning. Once more I felt I was the master of my life. When I came back to New York, I no longer lived at home, to my mother's deep dismay. My social circles, consisting of my New York friends of prewar days, my Albany friends, my Vilna friends, and my refugee friends, didn't always overlap, and I seldom brought them all together, for I didn't think they had much in common. As for myself, I felt that I belonged to two different worlds, and though I was at home in both, I was never quite content in either. Nor did I know, even within my own heart, where my deepest attachments lay.

The joys and satisfactions of my private life were darkened by the course of the war and the fate of the European Jews. Every day in the papers, at least in the Yiddish press, we read of new calamities and atrocities that the Germans inflicted on the Jews. In October 1940, just a year after Zygielbaum had made his impassioned speech urging passive resistance to ghettoization, the Germans actually created a ghetto in Warsaw and locked the Jews inside it. The *YIVO-Bleter* of November/December 1940 printed a small item about the ghetto and a map of Warsaw, on which I had drawn the boundaries of the ghetto, in accordance with the text of the German directive.

Britain continued to stand alone against the deadly bombing by the German air force. In November, the Germans stopped their raids on London and instead began bombing the industrial cities of the Midlands. Coventry was practically demolished. But improved British air defenses and nature's cooperation—shorter days and winter storms—soon succeeded in driving the Germans off. Meanwhile, Hitler had concluded a mutual assistance pact with Italy and Japan—the Berlin-Rome-Tokyo Axis, it was called. Then, one by one, Rumania, Hungary, and Bulgaria joined the Axis. Italy invaded Greece. We watched helplessly, as every country in Europe was being sucked into Hitler's orbit.

On December 29, 1940, in one of his famous radio "fireside chats," to which some 85 million people used to listen, Roosevelt warned the American people: "If Great Britain goes down, the Axis powers will control the continents of Europe, Asia, Africa, Australasia and the high seas—and they will be in a position to bring enormous military and naval resources against this hemisphere." On January 6, 1941, he sent Congress his proposal for Lend-Lease to the Allies, asking for authority and funds to manufacture war supplies "to be turned over to those nations which are now in actual war with aggressor nations." That talk boosted our morale. In it he articulated the hope for "a world founded upon four essential freedoms"—freedom of speech and expression, freedom of worship, freedom from want, and freedom from fear.

After the Lend-Lease Bill was introduced in Congress, the anti-interventionists launched a major campaign to defeat it. Most aggressive was the America First crowd, riddled with anti-Semites, whose spokesmen and supporters often singled out "Wall Street," "international bankers," or "international Jewry" as those who would plunge the country into war. But despite the venom that both the right and the left discharged into the public discussion, the urgency to help Britain and to build our own defenses had become apparent to most Americans. The House passed the Lend-Lease Bill early in February, 260 to 165. A month later the Senate passed it, 60 to 31.

Even so, Lend-Lease was poor comfort for what was happening across the Atlantic, where disaster followed upon disaster. In March, Bulgaria joined the Axis bloc. In April, the Germans invaded Yugoslavia. A German-Italian offensive in North Africa under General Erwin Rommel forced the British out of their outposts in Libya and back into Egypt. At the end of April, the Germans took Athens; Greece was divided into German and Italian zones of occupation. In May, the Germans invaded Crete. We didn't realize it, but Hitler was then ensuring the security of his southern flank in preparation for his next surprise move.

On May 27, Roosevelt proclaimed a state of unlimited national emergency and in June he ordered all German and Italian consulates in the United States to be closed. All this time the Communist-front American Peace Mobilization was engaged in a twenty-four-hour "perpetual peace vigil" in front of the White House, screaming that the Yanks were not coming. On June 21, they called off the vigil. Their timing turned out to be uncannily opportune.

The very next day, Tuesday, June 22, Germany invaded the Soviet Union. Like a murderer's knife penetrating his victim's heart, German armed forces plunged into Soviet-held territory along a 2,000-mile front. The Red Army was unprepared for the invasion and unprepared for war. It hadn't been adequately mobilized, even though, as we learned after the war, Churchill himself had sent a warning to Stalin about Hitler's imminent threat. Stalin's purges in the 1930s had decimated the Red Army's generals. What military equipment the Russians had was antiquated. They were short of weapons, ammunition, warm clothing.

The German invasion shocked us by its surprise, yet once we assimilated the news, we recognized its inevitability. We had always known that the Hitler-Stalin pact of August 1939 had been a cynical and temporary expedient on Hitler's part, into which Stalin had entered with equal cynicism. Now, overnight, the Soviet Union became just another one of Hitler's victims. Overnight the American Communists had to change their line. They had to change also the name of the American Peace Mobilization. That was easy. By renaming it the American People's Mobilization, they could keep the same acronym.

Overnight the Soviet Union became Britain's ally, a partner in the war against Germany. On July 12 both countries signed a mutual assistance pact. At the end of July, the Soviet Union reestablished diplomatic relations with Poland, now the Polish Government-in-Exile, and agreed to grant amnesty to all arrested and interned Polish citizens and to permit them to organize a Polish army. Such an army was formed, commanded by General Władysław Anders. Its units eventually left the Soviet Union and made their arduous way from Central Asia to the Middle East. They were later incorporated as the Second Polish Corps into the British Eighth Army.

The first good news which my refugee friends had about the Polish amnesty came in August with a report that Henryk Erlich had been freed from a Soviet prison. It was confirmed on September 22, when the *Forverts* received a cable signed by both Erlich and Victor Alter, which it published the next day. It read: "We continue the common struggle against Fascism and for Socialism. Convey our greetings to our comrades and friends." Their return address was Hotel Metropole, Moscow.

Meanwhile, the United States and Britain had organized a plan of aid for the Soviet Union and on October 1 a protocol was signed in Moscow, which provided that Britain and the United States would supply materials essential to Russian war efforts. At the end of October, the United States extended a credit of one billion dollars to the Soviet Union.

America was becoming more involved in defense preparations and aid to the Allies. In July Roosevelt had asked Congress for legislation to extend the length of conscription from twelve to eighteen months and in August Congress did so. The fury of the anti-interventionists intensified. On September 11, 1941, Charles A. Lindbergh, the aviator hero and the most popular speaker on the isolationist circuit, addressed an America First rally in Des Moines on the subject: "Who Are the War

Agitators?" He identified them readily: "The three most important groups who have been pressing this country toward war are the British, the Jewish, and the Roosevelt administration." The next day's papers were filled with denunciations of Lindbergh as an anti-Semite. He had not helped the isolationist cause, nor was it helped by unfolding events.

Just a week before Lindbergh's speech, a German submarine had fired at, but missed, an American destroyer. That had been the latest of a series of such episodes. The same evening that Lindbergh spoke in Des Moines, Roosevelt addressed the American people in a fireside radio chat. He told them that he had ordered the navy to shoot on sight at any German or Italian vessel within the Atlantic patrol zone. In October, to ensure that American military supplies going overseas to belligerents would reach their destinations, Roosevelt asked Congress to revise neutrality legislation so that American merchant ships could be armed. The bill passed the House by a generous margin, 250 to 138, and by a closer vote in the Senate.

By November, at the onset of the Russian winter, the Germans had advanced deep into Soviet territory. City after city had fallen like dominoes in a child's game. German armed forces took Vilna on June 24, Minsk on June 27, Riga on July 2. In July they captured Smolensk. At the end of August the Germans cut Leningrad's rail connections to the rest of the Soviet Union. The siege of Leningrad began. In mid-September, Kiev and all the Ukraine west of the Dnieper were in German hands. In October Orel, Bryansk, and Odessa fell. Our knowledge of Soviet geography improved, as we followed the disastrous course of the German conquest of Soviet cities. The German army in the north reached Moscow's outer fortifications; one unit, it was reported, could see the Kremlin's domes. In mid-October, Stalin ordered the government evacuated from Moscow to Kuibyshev, on the left bank of the Volga. The siege of Moscow had begun. At the southern end of the front, the Germans entered the Crimea. Over 1,500 factories, along with universities and scientific institutes, were moved from many cities in Russia proper eastward to the Urals, Siberia, the Volga, and Central Asia. By late October the Germans had taken nearly three million Russian prisoners.

The terrible war news had its Jewish parallels in the horrifying reports which we read in the Yiddish press about massacres of Jews wherever the Germans took over. News stories, based on underground reports received by the Polish Government-in-Exile in London, told about hunger and epidemics in the ghettos which the Germans had built in Polish cities. In October, London sources estimated that the Germans had murdered thousands of Jews in Poland and the Ukraine and gave specific figures for some cities. In Rumania, the native population didn't need help from the Germans to kill the Jews. They did it bloodily and of their own free will.

Wisps of news surfaced about Vilna. In July 1941, the *Forverts* published an item from the German-controlled radio in Warsaw to the effect that Germany's "expert on the Jewish question" was being sent from Warsaw to Vilna and Kovno "to solve the Jewish question." His name was Eichmann and he was said to have been in charge of Jewish matters when the Germans took over Austria in 1938. In August, we heard that a ghetto was being built in Vilna. In September, according to a Memel newspaper, the Germans were burning Jewish libraries in Lithuania. Two libraries were mentioned: the Mapu Library in Kovno and the Strashun Library in Vilna. In October, it was reported that the ghetto in Vilna had been completed. Ulica Niemiecka, German Street, which had been the heart of the Jewish retail trade, was now *Judenrein*, utterly without Jews. The news reawakened my tormented feelings. The nightmares returned. But the despair to which I had succumbed two years earlier gave way to explosive emotions of rage. The passion that devoured me was hatred for the Germans.

On December 7, 1941, a peaceful Sunday morning in Honolulu, at a little before 8 A.M., an armada of 353 bombers from six Japanese carriers attacked Pearl Harbor, destroying most of the American fleet within two hours. Tension between the United States and Japan had been intensifying in recent months and Washington had expected that Japan would attack an American target, but no one had foreseen that it would be Pearl Harbor or that it would come so soon and be so devastating. News of the attack reached Washington about twenty minutes later, where it was about 1:30 P.M. At about that time, an America First rally was getting under way in Pittsburgh. An hour or so later, when the speaker was deep into his talk, he was told that the Japanese government in Tokyo had announced a state of war against the United States and Great Britain. That was America First's last meeting.

On Monday, December 8, Roosevelt addressed a joint session of Congress. December 7, 1941, he said, was a date that would "live in infamy" and he asked Congress to declare that a state of war existed between the United States and the Japanese Empire. In the House, one die-hard isolationist cast a single dissenting vote against the declaration of war. The vote in the Senate was unanimous. The same day Great Britain declared war on Japan. Three days later, Germany and Italy declared war on the United States. Both houses of Congress then unanimously passed a joint resolution accepting the state of war "which has been thrust upon the United States."

For me it was a time of exhilaration, for I felt that at last we were participants in the struggle for the future of the world. The United States' presence, I was certain, would make it possible to prevail over Hitler. For the whole country it was a time of unaccustomed unity of purpose, high solemnity, and grim determination. Congress voted an appropriation of over ten billion dollars for America's defense and for Lend-Lease aid. Americans felt it was now their responsibility to rescue the world from the evil and murderous aggressions of the Germans and the Japanese. Soon the pro-Nazi German-American Bund was dissolved and, in an action of greater scope and little justifiability, the War Department, by order of the president, forcibly relocated some 110,000 Americans of Japanese ancestry living in the western states to internment camps in the interior.

The country geared up for war and buckled down to work. It had to make up for the effects of over a decade of disarmament and appeasement, the failure to have maintained an adequate military defense. Back in December 1940, Roosevelt had established an Office of Production Management to coordinate defense production and to make the United States "an arsenal of democracy." Since then many manufacturers had converted to war production, but the country's economy was still producing mostly civilian goods. After the shock of Pearl Harbor, war production moved into high gear. Factories retooled, workers retrained, work shifts expanded. Factories soon began operating on three eight-hour shifts. They were manufacturing mostly new products or new designs of familiar ones—planes, tanks, trucks, big guns, anti-aircraft weapons, bombs, radar, submarines, aircraft carriers, destroyers. Increasing numbers of women entered the industrial labor force, as more and more men were conscripted into the armed forces. Between 1940 and 1945, the United States produced 296,601 aircraft, 71,060 ships, and 86,388 tanks. In the first year after Pearl Harbor, when the war in Russia and in the Pacific was going badly for our side, American morale was boosted by the nation's ability to produce the goods that would provide the victory we were certain would eventually be ours.

The conversion from civilian to war production soon created shortages. In January 1942, the production of passenger cars was stopped for the duration of the war and in April so was the production of radios and phonographs. Refrigerators, vacuum cleaners, and washing machines ceased being manufactured. The mammoth demands of war production brought on shortages of steel, copper, tin, rubber, aluminum, leather. Soon we all enlisted in salvage drives, collecting old pots and pans, used tools and tea kettles, tin cans (emptied, rinsed, and flattened), toothpaste tubes, wastepaper. The most serious shortages affected people who depended on their cars. New ones were not being built; car rentals were frozen; tires became rationed. Gas was in shortest supply for civilians. People stayed home more, even though they had more money to spend than they'd had in a long time. They went to the movies instead, to dances and parties. They drank more.

Rationing went into effect in May 1942, when we received War Ration Book One, with twenty-eight ration coupons for sugar. Later there were ration stamps of different colors for butter, meats, coffee, canned foods, and even shoes. People grumbled and complained, but there were no real hardships. Cigarettes were in short supply, and though I smoked twenty to thirty cigarettes a day, I don't recall ever being out of them. At times, it was hard to get whisky. My friends and I were then drinking martinis; gin would do. Besides, a year in Vilna had accustomed me to vodka. We had plenty to eat, even when beef was scarce. When we ate out, as I began to do more frequently, we were seldom aware of shortages. In 1942 some restaurants, if I remember correctly, limited their customers to two cups of coffee. The stores were filled with goods. My Polish refugee friends, who had lived for a year under the Soviets, were bedazzled by the plenitude of food and the variety of merchandise in the shops.

Only the shortage of stockings bothered me. Silk stockings had become scarce even before Pearl Harbor and afterward we boycotted them. Nylons had just been introduced, but they, too, disappeared from the stores. In 1942 Du Pont needed nylon for parachutes. I was reduced to wearing rayon or cotton stockings. As soon as it got warm, I painted my legs with a liquid like suntan lotion. A bottle of Elizabeth Arden's Velva Leg Film cost one dollar and was good for twenty applications. Legs were important because hemlines were going up. Dress designers and manufacturers said they were doing it to save fabric. There was a war on. Men's trousers were being made without cuffs.

We began to buy war bonds and take part in civilian defense. In 1942, with the enemy everywhere on the offensive, we had air-raid drills, dim-outs, and blackout tests. Lights were ordered to be put out—house, street, traffic, and car lights. That summer night baseball was canceled. Still, in New York at any rate, we didn't take the idea of an air attack seriously. It was a far cry from the mood during the air-raid drills in Vilna in March 1939.

In 1942, two good friends, having completed their basic training, had gone on to officers' training—one into the air force, the other into the army's chemical warfare branch. They came to New York on leave with more money than they had ever had, because there was nothing to spend it on where they were stationed. We'd eat in expensive restaurants and sit in orchestra seats in the theater, enjoying our brief periods of afflu-ence.

Three days after Pearl Harbor, two great British battleships, the *Prince of Wales* and the *Repulse,* escorted by four destroyers, sailed out of Sin-gapore, heading north to halt a Japanese drive southward. In about two hours Japanese bombs and torpedos sank them all. Thereafter, the Japan-ese proceeded invincibly. Their forces took island after island and city after city on the mainland, just as easily as the Germans had taken the Russian cities. Hong Kong fell on Christmas Day 1941; Manila on January 2, 1942; the Solomon Islands later that month. In February the Japanese took Singapore and in March, after the battle of the Java Sea, captured Djakarta. The British evacuated Rangoon; the Japanese moved into Burma and closed the Burma Road. Now we had to learn the geography and geopolitics of the South Pacific.

Colonel Doolittle's daring bombing raid on Tokyo in April thrilled us, but it didn't stop the tide of Japan's conquests. That month American and Philippine forces on the Bataan Peninsula, which had been fighting a doomed last-ditch action, finally gave up. On May 6, the forces holding the island fort of Corregidor at the entrance to Manila Bay at last surrendered. Later that month, the Japanese took Mandalay. It was no longer just a name in a rowdy barrack-room ballad. In May, in the Battle of the Coral Sea, Allied naval and air forces halted a possible Japanese invasion of Australia and destroyed 100,000 tons of Japanese shipping between New Guinea and the Solomon Islands. In June, at the Battle of Midway, the United States forces drove off the Japanese attack. It was the first American victory in the Pacific and rendered a Japanese invasion of Hawaii unlikely. In August, Americans landed at Guadalca-nal, the largest of the Solomon Islands, and captured the Japanese airfields there, but the next day the Japanese sent reinforcements to their troops and counterattacked. Fierce and costly jungle warfare would continue for months.

In North Africa, the situation was tense that spring and summer of 1942. Rommel opened a new drive against Egypt in May and in a short time recaptured Tobruk from the British. By the end of June, the Germans had penetrated into Egyptian territory and reached El Alamein, only seventy miles from Alexandria. We knew that if the Germans would take Cairo, Palestine would easily fall into their hands. But the British managed to hold their positions at El Alamein and there at last they checked the German advance. During the summer the fighting ground to a halt, as both sides dug in and waited. In New York, we watched and waited, too.

The Russian front wasn't more encouraging. The Red Army's winter offensive had not succeeded in recapturing much territory from the Germans. In June 1942, the Germans returned to their conquering ways in a new offensive and started to push toward the Caucasus. After an eight-month siege, they seized Sevastopol on July 1, and then, in rapid succession, Voronezh and Rostov. In August, after taking Maikop, German forces crossed the Don River and opened their offensive against Stalingrad. On September 1, they crossed the Kerch Straits from Crimea and invaded the Caucasus. By mid-September, German forces had penetrated Stalingrad's defenses and were fighting block by block, building by building. But in October the Russians launched a pincer offensive to encircle and trap the Germans at Stalingrad. Then winter once more brought the fighting along the length of the Russian front to a standstill, except for the close combat that continued all winter in the streets of Stalingrad.

In those days we could take comfort only in the saturation bombing of Germany which the RAF launched on May 30, 1942. Over 1,000 planes crossed the sea to bomb Cologne, on which they dropped 1,445 tons of bombs. The next day another cohort of some 1,000 planes bombed Essen and the Ruhr. Later the RAF bombed Lubeck, Bremen, Berlin, Hamburg, Dortmund, Leipzig—"all on the Coventry scale," as Churchill later put it. I read of the destruction of those German cities with grim satisfaction.

CHAPTER 11

███████

New York 1942–1943: Death Watch

Hatred for the Germans consumed me that summer of 1942, as news about massacres and murders of the European Jews swelled. I read the papers even more obsessively than I had in 1939—the *New York Times* regularly, the New York *Herald Tribune* occasionally, and *PM,* a lively, brash, left-liberal paper that had begun to appear in New York in June 1940. In the YIVO, we read all the Yiddish papers, even the Communist *Freiheit.* We received bulletins and periodicals from the Jewish Labor Committee, the newly organized Bund in New York, and Polish exile groups. Among the magazines, the *Contemporary Jewish Record,* a bimonthly published by the American Jewish Committee, provided the most extensive English-language coverage. It printed substantial news chronicles based on the dispatches of the Jewish Telegraphic Agency (JTA) and articles by firsthand witnesses of the events in Europe, many of them translated from the Yiddish press. Being at the YIVO, I probably knew more than most other American Jews about what was happening to the European Jews.

When Weinreich wanted to publish a documented account of the German treatment of the Jews in occupied Poland, he turned to an old friend from Warsaw, Shlomo Mendelsohn, a political refugee, who'd been a Bundist educator and journalist. Mendelsohn had access to the reports sent by the underground Bund in Poland. He also gathered, bit by bit, the scraps and snippets of news from all sources, including official German records—directives, communiqués, and their press. He produced a chilling account of conditions in the ghettos in German-occupied Poland, with evidence of the hunger, disease, and mortality to which the Jews were succumbing, of the forced labor and murderous violence, the depredations and killings that had become their fate. When he read the paper at the YIVO's conference on January 11, 1942, people wept. We published it in the *YIVO-Bleter* and also as a pamphlet in English and Yiddish.

Early in June 1942, the most definitive news yet reached us about what was happening to the Polish Jews. It was a report which the underground Bund in Warsaw had sent through clandestine channels to the Polish Government-in-Exile in London. The two Jewish members of the Polish National Council, Shmuel Arthur Zygielbaum, who not long before had left New York, and Ignacy Schwarzbart, a leading Polish Zionist, transmitted the contents of the report to General Władysław Sikorski, the Polish prime minister, and also to British government authorities and the BBC. On June 10 a summary appeared in the *New York Times*. More than thirty years later, I included that report in a book of mine, *A Holocaust Reader,* a collection of basic documents about the murder of the European Jews.

The report estimated that at the time of writing—May 1942—the Germans had murdered 700,000 Polish Jews since June 1941, when they had invaded Soviet-held Poland. Cities where the Jewish population had been slaughtered were enumerated with the local statistics of murder. In Vilna, 50,000 Jews were said to have been murdered in November 1941; only 12,000 remained. The report also told of the annihilation of the Jews in that part of Poland which the Germans had occupied since 1939. In a place called Chełmno, people were being gassed, ninety at a time, in vans equipped with gas chambers. Later we learned that those were mobile gassing units with which the Germans were still experimenting. In Lublin, some 25,000 Jews were taken away in sealed railroad cars to an "unknown destination." Not a single Jew was said to have remained in Lublin. In Warsaw, on the night of April 17–18, the Gestapo had "organized a blood bath in the ghetto," seizing more than fifty Jewish men and women from their homes and murdering them on their doorsteps.

The German government was fulfilling Hitler's prophecy to annihilate all the European Jews, the report's authors wrote. They asked the Polish government to urge the Allied powers to adopt a policy of retribution against German citizens and fifth columnists living in their countries. "This is the only possibility," they concluded, "of rescuing millions of Jews from certain annihilation."

Within a few weeks, those terrible tidings were printed and reprinted in England, the United States and Canada, and in Palestine. We heard skeptical voices; people suspected the statistics were exaggerated. Their enormity made it hard for us to grasp their full implications, but I believed the figures. Still, my refugee friends continued to think—how could they not?—that their families and friends were still alive. I, too, thinking of Rivele and Kalmanovich and my other friends in the Vilna ghetto, visualized them suffering cold, hunger, sickness, gripped by fear and despondency. I didn't have so luridly inventive an imagination as to envision anything beyond the misfortunes which the history of earlier wars and enemy occupations had made familiar.

Nor did we try to make sense of the incoming information. No one I knew could understand why or how these murders were being committed. In the midst of a war, why should the Germans distract themselves with the Jews? We had known for years that the Germans were fanatical anti-Semites. But we hadn't known, until now, that they were murderers, mass murderers. The terrible news about the Jews fueled the explosive energy of my rage against the Germans. It was past my fathoming how even fanatical anti-Semites could become mass murderers, freeing themselves from the moral and religious restraints that had somehow held killer instincts in check.

Whether or not American Jews believed the statistics of murder, everyone acknowledged that Jews were being massacred on an unprecedented scale. Jewish organizations deliberated about what to do. A mass meeting at Madison Square Garden on July 11, sponsored by the American Jewish Congress, drew an overflow crowd of some 20,000. The big-name speakers included Governor Herbert H. Lehman, Mayor Fiorello LaGuardia, Senator Henry Cabot, William Green of the AFL, and Bishop Francis J. McConnell, besides Rabbi Stephen S. Wise and other Jewish spokesmen. Messages came from Churchill and Roosevelt. Roosevelt declared that the American people would "hold the perpetrators of these crimes to strict accountability in a day of reckoning which will surely come." Demonstrations and meetings were held also in Los Angeles, Boston, Chicago, Cleveland, and St. Paul, and probably in other places I hadn't read about. Rabbis called for fast days and memorial services.

Thereafter, the stream of terrible news about the Jews in German-occupied countries flowed relentlessly. From Soviet sources we learned that German SS troops, shortly after their invasion of Soviet-held territory in June 1941, had murdered thousands upon thousands of Jews in Minsk, Vitebsk, Kiev, Kharkov, Riga, Vilna, and countless other cities. These accounts corroborated the authenticity of the Bund report of June.

In July devastating news began to arrive about Warsaw. It was reported that old people were being killed, while able-bodied Jews were being deported "eastward to build fortifications for the Germans." Two weeks later, we read that Adam Czerniaków, head of Judenrat in the Warsaw ghetto, had committed suicide, because he had refused to approve the deportation of 100,000 Jews. It would take a long time before we realized that "deportation to the East" was a euphemism, that those hundreds of thousands of "deported" Jews had been sent to their deaths in specially constructed killing sites. We didn't yet know the name of Treblinka, where most of the Warsaw Jews were gassed. Nor had we yet heard of Auschwitz, Bełżec, or Majdanek.

On August 21, 1942, Roosevelt opened his press conference by reading a warning to the enemy nations. Obviously in response to the avalanche of news about the German crimes against the Jews, he reiterated a declaration which nine occupied European nations had issued the previous January. They had then stated that one of their principal war aims would be the punishment of the Germans for the barbaric crimes which they were committing against civilian populations. To this Roosevelt added that the United States had been aware of these crimes and welcomed further reports "from any trustworthy source" as evidence of such crimes. After the Allied victory, the United States would make appropriate use of this evidence against the Germans: "It seems only fair that they should have this warning: that the time will come when they shall have to stand in courts of law, in the very countries which they are now oppressing, and answer for their acts."

My friends and I were not impressed. We didn't think the German barbarians deserved fair warning or trials in courts of law. They were not entitled to be treated as members of a civilized society. I burned with an unquenchable passion for revenge. I wanted to see Germany bombed to dust, its cities obliterated, its people ravaged with fire and sword.

In September and October the bad news continued to pour in. Only 100,000 Jews were said to have remained in Warsaw. We learned from Shlomo Mendelsohn that Menahem Linder, my friend from Warsaw, had been murdered in Warsaw in April. There was no other information. He was the first person murdered by the Germans with a name and a face I could identify. I tortured myself with the thought that I, the last one of us at the YIVO to have seen him, had left him there to be murdered. Much later we learned that he had been one of some fifty Jews seized by the Gestapo late Friday night, April 17, 1942, in the "blood bath" mentioned in the Bund report released in London last June. On that bloody Friday, the Gestapo had rounded up printers and journalists who they suspected were producing the ghetto's underground press. Menahem had been shot in front of his house on Leszno 50. We knew nothing of the fate of his wife, Mira.

That fall of 1942, the Jewish Anti-Fascist Committee, a newly formed Soviet agency then headquartered in Kuibyshev, released a series of eyewitness accounts of German brutality against the Jews in Galicia and concluded that less than half of the Jewish population in the cities of Lwów, Tarnopol, and Stanisławów had survived. In November, the *Jewish Frontier,* a monthly Labor Zionist journal published in New York, put out a special issue entitled "Jews under the Axis." It contained eyewitness accounts of the slaughter of the Jews based largely on reports from underground Zionist sources in Poland. But the horrors reported in the *Jewish Frontier* had already been surpassed by more recent and more terrible tidings.

On November 24, the Polish Government-in-Exile released the substance of a firsthand report it had received from a trusted courier of the Polish underground state. His name, we later learned, was Jan Karski. He had told them that one million Polish Jews had already been murdered and that Himmler had ordered the annihilation of half of the surviving Jews in Poland by the end of 1942. As of October, when he had left Poland, only 40,000 Jews remained in the Warsaw ghetto, a terrible place to which he had been taken by two leaders of the Jewish underground. Other cities no longer had any Jews at all. The courier brought the first news of a death camp located at Bełżec, about 100 miles east of Warsaw. There the Jews were brought to be murdered in mass by quicklime and asphyxiation. The day after Karski's report was released, another report was released, which had come via Switzerland, to the effect that Hitler planned to murder some three and a half million to four million Jews in territory occupied by the Germans "to resolve once for all the Jewish question."

Those last days in November and early December were like a protracted Yom Kippur, a time of fasting and mourning which we all observed. It was as if the Jews in the United States were reenacting the events in the Book of Esther, when the Jews learned of the king's decree to destroy them: "there was great mourning among the Jews, and fasting, and weeping, and wailing; and many lay in sackcloth and ashes." Memorial services were held in synagogues and churches all over the country and on radio networks. The rabbis decreed a fast day. Across the nation, two-minute periods of silence were observed. In New York, half a million workers stopped work for ten minutes.

On December 8, 1942, a delegation from six Jewish organizations saw Roosevelt and left with him a memorandum describing the atrocities the Germans had committed against the European Jews. They asked him to do what he had already said he would do: hold the Germans to strict accountability for their crimes and set up a commission to gather and study the evidence of such crimes. On December 16, Premier Sikorski, then in the United States, visited Roosevelt and presented him with the Polish government's report on the German massacres of Jews and Poles.

Meanwhile, on December 9, 1942, Count Edward Raczyński, minister of state for foreign affairs in Sikorski's cabinet, addressed a diplomatic note to the Allied governments, summarizing the contents of the Polish courier's report and urging the Allied nations not only to condemn the barbarities, but also to find means "of offering the hope that Germany might be effectively restrained from continuing to apply its methods of mass extermination." At this time, as they had in June 1942, cynics in the British government and among all the Polish Jewish refugees I knew intimated that the Polish initiative was intended to lay to rest the persistent charges of anti-Semitism in the Polish Government-in-Exile, in the Polish underground in occupied Poland, and in the Polish army. But whatever the reason for Poland's uncharacteristic interest in its Jewish citizens, Raczyński's intervention proved effective.

The British Foreign Office, the State Department, and the Soviet foreign minister issued a declaration on December 17, the first public and official acknowledgment by the Allied nations of the mass murder of the Jews. This was its text:

> The attention of the Governments of Belgium, Czechoslovakia, Greece, Luxembourg, the Netherlands, Norway, Poland, the United States of America, the United Kingdom of Great Britain and Northern Ireland, the Union of Soviet Socialist Republics and Yugoslavia, and of the French National Committee has been drawn to numerous reports from Europe that the German authorities, not content with denying to persons of Jewish race in all the territories over which their barbarous rule has been extended the most elementary human rights, are now carrying into effect Hitler's oft repeated intention to exterminate the Jewish people in Europe. From all the occupied countries Jews are being transported, in conditions of appalling horror and brutality, to Eastern Europe. In Poland, which has been made the principal Nazi slaughterhouse, the ghettos established by the German

invaders are being systematically emptied of all Jews except a few highly skilled workers required for war industries. None of those taken away are ever heard of again. The able-bodied are slowly worked to death in labor camps. The infirm are left to die of exposure and starvation or are deliberately massacred in mass executions. The number of victims of these bloody cruelties is reckoned in many hundreds of thousands of entirely innocent men, women and children.

The above mentioned Governments and the French National Committee condemn in the strongest possible terms this bestial policy of cold-blooded extermination. They declare that such events can only strengthen the resolve of all freedom loving peoples to overthrow the barbarous Hitlerite tyranny. They reaffirm their solemn resolution to ensure that those responsible for these crimes shall not escape retribution, and to press on with the necessary practical measures to this end.

I sorrowed for the murdered European Jews, even if I didn't know the names of the people for whom I was mourning. Still the sorrow I felt did not interfere with the discharge of my family obligations or dilute the devotion I lavished on my work, nor was my personal life without its joys and pleasures even in those days of communal sadness. Somehow I felt as if I were living in disconnected universes—in a real world of normal obligations and pastimes and in a phantasmagoric world of my fevered imagination, in which I partook of its agony and death as if it were my real world.

Nor did mourning for the European Jews distract me or my refugee friends from following the course of the war. Only Hitler's defeat, we thought, could ensure the survival of the Jews. But in those days that defeat didn't seem likely to happen soon. All Europe was then Hitler's fortress, an impregnable empire that extended from the Atlantic Wall to the very gates of Leningrad, Moscow, and Stalingrad. Everywhere on the battlefields the Allies were losing to the Axis powers. Time seemed to stand still then, for there was nothing to look forward to. American morale was then at its lowest point since the war began. For over a year, Stalin had been pressing the British and the Americans to open a second front in Europe, but the Western Allies were not yet prepared to pay the costs in human life that such an offensive would entail. They were waiting to build up their military strength, to replenish their arsenals, depleted by a decade of disarmament.

Just when the revelations about the murder of the European Jews were agitating us, the tide of the war began to turn, distracting us, if only intermittently, from the news about the Jews. In North Africa, late in October 1942, the British Eighth Army, under General Bernard L.

Montgomery, launched a massive attack against Rommel's forces. Within days, Rommel lost 60,000 men, besides tanks and guns, and had started on one of the longest retreats in military history. Just as he was trying to establish a holding position, the British and Americans carried out an amazing landing on the North African coast on November 8, 1942. Protected by the U. S. and Royal navies, 35,000 American troops disembarked in Casablanca, 39,000 more in Oran, and a combined force of 33,000 Britons and Americans landed in Algiers, all under the command of a general we hadn't heard of before—Dwight D. Eisenhower. But the Germans, having been reinforced, persisted. Bitter fighting continued for months. By May, the Allied pincer movement, closing in from Casablanca and Cairo, at last trapped the German and Italian forces in Tunisia, who surrendered on May 12. That was the Western Allies' first major victory.

In the Pacific, bitter jungle warfare between American marines and Japanese forces was still being fought on Guadalcanal. In February 1943, the Japanese finally gave up and evacuated the island, leaving behind some 24,000 dead. The American losses were 1,750. That was the first land victory the Americans had won over the Japanese. In March, the Fifth U.S. Air Force destroyed a powerful Japanese convoy trying to reinforce Japanese garrisons on New Guinea, but Tokyo was still a long way off.

On the other side of the world, Russian forces had succeeded in encircling the Germans in Stalingrad, but fierce fighting continued. Finally, on February 2, 1943, the decimated German army surrendered amid the ruins of Stalingrad. German losses were about 300,000, Russian losses not much smaller.

After its victory at Stalingrad, the Red Army launched a westward drive, recapturing Belgorod and Kharkov in February. But the Germans fought doggedly and in March took back both cities. Not before the summer of 1943 could the Russians maintain their offensive against the Germans. By that time they were better prepared, the beneficiaries of a staggering amount of military supplies which the United States had meanwhile shipped—4,100 planes, 138,000 motor vehicles, steel, and industrial machinery for Soviet arms production.

Under Max Weinreich's direction, the YIVO in New York expanded rapidly. Its staff increased. Its library grew and improved in quality. Besides *YIVO-Bleter* and *Yidishe shprakh,* we published a number of books, mostly in history. Under Weinreich's supervision, I completed a comprehensive bibliography of YIVO's publications from 1925 to 1941, using the Library of Congress classification system, which Weinreich and I adapted to fit the needs of our Jewish material. Offset from my 211-page typescript, containing over 2,500 items, it was published in January 1943. Later that year, we began to put out a bilingual house organ, of which I became managing editor.

The space at 425 Lafayette Street had become inadequate and in the fall of 1942, the YIVO purchased a fine four-story building at 531–535 West 123rd Street, between Broadway and Amsterdam Avenue. (It no longer exists; it was razed in the mid-1950s to make way for a complex of high-rise apartment houses.) The building had once been the home of the Jewish Theological Seminary of America, which, having outgrown it, was now located across the street in a much larger red-brick quadrangular structure, with a tower over its entrance on Broadway. Just as the Seminary, in an earlier time, had moved uptown to assert its Americanness and its separateness from the East European orthodoxy of the Lower East Side, so the YIVO's uptown move symbolized its distinctiveness from the immigrant Yiddishist institutions in their shabby downtown quarters.

The move gave us room to grow. The library occupied the whole top floor; the expanding archival collections were located in the basement, which had been equipped with temperature controls. A large auditorium, a conference room, and administrative offices were on the main floor. The research operations occupied the second floor—offices, classrooms, and a lecture hall. Shortly after we moved in, we held an exhibit of Roman Vishniac's photographs of Eastern Europe. Afterward, the photographs remained with us to adorn the corridors of the building.

Max Weinreich strove to make the YIVO in the United States part of the universe of scholarship which was inhabited not only by the Jewish Theological Seminary, but also by Columbia University. It was his ambition to demonstrate to educated American Jews and to the community of American scholars that Yiddish was not just a vernacular of plain folk and women, as seventeenth-century Yiddish books used to advertise themselves, but was a tongue fit for scholars and intellectuals. He wanted to show that Yiddish could serve as a medium of high scholarship and that the language and its culture were themselves suitable subjects for high scholarship. Accommodating the principles of the Vilna YIVO to the realities of Jewish life in the United States, he succeeded in his ambition in a surprisingly short time. Even on alien soil, his willpower made the difference. He fought the paralysis of depression. By dint of his will, he made the YIVO in New York a memorial to the YIVO in Vilna.

Vilna was never out of his mind. Addressing some 2,000 people at the YIVO conference on January 8, 1943, he opened his talk with these words: "How else can one begin a report about YIVO activity in a year of destruction except by first confessing publicly to a sense of burning shame for living in peace in this blessed land, in security and in plenty, at a time when the murderers' long knives have already butchered so many of our brothers and sisters across the sea."

That YIVO conference adopted a resolution asking "all people of learning" to awaken the conscience of the world to the fate of the Jews. With that authorization, Weinreich prepared a petition to be addressed to President Roosevelt and to be signed by America's leading scholars and college administrators, many of whom he had by now come to know. I don't remember how many professors we canvassed, but I think that almost all of them signed the petition. Some later became members of YIVO's Academic Council. On March 22, 1943, we sent the petition, with its impressive list of 283 signatories from over 100 of America's top academic institutions, to President Roosevelt. This was its text:

Mr. President:

The undersigned scholars and scientists have become acquainted with the statement submitted to you on December 8, 1942, about the heinous crimes committed by the Nazis and their satellites against the defenseless Jewish population of the subjugated countries, above all in Eastern Europe. With pain and horror we have read that through planned starvation in slave reservations and through premeditated mass murder, almost two million Jewish men, women, and children have already met their death, and that Hitler has now issued an edict calling for the total extermination of the over five million Jews who may still be alive in Nazi-dominated Europe. Whoever knows Hitler's record will see the brutal reality of this threat unless immediate and effective action is taken.

Mr. President: We appeal to you to speak and to act.

We appeal to you to find the means to let every German know what is being perpetrated by his rulers and to warn the German people that for generations this guilt will rest upon them unless the hands of the murderers are stayed.

We appeal to you as soon and as effectively as possible to apply hitherto

unused methods to save the millions of European Jews doomed to death
by the enemy of civilization.

For all of his intellectual brilliance, Weinreich was just as helpless as
the rest of us when it came to practical suggestions on how to save the
Jews. He could only propose "hitherto unused methods," hoping that
Roosevelt's advisers would know how to implement his suggestion.

The flow of bad news did not let up during those months. Every day the
papers brought fresh statistics of death and destruction. Every day we
learned that towns and cities which Jews had once populated in Poland,
Lithuania, Russia, the Ukraine, Rumania no longer had any Jews left
at all. It was hard to assimilate this information, to absorb the statistics
of anonymous masses slaughtered. We couldn't grasp how so many
people could have been killed. Nor could we understand why. What
use was it to the Germans?

Early in February 1943 the Bund in New York received information
that the Bund in the Warsaw ghetto together with several Zionist
groups had formed a resistance organization, that they had obtained
weapons, and had actually battled the Germans in the ghetto in January.
The news electrified us. Yet I saw it then as a sign of ultimate despair,
an evocation of Masada. There, in 73 C.E., the beleaguered Jewish
fighters against Rome chose mass suicide instead of captivity. In 1943,
the Western Allies, with the enormous resources of the United States,
didn't yet dare to take on the entrenched strength of the Germans on
the European continent. What chance did the ghetto Jews have? About
a month later, Zygielbaum in London released a report from the Warsaw underground sent after that January battle. It was published in the
Forverts: "Alarm the world. Appeal to the Pope. The few hundred
thousand surviving Jews in Poland are in danger of being annihilated
soon. Only you can save us."

At times, when I woke after a fitful night, I thought that the news
about the European Jews was only a bad dream, a hallucination. Other
times, I'd be seized by the irrational notion that we were witnessing the
end of the world. Not our world here in New York, but the world from
which I had fled in 1939. In those moments, I'd try to imagine the
emptiness of Vilna's Jewish quarter with its crooked little streets. Vilna
had never in its history had a ghetto, but the Germans had made one
in those little streets. I tried to picture warfare in the streets of the

Warsaw ghetto. Instead I summoned up the memory of the bustle on Warsaw's Jewish streets, as I had seen them aswarm with people, buying and selling, bargaining, shouting, laughing. The end of that world had come without portents or prophecies, without visions or revelations. None of us had seen the heavens turn black, but in Europe I knew the earth was red with Jewish blood.

We were aware of our impotence. Powerless to avenge the murder of the Jews, we fell a-cursing like Hamlet unable to avenge his father's murder. Perhaps I'd come to believe that our curses had magical incantatory properties, that our damning words would destroy the Germans. The intensity of our hatred for them had an energizing effect. It roused us from despair. Anger, rage, fury were our antidotes against sorrow and despair.

All over the United States Jews went to mass meetings and public demonstrations, even children. In Chicago, on January 8, Jewish schoolchildren protested at the City Council in the name of the murdered Jewish children in Europe. In New York, the Jewish Education Committee organized memorial services at Mecca Temple (now the City Center) for some 3,000 Jewish schoolchildren. The American Jewish Congress called another mass meeting in Madison Square Garden on March 1, co-sponsored with the Church Peace Union and the AFL and the CIO, then separate organizations. Twenty thousand people filled the Garden and about 75,000 were massed outside, listening to the speeches on a loudspeaker system. An eleven-point rescue program which the Jewish organizations had worked out jointly was adopted. It offered some practical and realizable ideas—establishing sanctuaries in the United States and elsewhere, for instance.

Other proposals seemed utopian—such as asking the United States to revise its immigration laws and Britain to open the gates of Palestine, even though they'd resisted doing so for over a decade. But even if both governments would declare that an emergency situation existed and even if they would suspend their rules and regulations, we all knew in our hearts that the key proposal on which the rescue of the Jews hinged was utterly futile, an illusory expectation. The Jewish organizations wanted the Allies to urge the pope, the neutral governments, and the governments friendly to the Germans to ask the Germans to release the Jews and let them emigrate. How could anyone believe that Hitler would do that?

Yet just two days after the Madison Square meeting, the State Department announced that the United States and Britain would hold a joint meeting in an effort to find a solution to the refugee problem. They were obviously responding to public pressure in the wake of the terrible news about the murder of the Jews. With the unquenchable optimism that Jewish history has seldom justified, Jews suddenly felt hopeful. Perhaps, after all, something substantial would be done to save those Jews who could still be saved.

In the midst of the landslide of disastrous news, William Green, head of the AFL, jolted us with an altogether different tragedy. In response to his persistent inquiries about Henryk Erlich and Victor Alter, the two Bundist leaders who had been released from Soviet prison in September 1941 but had shortly thereafter again disappeared from sight, Soviet Ambassador Maxim Litvinov in Washington informed Green that both Erlich and Alter had been executed by the Soviet government. For well over a year, efforts had been made at the highest levels to learn of their whereabouts. In 1942, when Wendell Willkie visited the Soviet Union as Roosevelt's personal representative, he spoke to Stalin about them; Stalin assured him that they were both well. But Stalin lied. They'd long ago been murdered and Stalin knew it.

The official Soviet explanation for their execution was so bizarre that it triggered my remembrances of the Moscow trials of the 1930s. Erlich and Alter were executed, according to Litvinov, "for active subversive work against the Soviet Union. . . . including appeals to the Soviet troops to immediately conclude peace with Germany." Only the Communist Party and its mouthpiece, the *Daily Worker,* slavishly accepted the preposterous Soviet charges; Earl Browder, the party's boss, insisted that Erlich and Alter had been part of a plot to destroy the Soviet Union.

The news of this political murder deepened the political differences within the Jewish community and the labor movement, even among liberals. When David Dubinsky's International Ladies' Garment Workers organized a protest meeting, people high in government circles were rumored to have pressured Dubinsky to cancel the meeting on the ground that it was impolitic. Russia was our ally. But Dubinsky stood firm and the meeting took place on Tuesday, March 30, at Mecca Temple. About 3,500 people filled the hall. I was there, too. The speakers included Dubinsky and Abe Cahan, longtime editor of the *Forverts,* Mayor LaGuardia, William Green, and the CIO's secretary-treasurer James Carey. Sidney Hillman, head of the Amalgamated

Workers' Union, boycotted the meeting and Wendell Willkie, who'd been hoodwinked by Stalin, found some excuse not to come. The left-wing CIO unions denounced the meeting. Joe Curran, head of the National Maritime Union and a pro-Communist stalwart, had reportedly threatened to beat up Carey for taking part.

The Erlich-Alter murders and the controversy surrounding them were just an interlude in the relentlessly unfolding drama of the mass murder of the European Jews. In March and April memorial meetings and assemblies were taking place across the United States. The Senate and the House of Representatives adopted resolutions condemning the Nazi atrocities. A spectacular pageant called *We Will Never Die,* written by Ben Hecht and produced by Billy Rose, staged by Moss Hart, with a musical score by Kurt Weill, was given two performances in Madison Square Garden. On April 14, some 20,000 people in the Chicago Stadium heard a host of speakers, including the governor and a senator from Illinois. The Jewish organizations jointly submitted their program for the rescue of the European Jews to the top American and British officials who were to attend the Bermuda Refugee Conference, to open on April 19.

On April 8 a brief JTA news item "from somewhere in Europe" told of three large concentration camps—in Lublin, Auschwitz, and Birkenau—where the Nazis were sending the Jews of Poland for forced labor. It was the first time that we heard the name of Auschwitz. Even then, after the flood of news about vast numbers of Jews who were murdered, even after Karski's report about a death camp at Bełzec, the press and its readers, all of us, still clung to the belief that the Jews were being sent to forced-labor camps.

On Thursday, April 22, the third day of the Passover festival, the *Forverts* ran two banner headlines:

NAZIS SLAUGHTER LAST JEWS IN WARSAW
SECRET RADIO SAYS NAZIS BUTCHER LAST 35,000 JEWS

Datelined Stockholm, the story reported that two nights earlier, on the eve of Passover, the Swedes had picked up a broadcast from SWIT, believed to be an underground Polish radio operating out of Warsaw. This is what they heard: "The last 35,000 Jews in the Warsaw ghetto are condemned to death. Warsaw is once again deafened with the bursts of gunfire. People are being murdered. Women and children are defending themselves with their bare hands. Save us. . . ." At that point the radio went dead.

After two days the Polish Government-in-Exile reported that the Jews were engaged in an armed conflict with the Germans in the Warsaw ghetto. That was all. Something terrible was happening in the Warsaw ghetto, but we didn't know exactly what.

Most of my refugee friends came from Warsaw and nearly all still had family there—wives, children, parents, sisters, and brothers, to whom they used to send money and food packages. Since the summer of 1942, none had heard directly from family members in Warsaw. The news from Warsaw thereafter had been ominous. Most of the Warsaw Jews had disappeared into a void. Were they working as forced laborers somewhere to the east? Or had they been murdered? Now, it seemed, there were still Jews living in the Warsaw ghetto, Jews at war with the Germans. But how many and for how long? Every day, while my refugee friends waited to learn what was happening, the atmosphere grew tenser. All of us at the YIVO—including the Americans on staff—became caught up in their anxieties. For my part, I dreaded the news that we anticipated. I tried to visualize a battle in the Warsaw ghetto between Jews and Germans, but the only images I could summon up were Blakean, apocalyptic. The Germans were satanic, the forces of evil in the world.

While we waited for news, the Synagogue Council, an organization representing Orthodox, Conservative, and Reform Jews, announced that a six-week period of mourning for the murdered European Jews would begin on April 26, the seventh day of Passover, with memorial services in the synagogues. Christian churches had designated Sunday, May 2, for church observance as a "Day of Compassion." Meanwhile the Bermuda Refugee Conference had ended—ended in nothing for the European Jews.

At that time, Chaim Zhitlowsky, the Yiddishist philosopher and ideologue whom my father had once admired, died while on a lecture tour. It was comforting then, when we were confronting mass murder and mass suicide, to read of the natural death of one person who had died amidst his admirers in the fullness of time, at seventy-eight.

On May 12, two brief news items in the *Forverts,* one from Stockholm, the other from London, summarized a SWIT radio broadcast to the effect that the Warsaw ghetto had been "completely liquidated." The next day, we were shocked to read that Arthur Zygielbaum had died in London; the day after, the news was amended to say that he had committed suicide. No one knew why; it was rumored that he'd become depressed on learning that his wife and children had been murdered. On May 14, the New York Bund received reports about the uprising in the Warsaw ghetto which Zygielbaum had mailed before his suicide. That material began to circulate among the Bund's members.

On May 18, we read in a JTA item from London that Zygielbaum had killed himself as an act of protest against the world's indifference to the massacre of the Jews. He left a letter for the president and prime minister of the Polish Government-in-Exile. The *Forverts* printed the text of his suicide note on June 2, the *New York Times* on June 4. Zygielbaum charged the Germans with the murder of the Polish Jews, but accused the Allied governments, including the Polish Government-in-Exile, of not having done enough to rescue the Jews from the murderous hands of the Germans. Then he wrote:

> I cannot be silent. I cannot live while the remnants of the Jewish population of Poland, of whom I am a representative, are perishing. My friends in the Warsaw ghetto died with weapons in their hands in the last heroic battle. It was not my destiny to die together with them, but I belong to them and in their mass graves.
>
> By my death I wish to make my final protest against the passivity with which the world has witnessed and permitted the annihilation of the Jewish people.
>
> I know how little human life is worth today, but since I could not do anything during my lifetime, perhaps by my death I will have a share in dispelling the indifference of those who now, at the last moment, can still rescue the few surviving Polish Jews. My life belongs to the Jewish people and I therefore give it to them.

Zygielbaum's suicide astonished his friends and comrades, even those who had known him longer and better than I, who had seen only his frivolous side. None had been prepared for this noble death. After Jan Karski published his memoir, *Story of a Secret State,* I understood the enormity of the guilt which tormented Zygielbaum that last year of his life. Karski had given him the verbatim message which the two Polish Jewish leaders in Warsaw had sent to the Jewish leaders in the West. "Let them accept no food or drink, let them die a slow death while the world is looking on. Let them die. This may shake the conscience of the world." Zygielbaum had been a close friend of the Bundist in Warsaw who talked to Karski. He surely had taken that message as a charge to him personally. He faithfully carried out the mission the Polish Jews had imposed upon him.

At night I dreamed dark dreams about the Warsaw ghetto; in the daytime my head was often filled with monstrous visions. But soon the contours of the real events began to emerge. A few hundred Jews, members of an armed resistance organization, backed by the still surviving ghetto Jews, had opened fire on the SS forces who had entered the ghetto on April 19. The Germans had come to deport the remaining Jews and to liquidate the ghetto. That evening was the night of the first Passover seder. On the first day of the fighting, the Jewish combatants turned back the Germans. Then the Germans brought in reinforcements and heavy weapons. The fighting continued for weeks. In May, combat in the ghetto turned into house-by-house fighting. Then the Germans set fire to the ghetto street by street, building by building. There were not many survivors. Some 2,000 Jews were said to have been executed, 3,000 burned to death, and some 14,000 deported. The Jews had killed about 1,000 Germans and wounded about 2,300 more.

On June 19, the Jewish Labor Committee held a meeting in Carnegie Hall to honor the fallen Jews of the Warsaw ghetto. We went and we wept, yet there was pride in what the Polish Jews had done. For the first time anywhere during the German occupation of Europe, a civilian population had taken up arms against their German oppressors. Not just any civilian population, but the most oppressed, the most helpless, the most desperate.

In the next weeks, Bundist and Zionist underground reports from Warsaw reaching the West gave details of the fighting and listed the names of the dead and the few survivors. The people I knew had lost children, wives, parents, their dearest friends. One friend mourned his daughter, a member of the resistance organization, who had died during the fighting. I went to pay a condolence call. Other visitors were there. But he didn't speak to anyone. He lay on his bed, his face turned to the wall. For three days, he didn't eat, drink, or speak.

The events of the Warsaw ghetto burned into my consciousness. At times they seemed to replace the placid realities of my everyday life. They even pushed aside my real memories of Vilna. The Warsaw ghetto became a constant part of my internal life. I used to imagine myself there, test myself as to how I would have behaved. Would I have had the courage to fight? Would I have had the stamina against despair? When I was cold and reached for a sweater, I thought of winter in the ghetto. I developed a secret moral code of human behavior that depended on options open only to those imprisoned in the ghetto. A few years later, in 1948, when I was asked to do research for John Hersey on a novel he was writing about the Warsaw ghetto, *The Wall,* I was ready for the task.

In June 1943, Max Weinreich received a letter from Saul Reisen, then in Jerusalem. In it, he gave an account of his life since 1939, after he and his father, Zalmen, had been arrested in Vilna. They had been imprisoned together in Nowo Wilejka, a town near Vilna, where a Soviet garrison was stationed. In May 1940, Zalmen was transferred somewhere deep in Russia. Thereafter, all trace of him was lost. In July Saul was moved to a prison in Polotsk in White Russia; a year later, after the German invasion, he was evacuated to Tobolsk on the Irtysh River in western Siberia. In September 1941, Saul was freed in the general Polish amnesty. Through the newly appointed Polish ambassador he tried to learn of his father's whereabouts, but their inquiries were rebuffed. The Russians said that since Zalmen Reisen had come from Vilna, they regarded him as a Soviet citizen. Therefore, they would not tolerate Polish interference in this matter. Saul later made his way, southward on the Irtysh River, as a laborer and stoker on Soviet freight ships. After three months, he arrived at Semipalatinsk, in Kazakhstan, where he joined the Polish army. They left the Soviet Union and eventually reached the Middle East.

On leave in Jerusalem, Saul had news of Vilna from Bernard Singer, a Polish Jewish journalist and friend of the Reisens. Some months earlier Singer had sent a food package to Saul's mother, Miriam Reisen. Its receipt had been confirmed. Saul said that he wanted to believe that they were all still alive and together in Vilna—his mother, Stefania Szabad, Rivele, and Kalman—and that soon we'd all see one another. It was a hope I shared, but in which I had little confidence. The flood of bad news, especially about the Warsaw ghetto and Zygielbaum's suicide, made me doubt that anyone I knew had survived. To me, Poland had already become a mass graveyard.

That summer of 1943 was like an interminable Tisha b'Av—the most solemn fast day in the Jewish calendar, marking the destruction of the

Temple in Jerusalem. We were then still too close to the terrible events, too shocked by the immediate deaths and daily disasters, to realize that we were mourning the destruction of the 1,000-year East European Jewish civilization.

Those days I was desperate to escape from the burdens of our terrible Jewish sorrows and my own tormented mental life. I wanted to protect myself against the assault of bad news, the daily accounts of Jews murdered in the cities of Russia, Poland, and Rumania, and deported from France, Belgium, Holland, Norway, and Greece to mysterious places from which they were never heard from again. I wanted to obliterate the reality of the newspaper reports. I longed to erase from my conscience and consciousness the old guilt. Blake says "excess of sorrow laughs." I tried to cultivate an air of frivolity, of lightness, to keep me afloat on the ocean of Jewish suffering.

The movies provided the most acceptable form of escape, in which everyone indulged, especially my refugee friends. It didn't matter whether we saw silly comedies or war movies. We sometimes went to the theater in those days. I remember a mammoth and gripping production of *The Skin of Our Teeth* with Tallulah Bankhead and the romantic comedy *The Voice of the Turtle* with Margaret Sullavan. I even went to musical comedies—*Oklahoma* and *Lady in the Dark*. But more important to my emotional survival in those days were the dates, the flirtations, and the occasional romances which buoyed my spirits and distracted me from my feelings of despair about the European Jews.

While there was no real escape from the Jewish coil in which I was firmly held, I sometimes tried to blot out the Jewish bad news by concentrating on the war news. In the Pacific, Americans took a few islands in the Solomons during the summer and fall of 1943. In November they captured the Gilbert Islands.

Meantime, the war was spreading in the Mediterranean. On July 9–10, 1943, the U.S. Seventh Army, under General George S. Patton, Jr., and Montgomery's British Eighth Army, a total of some 160,000 troops, with tanks and vehicles, after having been transported from different ports on the Mediterranean by some 3,000 warships and landing craft, invaded Sicily. On July 25, with Italian morale collapsing, the Fascist Grand Council forced Mussolini to resign and replaced him with Marshal Pietro Badoglio, who right away began to negotiate for an armistice. By mid-August, the Allies held all Sicily. Though some 60,000 Germans had managed to escape across the Straits of Messina into Italy, they left 135,000 prisoners and 32,000 dead and wounded. The

Allies had about 22,000 casualties. The *New York Times* began to publish daily casualty lists.

Meanwhile, since the spring of 1943, the RAF and the AAF had been bombing Germany night and day. In July, Hamburg, Germany's principal seaport and center of its oil refineries, became the target of their round-the-clock bombing. When I read that thousands of Germans died in the bombing, I rejoiced. On August 17, 376 English bombers blasted Regensburg and Schweinfurt, the center of the German ball-bearings industry.

Late that summer a spate of divisive Jewish politics almost upstaged the war news. The disastrous news about the European Jews had galvanized the Zionists to form a broad-based organization to press the British to open Palestine to Jewish immigration, but it foundered on ideological and institutional differences. The Reform movement, too, divided on the issue of Palestine; anti-Zionist defectors formed the American Council for Judaism, which strenuously opposed the creation of a Jewish state. Since I wasn't a Zionist, I had little interest in those quarrels. At the time Palestine seemed irrelevant to me, of little use to the Jews in danger of being murdered. However justified the Zionist attacks on Britain's Palestine policy might be, I felt offended by its effect at that time, in the midst of the war. Where would we all be, were it not for the British? Churchill had transformed my literary Anglophilia into boundless admiration and gratitude to the British. They had stood alone against Hitler in 1940, when Russia was Hitler's ally, and they had prevailed. It was hard to reconcile the anti-Zionist aspect of British policy with its war policies, but I thought that the defeat of Hitler was the first priority for us as Americans and as Jews.

On August 28, 1943, at the age of sixty-two, Tcherikower died of a sudden heart attack. Riva was inconsolable. In the months that followed, I often stayed overnight with her, to share her sorrow and ease her loneliness. I thought of him as one of Hitler's casualties. Still, Tcherikower's three years in New York had been the most productive of his life. He had edited two volumes of studies on the Jews in France (the material had been almost ready for publication in Paris before the German invasion) and two volumes on the history of the Jewish labor movement in the United States, in addition to numerous short papers.

A few days after his death, on September 3, the Allies crossed the Straits of Messina and invaded Italy. Fighting was heavy all the way up the Italian boot. Badoglio surrendered, but the Germans swooped down from the north, kidnapped Mussolini from the prison where he'd been held, and reinstalled him as head of the Italian government. Hitler sent Rommel into Italy and soon all of north and central Italy were under German military control. Southern Italy was held by the Americans who had reached only as far as Cassino, about halfway between Naples and Rome. There they were halted by the winter, the mountainous terrain, and tough German resistance.

Meanwhile, the Red Army advanced. In August the Russians took back Kharkov for a second time and Taganrog in the south; in September, Bryansk and Smolensk. In the wake of every Russian victory we now came to await a replay of the same terrible news. In every city and town from which the Germans had fled they had left their murderous signature. Everywhere the Jews had been slaughtered. Usually a single survivor emerged from the rubble to tell a story whose contours had become familiar, even if unbearably horrible. Though I already knew what the terrible truth was, I couldn't stand to hear it, to read it. Sometimes I used to think that I could hear the ghostly silence that enveloped the places where Jews had once lived. My hatred for the Germans used to keep me awake. It even intruded unbidden in moments of joy.

In October the news from Denmark diverted our attention from the advancing Russian forces. The Germans had begun to round up the Jews in Copenhagen to deport them to Poland. On October 4, we read that the Germans had deported 800 Danish Jews to Poland, but many more had managed to flee to Sweden. A week later, the papers reported the astonishing news that 6,000 Danish Jews had reached safety in Sweden. That was the first information of the heroic rescue of the Danish Jews by the Danish people living under Nazi terror. Weinreich and I thought first of all about the people we knew, especially the Davidsohns. We were sure, given their connections and position, that they had made it to Sweden.

On October 29, a JTA dispatch from Stockholm in the *Forverts* cited a Moscow Radio announcement that the Germans had recently murdered the last 12,000 Jews in Vilna. That was the whole story, but we believed it, for the recurring accounts of mass murder were like German clockwork—regular, systematic, methodical, reliable. Why should Vilna have been exempted? On November 16, just ten days after the Russians recaptured Kiev, the Soviet news agency TASS reported that the Germans had murdered all the Jews in Kiev in 1941 in a matter of a few days.

At the YIVO, we were then deep in preparations for our annual conference to be held from January 7 to 9, 1944. At the closing session, Shlomo Mendelsohn read a paper on resistance in the Warsaw ghetto. The hall was jam-packed with several hundred listeners. People stood in the back and against the side walls. Mendelsohn began by enumerating and qualifying his sources—the underground Jewish and Polish reports to the Polish Government-in-Exile and to the Bund's representative in the Polish National Council (Zygielbaum's place had already been filled), the underground Polish press, documents issued by the Jewish resistance organization, even several eyewitnesses who had escaped from Poland. Then he described conditions in the ghetto up to 1942.

When he spoke about Czerniaków's suicide and the terrible deportations of the Jews from the Warsaw ghetto during the summer of 1942, the tension in the hall heightened. He spoke about the trains that brought the Jews to the gas chambers in Treblinka. Though he had no information about how the Jewish Combat Organization had come into being, he had reports of the Polish government and of the Polish underground press about the actual battles the Jews fought against the Germans. He quoted an appeal issued on the fifth day of the fighting by the Jewish Combat Organization to the Polish population:

> . . . every threshold in the ghetto has been and will continue to be a fortress. We may all perish in this struggle, but we will not surrender. Like you, we breathe with the desire for revenge and punishment for all the crimes of our common foe.
>
> This is a battle for our and your freedom.

In the crowded hall you heard only Mendelsohn's voice, punctuated by occasional sharp gasps among the audience, quick intakes of breath. The atmosphere was heavy with grief. When he finished, the hall was hushed. No one applauded. Spontaneously everyone arose to honor the fallen Jews of the Warsaw ghetto. Then someone said: "Let's recite Kaddish." From the other end of the room, a man began to intone the Jewish prayer for the dead. Everyone joined in, amid a surge of sobbing.

CHAPTER 12

___

New York 1944–1945: The Reckoning

On January 22, 1944, President Roosevelt announced that he had established a United States War Refugee Board "to take action for the immediate rescue from the Nazis of as many as possible of the persecuted minorities of Europe, racial, religious or political, all civilian victims of enemy savagery." The idea for such an organization had originated in the proposals for rescue which the Jewish organizations had submitted in March 1943 to the American and British officials who were to attend the Bermuda Refugee Conference. It was later pursued by a clamorous group of Revisionists-Zionists, whose supporters in Congress had introduced resolutions favoring the creation of a governmental rescue organization. But the creation of the War Refugee Board came about as a result of the initiative and persistent efforts within the Treasury Department and the ability of its secretary, Henry Morgenthau, Jr., to persuade Roosevelt of its necessity.

At the time, I thought that the War Refugee Board was little more than a symbolic gesture on Roosevelt's part in response to the magnitude of the Jewish disaster. I could not imagine that it would have any great consequence as a rescue agency. Most East European Jews had already been murdered. As for those still alive who were held in the vise of Hitler's SS forces, I couldn't see how the War Refugee Board could save them.

At the YIVO we were then preparing for a conference of representatives of Jewish *landsmanshaftn,* to be held on Sunday, March 19, 1944. *Landsmanshaftn* were organizations of Jewish immigrants from the same town in Eastern Europe whose purpose was to help their less fortunate landsmen back home. Most *landsmanshaftn* had been in existence for decades. Now that those European Jewish communities no longer existed, so Max Weinreich reasoned, the modest *landsmanshaftn* had become the repositories of the local lore and history of their destroyed homes. The YIVO wanted to enlist their support in creating a Museum of Jewish Homes of the Past, which would preserve the record of those communities and their culture, customs, and accomplishments. Therefore, Weinreich wrote in his letter of invitation, every bit of documentation about the life, history, and culture of the East European Jews had become precious and valuable. Every scrap of paper and every family photograph now constituted a national Jewish treasure.

The *landsmanshaft* conference endorsed the Museum of Jewish Homes of the Past and we embarked on a large-scale effort to collect photographs, documents, and local histories, descriptive materials that would serve as a historical record, testimonials to the existence of communities which we believed were already irretrievably lost. None of us expected that Jewish communities would ever again exist in Poland and Lithuania. It was then that I gave to the YIVO Archives my photographs of Vilna which Saly, the refugee from Germany whose last name I had forgotten, had taken for me in the summer of 1939.

The day our *landsmanshaft* conference met in New York, German armed forces marched into Hungary and occupied it. Though Hungary was part of the Axis, Hitler feared that Hungary would betray him, now that the Russians were near. Overnight, the 650,000 Jews in Hungary, who had been safe from the reach of Hitler's executioners despite the hardships under which they lived, had been put in the grip of the Nazi murderers. On March 24, Roosevelt issued another statement of warning. It had Churchill's and Stalin's full knowledge and approval:

In one of the blackest crimes of all history—begun by the Nazis in the day of peace and multiplied by them a hundred times in time of war—the wholesale systematic murder of the Jews of Europe goes on unabated every hour. As a result of the events of the last few days, hundreds of thousands of Jews, who while living under persecution have at least found a haven from death in Hungary and the Balkans, are now threatened with annihilation as Hitler's forces descend more heavily on those lands. That these innocent people, who have already survived a decade of Hitler's fury, should perish on the very eve of triumph over the barbarism which their persecution symbolizes, would be a major tragedy.

It is therefore fitting that we should again proclaim our determination that none who participate in these acts of savagery shall go unpunished.

Hitler is committing these crimes against humanity in the name of the German people. I am asking every German and every person of any other nationality everywhere under Nazi domination to show the world by his action that in his heart he does not share these insane criminal desires. Let him hide these pursued victims, help them to get over their borders, and do what he can to save them from the Nazi hangman.

In those days, momentous events hurtled through time with the rapidity and violence of rock landslides. We had no respite from their relentless assault on our eyes and ears, upon our consciousness. Everything that happened in the world affected us. On Saturday, April 15, we were astonished by a story on the third page of the *New York Times,* with the byline of its Moscow correspondent, Ralph Parker. It was headlined: "Poet-Partisan from Vilna Ghetto Says Nazis Slew 77,000 of 80,000."

The poet-partisan was Abraham Sutzkever. He was "in a Lithuanian detachment which he had joined with a few hundred other Jews who had crawled from the ghetto via sewers." Sutzkever told Parker that the Germans had established two ghettos in Vilna and had then, over a two-year period, murdered its Jews. Two months ago, he said, only 3,000 Jews were still alive in Vilna. Sutzkever talked about the SS officer Kittel who liquidated the Vilna ghetto and described the organization of Jewish resistance in the Vilna ghetto, something we hadn't known about at all. He also showed Parker a letter written by Maxim Gorky, which he, Sutzkever, had brought to Moscow. He had smuggled it out of Vilna's "famous Jewish Museum"—we didn't know precisely what he meant, but suspected that he was referring to the YIVO. He said he had also saved "many other valuable relics."

Weinreich and I cried and laughed. This was the first news we'd had of anyone we knew in Vilna, even if it was a story that begged for further explanation. How had Sutzkever gotten from Vilna to Moscow? But no matter. Our Jewish optimism easily revived. Once more we allowed ourselves to hope that the people we loved might still be among those 3,000 survivors Sutzkever mentioned. Every day thereafter I reached for the papers with feverish intensity, but there was no more news from Vilna.

The RAF and AAF continued to bomb Germany without letup. In the last week of February, they sent 6,100 bombers to destroy the German aircraft industry. Then they took to bombing western German and French railroad installations. They sent bombers across vast stretches of enemy territory to blow up the oilfields at Ploesti. In April, day after day, fleets of thousands of planes smashed Hitler's Reich. On April 14, Drew Middleton, reporting from London, described an attack by 3,000 American planes as "the greatest concerted aerial operation of history." It was the climax of a six-day offensive against the German aircraft industry, the Luftwaffe's airfields, and Germany's supply lines. No war communiqués gave me greater satisfaction than those describing the havoc which our planes wreaked on Germany and the Germans.

No matter how secret the Allies' plans for the invasion of Europe were, they could not conceal the bulging evidence that Britain had become one vast military camp. Invasion fever seized us. We read that Britain was thronged with millions of troops, not only their own, but Canadians, Australians, New Zealanders, and, most of all, Americans. British ports were filled with ships, loading and unloading cargoes. London streets rumbled with the traffic of long caravans of tanks and trucks, cannons and machine guns on their way to park in the nearby countryside. We were not the only ones excited by the military buildup. The Germans watched, too. Rommel, who had been transferred to France, predicted that the Allies would invade France any day. Like everyone else, I was all keyed up about the imminence of the invasion, even if it was coming too late to save the Jews. We had to win the war; we had to defeat Germany. I wanted to see Germany utterly destroyed. I wanted revenge.

Meanwhile, in the Pacific our forces kept up their island hopping. They'd taken the Marshall Islands and were fighting in New Guinea. In May the Russians retook Sevastopol and cleared the Crimea of Nazis. In Italy, after two months of stubborn fighting, the Allies took Cassino on May 18, and continued to push northward. On June 4, they finally took Rome. It was a triumphal victory, but the excitement it generated was almost overnight eclipsed by even more momentous news. For just two days later, at dawn on Tuesday, June 6, Allied forces began landing on the beaches of Normandy. By nightfall nearly all the Allied troops were ashore. It was a mighty host—176,000 men, 20,000 vehicles, and 1,500 tanks, all protected by 12,000 planes. After a few days, sixteen divisions had landed in Normandy. By the end of June, the Allies had a million men pushing forward in Brittany and Normandy.

In July we turned our attention back to the eastern front. The Russians were advancing on Vilna and we followed the military communiqués. On July 6, General Ivan D. Chernyakhovsky's Third White Russian Army was forty-five miles away; on July 7, twenty-five miles; on July 8, twenty miles. The next day, they entered Vilna, but the Germans did not give up easily. For five days, the Russians and the Germans battled in Vilna's streets. It was hard to imagine that armies could fight, house by house, in Vilna's narrow and ancient streets. Finally, on July 14, the Russians took Vilna. Its capture was front-page news in the *New York Times* and *Herald Tribune.* Headlines in both papers reported that 8,000 Germans were killed and 5,000 taken prisoner.

But there were no Jews left after the Germans had been driven out. *Izvestia,* following Soviet policy in not mentioning that the victims were Jews or mostly Jews, reported that the Germans had murdered "over 100,000 people" in Vilna. Most of the murdered were buried at Ponary. That was the first time I heard of this desolate village, about ten kilometers from Vilna, which, we later learned, had become a vast killing ground for the Vilna Jews and had earned its geographic notoriety as the locale of massive death pits filled with tens of thousands of rotting corpses.

Soon thereafter we learned that some 2,500 or so Vilna Jews had survived, one-third of them in the forests, a small number in hiding in Vilna and its environs, and the rest in the Soviet Union. Some 300 Jewish partisans who had been in the forests were among the first to reenter Vilna by the end of July. Among them were Shmerke Kaczerginski and Abraham Sutzkever. Both had been in the ghetto until September 1943, when they escaped to join up with the partisans. Reports began to appear in the Yiddish press about Vilna. In a few weeks other survivors returned. We soon learned that Rivele Kalmanovich, Stefania Szabad, and Miriam Reisen were no longer among the living. In September Chaim Grade, who had been in the Soviet Union, came back to Vilna. We began to keep lists of those few who had survived and of the many who had not.

We had some bits of news about the YIVO itself. We put together what we knew in a small item titled "What Is Left of the YIVO in Vilna?" and published it in the September issue of the *News of the YIVO*. According to a Jewish Telegraphic Agency account, the Germans had blown up the YIVO building just before they left. A dispatch from Moscow in the *Herald Tribune* of July 15 mentioned two Germans whom the Russians identified as "robber professors," whose task was to confiscate and dispose of cultural treasures in Vilna. Some of those cultural treasures were sold to paper mills, but the rest were apparently shipped to Germany. We presumed that most, if not all, of these materials had come from the YIVO's library and archives.

While we were gripped by the news of Vilna, we were nevertheless aware of the rush of other events around us. At home the Republicans had nominated as their presidential candidate Thomas E. Dewey, a former New York City district attorney and governor of New York. On July 20, 1944, the Democratic National Convention for the fourth time nominated Roosevelt as its presidential candidate. Harry S. Truman, senator from Missouri, was the Democratic vice-presidential candidate. During the convention, Roosevelt was reported to have suggested that Truman's candidacy be checked with Sidney Hillman, the CIO's political power broker. Roosevelt's instruction, "Clear it with Sidney," became the target of a vicious anti-Roosevelt, anti-labor, and anti-Semitic election campaign.

The same day that Roosevelt was nominated in Chicago, an unsuccessful attempt was made in Berlin to assassinate Hitler. Too bad, we thought, the would-be assassins had bungled the job. But why had they waited so long to do this? It was then the twelfth year of Hitler's murderous regime. Had they decided to kill Hitler because he hadn't delivered the victory he had promised? I didn't care a whit that those failed assassins were rounded up, arrested, and executed. As far as I was concerned, all Germans were murderers. It didn't matter anymore whether Hitler lived or died. He had already fulfilled his prophecy to destroy the European Jews. He had even seen to it that most Hungarian Jews had been murdered, just in these last two months, in the full view of the Western world. Anyway, I didn't think that Hitler had long to live, for though the German armed forces were still fighting stubbornly in France, we knew that Germany would soon be defeated, that victory would at last be ours. People were predicting that the war would be over by October.

That summer the Russians kept advancing at high speed, pushing west-ward into territory that had been Poland before 1939. In every city and town from which the Germans had fled, the story was the same. A few survivors who had been in hiding or in the woods emerged to tell the terrible story of how all the other Jews had been murdered. Soon the *Forverts* began to print lists of survivors in search of relatives in the United States. I began to read these lists. I never found a familiar name.

On July 22 the Red Army entered Lublin. There the Russians set up the Polish Committee of National Liberation. It was not just a commit-tee to preside over Polish liberation, but a provisional Polish govern-ment under Soviet auspices. Its creation would soon dispel whatever hopes the Polish Government-in-Exile had about returning to Poland and resuming its political leadership.

Two days later, the Russians liberated Majdanek, a death camp on the outskirts of Lublin. We began to learn about the German system of mass murder. In August American correspondents visited the camp and described it as a "highly systematized place for annihilation," where 1.5 million men, women, and children had been murdered, most of them Jews. The grounds at Majdanek were covered with masses of corpses. The journalists saw hermetically sealed gas chambers in which the victims were asphyxiated and five furnaces in which the bodies were cremated. Warehouses on the premises bulged with the accumulated loot taken from the murdered Jews. A correspondent for *Life* magazine reported "that the shoes had burst out of the building like corn from a crib. It was monstrous." I couldn't stand to read about it, but I did. We all read the newspaper reports, but we never spoke about them. I was deafened by the silent screaming inside my head.

Barely a few hundred Jews survived. One of them, whose wife, son, and parents had been killed, told the journalists: "I have nothing to live for except revenge." The New York *Herald Tribune* editorialized: "A regime capable of such a crime deserves annihilation on the same scale."

On Monday, July 31, Soviet tanks were reported to have entered Praga, a Warsaw suburb on the far side of the Vistula. The Polish Home Army, the underground Polish nationalist army of the Polish Government-in-

Exile, had been waiting for the opportune moment to stage an uprising against the Germans. Believing the moment had arrived and that the Red Army would cross the Vistula and ensure the liberation of Warsaw, the commander of the Home Army ordered the general uprising to start the next day. But the Red Army did not come to the aid of the Polish nationalists and had likely never planned to. After all, the Soviet Union had already created the Polish Committee of National Liberation, which would serve as its puppet Polish regime.

Though the 150,000 Polish resisters had insufficient military equipment and resources, they fought the Germans with spirit and courage. In mid-September, Allied planes, flown by Polish pilots, made hundreds of drops of arms and food to the beleaguered fighters, but most fell into German hands. On October 2, the Polish Home Army capitulated. It had lost some 20,000 men. Over 200,000 Polish civilians had been killed. The Germans emptied Warsaw of its surviving residents, sending over a half million Poles to concentration camps and some 150,000 to Germany for forced labor. Then, obeying Hitler's orders, German troops utterly demolished the city of Warsaw, dynamiting every building that had still been standing.

Hitler had ordered a similar fate for Paris in the event of a German retreat, but the commanding German general there was less compliant than the one in Warsaw, preferring to negotiate a withdrawal of his forces. Thus Paris was spared. On August 25, the Free French forces in the vanguard, followed by the U.S. Fourth Infantry Division of Patton's Third Army, liberated the city.

A week later Brussels was liberated. Meanwhile, Rumania had surrendered the day before Paris's liberation. In September Soviet troops entered Bulgaria; in October they were in Belgrade. Hitler's Fortress Europe was crumbling. Yet all through this period, the Germans kept sending Hungarian Jews to their deaths in Poland. Mass protests in New York and warnings from Churchill and Roosevelt that they would hold the perpetrators responsible for their crimes did not deter the Germans from their murder operations.

The predictions that the war would end in October were not fulfilled. Britain's First Airborne Division had suffered catastrophic losses in September while attempting to seize the Dutch town of Arnhem. The Germans continued to put up stiff resistance. They could not yet be counted out. Just then, stories appeared in the Washington and New York press about disagreements within Roosevelt's cabinet as to how to deal with Germany after the war. The subject, which seemed premature at the moment, had been on the agenda of the Roosevelt-Churchill meeting in mid-September in Quebec.

Henry Morgenthau, secretary of the treasury, had been asked by Roosevelt to present his proposal to deindustrialize Germany and turn it into an agrarian nation, so that it would no longer threaten world peace. In a column in the *New York Times* on September 22, the Washington journalist Arthur Krock said that reports of the Morgenthau Plan had reached the top Nazis in Berlin and he insinuated that those reports had consequently hardened German resistance to Allied troops and thus cost American lives. The 1944 election campaign was then in full swing. The anti-Semitic innuendos about "Clear it with Sidney" were being reinforced with whispered and shouted charges that the Morgenthau Plan was an expression of Jewish vindictiveness against the Germans.

Why should the Jews not have felt vindictive against the Germans? Everyone I knew hated the Germans and wanted revenge. Yes, we were the people who wanted an eye for an eye. To be sure, my circle of friends and acquaintances was limited, almost entirely Jewish. Even Jews with minimal Jewish commitments hated the Germans and felt a passion for revenge. We all feared for the world's future, lest the savage and murderous Germans raise new generations to follow in their savage and murderous ways. The Morgenthau Plan, I thought, was too generous.

In those days I was possessed by visions of an Armageddon soon to come. When the fighting would end, I envisioned a new war on the European continent, expecting the occupied peoples of Europe to rise up against the Germans and their collaborators. It seemed to me then that all of them—Frenchmen, Belgians, Italians, Danes, Norwegians, Czechs, Poles, Serbs, Greeks—would want to exact revenge for their ravaged homes, their slave labor, their destroyed families. In my daytime fantasies I'd imagine that I, too, in Europe searching for my friends, hoping they had survived, would kill a German or two. I never quite pictured how I'd do it, but the fantasy comforted me in my frustration, in my hopelessness.

The terrible news about how many Jews the Germans had murdered continued to pile up, with reports from every town in Europe which the Allied armies liberated. On Friday, October 6, 1944, I read an account in the *New York Times* of a death camp in Estonia, in a place called Klooga. Here, the correspondent W. H. Lawrence reported, the Germans had built what was originally a labor camp to house the last survivors of the Vilna ghetto. "Here," Lawrence wrote, "I have seen and counted recognizable parts of 438 complete and partly burned bodies of men, women, and children." He described three huge funeral pyres, where he "counted the recognizable parts of at least 215 bodies, and an unknown number of other skeletons." These had been reduced to bone ash by a fire made by "burning pine logs and bodies soaked in gasoline."

I had to pause in my reading, unable to continue, feeling hot and cold, nauseous, my insides in spasms. I had heard that Zelig Kalmanovich had been deported to Estonia. Without any evidence, I began to believe that he had been in Klooga. My mouth was dry, my eyes burned. I was reading about the bone ash of people I had known, people I had encountered somewhere in Vilna, people I loved and people I hadn't cared for, like the loud-mouthed woman who owned the little grocery on Makowa Street, the street where I used to live. This camp at Klooga was Ezekiel's valley of dry bones, a valley of bones of death. But no divine presence had appeared in Klooga to lay sinews upon those dry bones, to bring flesh upon them, and skin, and to breathe life into the slain. At Klooga there was no resurrection.

About half of the 3,000 or more slave prisoners in the camp had been Vilna Jews; the rest had been Soviet war prisoners and Estonian political prisoners. The correspondent said that only eighty-five persons had survived; he had talked to a few of them, one a thirty-one-year-old Jewish lawyer from Vilna whose name was unfamiliar to me. He provided a capsule history of the Jews in Vilna under the Germans, adding a few more facts to what we had learned from Sutzkever's account in the *New York Times* last April. There had been 70,000 Jews in Vilna when the Germans came in, the lawyer said. During the first six weeks of their occupation, special squads of Germans used to seize Jews at night; thousands disappeared. Only 37,000 Jews remained when the ghetto was established—two ghettos in fact, one inhabited by some 25,000 people who had occupational skills and the other by 12,000 persons without such skills. The smaller ghetto was liquidated on October 21, 1942; its inhabitants were murdered at Ponary. For the next year, the survivor related, he, his wife, and his parents continued to live in the ghetto. On September 24, 1943, they were ordered to pack their things to leave. At the railroad stations, he and his father were separated from his mother and his wife. He never knew what had happened to them.

Later, when we became familiar with the history of the Vilna ghetto, we learned that the ghetto had been liquidated on September 23–24, 1943, when some 10,000 Jews were still alive. Men and women were suddenly and forcibly separated. Some 2,000 able-bodied men were sent to labor camps in Estonia, some 1,700 able-bodied women to camps in Latvia. About 5,000 women and children were brought to Majdanek, and a few hundred old and sick Jews were shot at Ponary.

Weinreich and I never talked about this story. Nor did I ever discuss these horrors with anyone. We had learned to control our physical revulsion and to stifle our grief. We endured our despair in silence. It was as if these events were off-limits for human intercourse, as if the world we had once known and now read about had been sucked into a terrible pit of nothingness. Compared to the realities of Majdanek, Ponary, and Klooga, Dante's vision of Inferno was a place of comfort. According to his Christian view of sin and punishment, the inhabitants of his Inferno deserved the punishment given them. Dante's poetic vision of hell after death paled before the horrors of hell on earth we read about in the straightforward prose of news reporters. They were the witnesses who had glimpsed the end of the world.

Not long afterward, late in October 1944, the YIVO received from the Ministry of the Interior of the Polish government in London a report about Jewish cultural work and self-help activities in the Warsaw ghetto, which had arrived through underground sources. Dated March 1, 1944, it had been written by the Warsaw Jewish historian Emanuel Ringelblum and his friend Adolf Berman. Just six days after he wrote the report, Ringelblum and his family were murdered by the Gestapo. A Pole, in a fit of drunken rage, had betrayed the location of their underground bunker on the "Aryan" side of Warsaw. Berman added this information to the report on May 20 and then forwarded it to London. We published it in the *News of the YIVO*, November 1944.

In Vilna I had once met Ringelblum. Early in January 1939, during the winter school recess, he had come from Warsaw to deliver a series of lectures to the teachers in the Yiddish schools. That particular evening I had worked late with Weinreich at the YIVO. When we finished, he proposed that we go to Velfkeh's. There we met Ringelblum. I wrote home late that night in a mood of high excitement, describing the evening. I closed: "We were joined by Saul Reisen and some of the actors who will appear in *The Tempest* which is opening tomorrow. It was a wonderful evening; Weinreich, Saul Reisen, and Ringelblum walked me home."

Ringelblum had been at the center of Jewish cultural life in Warsaw before the war. In the ghetto he founded a group with the code name Oneg Shabbat (Society for the Pleasures of the Sabbath). Its purpose was to gather documentation about the life and sufferings of the Polish Jews during the German occupation. The report that was sent to the YIVO described Oneg Shabbat and other cultural and social-welfare activities in the Warsaw ghetto and elsewhere.

Oneg Shabbat's collections became one of the primary documentary sources for the history of the Jews in the Warsaw ghetto and in other places in Poland during the German occupation. In August 1942, when most of the Warsaw Jews were being deported to Treblinka, the massive documentation which Oneg Shabbat had accumulated was buried in the ghetto. Most of the metal containers were found after the war and many original documents found their way to the YIVO Archives in New York. Years later, I published some of them in *A Holocaust Reader*.

Meanwhile, the fighting continued. In the Pacific, the Allies were making headway against the Japanese. In October 1944, General Douglas MacArthur, who had promised to return, launched the long-awaited invasion of the Philippines. The Japanese put up tremendous resistance and in the battle for Leyte Gulf loosed their secret weapon—the kamikaze, or suicide, planes and their pilots. But by the end of the year, Japanese resistance on Leyte had been broken. The Japanese had lost over 56,000 men; the Americans, 2,888. MacArthur was readying his attack on Luzon and Manila.

On the western front, the defeat of Germany continued to elude us. On December 16, Germany launched a stunning counteroffensive in Belgium's Ardennes Forest, said to have been masterminded by Hitler himself. German armed forces trapped the thinly held American positions. About 8,000 Americans surrendered. Other Allied armies raced to reinforce their lines. The Battle of the Bulge lasted for about a month. Finally the Germans withdrew after costly losses. In January 1945 the front was back where it had been in December.

On Friday evening, January 5, 1945, my former Mitlshul teacher Leibush Lehrer opened the annual YIVO conference. He invoked a byword attributed to a hasidic sect, said to have been inscribed on a wall in the Warsaw ghetto: "Jews, don't despair!" In keeping with that upbeat note, my other Mitlshul teacher, Jacob Shatzky, read a paper on 150 years of

Jewish resistance in Warsaw. He was then working on a history of the Jews in Warsaw. But other sessions of our conference more truly reflected our mood of despair and sorrow. Jacob Lestchinsky presented a statistical study of Jewish losses in Europe. According to his data, some five million European Jews had been murdered. They had constituted 60 percent of the Jews in German-occupied countries. No more than 10 percent of Polish Jewry survived.

The conference closed on Sunday, January 7, with a lecture by Abraham Joshua Heschel. Heschel, then in his late thirties, had left Warsaw shortly before the German invasion and was teaching at Hebrew Union College in Cincinnati, the Reform rabbinical seminary. He himself was a fully observant Jew. When he agreed to speak at our conference, my first obligations were to see that he was housed within walking distance of Hunter College, where the YIVO conference opened on the eve of the Sabbath, and that he would have kosher meals. Heschel delivered a eulogy for East European Jewry, a funeral oration that combined scholarship and poetry. His Yiddish was exquisite. His talk, "The East European Era in Jewish History," was published in the *YIVO-Bleter* in 1945 and a year later, in an English translation, in the *YIVO Annual of Jewish Social Science.* He closed with these words:

> When Nebuchadnezzar destroyed Jerusalem and set fire to the Temple, our forefathers did not forget the Revelation at Mount Sinai and the words of the Prophets. Today the world knows that what transpired on the soil of Palestine was sacred history, from which mankind draws inspiration. A day may come when the hidden light of the East European era may be revealed.

Max Weinreich sat in permanent silent mourning for the Vilna YIVO and its murdered staff. Yet he clung to the belief that some relics of the Vilna YIVO might still survive. The thought of recovering that part of the YIVO's library and archives which the Germans had carted off from Vilna haunted him. If even a small portion of the YIVO library would be found among the ruins in Germany, it would be a sign that the Jerusalem of Vilna would yet rise phoenix-like from the ashes, that it would reestablish its earthly presence. Finding the library would be a token of redemption.

As early as May 1944, soon after the interview with Sutzkever had appeared in the *New York Times,* Weinreich began to stake out YIVO's claim to whatever might turn up in Germany of the Vilna YIVO's cultural property. He corresponded with the State Department's Special War Problems Division and with a government advisory body dealing with these matters. Meanwhile, by the year's end, we had accumulated some basic information about the history of the YIVO library during the German occupation. At the time, Weinreich was writing a book about anti-Jewish scholarship in Nazi Germany and his Nazi sources unexpectedly provided clues to the fate of the YIVO library.

One of the Nazi institutions Weinreich described in his book, *Hitler's Professors* (which the YIVO published in 1946), was the Institut zur Erforschung der Judenfrage (Institute for the Study of the Jewish Question), headed by Alfred Rosenberg, one of Hitler's early mentors and the ideologue of the Nazi movement. Rosenberg's institute was intended to be part of a grandiose "center for National Socialist ideological and educational research" which Hitler himself authorized. It was headquartered in Frankfurt, because the city's mayor had confiscated the magnificent Judaica collection of Frankfurt's Municipal Library and offered it to Rosenberg for the privilege of having the institute located in his city. That Judaica library, a gift of the Rothschilds to the city of Frankfurt in 1928, was then housed in a grand building on the Main, once known as the Rothschild-Palais.

With the Frankfurt Judaica library as his institute's core collection, Rosenberg then confiscated the libraries of the Berlin Jewish Community, the Breslau Rabbinical Seminary, the Vienna Jewish Community, and the Vienna Rabbinical Seminary. In 1940, the looting operations were conducted by the so-called Einsatzstab Reichsleiter Rosenberg für die besetzten Gebiete—ERR (Reich Leader Rosenberg's Special Task Force for the Occupied Areas); its function was to scour the occupied areas for documentation to justify the Nazis' ideological war against Jews and Freemasons. In September 1940, Goering extended the ERR's authority to include also Jewish art collections. Armed with authorizations from Hitler and from General Wilhelm Keitel, chief of the German armed forces' High Command, the ERR task forces moved freely into areas of military operation and occupation. They seized the libraries of the Alliance Israélite Universelle and the École Rabbinique in Paris and the Rosenthaliana collection in Amsterdam. They seized the Rothschild art collection in Paris and other private and public collections in France and Holland.

In August 1941, barely two months after the German army had

entered Vilna, an ERR task force arrived there. Right away they began ransacking the Strashun Library for incunabula. Then the ERR team commandeered the YIVO building as a central collecting place for all the looted books from the area. In January 1942 a new ERR task force arrived, headed by a Dr. Johannes Pohl, whom Rosenberg had appointed on March 1, 1941, as Hebraica chief at the Frankfurt institute. Pohl conscripted twenty workers from the Judenrat, specifying that at least five were to be experts in Judaica. Kalmanovich was chosen as one of the experts; other workers included Sutzkever and Shmerke Kaczerginski. Their task was to sort hundreds of thousands of books and documents, as instructed, by century. From this mass, books were selected for shipment to Germany, catalogued, and then packed. Most went to Frankfurt; some to Berlin. What the Germans didn't want, they sold for scrap and used for heating. They destroyed irreplaceable cultural treasures and historical documents as recklessly and ruthlessly as they murdered people.

Anguished by the wanton destruction of precious books and manuscripts, the Jewish staff undertook to rescue what they could by smuggling material out of the YIVO into the ghetto and concealing it there in a secure place. It was a hazardous procedure. On one occasion Sutzkever obtained written permission from an ERR officer to take some "scrap" from the YIVO to use for heating in the ghetto. He and his friends used that permit over and over again to bring books and documents "legally" into the ghetto. When smuggling became too dangerous, the Jewish staff created hiding places in the YIVO's basement and attic, where they reportedly stowed about 5,000 books. Kalmanovich didn't approve of their efforts. According to Shmerke, Kalmanovich held that the way to save the books was to impress the Germans with their scholarly importance and even their financial value. The Germans would then likely ship them all to Germany, where, he argued, the books and manuscripts had a better chance of surviving.

During the last year of the ghetto Kalmanovich kept a diary, which Sutzkever found and sent to the YIVO in 1947. (It was published in the *YIVO-Bleter* in 1951 and later in an English version.) An entry dated August 26, 1943, written shortly before the liquidation of the ghetto, described his despair amid the looted books: "Heaps of books lie on the floor of the YIVO's reading room—a graveyard of books, a mass burial plot, casualties of the war of Gog and Magog, just like their owners." Years later, we learned that in the ghetto people called Kalmanovich "the prophet." In the matter of the books, his prophecies came true, for only a small part of the books and documents which Sutzkever and his friends had hidden was ever recovered.

On February 4, 1945, Churchill, Roosevelt, and Stalin met for a week at Yalta, on the Black Sea, in the Crimea. The front-page photograph of the three leaders showed the unmistakable ravages of illness on Roosevelt's face. There, at Yalta, the Big Three made clear to the world and to the German people what the terms of "unconditional surrender" meant. On February 13, the day after the conference closed, the *New York Times* published an account based on the final communiqués. "Nazi Germany is doomed," read the Yalta communiqué. "Only when Nazism and militarism have been extirpated will there be hope for a decent life for Germans, and a place for them in the comity of nations." Germany, after its military defeat, was to be divided into separate occupation zones, coordinated through a commission of the Supreme Army Commanders sitting in Berlin. Germany would remain under strict control until its armed forces would be disbanded "for all time," its war industries eliminated, every vestige of the Nazi Party and its doctrines eradicated, and other necessary measures taken "to insure that Germany will never again be able to disturb the peace of the world." Germany would also have to pay war damages and reparations. The conferees also agreed that they, together with China and France, would sponsor the founding conference of the United Nations Organization, to convene in San Francisco on April 25.

Meanwhile the Allied armies were closing in on Germany. On March 7, the U.S. First Army crossed the Rhine at Remagen. That's when we at the YIVO started a new vigil—waiting for the Allied seizure of Frankfurt. On March 29, the U. S. Third Army's Fifth Division at last took the city. Most of it had been flattened into rubble. The *New York Times* correspondent reported that you could stand in the center of the city and, looking as far as the eye could see, you would not spot a single undamaged building. Usually Weinreich and I took pleasure in such reports, but not then, not about Frankfurt. For the sake of the YIVO's library, we hoped that Rosenberg's institute had remained intact.

On April 4, the *Times* reported on a survey made for the State Department's Division of Cultural Cooperation about the hundreds of European libraries which the Germans had devastated. That news story and his own barely disciplined impatience spurred Weinreich to write that very day to Archibald MacLeish, then under secretary of state in charge of the Division of Cultural Cooperation. Weinreich's three-page single-spaced letter, which I typed, recounted the history of the looting of the European Jewish libraries for Rosenberg's Frankfurt institute, with particular attention to the YIVO. He raised the possibility that the Germans might have removed the institute's library from Frankfurt to a safer place. But if they had not done so, he cautioned that valuable materials might now likely be buried beneath the ruins of Rosenberg's institute. He stressed the urgency of safeguarding them from further injury and from souvenir hunters. He raised the question of the eventual disposition of the materials and made the case for the YIVO in New York as the rightful owner.

Just days later, we read in the press that a detail of the U.S. Third Army's Fifth Division had discovered a huge collection of Jewish books, manuscripts, and artworks in an ancient castle at Hungen, thirty-two miles from Frankfurt. Those treasures, the papers reported, had been collected under the direction of Alfred Rosenberg and had been looted from Jewish institutions in Russia, Poland, Greece, France, Holland, and Germany. Those news stories were like omens from heaven, heralding good news yet to come. Weinreich's speculations had at last been confirmed. Now we had a realistic basis for our unrealistic hopes. Perhaps we could now recover the remnants of the YIVO library.

On April 12, Roosevelt died suddenly. He had not lived to see victory. We wept that day for his death. I remember my own feelings of loss, for I—and everyone I knew—had seen him as our protector, the president who shared our hatred of Nazi Germany and who had made possible its military defeat. That day Harry S. Truman was sworn in as the thirty-third president of the United States. He told the press: "Please pray for me."

As the Americans, British, and French pushed into Germany, they came upon more evidence of German atrocities. Before those days in April 1945, most of the evidence for the evil things the Germans had done came to us secondhand, relayed by journalists from accounts of a handful of survivors they had interviewed. Only a few times had Western journalists themselves seen at first hand places like Majdanek and Klooga. Though we had read a detailed report about Auschwitz, no one we knew had actually seen it. Now, as American and British armies entered Germany, they saw for themselves sights that surpassed in horror anything they had heard about or ever imagined. They came upon mounds of corpses, bodies piled high on rotting bodies. They also found living survivors of these horrors, only barely alive. Many did not survive their liberation.

Allied troops liberated prisoner-of-war camps and concentration camps at Siegenhain, Langenstein, Buchenwald, Belsen, Erla, Nordhausen, Flossenburg, Ohrdruf, Altendorn, Landsberg, Langwasser, Dachau—places no one had ever heard of before. Every day we read accounts of different camps in the daily press and the weekly news magazines. A correspondent for *Time* magazine described what he saw at Belsen:

> The magnitude of suffering and horror at Belsen cannot be expressed in words and even I, as an actual witness, found it impossible to comprehend fully—there was too much of it: it was too contrary to all principles of humanity—and I was coldly stunned. Under the pine trees the scattered dead were lying, not in twos or threes or dozens, but in thousands. The living tore ragged clothing from the corpses to build fires over which they boiled pine needles and roots for soup. Little children rested their heads against the stinking corpses of their mothers, too nearly dead themselves to cry.

Everywhere the accounts were the same, as reporters struggled to find words to portray the horrors they saw and the revulsion they felt. They, too, wanted to share their hatred of the Germans. When the American and British liberators had come upon the camps, the SS troops who had operated them had already fled. The Allied officers first of all rounded up the German officials of the towns where the camps were located and brought them to witness the criminal deeds which they and their government had committed, to compel them to look at the end results of Nazism. Then the Germans were forced, sometimes at rifle point, to bury the bodies. Everywhere the reporters went, they said the Germans denied they'd ever known anything of these terrible crimes, even though the smell of death and the smoke of burning bodies polluted the air for miles around.

General Eisenhower had seen the camp at Ohrdruf, near Gotha, and afterward cabled Chief of Staff General George C. Marshall, urging him to invite twelve congressmen and twelve American editors to make personal inspections of the camps. He telephoned Churchill on April 18 and extended the same invitation to Members of Parliament and British journalists. The next day Churchill addressed the House of Commons about the horror "at the proofs of these frightful crimes now coming into view" and proposed that eight members of the House of Commons and two of the House of Lords form a parliamentary delegation to leave immediately for their grisly tour of inspection. A London paper reported that "Eisenhower had ordered that every man who could be spared should visit German concentration camps near his unit so that he could tell people at home what the Germans are like." Years later, I read a letter Eisenhower wrote to General Marshall about his visit to the camp near Gotha:

> The things I saw beggar description. While I was touring the camp I encountered three men who had been inmates and by one ruse or another had made their escape. I interviewed them through an interpreter. The visual evidence and the verbal testimony of starvation, cruelty and bestiality were so overpowering as to leave me a bit sick. In one room, where there were piled up twenty or thirty naked men, killed by starvation, George Patton would not even enter. He said he would get sick if he did so. I made the visit deliberately, in order to be in position to give *first-hand* evidence of these things if ever, in the future, there develops a tendency to charge these allegations merely to "propaganda."

At exactly the same time Allied army units were uncovering the German concentration camps with their grisly corpses and skeletal survivors, other Allied army units were uncovering caches of artworks, valuable books, manuscripts, even of gold, all of which the Germans had plundered from their victims. It was a macabre parallel. Our intentness in searching for YIVO's library helped to sustain us then against the horrors of the camps, horrors which we had internalized from accounts we had read back in 1944. The recovery of the looted art treasures gave us hope. We were now convinced that we would find remnants of the Vilna YIVO library at Hungen or in the rubble of Frankfurt.

The end of the war was in sight. On April 28, Mussolini, attempting to escape, was shot by Italian partisans. On April 30, Hitler committed suicide in his bunker in Berlin, as all around him the savage battle for Berlin raged on the streets between the Germans and the Russians. The city was in flames. Berlin fell on May 2. German forces in Holland and Denmark were surrendering. On May 5, German forces in Austria capitulated. On May 7, German generals surrendered at Rheims to Allied officers. They were informed of the terms of unconditional surrender. The next day Truman and Churchill proclaimed the end of the war in Europe. May 8 was V-E Day, the day of victory in Europe. It was a time of muted joy for us, for the war had ended too late for the European Jews.

In June an American sergeant wrote his wife to tell the YIVO that he had found part of its Vilna library at Frankfurt—about 100,000 books packed in some 1,000 crates. The YIVO books were together with books from the École Rabbinique in France, from the Rabbinical Seminary of Amsterdam, and from private libraries. He said that he was trying to convince military government authorities to safeguard "this priceless treasure" and remove it "to a more appropriate place." The news electrified us. At last our expectations had been realized. At last a remnant of the YIVO had survived amid the ruins. It was the only good Jewish news we had had.

Weinreich now concentrated his energy on the recovery of the remnants of the YIVO library. He dictated, and I typed, a new series of letters and memoranda to various government agencies. A month later, we received official confirmation from the State Department's Division of Economic Security Controls. Dated July 23, that letter quoted several paragraphs from a report which General Lucius D. Clay, then deputy chief of the U. S. military government in Germany, had sent to the War Department. The YIVO's collections which had been incorporated into Rosenberg's institute had been uncovered, along with books from other libraries, in two repositories—one, with about 100,000 volumes, in the cellars of the institute's building on Buckenheimer Landstrasse 68–70, in Frankfurt; the other, at Hungen, where over 350,000 volumes were stored. Steps were being taken to ensure the preservation and security of the collections. They were, Clay reported, eventually to be consolidated at one collecting point where they would be sorted and made accessible for later examination. The suggestions made by the Department of State, he added, were being given careful consideration.

At that time, the army had decided to store the Judaica collections in the former Rothschild-Palais, the original home of the Frankfurt Judaica library, then undamaged.

There was still a war to be finished with Japan. That Pacific war had never enlisted my passion as had the European war, but like everyone else I wanted it over. I wanted my friends to come home. That summer Japan fought on, without allies. American forces had taken Iwo Jima and Okinawa and were now closing in on Japan itself. From May to August U.S. battleships shelled Japanese cities and the Twentieth Air Force dropped tens of thousands of tons of bombs on Japan's industrial cities. On July 26, the Big Three—Churchill, Truman, and Stalin—in the last of the war's summit conferences at Potsdam, issued the Potsdam Declaration, an ultimatum which offered Japan a choice between unconditional surrender and total destruction. (Later we learned that during the conference Truman received word that the first atomic test explosion in Alamogordo, New Mexico, had been successful.)

Japan's rulers chose to fight on. On August 6, the first atomic bomb was dropped on Hiroshima. More than half the city was destroyed. But the Japanese still refused to capitulate. On August 9 the second atomic bomb was dropped on Nagasaki. The next day the Japanese Supreme War Council made an offer of surrender. After the Allied terms of unconditional surrender were communicated to them, the Japanese surrendered on August 14. The next day we celebrated the victory over Japan, V-J Day. The war was over.

As 1945 came to a close, we still had no assurance that the YIVO in New York would get back the surviving remnants of its Vilna library. But before the year's end we received a tangible token of the Vilna YIVO's library. It came from Sutzkever. When he was in Moscow, he met several Western journalists and enlisted their aid in getting some of YIVO's materials out of the Soviet Union. Ella Winter, Lincoln Steffens's widow, long reputed as a pro-Soviet journalist, brought the first package late in 1945. She called Weinreich from the downtown editorial offices of a Yiddish newspaper—it was the only address in New York that Sutzkever remembered. Weinreich went there to meet her. The package contained some of Weinreich's own manuscripts and the original manuscript of *Serkele,* a Yiddish drama written in the mid-nineteenth century by the poet and playwright Solomon Ettinger, whose collected works Weinreich had edited.

A few weeks later, the *Herald Tribune*'s Moscow correspondent telephoned and asked Weinreich to pick up a package he had brought from Sutzkever. Weinreich sent me to that West Side apartment, not far from where I was then living. I rang the bell to the journalist's apartment. When he opened the door, I identified myself. He grunted and handed me a small package as I stood in the dimly lit hallway outside his door.

I said "Thank you" and left. He must have been afraid of the Soviet secret police.

That package contained a copy of Volume II of YIVO's *Studies in Psychology and Education*. Leibush Lehrer had edited the manuscript in New York in 1938 and had sent it to Vilna, where it had been set in type in the summer of 1939. In August 1940, the book was printed under Soviet Lithuanian auspices in an edition of only forty copies. The next morning, when we unwrapped the package in Lehrer's presence, was an occasion for tears.

In the spring of 1946 we learned that all the Judaica collections found in Germany which had been stored in the former Rothschild-Palais in Frankfurt had been transferred to a huge collecting point in Offenbach, just across the Main River. They were now the responsibility of the Office of Military Government of the United States (OMGUS), in the section known as Monuments, Fine Arts and Archives (MFA&A), whose men and officers were specialists in art, archives, and libraries attached to field commands. It was their task to advise the military on how best to ensure the security of such valuable properties, protect them from further deterioration, and identify their former owners.

In accordance with the declarations made during the war, the Allied powers established an International Military Tribunal "for the just and prompt trial and punishment of the major war criminals of the European Axis." On November 21, 1945, in his opening address at the International Military Tribunal at Nuremberg, Justice Robert H. Jackson, chief prosecutor for the United States, spoke about the crimes committed against the Jews. His statistical estimate of the number of murdered Jews exceeded Jacob Lestchinsky's. This is what Jackson said:

> Of the 9,600,000 Jews who lived in Nazi-dominated Europe, 60 percent are authoritatively estimated to have perished. 5,700,000 Jews are missing from the countries in which they formerly lived, and over 4,500,000 cannot be accounted for by the normal death rate nor by immigration; nor are they included among displaced persons.

At the YIVO, we, too, were making our reckoning. From the handful who had survived—Sutzkever, Kaczerginski, Grade, and others whom Weinreich knew—we recorded as best we could our losses. The list of those who were alive was short. I heard that the actor Abraham Morewski had been in the Soviet Union. Later he returned to Poland. Hertz Grossbard had been touring in South America when the Germans invaded Poland and had remained in Argentina during the war years. Elihu Yonas, the *pro-aspirant* whom we all loved, had also been in the Soviet Union. My friend the composer and conductor Elya Teitlebaum had survived in the Soviet Union, but we never heard anything further about him. Years later I found his name in a book about Jewish music in Poland. The information was sparse: He had become music director of a Russian theater in Minsk and had died "forlorn" in 1967.

Most of my Vilna friends and acquaintances had been murdered.

Early in September 1943, Zelig Hirsch Kalmanovich was deported from the Vilna ghetto to Estonia. He was sent first to the headquarters of the SS slave-labor camp at Vaivara, then transferred to the camp at Ereda, and finally to the labor camp at Narva. There he died early in 1944 of hunger and disease. His body was burned in one of the crematoria at Narva.

Rivele Kalmanovich left Vilna a few days after her husband, purportedly to join him, but she was taken to Ponary and shot in September 1943.

Stefania Szabad was deported from Vilna and gassed in Majdanek in 1943. In the Vilna ghetto it was said that she conducted herself with dignity and courage.

On November 12, 1943, the Germans uncovered the hiding place in which Miriam Reisen and a dozen others had concealed themselves after the liquidation of the Vilna ghetto. Presumably she was arrested and then shot. It was said that a Yiddish inscription was found scratched on the wall of a Gestapo cell: "I bless my sons Saul and Leibe and my beloved husband Zalmen. I die in peace. Miriam Reisen."

David Kaplan-Kaplansky and his son Saul were deported to labor camps in Estonia in September 1943. In 1944, as the Russians approached, they and other surviving prisoners were evacuated to a camp in Germany, where David died of dysentery late in 1944. His son, too, died. Taybe Kaplan-Kaplansky was deported to Majdanek and gassed there.

Ber Schlossberg, his wife, and their infant were shot at Ponary in September 1943.

Chantche Piszczacer Mann and her daughter Esther lived in the Vilna ghetto after her husband Isaac was seized by German squads in July 1941 and murdered at Ponary. She and her daughter took part in the abortive Vilna resistance of September 1943. Both were deported to Majdanek and gassed there.

Nechama Epstein and Shmuel Zeinvel Pipe were married in Vilna in August 1939. He returned to Sanok for a brief visit, but the German invasion of Poland prevented his return. He probably was murdered during the liquidation of the Sanok ghetto in September 1942. Nechama Epstein was imprisoned in the small Vilna ghetto and, upon its liquidation, shot at Ponary.

Esther Schindelman and her mother were murdered by peasants in a village near Shavli, a town in Lithuania, right after the Red Army retreated from the German invasion in June 1941.

Chaim Munitz and his wife had returned to his native Brasław. There he became secretary of the local Jewish Council. He, his wife, and their family were murdered in the massacre of the Brasław Jews in June 1942.

Joseph Davidsohn and his wife Fania, my friends in Copenhagen, never reached Sweden. In October 1943 their bodies were found in woods near Copenhagen.

Moshe Lerer, the staff member of the YIVO who had abused Kalmanovich during the Soviet period, was deported to Estonia during the liquidation of the Vilna ghetto. At Narva, by a strange twist of fate, his bunk was next to Kalmanovich's. When Lerer became ill with typhus and dysentery, Kalmanovich cared for him, though until then he'd not forgiven Lerer for the wrongs which Lerer had done him during the Soviet period. Lerer died before Kalmanovich; his body was cremated in the camp ovens.

Joseph Gerstein, the conductor of the choir whose performances I often heard, fell into despair in the Vilna ghetto. He became ill and died in the ghetto hospital on September 27, 1942. Kalmanovich was one of those at his death vigil. David Kaplan-Kaplansky spoke at his funeral and Sutzkever read a poem he'd written in his memory.

Wolf Ussian, whom we all knew as Velfkeh, the proprietor of the restaurant where we spent many of our liveliest evenings, was seized late in August 1941 and shot at Ponary.

Sutzkever's mother was shot at Ponary in 1941.

Chaim Grade's mother was in the small ghetto and was shot at Ponary, perhaps on Yom Kippur 1941. His wife, the nurse, worked in the children's ward of the ghetto hospital. She was probably murdered when the Vilna ghetto was liquidated in September 1943.

All the others disappeared without trace. Those who had lived in

Vilna were likely to have been shot at Ponary in 1941, 1942, or 1943, or deported to Majdanek and gassed there. A few thousand were deported to Latvia and Estonia. Those who had lived in Warsaw were likely to have been deported to Treblinka and gassed there. They were among the six million.

May their souls be bound up in the bonds of eternal life.

PART III

CHAPTER 13

━━━

In the Land of Amalek

On September 30, 1946, I sailed from New York on the *Marine Marlin,*
a converted Liberty ship, on my way to occupied Germany to work
among Jewish survivors in the displaced persons camps. Once again I
had embarked on a perverse journey, once again I was traveling against
the traffic. Germany had become the Jews' most implacable foe since the
Romans had destroyed the Second Temple in 70 C.E. In the Bible,
Amalek, who warred against the people of Israel, was the national
enemy of the Jewish people. The Bible enjoined Jews to remember the
deeds of Amalek. In the course of time, Amalek's name entered Jewish
historical consciousness and Jews came to regard their direst enemies as
descendants of Amalek. After 1933, Jews everywhere referred to Germany as Amalek.

Hatred for the Germans continued to consume me, even after the war,
though my rage was somewhat appeased by the knowledge that Germany was a defeated nation, its cities in ruins, its land divided into four
zones and occupied by the victorious Allies. When I embarked on my
journey to occupied Germany, I knew that I would not be among
Germans, but would be part of the American occupation. I told myself
that I was going not to the land of Amalek, but to the realm of Jewish
survivors.

The idea of working among Jewish survivors in Germany had first been broached to me late in 1945 by Koppel Pinson, a professor of German history at Queens College in New York and a close associate of YIVO during the war years. He was then education director of the American Joint Distribution Committee (JDC) in occupied Germany. In his letters to me, usually about YIVO matters, he urged me to enlist in the JDC and come to Munich as his assistant. The possibility that I could be hired for work among Jewish survivors in the camps at once agitated and exhilarated me. If I returned to Europe, I might at last realize the dark fantasies which had obsessed me since 1940, those nightmarish visions in which I saw myself in war-torn Poland in search of Rivele and Kalman. Even long after I knew I'd never again see them, never again embrace them, those dreams continued to haunt me. Going to work among the surviving Jews would be like embarking on a pilgrimage of homage to the dead.

Going to Europe would also resolve my personal dilemmas. Most of my friends were then settling down to normal lives, after their husbands or boyfriends had returned from the war. I, too, had a friend who had returned from the Pacific war theater, but I was no longer the same person I'd been when we had seen each other last in 1942. Driven by memories not rightfully mine, I now inhabited a shadow world of murdered European Jews. I could not share a life with someone who did not share my Jewish perspective. Nor was I ready to share a life with my refugee friend, though we had the same Jewish perspective.

After more than five years at the YIVO, I had become restless. I felt I had come to a dead end. Early in 1945 I had returned to Columbia University on a part-time basis to study Jewish history with Professor Salo W. Baron, the most erudite of Jewish historians. That was my signal to Weinreich that I was unwilling to serve the life term of discipleship he demanded. In Vilna, I recalled, Ber Schlossberg and my friend Chantche Mann had both been utterly devoted to him for years. It was not my nature to offer such fealty and it was not his to encourage the independence I wanted.

In the spring of 1946, as I was completing my course work for a master's degree in Jewish history, I decided to apply to the JDC. They took me on as an education officer. I had to commit myself to at least eighteen months of service. Weinreich was shocked by my decision to leave the YIVO, regarding my departure as a form of apostasy. Thereafter, though we maintained cordial relations until his death in 1969, the warmth that had once existed between us cooled.

Signing up with the JDC for work in Germany was almost like enlisting in the army. You needed more than a passport and evidence of good health to get into Germany. It was then under Allied military government, whose top authority was the four-power Allied Control Council, consisting of the commanders-in-chief of the occupying powers sitting in Berlin. The JDC was one of the Allied voluntary welfare agencies authorized to operate in occupied Germany and Austria under the aegis of the U.S. Army and UNRRA, the United Nations Relief and Rehabilitation Administration. To enter Germany I needed, and received, military clearance and a military permit issued by the Joint Chiefs of Staff for the American zone of occupation. I got another permit for the British and French zones. (The Russians kept their zone off-limits to Westerners.) UNRRA issued me a certificate of identity; since it was preparing to liquidate in 1947, I received an identity card also from its successor organization, the Preparatory Commission for the International Refugee Organization (PC-IRO). Being, as it were, a subordinate of the U.S. Army, I was required to outfit myself with an olive-drab wardrobe of a U.S. Army officer. We wore blue-and-white chevrons, with the letters AJDC, on our uniforms. My rank was equivalent to that of army major and I was entitled to its privileges and priorities.

Once you had the necessary permits and identity cards, you needed travel orders. These were issued by the army, military government, or UNRRA and specified your destination, the purpose of your journey— duty or leave—and the agency to be charged for your fare, UNRRA, in my case. You had to have a persuasive reason to travel; otherwise you didn't always get to go when and how you'd like, for trains were then in short supply. Only a third of Germany's locomotives and railway cars were serviceable, the rest having been heavily damaged by Allied bombings. Military trains—first-class coaches and sometimes sleepers, exclusively for personnel of the Allied military forces and of Allied voluntary agencies—were often overcrowded, with soldiers and noncoms sitting on their baggage in the passageways. Food was not available on any trains. On my first trip into Germany, UNRRA supplied me with a day's K rations. At some stations, the army distributed sandwiches and canned juice; at major terminals, the army's Rail Transportation Office served hot meals in what had once been the German passengers' railroad buffet.

My first destination was Heidelberg, where I had to clear my orders at UNRRA headquarters. That didn't take long: I was given travel orders to Frankfurt, where I would get my JDC assignment. Before my train left, I had time to walk around and lunch at an officers' mess. Except for a couple of damaged bridges, Heidelberg had emerged unscathed from Allied bombings. It was a picturesque medieval town with a castle or two nestled in the hills overlooking the Neckar River. I found myself resenting its loveliness. I'd associated Heidelberg in the days before Hitler with beer-drinking dueling students, romance, and operettas. But those exuberant students had overnight become Nazis. I could no longer think of Heidelberg as a place of waltz-time marzipan sentimentality. Those fun-loving Heidelbergers had burned down the synagogues during *Kristallnacht* and deported to their deaths the Jews who had lived there for generations.

To me Heidelberg, like every place I would see in Germany, had become a site of blood and ashes. The whole time I was in Germany I couldn't bring myself to photograph anything but its ruins and devastation. Everywhere I felt the presence of Nazism as a palpable reality. After all, one of the Allied military government's primary tasks was to de-Nazify the Germans, an undertaking that evoked my skepticism. The moment I arrived in Heidelberg, I was seized by anxiety in case I'd have to speak to a German. I used to imagine all sorts of things I would say or do, sure that any German I might meet would likely have been a Nazi. Nor would it be unlikely that he'd had a hand in murdering Jews.

Heidelberg was then headquarters for the U.S. Third Army as well as UNRRA. Consequently I saw only uniformed Allied personnel everywhere I went. Whatever Germans I encountered were porters and sweepers at the railroad station, chambermaids in the UNRRA billets where I stayed overnight, and waiters in the UNRRA and army messes where I ate. I didn't need to converse with them. I took pleasure seeing them in their menial positions. The Germans at last were being penalized for the evils they had committed. They were no longer the master race. In occupied Germany, the Allied commanders-in-chief were the supreme authorities.

The first bombed building I saw in Germany was Frankfurt's main railroad station. A massive, three-domed structure, it had a roof that looked like the skeleton of a gargantuan monster, for only its steel ribbed framework remained. Even the girders supporting the roof were skeletal. The platforms and train tracks were exposed to the elements. A JDC driver picked me up in a jeep to take me to the JDC office. On the way we passed mounds of rubble and a landscape of gutted hulks of buildings. My driver, a Polish Jewish survivor, told me that even native-born Frankfurters now lost their way around the bombed-out parts of the city.

Frankfurt had been about 65 percent smashed or destroyed by Allied bombs, incendiary raids, and artillery. About half the residential buildings had been totally destroyed and about 10 percent of those still standing were uninhabitable, except in the summer. Their roofs were gashed open, gaping holes where windows and doors had been. I rejoiced in Frankfurt's devastation and the knowledge that many Germans now had to live in cellars. It was little enough punishment for having driven millions of Jews from their homes before murdering them. When I saw the shell of St. Paul's Church, I thought of the thousands of synagogues all over Europe which the Germans had desecrated and then destroyed. It didn't bother me that barely a wall was left standing of the house where Goethe had been born. Frankfurt was famous as Goethe's birthplace, but to me it was the site of Alfred Rosenberg's infamous Institut zur Erforschung der Judenfrage, for whose racist pseudoscholarship the Jewish libraries of Europe had been plundered.

That evening I met Dr. Joseph Schwartz, the head of JDC's European operations. He confirmed my assignment as an education officer in JDC's headquarters in Munich. The next morning UNRRA gave me travel orders to Munich, but before my train left I had the whole day to see Frankfurt.

The Americans chose the undamaged part of the city to establish their military headquarters for the American zone. Its operational center was then named USFET (U.S. Forces European Theater). It was located in the massive complex of buildings with over 1,000 rooms that had been the headquarters of I. G. Farbenindustrie, the huge chemical cartel, notorious for having fueled Hitler's war machine with slave labor supplied by the SS.

The Americans lived near their workplace, in a vast compound of good modern housing adjoining the I. G. Farben complex. Except for its barbed-wire fences and gates, it resembled a suburban American community with its landscaped grounds and quiet streets. The only Germans there were servants and laborers. The compound was provided with many amenities of life back home—a commissary, a post exchange (PX) for shopping, a pharmacy, beauty parlor and barbershop, schools for the dependents' children, movies. A community center was then under construction. One enormous Farben building had been converted into an officers' mess, called the Casino, with a cafeteria and a club.

All over Germany, the American occupation authorities had created a militarily secure and materially comfortable society for the 150,000 Americans working in the army, military government, and Allied voluntary agencies. Without intending to, they had also created a caste system in Germany. Frankfurt, where the separation of Americans and Germans was most conspicuous, introduced me to the most polarized society I had ever known. The dichotomy between the powerful and the powerless in occupied Germany, between the privileged and the unprivileged, was starker than any disparities between rich and poor that I had seen in New York or between Jews and Poles that I had observed in Vilna. Created by the Allied military occupation, this dichotomy had nothing to do with traditional hierarchies of class or the oppression of a minority by a majority. Instead, it summoned up the image of the Raj, the British reign in India. In Germany the Raj was the consequence of Germany's unconditional surrender and the determination of the Allied military government that Germany would never again become the scourge of the world.

To create its European version of the Raj, the Americans took from the Germans housing, fuel, and rolling stock, but they brought in everything else they needed for themselves, including food and gasoline. Americans ate in their own messes and shopped at army commissaries and PXes. There they could buy canned and packaged foods, instant coffee, peanuts, chocolates and candies, soft drinks, cigarettes, liquor, soap, towels, toilet paper and cleansing tissues, clothing, writing supplies—all at prices well below those in the United States. On the highways, they had their own gas stations and snack bars. Americans even had their own monetary system. In September 1946, just before I arrived, the authorities introduced military scrip with which to pay American personnel.

Everywhere in Germany, the army set up its own recreational facilities—movies, theaters, dances, sports, even travel organizations. It maintained service clubs, canteens, snack bars, and doughnut shacks, some run by the Red Cross. The army published its own daily newspaper, *Stars and Stripes,* and operated its own radio station, the Armed Forces Network, which broadcast news, music, and major-league baseball games. I became a grateful patron of the army's installations, relishing the doughnuts and good coffee at the Red Cross, dependent on the soap, tissues, peanuts, cigarettes, and whisky I bought in the PX, thriving on the Coca-Colas and hamburgers I ate in army canteens, and attending army movie theaters. That was the way to ease homesickness and relieve the sense of dislocation created by the bizarreries of living in the desolate bombed-out cities of occupied Germany.

In October 1946 I arrived in Munich, my post for the next half year. Situated on the banks of the Isar River, once the capital of the Kingdom of Bavaria, Munich was better known as the cradle of the Nazi movement. There, in 1919, Hitler used to make speeches in the Schwemme, the ground-floor poor-man's beer cellar of the Hofbräuhaus. There, in 1920, in that same Hofbräuhaus, he took over the leadership of the National Socialist Party. There, in 1923, using that same Hofbräuhaus as headquarters for one of his battalions, he launched the Putsch that failed. In 1930, as the Nazi movement grew, the party purchased for its headquarters the Barlow-Palais, formerly the Italian embassy, at 45 Briennerstrasse, one of Munich's two most imposing streets, right near the Königsplatz, an equally imposing square. After they came to power, the Nazis made the area even more grandiose. Hitler's architect, Paul Ludwig Troost—Albert Speer's predecessor—enlarged the Barlow-Palais and then, by paving over the wide grassy plots of the Königsplatz with stone, created a mammoth parade ground for flaunting Nazi military strength.

Munich was Heinrich Himmler's birthplace and he, too, made history there. In March 1933, when Himmler headed not only the SS, but also Munich's provisional police, he created a new institution and invented a name for it—"concentration camp." The first concentration camp in Nazi Germany was built at Dachau, just ten miles northwest of Munich.

In 1946, little of Munich's early Bavarian splendor or Nazi grandeur was to be seen. About 75 percent of the city had been damaged or destroyed. Even after more than a year of clearing the debris, some streets were still impassable because of the piles of smashed brick, blasted stone, shattered glass, and twisted iron and steel. Ruins of buildings leaned at precarious angles, their roofs and windows gone, their insides hollow. But some historic places had survived with little or no damage.

The Hofbräuhaus had become a Red Cross center where you could get hot dogs, ice cream sodas, and other American fare. The Haus der deutschen Kunst, on Prinzregentenstrasse, Troost's first exercise in megalomaniacal architecture, completed after his death, had been turned into a U.S. Army officers' mess and club. The Nazi Party building on Briennerstrasse had been requisitioned by the military government's Monuments, Fine Arts and Archives (MFA&A) section to serve as a collecting point for the art and sculpture which the Nazis had robbed from museums and private collections throughout Europe. The Deutsches Museum, a large complex on an island in the Isar, was used by Allied personnel as well as Jewish and Polish survivors as an information center to trace missing relatives and friends. Dachau, from which the Americans had liberated its prisoners in April 1945, had been taken over by the Americans as a prison for Nazis and SS men.

Munich was JDC's headquarters for the American Zone of Germany, because it had the largest concentration of Jewish displaced persons in occupied Germany. "Displaced persons" (DPs) was the term for the more than 6.5 million non-Germans from all over Europe whom the Germans had brought into Germany during the war as forced laborers or concentration-camp prisoners. By dint of a stupendous effort, the U.S. Army, assisted by UNRRA, managed to repatriate about 6 million of them by the end of 1945. More than 500,000 remained in the American zone. They were the ones who would not or could not return home. Most were Poles and Balts; about 100,000 were Ukrainians who feared they'd be tried and punished for their wartime collaboration with the Germans.

About 156,000 of the unrepatriable DPs were Jews, who no longer had any homes to return to. Some 50,000 of them had been found alive in concentration camps by the liberating Allied armies. Then, in 1946, about 100,000 Jewish refugees poured into the American zone from the east. Many had been in the Soviet Union during the war and were repatriated in 1945 to their homes in Poland and Rumania. Back home, they found that their families had been wiped out and their property stolen. Everywhere they faced open anti-Semitism. Once again they set out, in an unprecedented mass movement, traveling westward across the Polish border, through the Soviet zone of Germany, into Berlin, or—a later route—through Czechoslovakia into Bavaria. After the pogrom in Kielce on July 4, 1946, when the Poles murdered forty-two Jews only because they had returned home to start new lives and rebuild their community, the flow of refugees from Poland turned into a torrent and continued until the winter set in. In mid-1947, according to UNRRA, about 156,000 Jewish DPs lived in the American zone, 15,000 in the British zone, and 2,000 in the French zone.

In the American zone, the U.S. Army was responsible for housing, feeding, and clothing the DPs. Housing was mainly in the comfortless former German barracks of what had been prisoner-of-war, forced-labor, and concentration camps. The food which the army requisitioned for the DPs came from German agricultural production. According to the provisions of the Potsdam Agreement, the Germans had to provide food not only to the countries they had ravaged, but also to the DPs, who were entitled to receive the equivalent of 2,000 calories daily. Food was then rationed in Germany. The Germans themselves were restricted to a daily diet of 1,500 calories, for the Allied victors had stipulated that Germany's standard of living was not to be higher than the rest of Europe. A diet of 2,000 calories was barely enough for people to live on, especially if they'd been starved for years. Nor was the food sufficiently nutritious, consisting as it did mainly of potatoes, turnips, bread, and ersatz coffee. The army and UNRRA, whose personnel administered the DP camps, as well as private social-service agencies, provided supplementary food and clothing.

The JDC was the principal institution to care for the Jewish DPs. Since 1915, the JDC, based in New York, had been helping the Jewish poor, homeless, sick, and war-stricken throughout the world, but never in its history had the agency faced such monumental tasks. Everywhere in Europe the surviving Jews were in need, but the displaced Jews in Germany, Austria, and Italy were the most distressed of all. The JDC provided food, clothing, and medical care, and a host of other services. It shipped staggering amounts of relief supplies to Europe—nearly 30,000 tons in 1946 and over 40,000 in 1947. Most of the tonnage was high-energy foods to supplement the local diet: canned fish and meat, butter, fats, sugar. The balance consisted of clothing and shoes, blankets, medicines, surgical equipment, even textbooks and educational materials for the over 10,000 children in schools which the survivors established in the camps. JDC's major service was in emigration assistance, though visas to anywhere and certificates to Palestine were in short supply. With the support of the army and UNRRA, JDC also provided for the cultural and religious needs of the DPs—provision of *shehitah,* kosher canteens, facilities for religious services, prayerbooks, religious texts, special foods for Jewish festivals, newspapers, and libraries.

To carry out these functions, JDC hired an unprecedently large overseas staff; in Germany alone it numbered nearly 150. They consisted of doctors, nurses, social workers, child-care workers, emigration specialists, educators, administrative and secretarial personnel. More than half were Americans; the rest, British, Belgian, French, South African, and Canadian nationals. The overseas staff, all entitled to the privileges of U.S. Army officers, were graded as Class I personnel. JDC also hired staff from among the Jewish DPs. Graded as Class II, they received minimal salaries in dollars and Reichsmarks.

Because its staff in Munich was large, JDC had its own billets and mess. We, the Class I personnel, lived in a modern four-story apartment house on Schumannstrasse, a quiet street in the Bogenhausen section of Munich, next to Red Cross regional headquarters and just three blocks from JDC headquarters. Each of us had our own room in one of the building's ten or so four- or five-room apartments, sharing a kitchen, bathroom, and toilet. The winter of 1946–1947 was said to have been the coldest for the last fifty years, but we had plenty of heat and hot water. We also had German maid service. The only thing we didn't have was privacy—we called our billets *Schumannstrasse Kaserne,* Schumann Street Barracks. Our mess, a requisitioned German villa on Möhlstrasse, just a block from the office, fed us plentifully, though not always to our satisfaction. We had PX privileges and we, too, lived in a modest version of the Raj, not quite on the scale of the brass in Frankfurt.

On the way to work at our offices at 3 Siebertstrasse, just off a pretty little park facing the Isar, we passed shells of bombed-out buildings and mounds of rubble. JDC was housed in a three-story brick building, which, like our mess and the other impressive villas erected in the area at the turn of the century, was set back from the street, its grounds enclosed by a high iron fence. Until recently it had been the residence of a top Nazi. The villa's grounds had space enough for our motor pool, with its jeeps, small trucks, and ambulances.

JDC headquarters in Munich was responsible for the Jews in the American zone, an area of 47,000 square miles in southeast Germany, comprising the states of Hesse, Wuerttemberg-Baden, and Bavaria. The American zone had only two large cities—Frankfurt and Munich—lots of scenery, and an enormous number of Jewish installations—about sixty camps, small DP communities in over a hundred towns and cities, about a dozen children's centers, several Jewish hospitals and sanatoria, and thirty farms used as training centers for would-be emigrants to Palestine (one was on the estate and farm of the notorious Nazi leader Julius Streicher). Because rail service was limited, the mails were slow,

and making telephone connections was time consuming, the JDC maintained a courier service to keep in touch with its regional offices and
larger DP installations.

Twice weekly, a driver set out at 6 A.M. in an ambulance, carrying
mail and supplies. It was an eleven-hour trip from Munich to Frankfurt
by way of Landsberg, Leipheim, Ulm, Stuttgart, and Heidelberg. The
return trip from Frankfurt went through Aschaffenburg, Würzburg,
Bamberg, Fürth, and Nuremberg. On two occasions, when I needed to
visit some camps, I traveled with the courier. The Autobahn, with its
army gas stations and snack bars, reminded me of the Merritt Parkway,
except for the occasional detours because of bombed-out bridges and the
infrequent sights of a rusting tank or disintegrating plane in a field. On
the road between Stuttgart and Heidelberg, we passed Bruchsal. It was
a ghost town, the most devastated place I ever saw in Germany, including Berlin. Later I learned that it had been a railway junction.

We, the overseas staff, were a motley lot. Most of the men had been
recruited in France or Germany, after they left the army or had done
a stint for UNRRA. Those who'd been with the army in Germany were
likely to be free-wheeling, experienced in "organizing" or "liberating"
food, shelter, and other necessities for the Jews they had liberated. Like
contemporary Robin Hoods, they were—or acted as if they were—
tough and unsentimental, working hard and playing hard. They hardly
ever spoke about the murder of the European Jews, but they were
indelibly marked by its horror. Not many were knowledgeable about
Judaism and few knew Yiddish well or even at all. The women on our
staff, in contrast, had been recruited in New York or Johannesburg and
were, for the most part, trained social workers. A few were top-notch
secretaries. More earnest than the men, the women were more articulate
about their Jewish commitments, which had brought them to the JDC.

The director of JDC's operations in the American zone was Leo W.
Schwarz, a writer whose anthologies of world Jewish literature, published in the 1930s, I had long admired. When I met him, Leo was about
forty, a dark-haired, handsome man of medium height, with a cigarette
always dangling from his lower lip. He had received a battlefield
commission in Normandy and after the liberation of Paris became a
medical administrative officer of a U.S. Army hospital in France. A
deeply committed Jew, it was inevitable that he would sign up with
JDC after he was demobilized. Leo was driven by nervous and seem-

ingly inexhaustible energy. His restless mind was prodigal with ideas for
projects to help the Jews. He knew army channels inside out and could
maneuver through the military government network; he had connections everywhere. When he returned from a trip, he usually brought
back supplies which he had wangled out of the army or even out of
JDC in Paris—paper stock for printing books, Yiddish typewriters, a
huge supply of army blankets to make coats for our DPs.

The head of JDC's Education Department was then Philip Friedman,
a historian from Lwów, who, before the war, had been a colleague of
Emanuel Ringelblum and Raphael Mahler. (Pinson had returned home
just a month before I came to Munich.) Friedman had just come from
Poland. In Munich, his tasks were to shape educational programs for the
Jewish schools in the camps and to work with the Central Historical
Commission, created by Jewish survivors, which gathered eyewitness
testimonies of German crimes against the Jews. I was assigned to the
department's practical operations—getting supplies for the educational
and cultural institutions which the Jewish DPs had themselves created.

They had, by October 1946, built up an extensive—if primitive—
network of institutions. They had begun at the top, when, in the summer
of 1945, a few months after liberation, they had created the Central
Committee of the Liberated Jews of the American Zone of Germany,
to represent their interests. In September 1946, just before I came to
Munich, the Central Committee had accomplished something remarkable. It had received recognition from the military government as the
representative body of the Jews in occupied Germany. A month later,
the military government appointed Colonel George R. Scithers as liaison officer to the Central Committee.

By that time, the Jews in occupied Germany had established over
sixty schools with 10,000 pupils, about twenty libraries, a historical
commission with many local and regional groups, four newspapers and
one journal, and several dramatic and musical groups. To run these
institutions they needed classroom equipment and educational materials,
books for libraries, newsprint and printing facilities, resources for dramatic and choral groups. It became my responsibility to get what I could
for them from sources available to us.

One of my first assignments was to check on the status of licenses for the
Yiddish camp newspapers. Under military government regulations, no
paper could be published without its permission. The policy had been

established primarily to encourage the democratization of German public and political life, but was applied also to DP publications. To foster
the rise of a free press, licenses for newspapers and journals were issued
only to such persons who demonstrated "an active devotion to democratic ideals." The editors of licensed papers obligated themselves not to
publish news that would endanger military security. They could not
advocate Nazi, Pan-German, militarist, or undemocratic ideas, nor could
they disseminate malicious criticism of occupation policies or personnel.
Licenses were issued by the Information Control Division (ICD) of the
Press Division of the Office of Military Government for Bavaria
(OMGB) and had to be approved by USFET in Frankfurt. The Office
of Military Government United States (OMGUS), with its headquarters
in Berlin, was responsible for civilian matters under the occupation, but
USFET, part of the General Staff, retained control of legal matters,
public health and welfare, and public safety.

In October 1946, only one German newspaper, besides a dozen or so
journals, was then being published in Munich—*Die Neue Zeitung*. Because of the shortage of paper, it appeared just three times a week. The
following month the military government approved the license for a
second newspaper, the *Münchener Mittag*. *Die Neue Zeitung* was, in
effect, an organ of the American occupation. Its editor-in-chief, Hans
Wallenberg, a German Jew, had been an editor and journalist in Berlin,
who had emigrated to the United States in 1937 and was drafted into
the U.S. Army in 1942. In 1945 he and the novelist Hans Habe founded
the first postwar newspaper in Germany, *Die Allgemeine Zeitung,* published in Berlin by the U.S. Army. In 1946 he came to Munich to run
Die Neue Zeitung. It was natural that the military government should
have taken advantage of his journalistic experience and political reliabil-
ity.

The shortage of printing facilities limited the issuance of licenses.
Many printing plants had been damaged. The military government
needed permission from the previous owners—in some cases, Jews
whom the Nazis had expropriated—to repair and use their presses. The
shortage of paper was also a factor in licensing newspapers and, once
a license had been issued, in determining how frequently a paper could
appear and in how many copies. Each publication needed, along with
its license, also an allocation of paper from OMGB.

The licenses for our DP publications had expired at the end of
October. One camp newspaper was then ready to go to press, waiting
only for the ICD-OMGB imprimatur. On November 2, I went to

OMGB headquarters, nervous at the prospect of confronting a fierce colonel who'd give me a hard time. Instead I found a pleasant young major. We talked of this and that for a while; he had once worked for B'nai B'rith Hillel Foundation in the States. We had much in common. He was eager to help me, but couldn't find any record in his files of the disposition of our application. He'd have to check, but he proposed—off the record—that our paper go to press as of October 31.

Back in my office, I was not quite satisfied with the outcome. I called a woman I'd met in Heidelberg, who was UNRRA liaison in the cultural and educational field. Right away she checked out the status of our licenses and informed me that USFET in Frankfurt had approved their renewals. The telegram of authorization had got lost somewhere in the shuffle of papers. It would take a few more days until we had the licenses in our possession, but we could go ahead and publish. That was an instance of a snafu, a frequently used army term, an acronym for *s*ituation *n*ormal, *a*ll *f*ouled *u*p. People used to say there were two ways of doing things—the right way and the army way. The army didn't always know what the military government was up to, the military government didn't know what UNRRA was up to, and UNRRA didn't necessarily know what the others were doing.

A month later, using the contacts I had already made in OMGB, I approached the Press Division with the request for the use of a linotype machine for a DP Yiddish journal, then being set by hand. (One set of Yiddish linotype matrices, which had been obtained from the United States, was then available in Munich; I was trying to get several more sets.) My inquiries soon brought me to the editor-in-chief of *Die Neue Zeitung,* U.S. Major Hans Wallenberg. At the time, I didn't know all of his history, but our conversation gave me some clues. My negotiations turned out to be easier than I had anticipated. Our journal was given the unlimited use of a linotype on the premises of *Die Neue Zeitung*'s plant. That meant our editors and their typesetter could make use of the plant's other facilities. It was the largest printing plant in the area, the former home of the official Nazi Party paper, the *Völkischer Beobachter.*

For Jewish survivors to have access to the facilities of the press that had once been the disseminator of vicious anti-Semitic propaganda seemed to be a grotesque historical irony. Aware of my own thrill of triumph in getting the use of those facilities for Jewish survivors, I wondered what Wallenberg's private thoughts might have been in those circumstances. He, who once had been a pariah in his fatherland, now wielded editorial power over those who had persecuted him. In his American officer's uniform, ensconced in the former citadel of Nazi propaganda, he was now shaping Germany's future. One thing I knew for sure. He must have felt that history had at last rewarded him.

My most complicated and distasteful task was getting textbooks printed for the camp schools as well as other materials as the occasion required. Though I was at home in printing plants in New York, familiar with their operations since my high school days, that experience was not much help to me in maneuvering through the hazards of the German economy.

Germany was then industrially crippled, nearly prostrate. Hitler had had a share in its incapacity, for it was he who had driven the Germans to fight to the last and thereby invite Germany's utter devastation. After Germany's surrender, the Allies set limits on its industrial capability. At Potsdam they agreed that Germany's economy would be based on agriculture and peaceful domestic industry, thereby ensuring that Germany would remain disarmed and never again become a military threat. German industry was to be demilitarized, decentralized, and decartelized. War plants and their industrial equipment were to be removed and transferred as reparations in kind to liberated countries and to the Soviet Union. (The Russians were thorough in dismantling German industrial plants in their zone.)

Coal was Europe's basic source of heat and energy, for fueling industry. Most of Germany's coal deposits were in the industrial Ruhr valley, in the British zone in northwest Germany. The French zone, in the southwest, had some coal in the Saar region and the Russian zone, to the east, had the Silesian coal fields. The American zone, with scarcely any coal deposits, had to get coal from the British.

The shortages of coal, gas, and raw materials impeded the restoration of industrial production. In the American zone, which had a moderate amount of industry, only about a fifth of the industrial plants were operating. A rich timber area, it had many sawmills, but fewer than half were functioning. No more than 25 percent of the factories producing textiles, clothing, and household commodities were at work. That bitterly cold winter of 1946–1947, electric power was rationed, with power shut off at specific times (*Stromsperre*). Factories and offices operated only three days a week. (In our office, we worked by candlelight at those times.) No fuel at all was available to industry during the week between Christmas and New Year's Day; all factories in the American zone were shut down.

The military government's first priority in restoring Germany's industrial plants to productivity was to meet the military needs of the American occupation forces. Its second priority was to fulfill the schedule of German reparations to provide food, fuel, and industrial goods for the liberated countries and also for the DPs inside Germany. Only thereafter, as the lowest priority, could German industry start providing the minimum essentials for German civilians.

The Germans needed food, clothing, soap, and cigarettes, but since these were not being produced in sufficient quantity, German stores had nothing to sell. Americans, however, had what the Germans wanted. Because Americans had no use for the German Reichsmarks, which could not buy anything anyway, the Germans began to empty their closets and cupboards to barter their possessions. The Americans, for their part, were ready to trade their supplies for Leica cameras, Bausch & Lomb binoculars, microscopes, Dresden figurines, Meissen and Rosenthal china and porcelain, crystal, paintings, *Lederhosen,* even Nazi mementos.

American cigarettes—Lucky Strike, Chesterfields, Camels, Philip Morris—became the universally accepted coin of the realm, the standard unit of exchange. A black market existed in every country in Europe, but only in occupied Germany did it become the basis for the economy's operation. On the official exchange, a dollar would get you ten Reichsmarks, but a pack of American cigarettes, which cost five cents in the PX or about fifteen cents in the States, would net you seventy Reichsmarks. In Berlin a carton of American cigarettes sold for fifteen dollars, in real money or military scrip. (Scrip, too, had worked its way into the black market, into the illegal possession of Germans and DPs.)

Cigarette butts became a barterable commodity and created a new entrepreneurial class—*Kippensammler,* collectors of cigarette butts. Seven butts could be made into one cigarette; one cigarette could buy a meal. Germans loitered wherever Americans congregated, near PXes, Army movie theaters, Red Cross snack bars. They were coiled to spring for cigarette butts. Sometimes they'd bump their heads, dashing for the same butt. German children everywhere learned to trail American soldiers, collecting their discarded butts.

As the demand for American cigarettes accelerated, Americans began to send home for cigarettes, because the PX ration was limited to one carton a week. A network of mail-order houses, situated mostly on the

East Coast, specializing in shipping cartons of cigarettes and other desirable barter items to Germany, soon came into existence.

Cigarettes could buy you anything on the black market from a loaf of coarse black bread to a Persian rug. One of my colleagues bought a prewar German portable typewriter in good condition for five cartons; another bought a German radio for five cartons. With enough cigarettes you could acquire a fine leather suitcase or a stolen original artwork. I heard that in Marburg, where Max Weinreich had once earned his doctorate, you could buy a doctoral degree for cigarettes. For Hebrew lessons which I was taking three times weekly with a survivor employed in the Central Committee's Education Department, I paid one pack per lesson. Cigarettes bought labor, for nothing could be produced without cigarettes, whether it was a small personal service or large-scale manufacture. I used to get my snapshots developed in a couple of days, despite the paper shortage, for a handful of cigarettes and I had a desk made for my room in Schumannstrasse for three packs of cigarettes.

Cigarettes gave the Germans more incentive to work than Reichsmarks. The food they obtained on the black market gave them the strength to work harder and the opportunity to earn still more cigarettes. I once read in *Stars and Stripes* that, according to statistics of the Frankfurt Health Department, Germans were eating 40 percent more than their authorized food ration. Cigarettes were the real stimulants of the German economy.

The JDC officially allocated cartons of cigarettes to each of its operating departments to enable us to get things done. We also had an expert on procurement on our staff—a survivor of Dachau, who knew his way around the industrial plants in Munich. The staff called him a BTO— Big-Time Operator. Alas for me, he was in hospital when I came to Munich. For two months, I had to learn by trial and error how to get books printed under the bizarre conditions of the German economy.

The textbooks, mainly Hebrew primers which had been chosen by the Zionist-minded survivors in charge of the camp schools, were to be reproduced by offset lithography. To get our books printed, we needed, first of all, a license from ICD, which was contingent on the availability of paper. Even though Munich, as the industrial center of a substantial timber industry, had many paper factories, their production was small, since they were short of fuel, equipment, and raw materials, like the rest of Germany's industrial enterprises. JDC solved our paper problem by bringing in American paper, usually donated by American Jews in the business. The paper I found in JDC's warehouse was heavy coated stock of superior quality. We couldn't use it, but we bartered it for larger quantities of cheaper paper, suitable for our textbooks and for school copybooks. I used to worry that sharp German businessmen were cheating me on the barter. As soon as our BTO procurement officer recovered his health, I enlisted him to help me bargain with the Germans.

Offset lithography required film, which we didn't always have. I used to complain to New York that when the film did arrive, it was the wrong kind. But we bartered what we had or compensated for what we didn't have with cigarettes. My first accomplishment was the printing of a 200-page textbook in an edition of 5,000 copies. It cost JDC about $500 in Reichsmarks, plus several cartons of cigarettes and a few food packages out of our supplies.

Before Hanukkah, I worked long hours to produce a bulletin, in Yiddish and Hebrew, with appropriate materials to celebrate the festival in the camps—popular history, songs, and stories. Our staff typed some thirty-five stencils. A German firm printed about 1,000 copies, and collated and stapled the pages in just a half day. It cost, besides the nominal Reichsmarks, three packs of cigarettes and one chocolate bar.

By February, I had four printers and engravers working for us. We needed that many to make up the time lost by the power shortages and the short workweek. We printed 20,000 Purim *megillot* practically overnight so that the Religious Department could get them out in time. Not wanting to be late for Passover, I had the plates for the Haggadah ready in February. Including the prayerbooks printed before I came, the JDC published over 300,000 copies of religious and educational books in the period I was there.

Several months later I succeeded in getting Yiddish matrices for linotype machines. After we had obtained access to the linotype machine at *Die Neue Zeitung,* we lined up machines on a similar basis in Stuttgart and Frankfurt. For these we needed additional sets of Yiddish matrices. The largest type foundry in Germany, I found out, was Stampel in Frankfurt. Astonishingly, they still had the fonts for Yiddish type, which they used to produce before 1933. In February I went to see the plant's manager, who told me the plant was shut down for lack of coal. Eager for the opportunity to exploit the rich Jews and the U.S. Army, he proposed to make as many sets of Yiddish matrices as we could use, if we supplied him with 100 tons of coal to operate the plant. Knowing that JDC could never justify such a request to the army, especially during that bitter winter, we decided to wait until warm weather, when the need for coal would not be so acute. Early in July, I picked up from the factory four full sets of Yiddish matrices. They had cost us 2,000 Reichsmarks, plus the obligatory cigarettes and chocolate to induce the Germans to work.

Getting the printing done was distasteful to me, not just because I disliked bargaining and bribing the German factory managers, but because I hated the Germans and hated to do business with them. I came to their plants, wearing my U.S. Army uniform with its AJDC chevrons, disciplining my feelings with a brisk business-like manner. Whenever possible, I spoke English, unwilling to give the Germans the satisfaction that I knew their mother tongue. Without exception, every single German businessman I met used to express his admiration and respect for the Jewish people, avow that he had never been a Nazi, and that he had never known of the terrible things that the Nazis had done to the Jews. The litany became familiar. I never responded. Instead I'd say: "Never mind. What about this deal?" I'd then put a deposit, as it were, on the table—a couple of packs of cigarettes, a chocolate bar. The eagerness with which they reached for the "deposit" reinforced the contempt I had for them. I enjoyed seeing them quiver in anticipation for more, as we haggled. My hatred must have been evident. Though they behaved cravenly, obsequiously, they were duplicitous. They hated us, too.

I must have dealt with dozens of Germans in the printing and paper business, yet I cannot summon up a single name, a single face. Even when I was negotiating with them, I blocked them out of my mind. How could I possibly have confronted them as people? They were all the right age to have murdered Jews. I had no idea of their histories. Surely they had strutted on Munich's broad avenues singing "Horst Wessel." How many of them, I used to wonder, had been on the Russian front, helping the SS shoot down Jewish men, women, and children?

To be sure, I knew that the Allied occupation had outlawed national socialism and dissolved the Nazi Party and its affiliates. Nazi legislation was annulled. Leading Nazis had been arrested and were being tried for their crimes. On September 30, 1946, the day I sailed for Europe, the International Military Tribunal at Nuremberg had already delivered its verdict on twenty-two major Nazi war criminals and had found them all guilty on one or more counts of war crimes and crimes against humanity. I knew that Dachau had become an internment camp for thousands of Nazis in this region—SS men and officers, party functionaries and government officials, all awaiting trials, hearings, or de-Nazification proceedings.

Even so, I was convinced that Munich, as indeed all of Germany, was aswarm with former Nazi Party members and sympathizers, all at liberty, their minds still filled with the lurid anti-Semitism in which they had been indoctrinated for over twelve years. How could all that be eradicated overnight? Under the military government, Germans who had been more than nominal members of the Nazi Party were excluded from political activity and from places of prominence in public and private life. Yet a neo-Nazi party, Die Sozialistische Reichspartei, had already come into existence, peopled with the old Nazis still at large.

Millions of Germans had to be brought before the de-Nazification courts, over which the Americans presided. The procedures soon taxed American manpower resources and in June 1946, the Americans turned those proceedings over to German tribunals, whose members had already been de-Nazified. The German-run tribunals functioned under Allied supervision. In January 1947, some 450 de-Nazification tribunals were in operation. Over 200,000 cases had already been tried; about 370,000 Nazis had been removed from their positions; about 1,300,000 remained to be heard.

Even Germans were skeptical about the efficacy of the tribunals, questioning the honesty of the tribunal examiners. It was said they were corrupt, sympathetic to the Nazis, easily bought. Once, in November 1946, I saw a German cabaret skit lampooning the de-Nazification proceedings. A friend from my years at the Sholem Aleichem Mitlshul, the son of a Yiddish poet, was then working for the military government, in ICD's German Re-education Program. He supervised the content of German theatrical productions and of the literary-political skits of cafes and cabarets. One evening, he invited me to visit such a cafe.

The place was tiny, not much larger than a spacious living room, the stage about six feet square. The two-hour program included several political sketches, one about de-Nazification proceedings. It went like this: A tribunal examiner faced the audience, arms akimbo. A woman entered. He asked: "Waren Sie [Were you] . . . ?" It wasn't necessary to finish the question. She answered that she was just an ordinary person and didn't know about anything. He fined her 1,000 marks and let her go. A man entered. "Waren Sie . . . ?" "No, certainly not," he replied, but it turned out he was one of Hitler's Reichministers, though he protested his innocence of all crimes. The examiner let him off scot-free. A third person entered, slipped some money into the examiner's hands, and went out. Looking all around, the examiner asked the audience if they'd seen anyone in the room.

The American military government had also undertaken to educate the Germans in the principles of democracy, to introduce them to the ideals and practices of representative government and free elections. Under American supervision, democratic political parties were established with the rights of assembly and free speech. In January 1946, in an effort to decentralize Germany's political structure and develop greater local responsibility, elections were held to choose local councils. This was the first step in turning back the day-to-day running of local administration to the Germans, though the military government still continued to supervise their activities.

In the American zone, the local authority the Germans wielded did not extend to the Jewish DPs or their institutions. German police were not permitted to enter Jewish camps; Jews charged with crimes in the camps were not tried in German courts. Instead, the Jews were allowed to have their own police organizations in the camps and establish their own courts. (Jews living in the cities were, perforce, under the jurisdiction of the German police and German courts.)

Only once, in the time I was in Germany, did I have a run-in with a German police officer. In June 1947, I took a transport of Jewish emigrants from Frankfurt to Paris. They were no longer DPs, for they were on their way to new homes and new lives. It was my task to shepherd them through the journey. I was responsible for their papers and safety, solicitous of their comfort, and obligated to deliver them in Paris to a JDC shelter.

This transport consisted of thirty-one adults, one child, and four infants. The French Rail Travel Office and French liaison had provided a third-class coach (wooden seats) exclusively for us. It was attached to a German civilian train going as far as Saarbrücken in the French zone. Our coach was to be disconnected from the German train at Ludwigshaven, on the French side of the zone border, and attached to a French civilian train bound for Paris. Since the train had no food or water, I had ordered a couple of GI water tanks. My passengers brought their own food; UNRRA gave us some cans of salmon and crackers. Knowing we had children aboard, I used up my month's PX ration and brought canned milk, chocolate, candies, chewing gum, and a couple of cases of Coca-Cola.

The back door of our coach was kept locked, but the front door was open. It was my responsibility to keep unauthorized people out. I was there to represent the authority of the United States and protect my flock from unwarranted searches. Whenever the train pulled into a station, I stationed myself at the door. At Mannheim, the last stop in Germany, a German policeman came to the door. I asked him what he wanted. "Deutsche Kontrolle," he replied. I asked him what he wanted to check. He said he had to check papers before the train entered the French zone. I told him that ours was an international coach, that German police were not permitted to enter. He became enraged, sputtering angrily. I stood impassively at the door. He didn't dare touch my American officer's uniform. I had humiliated him, injured his German dignity, hindered his officiousness. He said, in as threatening a manner as he could, that he would get an MP. I replied, quite coolly: "You do that." He left, red-faced. He never returned, with or without an MP. Ten minutes later the train pulled out. My passengers, who probably hadn't expected much protection from their barely five-foot American escort, now accepted me as one of them. It was a small victory, but I felt as if I had triumphed over Amalek in this hated land.

CHAPTER 14

▬

Saving Remnants

Classified as "displaced persons," a euphemism for uprooted people, the Jews in occupied Germany thought of themselves not as displaced, but as outcast. Having survived Hitler's murderous cosmos, they had taken shelter in the comfortless climate of his devastated Reich. Now, as inmates of DP camps, they were suspended between an unspeakable past and an uncertain future, their existence like a time-out of history.

They described themselves officially as "liberated Jews," but among themselves they were *katsetlers* or *katsetnikes,* concentration-camp inmates. The name came from KZ (pronounced *ka-tset* in German), the abbreviation for *Konzentrationslager.* Those were the people with the Nazi numbers tattooed on their forearms. They also spoke of themselves as *amkho. Amkho* was a biblical word which meant "Your people," that is, God's people. Over the centuries that word also came to mean "the common people." During the war, *amkho* became a watchword for Jews on the run, in flight from the Germans or other enemies, to signal one another that they were Jews, even when disguised as non-Jews.

They had still another name, a more exalted one, resonant with the consciousness of their place in Jewish history—*Sheerit ha-Peletah,* a biblical reference to "the remnant that was saved." In the course of centuries, the phrase had taken on a thicker symbolic meaning—"the saving remnant." When Leo Schwarz wrote a book about the survivors, he titled it *The Redeemers*.

What they called themselves mattered less than what they were. For me they were exemplars of suffering and endurance. Because of the horrors they had witnessed and experienced, horrors which I could scarcely imagine, my feelings for them verged on reverence. When I came to Munich, I wanted to be with them, to hear their stories, to enter vicariously into the dark world of their torments.

The first survivors I met were among my JDC colleagues, the so-called Class II personnel. Some of them had responsible positions, like the BTO who headed our Procurement Department. Others were drivers or worked in JDC's warehouse. My circle of acquaintanceship with survivors expanded when I met members of the Central Committee of Liberated Jews and its subsidiary institutions, mainly in the cultural and educational departments. On my visits to camps, I encountered survivors, especially those aggressive enough to come forward to complain about the Central Committee or the JDC. My fluent Yiddish gave me access to them. They would ask where I had learned it and I'd tell them about Vilna. That helped to establish my credentials among them; they were more likely to trust me. I met a number of survivors of the Vilna ghetto, but it invariably turned out that our paths had never crossed before the war. All we had in common were memories of Vilna's crooked little streets and of its now extinguished life force.

Many of the Jews liberated at Dachau were from Lithuania and most came from Kovno, its prewar capital. When the Germans liquidated the Kovno ghetto and its concentration camp in July 1944, just before the Red Army captured the city, they moved the surviving 8,000 Jewish forced laborers to Germany—the men to Dachau, the women to Stutthof, a camp near Danzig. Though barely 20 percent of the Dachau inmates lived long enough to be liberated by the Americans in April 1945, the survivors from Kovno soon became a visible presence among the Jews in Munich. They made up the leadership of the Central Committee of Liberated Jews in the American zone. They became the elite among the survivors.

Kovno had been Vilna's sister city, though it never attained Vilna's venerable reputation. Both cities shared the same religious, cultural, and social traditions. Both were strongholds of the *litvak* Jew. Kovno had had its share of great Talmudic scholars and rabbis, though none with the stature of the Vilna Gaon. The *musar*-yeshiva, which had produced Chaim Grade, had deep roots in the Kovno area. Alongside Kovno's religious life, secular Hebrew and Yiddish culture had also flourished. When I heard the survivors speak their Lithuanian-accented Yiddish, I was reminded of Vilna.

The will to live asserted itself in most survivors, despite their losses and the unforeseeability of their future. They began to get married, to have children, to look toward a future. They built the institutions they needed, knowing well that their camp committees, political parties, schools, newspapers, theatrical groups, and sports clubs were only for the time being, that their presence in the land of Amalek was only for the time being. Even those who before the war had not been Zionists had been persuaded by their wartime experiences to become impassioned Zionists. They were convinced that only in a state of their own could Jews as a people achieve a secure existence. They were eager to go to Palestine, though their chances were slim because the British issued a small number of certificates. Jews who tried to enter Palestine without certificates were interned by the British in detention camps on Cyprus.

In refashioning their lives, the survivors had to cope with their physical and emotional frailties. Years of starvation and debilitation had impaired their bodily health. Tuberculosis was a common ailment and an obstacle to their emigration. They suffered from weak hearts, high blood pressure, stomach illnesses, tension. All sorts of physical and neurological disorders plagued them not only while they remained in Germany, but for the rest of their lives. Their days were haunted by their memories and their sleep disturbed by their nightmares. Once while visiting a camp, I met a young man, a survivor of the Warsaw ghetto. His arms and hands were freshly bandaged. Responding to my query, he told me that he was frequently tormented by nightmares about the roundups in the ghetto. That was when he had lost his parents. During a hallucinatory dream a few nights earlier, he had leaped out of bed and jumped through the window. Since his room was on the first floor, the cuts to his arms were the most serious injury he sustained.

Many survivors I knew were driven by a sense of guilt, by what psychologists now call "survivor guilt." It was a wound of conscience. They believed that because they had outlived their parents, mates, or children, they were somehow to blame for their deaths. In Munich I became friends with Sophie B., a twenty-year old girl from Vilna, a candidate for a college scholarship in the United States. The JDC was then sponsoring a scholarship program which had been initiated by the

B'nai B'rith Hillel Foundation. I had been assigned to work on it. Sophie had done well on the qualifying exam and was soon thereafter accepted at Sarah Lawrence College. While in Munich, she'd talk freely to me. She was persuaded that because she had been provided with a safe hiding place, another member of her family had been deprived of it. At times she seemed to be a normal young person, who enjoyed gaiety and fun, but depression and guilt feelings were her more frequent companions. After Sophie received her student visa to the United States, she left Munich. After I had returned to New York, I used to see her with some regularity. She was doing well at Sarah Lawrence and had made friends. But before she was graduated, she took her own life.

Many survivors had unrealistic expectations of how they would be treated after liberation. In the bleakness of the concentration camp, they had sustained themselves with daydreams of being rewarded after the war for their sufferings and losses. They thought that the world and particularly the Jews who had lived comfortably in the West owed them recompense. But after liberation, realizing that they would not be rewarded, they became embittered and cynical. In occupied Germany they confronted new authorities and bureaucracies that exercised control over their lives, whom they uniformly distrusted. Almost to a man, the survivors regarded all *goyim*—non-Jews—as unmitigated anti-Semites. They were convinced that they all would, sooner or later, even in the United States, do to the Jews what the Nazis had done. They were contemptuous of American Jews, including us in the JDC, despising us as rich and self-satisfied. They called us *amerikaner khazeyrim* ("American pigs"). They resented being dependent on our handouts. Most of all they hated the functionaries of the Central Committee and the camp committees, believing them to be crooked and corrupt.

The survivors I knew hated the Germans and avoided them. Yet I always heard stories about Jews who were doing black-market business with Germans and who slept with German women. It was said they did it for revenge. The desire for revenge always simmered beneath the surface. Sometimes it erupted in violence. I had heard about fights—not with Germans, but with Balts or Ukrainians, who were often housed in adjoining DP camps. Once I witnessed an episode of brutal rage. While I was at a meeting at the Central Committee offices, we were disturbed by a sudden explosion of yelling and screaming. We went downstairs to see a swarming pack of some thirty or more survivors—all men—milling around a bloodied man prostrate in the vestibule.

He was a Ukrainian, we were told, who had been a guard in a concentration camp. He was notorious for beating Jews. Some survivors recognized him on the street and attacked him with their bare hands. Then they dragged him, unconscious, to the Central Committee building, hoping perhaps that the jurisdiction of the German police would not extend to these official Jewish precincts. The vestibule was literally awash in the Ukrainian's blood. The Central Committee functionaries made space around him and called for a doctor. I managed to get a look at the inert figure; the sight made me feel ill. His face was so battered, I couldn't make out his features any more.

Survivors had a compulsion to talk. Telling their story helped them to expiate the guilt feelings that tormented them. They wanted to talk about their losses—of parents who perished, sisters and brothers who vanished, even of their own children who were murdered. In the time I spent in Germany, I must have heard hundreds of their stories. Once a seventy-one-year-old observant Jew from White Russia told me about his family of sixty, of whom only ten had survived and were now scattered in camps throughout Germany. Like hundreds, perhaps thousands, of Russian Jews, he had clandestinely joined the stream of repatriated Polish Jews leaving Russia, probably as part of an underground movement of the Lubavitch hasidim. He had a sister who, having emigrated in the 1920s to Montevideo, had now sent him a visa to Uruguay. He alone among his relatives had papers to emigrate. He cried as he talked, for he knew that, in leaving them behind, he'd never again see the remnants of his family.

In telling their stories, the survivors liked best of all to talk about their former lives, to describe the houses they lived in, the family businesses, their schooling, their place in the community. By defining themselves in their previous existence, they were confirming their identity as individuals entitled to a place in an ordered society. They had not always been outcasts.

When they talked about the terrible deeds the Germans had done, how the Germans, assisted by Lithuanians, separated husbands from wives and children from parents, abused them, murdered their families, they wept. Crying came easily to them. But they wanted more than pity. They wanted the Germans punished for their crimes. In Munich, at the end of 1945, when the Americans brought to trial the Germans who had been in charge at Dachau, many survivors told me that they had testified. A young man who worked for the JDC said that he had felt obliged to do so, no matter the emotional cost.

The survivors told their stories to each other, to listeners like me, and in court. But they wanted also to record their experiences, to preserve them for history and posterity. In occupied Germany they did so under the guidance of the Central Historical Commission, a subsidiary of the Central Committee of the Liberated Jews in the American Zone of Germany. The Central Historical Commission had been organized in August 1946 in Munich by two survivors—Moshe Feigenbaum, who had come from Poland, and Israel Kaplan, liberated at Dachau. I met them soon after I came to Munich, for it became my task to help them publish their journal, *Fun letstn khurbn* (*Out of Our Most Recent Catastrophe*). It was for them I obtained the use of the linotype in the plant of *Die Neue Zeitung.*

Feigenbaum was thirtyish, tall, brown-haired, brown-eyed, with a bushy mustache, a vigorous man, whose modesty belied his initiative and energy. He came from Biała Podlaska, a town in Poland, where he had been a bookkeeper. He and three friends had survived by hiding for almost a year in a farmer's orchard in an underground bunker they had dug and outfitted. The Polish farmer who owned the property had helped them. After the Germans were driven out of Poland, Feigenbaum went to Lodz, where he worked with the newly established historical commission. In December 1945 he came to Munich and soon after proposed to the Central Committee that a similar historical commission be created in occupied Germany. Its main function would be to gather testimonies of the experiences the Jews had endured under the Germans. Feigenbaum was then writing his own story. It was later published in Yiddish; one chapter, which I translated, appeared in *The Root and the Bough,* an anthology of survivor accounts edited by Leo Schwarz and published in 1949.

Israel Kaplan had been a journalist in Kovno before the war. When I met him, he was a small lively man, probably fortyish, prematurely gray. He had weighed sixty pounds at the time of his liberation. He wore thick-lensed glasses to improve his poor vision. He was a man of many words, whose sardonic humor made his loquacity entertaining.

The Central Historical Commission had its offices in the headquarters of the Central Committee of Liberated Jews, a requisitioned German villa on Möhlstrasse 12A, a block from the JDC offices. A large room on the first floor, once no doubt an elegant drawing room, served as a library, meeting room, and rehearsal space for a theatrical group. The people who hung around used to eat their lunch on a grand piano, no longer in good condition. The Central Historical Commission, on the top floor, had three rooms—one for its office; one for receptions, exhibitions, meetings; and a tiny room cluttered with piles of archival materials, handwritten eyewitness accounts by Jewish survivors and German documents found in the bombed-out Nazi chancelleries in Munich.

At the end of 1948, the Central Historical Commission closed down, as Feigenbaum and Kaplan prepared to emigrate to Israel. In its barely three years of existence, it had established a network of some fifty historical committees in the camps and cities throughout occupied Germany and gathered over 2,500 survivor accounts, more than 1,000 photographs, statistical materials, and an archive of ghetto and camp folklore. The Commission's collections were transferred to Israel and deposited with Yad Vashem, Israel's national institution to commemorate and document the Holocaust.

Some survivors could not tell the whole of their stories. Though I encouraged them to talk, I never dared probe, for fear of clawing at open wounds. The survivors wanted to express their grief and release their feelings of loss, but they could not—or would not—unlock memories that would expose their shame, humiliation, or bad conscience. One survivor of Dachau I knew, who had lost his parents and his young wife in Kovno, always seemed happy-go-lucky, enjoying a good time, dancing, drinking. He reminded me of the prewar *goldene yugnt* I had met in Vilna. I could never fathom if his insouciance was a willed repression of his despair over the losses he had suffered or a way of concealing a dark secret.

Among us, on the JDC staff, was a man whose dark secret surfaced when I was in Munich. Years later I found his story documented in history books with a fullness of detail absent from the hearsay and rumor bruited about. Robert Prochnik came from Vienna and was one of the few survivors of Theresienstadt, a concentration camp near Prague, which the Germans operated ostensibly as a show-camp, where on a few selective occasions they displayed the humane treatment they accorded the Jews in their custody. But that was a false front, for nearly all of Theresienstadt's inmates were deported to Auschwitz. When I first met Prochnik, he was working in JDC's Immigration Department and was said to be able and dedicated, knowledgeable about the ins and outs of getting visas, permits, travel accommodations, travel routes. My work didn't bring me in contact with him, but we used to meet in the mess, at meetings, or at parties. Of medium height, heavyset, tending to fat, with a high forehead and a receding hairline, with a large bulbous nose his most prominent facial feature, he was not an attractive man. After a while I heard whisperings about him. It was said that he'd made up lists of Jews for deportations when he was in Vienna and also, more ominously, in Theresienstadt. In response to pressure from survivors in Munich, the JDC transferred him from Munich to its Paris office.

In June 1947, while I was in Paris on JDC business, I ran into Prochnik at the office. I had heard that his past pursued him like an avenging ghost. He greeted me like an old friend and wanted to take me to dinner. He said he had to talk to me, to tell me the truth about himself. He wanted to enlist me on his side. He talked and I listened. In Vienna he'd worked for Rabbi Benjamin Murmelstein, who headed the emigration section of the Israelitische Kultusgemeinde Wien, the officially recognized Jewish communal organization of Vienna. Prochnik told me how desperately he tried to find ways to get Jews out of Austria, out of Hitler's reach, to safe havens in South America or any other place where one could get papers and passage. I asked him what he had done at Theresienstadt, after he and his boss had been sent there. He replied that he had no choice but to work for the Germans under their orders. He repeated again and again that he had tried to save Jews, not to harm them.

I suspected that he was withholding, concealing—what, I feared to imagine. At the end I told him I couldn't defend him, but neither would I join the campaign to get him fired from JDC. I never saw him again. I heard that he got a job with a business firm in Alsace. Years later I found his name in accounts about Theresienstadt and in a history of the Jews in Austria. Part of what he had told me was true. In the early years, he had worked assiduously to get Jews out of Austria. But the situation changed in 1941. He then turned his talents to serving the Germans, through his boss Murmelstein, who had connections with Eichmann. Prochnik made lists of Jews to be deported to the Lodz ghetto, to Theresienstadt, and to Auschwitz. The author of one book described him as Murmelstein's "evil spirit."

Long before my last encounter with Prochnik, I had already realized that I was sentimentalizing the survivors as a class, endowing them not only with courage and endurance, but with mythical properties as the last bearers of a world that had been extinguished, verily as the saving remnant. Some survivors I knew were indeed just that, but as I came to know more of them, I saw that not all were stamped from the same mold. Suffering, I learned, did not always ennoble. The experiences of suffering were more likely to bring to the fore the dominant elements in a person's character, the good or the bad, selflessness or ruthlessness. Among the survivors I came to know were some to whom I'd trust my life and others with whom I didn't want to be in the same room. I began to be more discriminating and sober in my individual assessments, wary of silences and blank spaces in a story, suspicious of dark secrets. Even so, I never could look at a tattooed forearm without feeling a sense of humility.

In December 1946, barely two months after I had arrived in Munich, I learned that my Vilna friends—Chaim Grade, Shmerke Kaczerginsky, and Abraham Sutzkever with his wife and baby—had arrived in Paris from Poland. When I was still in New York, I knew that they had left Vilna, which the Soviets had once again reinstated as the capital of S.S.R. Lithuania. Their first way station had been Lodz, where they applied for visas to Paris. Sutzkever was corresponding with Weinreich, who kept me informed of their movements. Soon I was writing Chaim Grade directly. The anticipation of a reunion stirred me to fever pitch. My yearning to recover at least a remnant of Vilna was at last to be fulfilled. It took nearly four weeks before I could get leave and I burned with impatience while I waited for my travel orders. Finally I left for Paris on January 19, 1947.

Even in my agitation about my Vilna encounter, I was happy to return to Paris, where I had stayed for two weeks the previous October, before entering Germany. Paris had been in my dreams as far back as July 1939, when I was figuring out when and how I'd return home from Vilna, hoping that I might get to Paris and board my New York–bound Polish liner at Cherbourg. But things hadn't worked out that way. The Paris I had wanted to see in 1939 was the fabled City of Light, the mecca of artists and writers, the center of elegance and fashion, the cradle of Liberté, Égalité, Fraternité. In 1946 Paris evoked other associations. Even in this vaunted site of political liberty and fraternity, Jews had been persecuted and hunted. Tens of thousands of Jews had been deported from Paris and sent to Auschwitz. Hardly anyone returned. For me, Paris, like other places in Europe, was haunted by the specters of murdered Jews.

In 1946 Paris was still trying to recover from the ravages of the German occupation. Food and fuel were in short supply. In October, with a chill already in the air, buildings were unheated. At night, the city was dimly lit, the streets exuding a lusterless brownish light. Milk, cream, butter, and meat were scarce; people didn't starve, but they weren't adequately nourished. Because of the shortage of grain, French bread, once legendary for its whiteness, was coarse and as dark as the streets at night. Everyone still talked about the German presence and Parisians would point out buildings which the Germans had taken over. The elegant building on 19 avenue Foch, which then housed the JDC's French Department, had been a Rothschild mansion, but the Gestapo had taken it over during the occupation. (Some years later, it reverted to the Rothschild family.)

When I first came to Paris, I had many people to look up. Weinreich asked me to look up the YIVO's Paris representative; Riva Tcherikower wanted me to see her friends, all survivors of the German occupation. I visited them all and listened to their stories. I became good friends with one, Sonia Ryback, the widow of Issachar Ryback, an artist who had died in Paris in 1935. When Riva first mentioned her name, I recalled I had met Sonia in Vilna in September 1938 at a dinner party at the Reisens' house. When we met again in Paris, she was in her late forties, a fine figure of a woman—tall, blonde, handsome. She lived in Passy and was an art dealer. Her large apartment was filled with unframed paintings leaning against the walls and art books piled high on chairs and tables. She still had some of her husband's work—paintings, drawings, etchings, and painted wooden sculptures depicting East European Jews at their traditional occupations.

Sonia became my guide through the Paris of my dreams. We visited museums and art galleries, dined in bistros, sipped wine in outdoor cafes where Jean-Paul Sartre and his friends congregated, but we'd not yet heard of him. We walked tirelessly, from the Bastille to the Bois de Boulogne, from Montparnasse to Montmartre, up and down the banks of the Seine. We rode to the top of the Eiffel Tower. At the Louvre I paid homage to the *Venus de Milo* and the *Mona Lisa*. At the Musée de l'Orangerie I saw paintings which the Germans had stolen during the occupation and which had just been restored by the U.S. military government—no doubt by MFA&A, now in charge of the remnants of the Vilna YIVO library still in Germany.

By myself I made a pilgrimage to Drancy, a small town just northeast of Paris. There, an unfinished housing project, windowless, barracks-like, had been taken over by the Germans to intern French Jews whom they had rounded up. The Jews were then deported to Auschwitz. Now one of the buildings had been converted into an elementary school. As

I walked around the dismal grounds, I could hear the voices of children in their classrooms. Their laughter and singing sounded grotesque in that somber setting. Only three years earlier, Jews had been sent to their deaths from here. I photographed a large wooden sign, bearing a short text that a monument would be erected on the site to memorialize the 120,000 deportees from the Drancy camp, "victims of Nazi religious persecutions."

Several times I visited the Centre de Documentation Juive Contemporaine, a new institution for research and documentation of the Jewish experience under the German occupation. The Centre had been founded in Grenoble in 1943 and moved to Paris after the liberation. I was impressed by the Centre's founder and president, Isaac Schneersohn, its staff, its archives, and research program. I pored over the collections of German documents, making notes, and wrote Weinreich about what I had seen. (About ten years later the Centre moved to a larger building in the Marais and there erected a stunning memorial and crypt dedicated to the Unknown Jewish Martyr.)

Paris in January 1947 seemed an inappropriate setting for the drama of my Vilna reunion. Even rue des Rosiers in the old Jewish quarter, where Yiddish could sometimes be heard on the streets, could not evoke the least remembrance of Vilna. By then Vilna seemed to have taken on a ghostly extraterrestrial character, as if it belonged not just to another time and place, but to an altogether alien planet.

I had arranged to meet my three friends—Chaim, Shmerke, and Abraham—at the JDC building at avenue Foch. Perhaps they had some business there. My memory of that first encounter is like an old silent film of a dream sequence. The images I summon up have a disembodied quality, as if all of us were floating just barely above the ground, enshrouded in silence. We met in a large room, no doubt once a grand salon, now utterly without decoration. Its only furniture were armless chairs lined against the walls, as if there had been a ball the night before. We were not alone in the room. Little clusters of people dotted the space, each far enough from the other to ensure privacy.

We embraced each other, scanned one another's faces, as if to see whether the loss of Vilna had aged our faces and creased our features. Shmerke was still the same tough little fellow. He seemed not to have changed since I saw him in 1939. It was natural that he should have joined up with the partisans. That kind of warfare, I thought, was a military equivalent of street fighting. Sutzkever, tall, thin, and pale, had also been a partisan, though I could never quite picture him in that role. Now, as in the old days in Vilna, he still looked like the persona of a poet. Chaim Grade was thinner, paler than he'd been in Vilna, but he still displayed the same volcanic verbal energy and passionate temperament that had distinguished him in the past.

We laughed a little, winked away tears, but our conversation was stiff. We were, I felt, collectively embarrassed. An abyss of death and destruction yawned between me and them. I could not find a way to bridge it. All I could do was teeter uncertainly at the edge of the abyss and stretch out a hand. Had I met each one individually that first time, it might have been easier. I found it too difficult to talk about Vilna and instead asked each one about his future plans and his work. They all hoped to come to the United States and had enlisted their American friends and admirers to help them. Shmerke had already completed a book called *Khurbn vilne* (*The Destruction of Vilna*), to which Max Weinreich had agreed to write an introduction. It was published in New York later that year. He was next going to write a book about the partisans. Sutzkever had published an account of the Vilna ghetto and was then writing poems about his ghetto experiences. Chaim had continued to write even after he had left Vilna on foot in June 1941, just a little ahead of the Germans. In 1945, he had already had a volume of verse published in New York, which contained some of his prewar poems as well as poetry he had written while in the Soviet Union during the war years. He was then writing a long narrative poem about Vilna.

Conversation was liveliest when Sutzkever told me about the several suitcases he had containing books and documents which he and Shmerke had smuggled out of the YIVO and hidden in the ghetto. They had also amassed a collection of documents about life and death in the Vilna ghetto. In the months to come, Sutzkever mailed these materials, envelope by envelope, to the YIVO in New York. They became the Sutzkever-Kaczerginsky Collection of the Vilna Ghetto in YIVO's Archives. I used them when I was writing *The War Against the Jews*.

In the course of my nine-day stay in Paris and in subsequent visits in June and July, I saw my friends individually. It was easier that way to reestablish our relations, though they never became as close and easy as they had been in Vilna. Chaim Grade still appealed the most to me. He'd become more worldly than I remembered him to have been and more aggressive in his quarrel with the world of Jewish tradition. The confrontation between modernity and tradition, whose battle lines he had drawn before the war in his poem *Musarnikes,* soon found its most powerful expression in the first story he ever wrote, "My Quarrel with Hersh Rasseyner," with postwar Paris as its locale and the murder of the European Jews now the centerpiece of the war between the believer and the denier. On one occasion in Paris he read me extracts of a long narrative poem about prewar Vilna which he'd been working on for the last three years, ever since his return to the ruins of Vilna in 1944. Deeply moved, I told him that if he kept working, he'd become one of our great Yiddish poets. He gave me a withering look and asked, expecting no answer: "And what do you think I am now?"

For a while I did not see that my unrealistic expectations had turned my Vilna reunion into disappointment. I had hoped that somehow, in the company of the survivors of Young Vilna, I would recover the essence of the old Vilna. But I came to realize that I could never restore the past to life. At that first reunion, I could not yet face the truth that we—the three Vilna survivors and I—had become dealers in remnants. We were like old-clothesmen who traded in our memories, shining and polishing them to high luster. Our wares were not as shabby as those in Vilna's wretched *durkhhoyf,* but our business was much the same— dealing in miseries, however sweet our recollections of the beloved world that had been shattered.

We, too, were part of the wreckage. Even if all of Vilna's survivors were to be assembled in one place, they would still be only fragments, from which no one could ever put Vilna together again. All we could do was to remember it, to continue to deal in our memories, to create out of them poems and stories, history and reminiscences. It was the only way through which that irrevocably destroyed past could survive. Vilna had once been a red giant star in the firmament and had once illuminated the Jewish universe. It had now been extinguished. It had become a white dwarf star, emitting a feeble light visible only to those who knew of its existence.

Late in 1947, Abraham Sutzkever and his family emigrated to Palestine and settled in Tel Aviv. In 1949 he established a world-class Yiddish literary journal, *Di goldene keyt* (*The Golden Chain*), which he edits to this day. The poetry he has written in the last forty years exhibits the same commitment to language, form, and style that marked his work in Vilna, but it has grown deeper, richer, more subtle. In 1948, Chaim Grade came to the United States, where he continued to produce masterful poetry and fiction in rich abundance. Having lost his earthly Vilna, he spent the rest of his life, until his death in 1982, recreating a heavenly Vilna out of his memory and literary imagination. Shmerke Kaczerginski settled in Buenos Aires. His book about the partisans was published in 1952. Two years later he died in a plane crash in Argentina.

At the end of January 1947, chastened by the disappointments of my Paris reunion, I returned to Munich. I was ready to get back to work and start a new task. I was going to get reading material for the camps. *Amkho* needed books to read, to pass the time, to study something useful, like English or Hebrew. The children and teachers in the camp schools needed texts.

JDC's records showed that some twenty larger camps had libraries of a sort. Later, on visits to the camps, I found those libraries to be haphazard collections of Yiddish, German, and English books, interspersed with old issues of the *Reader's Digest* and *Life* magazine. When I inspected our department's supplies in JDC's warehouse at Schleissheim, just outside Munich, I found several hundred books that were still to be distributed to the camps. These, like most books already in the camps, had been part of an immense borrowing by Koppel Pinson from the Offenbach Archival Depot, the collecting point for the books which Rosenberg's task force had robbed from the Jewish libraries of all Europe, the same place where the remnants of the YIVO library were being held.

Pinson first thought of drawing books for the camps back in November 1945, when he visited the former Rothschild-Palais in Frankfurt, the MFA&A's first storage place for Rosenberg's stolen goods. He applied to General Lucius D. Clay, head of OMGUS, which was responsible for carrying out United States restitution policy, for permission to draw 25,000 nonvaluable books for use in the camps. Then, at the end of November 1945, when I was still working for YIVO in New York, Pinson asked the YIVO to authorize him to take nonvaluable books that might belong to YIVO's Vilna library and promised that he would proceed "with great caution and respect for YIVO's aims and rights." Pinson's request had displeased Weinreich and increased his anxiety about the security of YIVO's property. But after some back-and-forth cables, Weinreich reluctantly gave Pinson the permission he wanted.

In mid-December 1945, General Clay rejected Pinson's application, but Pinson didn't give up. He found an advocate for his project in Judge

Simon H. Rifkind, on leave from the federal bench and then Adviser on Jewish Affairs to General Eisenhower, commander, USFET. On January 7, 1946, Rifkind requested General Clay to reconsider the loan of 25,000 volumes for use in the Jewish DP centers. He proposed specific guidelines for the selection of the books: No irreplaceable, unusual, or valuable book would be borrowed and no book, if established to be the property of any known institution or individual, would be withdrawn. He stressed also, for the protection of possible owners of the books, that the JDC was a financially responsible organization. On January 12, General Bryan L. Milburn, on behalf of General Clay, authorized the loan of 25,000 volumes to the JDC, in accordance with the conditions set forth in Rifkind's letter.

MFA&A was then in the process of transferring the mountain of several million items of Judaica—books, manuscripts, and ritual objects—from the cramped quarters in the Rothschild Library to a spacious warehouse in Offenbach, just across the Main River. Rifkind and Pinson, meanwhile, concerned about the care and ultimate disposition of this vast Jewish cultural treasure, persuaded military government authorities to appoint someone with archival experience to operate the new installation, the Offenbach Archival Depot (OAD). Major Seymour J. Pomrenze, formerly an archivist with the National Archives in Washington, then serving as an MFA&A officer in Germany, was drafted for this position. He knew German, Hebrew, and Yiddish, and was familiar with Jewish cultural matters.

In March 1946, the OAD was officially opened and that month Pinson began to select books for the camps. Before he returned to the States, he had drawn about 20,000 volumes. While he worked at the OAD, JDC's regional office in Frankfurt had served as Pinson's headquarters and Sadie Sender, JDC's regional director in Frankfurt, was familiar with his work. In January 1947, she sent Leo Schwarz a memo reminding him that JDC could still draw 5,000 books from Offenbach under General Clay's authorization. Leo gave me the assignment. Getting 5,000 books at one fell swoop was like manna from heaven. I asked Sadie to make the necessary arrangements for me to visit the OAD early in February.

Though the disappointment of my Paris experience restrained my flights into nostalgia, I was keyed up by the prospect of holding in my hands the remains, as it were, of the civilization of the East European Jews. I was even more agitated by the thought that I might see the remnants of the YIVO library. But I resolved to keep cool, to stay within the limits of my JDC task, separating myself and JDC from the affairs of YIVO's library. On Tuesday, February 4, 1947, I presented myself at the Offenbach Archival Depot as JDC's representative hoping to be permitted to borrow 5,000 nonvaluable books from among the still unidentified volumes.

Offenbach, a medium-sized city, had been an industrial center, known for its chemical industry and more famously for its leather goods. During the war, it had been heavily bombed. Some areas looked as desolate as Frankfurt. Dramatic profiles of roofless hollow shells were visible on every street. It was common to see buildings with only one or two of their sides still standing. On some streets, half the buildings had crumbled into rubble. Offenbach's pre-Hitler Jewish community of about 1,400 had dwindled to 500 by 1939 and after 1941 they were all deported. A few survivors returned after the war to rebuild their community.

The Offenbach Archival Depot was housed in a warehouse of the Naphtol-Chemie plant, the property of the local I. G. Farben factory. The ugly five-story reinforced concrete loft building on 169 Mainstrasse, a wide cobbled street, extended for the length of a Manhattan city block, with the entrance at the center and five or six truck-loading platforms to the left. At the rear of the building were more loading platforms and two or three sets of railway track sidings.

The Depot's director, the third in the succession of directors, was Joseph A. Horne, called Tony by his friends. Before the war, he'd been on the staff of the Library of Congress's photographic division. Transferred from MFA&A in Berlin, he was then new to the Depot, having taken over his duties barely two weeks before my visit. About thirty, very tall, thin, lanky, and blond, he was the only American there. He was in charge of a staff of some forty Germans.

When I came, Horne was already familiar with the details of the JDC loan. After Sadie Sender had arranged for my visit, he had checked with his MFA&A superiors in the Restitution Branch of OMGUS in Berlin. They gave him permission to let me, as JDC's authorized representative, start selecting those 5,000 books. Horne and I talked about what I would be doing. It looked as if we'd get along. Afterward he showed me around the Depot.

The OAD then had on its premises about 630,000 items—books, manuscripts, religious objects. Nearly two million items had already been shipped out by the two previous directors, Major Seymour Pomrenze and Captain Isaac Bencowitz. Those materials had been restituted to the countries of their owners—France, Belgium, the Netherlands, Italy, the Soviet Union, Poland.

Only about half the books still in the Depot had been identified. Among these were 347 cases containing an estimated 76,000 items belonging to the YIVO. The restitution of Jewish materials from Germany, Austria, Czechoslovakia, Estonia, Latvia, Lithuania, and Poland, even of those whose original ownership had been established, was then being held up, pending determination of United States policy on heirless Jewish property. From my days at the YIVO, I knew of differences on the highest government levels as to the disposition of heirless Jewish property. The War Department had been committed to a policy of restitution to nations, not to individual owners. The State Department, on the other hand, had long ago recognized YIVO's claim to its library. On my first day at the OAD, I heard about an idea afloat in MFA&A that the heirless Jewish property might be constituted into a comprehensive Jewish library under some international scholarly Jewish auspices.

The hundreds of thousands of books, brought from all over the American zone, stretched wall to wall in a continuing vista of wooden boxes on two floors of the Depot. When the books arrived, each case was opened and examined to check the condition of its contents. The Depot maintained a Care and Preservation Room to dry wet books and manuscripts and to make minor repairs. After the preliminary inspection, the cases were moved to a general sorting area where they were divided into books in Western languages and books in Yiddish and Hebrew—languages which the German staff was unable to decipher. The next step was to set aside the identified books from the unidentifiables.

The previous director had devised a procedure for identifying the Hebrew and Yiddish books. He had compiled an assortment of the more common and decipherable library stamps, *ex libris,* or other identifying marks found in the books and reproduced them in a booklet as a guide to the twelve German sorters. For Vilna collections alone, he had assembled 175 different *ex libris.* The sorters worked at enormous tables, examining book by book, for recognizable designs or symbols, stacking thousands of books in high piles, according to their identifying marks. The work areas were heavy with the dust that the books had accumulated in the ancient castles, caves, and tunnels where the Germans had stowed them. After this sorting, the books were recased, relabeled, and sent to another floor. The Depot maintained a carpentry shop to make new cases for shipping books.

The Torah Room contained the OAD's most valuable materials—over 750 manuscripts, incunabula, books printed between 1650 and 1800, and rare editions, which were kept in locked cabinets. About 600 were unidentifiable. Over 500 Torah scrolls and 200 *megillot* (mostly scrolls of the Book of Esther) were neatly stacked crosswise. Some handsomely embroidered and decorated ark curtains and Torah wrappers hung on the walls, while hundreds of brass and silver menorahs were lined up on long shelves, as if they were for sale.

The smell of death emanated from these hundreds of thousands of books and religious objects—orphaned and homeless mute survivors of their murdered owners. Like the human survivors, these inanimate remnants of a once-thriving civilization had found temporary and comfortless shelter in the land of Amalek. The sight of these massed inert objects chilled me. I didn't yet know that I would soon be spending my time in this mortuary of books.

The next day I returned to the Depot, rolled up my sleeves, and set to work. It was my plan to work for four days of the week at Offenbach, commuting from Frankfurt, until I finished the selection of the books. (The other three days I spent in Munich.) I slept on the living-room couch in Sadie Sender's billets in Frankfurt and used JDC transportation to get to Offenbach. Horne arranged for me to lunch at the officers' mess in the house where he was billeted with officers in other branches of the military government.

Before I had come to the OAD, I had promised myself that I would do my best to safeguard the rights of possible owners and heirs. I would evaluate every book as to its actual or potential scholarly value. Since the Jewish culture which had flourished in Eastern Europe had been wiped out and since it was unlikely that Hebrew and Yiddish books would ever again be published there, every surviving book from that world had become a historical document, a cultural artifact, specimen, and testament of a murdered civilization.

I set up strict guidelines for the selection of books. I would take only ownerless books in the following categories: (1) textbooks and belles-lettres published in the United States; (2) belles-lettres and texts published in prewar Poland, copies of which were likely to have been sent abroad to the United States or Palestine; (3) all Palestinian publications; and (4) some belles-lettres published in the Soviet Union. Even though the 5,000 books would be taken as a loan, I knew it was unlikely they would ever be returned. In occupied Germany you couldn't prevent books from disappearing. Wherever there were books—in army lounges and Red Cross reading rooms, in DP camps and in our own billets—people pocketed them and carried them off.

Horne organized the procedures for my work and supervised the German staff. I was given a whole floor to myself, where the unidentifiable books in Yiddish and Hebrew were stored. The boxes were marked *Hebräisch O.B.*, "Hebrew ownerless" (*o.b.* = *ohne Besitz*), though they were both Hebrew and Yiddish, for the German staff couldn't distinguish one language from the other. A young German, no more than seventeen or eighteen, worked with me, bringing several boxes to the work area, unpacking them, and shelving the books. Each case was estimated to hold 200 books, but that was an arbitrary figure. Cases with volumes of the Talmud held only about 100 books; cases with unbound periodicals, paperbound books, and pamphlets held about 500 items. The books in the cases I worked on were counted by the German workers, who kept records of the numbers of books as I worked and sorted them in new categories. I sat or stood at an enormous square table on which the boy would put piles of books, which I would then examine. The dust floated up from the opened boxes and the opened books. The air was musty. Everyone wore a smock in the work areas.

By the end of my first week in Offenbach, I had selected nearly 2,000 books. But before I left for Munich, OMGUS in Berlin apparently had had second thoughts about the JDC loan. Before they would agree to release the 5,000 books, they wanted an accounting of the 20,000 books which Pinson had borrowed. They also wanted a catalogue of the 5,000 books I was to borrow. That weekend I consulted Sadie Sender and then Dr. Friedman in Munich. We agreed to go along with those conditions. My search of the JDC files for records of Pinson's loan of the 20,000 books yielded only a list of the camps to which books had been distributed, which I forwarded to Berlin. As for the catalogue, with Horne's help, we decided to prepare index cards with the bibliographical details in Latin letters. The German staff would alphabetize the cards and type the catalogue.

When I returned to Offenbach on February 11, I learned that though OMGUS had officially accredited and approved me as JDC's authorized representative to draw books for the use of displaced persons, they wanted me to come to Berlin for an interview about the JDC loan. Horne said he'd arrange the date and get me the necessary clearance from USFET.

In a matter of days, my good intentions not to entangle my JDC work with the affairs of the YIVO library collapsed. While examining the books designated as unidentifiable, I found that I could identify some—they belonged to the YIVO. I was in a state of exaltation. I wrote home that when I came upon those YIVO books, I had "a feeling akin to holiness, that I was touching something sacred." I reported my discovery to Horne with a tingle of triumph. Each day thereafter I continued to uncover books that were YIVO's. I came across the familiar forms of the Vilna YIVO's Periodical Division in volumes of bound periodicals, their entries indicating how many issues of that periodical had been published. In some books I found the double perforated labels with the YIVO library's accession numbers. Other books were inscribed in Yiddish or Hebrew to the YIVO or to Zalmen Reisen. I found books with Weinreich's name in them or marginal comments in his distinctive handwriting. I turned up an edition of Weinreich's sociopsychological study of Polish Jewish youth, *Der veg tsu undzer yugnt,* which had been republished in 1940, with a Lithuanian title page.

Many books which I could identify came from the Strashun Library. They reminded me of a strange story Weinreich had told me back in 1940, when we had begun to work at the YIVO in New York. Soon after the Soviet occupation of eastern Poland, when the Russians had given Vilna over to the control of Lithuanians, Kalmanovich had cabled Weinreich, then in Copenhagen, and the New York YIVO, proposing that they get the YIVO library out of Vilna. It was an idea born in desperation. The trustees of the Strashun Library, also fearing for the safety of their library, asked the Vilna YIVO to ship their library, too, and to become responsible for its security. On that basis, I told Horne, the remains of the Strashun Library ought to be considered as YIVO property, since Strashun no longer had any owners or heirs.

Horne and I were becoming friends. To explain my YIVO connection, I had told him about my year in Vilna. We used to talk about the life of the Jews in prewar Poland. He had come to believe that a renewal of Jewish life in Poland was unlikely and that the mass of heirless Jewish books, manuscripts, and ritual objects at the Depot ought to be restituted to Jewish institutions in the West and in Palestine.

The second week I was at the Depot, Horne told me that a decision about the disposition of the YIVO library was imminent and that the YIVO's chances were good for the return of its property and the remains also of Strashun. He proposed that I might strengthen YIVO's case when I would be in Berlin to discuss the JDC book loan with the OMGUS Restitution Branch. The date for my visit had been set for March 10.

On the strength of Horne's information, I cabled Weinreich on February 14 that the chances were fairly good for the return of the YIVO library together with Strashun and asked him for documentary support to present in Berlin. I followed the cable with a letter describing the situation at the Depot.

A rapid exchange of cables and letters between us followed. Weinreich wrote that he had enlisted Seymour Pomrenze, the OAD's first director, who had returned to the Library of Congress, on behalf of the YIVO library. Pomrenze had been negotiating with the State Department. Just then they had high expectations for the return of the YIVO library. Pomrenze, as part of a Library of Congress mission, would likely be authorized to bring YIVO's property from Offenbach to New York. Weinreich preferred to let the present course continue.

Meanwhile, at the OAD, I continued to examine books by the hundreds and thousands. By the end of February, I had accumulated 5,000 books suitable for the camps. The catalogue was still to be completed. I was planning to return to Munich after my trip to Berlin. Horne urged me to stay on at the Depot. It would serve the YIVO's interest, he argued, as well as the OAD's. The possibility that I might play a role, however minor, in the return of the YIVO library reawakened my old rescue fantasies. I no longer dreamed of rescuing Rivele and Kalman from the flames of war, but now I had become obsessed with saving as many remnants as I could of the Vilna YIVO's books and manuscripts. I wanted to have a share in restoring them to their transplanted home in New York. I did not confide my fantasies to Horne. Instead I told him that the decision was not mine, but the JDC's to make.

Saturday evening, March 8, I took the night train to Berlin. The following morning, as we traveled through the Russian zone, I photographed the Russian military signs on the way. At the Berlin station, a JDC driver was waiting to take me to the JDC office. We drove through silent snowy streets. Not a living creature was to be seen. Hardly a building had been left standing. I had not been in Berlin since August 27, 1939, when I was in flight from Vilna, on my way to Copenhagen. Driving through those dead streets, I recalled images of jubilant masses of soldiers rallying for the invasion of Poland. In the mournful silence in that desolate city, I heard echoes inside my head of the fortissimo singing and the tumultuous cheers of Hitler's Wehrmacht. That Sunday morning, eight years later, I took grim satisfaction in Berlin's wreckage.

The JDC office was located on Kronprinzen-Allee, in Dahlem, a residential district of Berlin, not too badly damaged by the bombings and shellings. The building resembled a suburban residence. There I met JDC's Berlin director, Henry Levy, and his staff. Henry said he had a surprise for me. Opening a side door, he called in a young man, who grinned at me. His face was familiar. It took a moment before I recognized Elya Yonas, the *pro-aspirant* in the Vilna YIVO who'd been our darling. With tears and laughter we embraced. During the war he'd been in Russia, as I had heard. When he returned to Vilna, there was no longer anything for him to stay for. He made his way out of Poland through the Soviet zone of Germany into Berlin. He was working for JDC. We talked for a while. I told him I'd seen the writers of Young Vilna in Paris. Soon we ran out of conversation. The next day, before I left for Frankfurt, I said goodbye to him. I heard that he later settled in Israel.

On Monday morning, a JDC driver brought me to OMGUS headquarters. Located on a broad avenue, later renamed Clay-Allee, in Dahlem, the palatial building was set back from the avenue, behind a high fence and an enormous courtyard with a double driveway, with lawns and rows of trees, almost like a park. An American flag on a tall pole fluttered high above the wide three-story building with its two wings at right angles. Inside, between two graceful ascending staircases, stood a statue of an American soldier in combat gear, at ease, his gun at his side.

My conversation with the officers of the Restitution Branch was mainly about the disposition of the books Pinson had borrowed. His report which I had sent to them showed that he had shipped books to the DP camp at Bergen-Belsen in the British zone. They said he had had no right to send books out of the American zone and wanted an accounting of those at Belsen. Only then would they release the 5,000 books I had selected. When I inquired about the disposition of the YIVO library, they said a decision would be made soon.

That decision came sooner than I expected. Three days after I was back in Offenbach, we were informed that the return of the YIVO property to the YIVO in New York had been approved. I cabled Weinreich: "USFET clearance to OMGUS already here. Strashun et alia assured. Congratulations do not seem premature." Meanwhile, the YIVO had heard from Assistant Secretary of State J. H. Hilldring that "the Office of Military Government for Germany is being authorized by the War Department to release the works in question for transfer to the United States through the facilities of the Library of Congress Mission." The wording of my cable and Hilldring's letter reflected the tangle of relations between the military and the civilian institutions and their channels of instruction, even in so small a matter as the YIVO library. The lines of communications between the State Department and OMGUS, responsible for the civilian affairs of the American occupation, were often routed through the War Department and its direct channel, USFET. Policy differences between State and War departments compounded the bureaucratic complications. On March 19, I cabled Weinreich that OMGUS had approved the Library of Congress mission. At last, the YIVO books, like survivors with visas and travel permits, would soon be en route to a new home and a new life.

My work at the OAD was coming to an end. The card catalogue for the 5,000 books, which I had completed, was being alphabetized by the German staff and the books were being numbered. Soon they would be packed. I had applied for travel orders to Bergen-Belsen to check on the books for OMGUS.

Horne and, at this time, also Weinreich urged me to stay on at the Depot, to continue my examination of the still unidentified books. Though I didn't look forward to staying at the Depot, my intense obsession with the rescue of the remnants of the Vilna YIVO gave me no respite. I felt compelled to stay on. I felt I had a mission to fulfill.

I decided to ask the JDC if they'd keep me on while I worked for the YIVO. In case they refused, I thought of asking for leave without pay. When I went to Munich late in March, Leo Schwarz had already departed for the States. But his deputy, responding to the intensity of my pleading, gave his oral permission for my unorthodox and irregular proposal and soon thereafter, JDC headquarters in Paris agreed to keep me on salary for the next three months while I worked at the Depot on behalf of the YIVO. Afterward, I'd be given a new assignment.

While I was working at the Depot in February and March, commuting daily from Frankfurt and weekly to Munich, I lived an unsettled life. Part of my belongings were in Munich and part in Sadie Sender's closet. But harder to bear than the discomfort of being unhoused and the weariness of constant travel was the constant presence of Germans in my working time. In Offenbach it was more difficult for me to treat them, as I had in Munich, as faceless, nameless creatures. They moved boxes and books for me. They brushed the dust from my uniform. They even polished my shoes. They chauffered me around and did my errands. Horne's secretary made my long-distance telephone connections. Whenever I returned from a trip, she'd have some fresh flowers on my desk. The cook at the military government mess saw that my laundry was done, my clothes cleaned, and my shoes repaired. The men in the OAD's Photographic Room developed my film.

Still, except for the secretary, who made tea for Horne and me every afternoon, I never addressed anyone by name. I was usually rigid and tense, trying to remain correct and polite, yet impersonal, distant. Even though I admitted to myself that the seventeen-year-old boy who worked with me was too young to have had a hand in murdering Jews, I never once asked him about himself or how much schooling he had had. In some unspoken way, the Germans conspired with me in this guarded and uncommunicative relationship, for they were always servile and fawning, bowing and scraping. I was generous with cigarettes. That enabled me to retain my contempt and hatred for them.

Early in March, just before I went to Berlin, the German staff at the Depot had a party to celebrate the Depot's first anniversary. They had reason to celebrate. They had good jobs, with a mess of their own provided by the military government. They had access to Americans and their cigarettes. For the party, they decorated one of the less dusty work areas where they set up a long table, banquet style. The cookies and wine were from army supplies. I was seated next to Horne at the head of the table. They presented Horne with Copy #1 of a mimeographed Festschrift they had prepared and me with Copy #2. I sat through the evening aloof and expressionless. The Depot, I wrote home, is the last place in the world where I can forget the crimes the Germans committed against the Jews.

When I worked, holding the orphaned books in my hands, I often thought that it was easier to be with *amkho,* with living people, than with these inanimate remnants of the world the Germans had destroyed. The human survivors had a will to live and even, at times, a will to forget, but the books had been dumb witnesses to mass murder. They were the relics of six million murdered Jews. Such thoughts continued to haunt me at the Depot and never more insistently than at that Depot party.

At the end of March, when it was decided that I'd stay in Offenbach until the YIVO library was shipped out, I tried to get billets in Offenbach.

But the military government had billets only for men. To meet my needs, Colonel Rose, the top-ranking military government officer in Offenbach, officially assigned me to a room in the Euler Hotel, a German establishment, normally off-limits for U.S. personnel. It was a couple of blocks from the military government house, where I was now taking three meals a day. The hotel fulfilled my expectations of German cleanliness. My room was large, sunny, and airy. The proprietor provided me with a desk. He was ingratiating, bootlicking, solicitous about my comfort and well-being. He once invited me to go bowling with him.

When I told Horne that my hotel room was unadorned, he offered to lend me a menorah from the Torah Room. I chose a simple brass one and put it on my desk. Two weeks later I returned it. Every time I looked at the menorah, I invented another history for it, imagining to whom it might have belonged, where it had stood in that home, and what had become of its owners. I felt as if these imagined people had moved into my hotel room.

During the week my social life was limited to the officers at the mess. Besides Tony Horne, there was a captain, about twenty-five, in the military government's Liaison and Security in Offenbach, whose interests were fencing and women. Another, a lieutenant about thirty-five, formerly in the air corps, was now in De-Nazification, even though he didn't know a word of German. His interests were flying and politics. I spent my evenings in my room. Besides reading and listening to the Armed Forces Network's American jazz programs, I wrote letters and was absorbed in translating survivor accounts that had been published in *Fun letstn khurbn*. I thought they might make a book that I'd complete in New York. (Instead, I gave Leo Schwarz most of the pieces I had translated for his anthology *The Root and the Bough*.) Weekends I often spent in Frankfurt with Sadie Sender, with whom I'd become good friends.

Weekdays in Offenbach I continued my dusty examination of thousands of books. The work fatigued me and often bored me, as I grouped the identifiable books in three piles: YIVO, Strashun, and other. Those I couldn't identify were arrayed in four piles: secular Hebrew, secular Yiddish, religious works, and Western-language books which had not been weeded out before. From time to time I'd come across a box of books that had been looted from publishers' stocks, as when I found dozens of paperbound copies of Israel Zinberg's eight-volume Yiddish-language history of Jewish literature. The OAD's monthly report for April described my work as a "thorough study of the unidentifiable

Hebrew and Yiddish materials." I also turned up a number of manuscripts and early prints.

Not all days were boring. Once I came upon a case which contained the Vilna YIVO's records—files of correspondence and even photographs. That discovery agitated me more than any other find from the YIVO library. I felt as if I had uncovered a part of my life that I had left behind in Vilna. I trembled as I picked up each new folder, tense with anticipation, though it's hard now to fantasize what I expected to find—perhaps a sign that there was life after death. I pored over every sheet of paper, searching for a familiar handwriting, for a message from the dead. I was reluctant to let any piece of paper pass out of my hands. I found photographs of people I knew. I came across some notes written by Zalmen Reisen late in August 1939, in preparation for the Aspirantur of 1939–1940. My name was on a list, with a check next to it. I found several autobiographies which had been submitted to a YIVO contest in the mid-1930s to provide Weinreich with documentary material for his book *Der veg tsu undzer yugnt.* I uncovered several Aspirantur studies and their raw data. The papers were all mixed up. I tried to imagine how they had been dumped out of their files in Vilna.

But after a day's delving into the very bowels of the Vilna YIVO's past, I was exhausted, drained of feeling. I wiped away my tears and went back to my hotel room. I had come to see that Vilna had been reduced to fragments of paper and fragments of memory. I knew that whatever I rescued from oblivion was all that could ever be rescued from the ruins of Vilna. I knew that I had completed the mission I'd imposed on myself.

In mid-May Weinreich wrote me that Pomrenze had received military orders and was traveling on government (Library of Congress mission) business. He would take over the YIVO books and organize their transportation to New York. He was due in Offenbach about June 20. A few days later OMGUS notified Horne of Pomrenze's arrival and instructed him to do everything to expedite Pomrenze's mission. I had already decided that I would wind up my work there by the time Pomrenze arrived, even if YIVO books might yet be found among the unidentifiables. By the end of May, according to the OAD monthly report, I had examined 162,683 Yiddish and Hebrew volumes, about half the unidentifiables at the Depot, and I had identified 32,894, about 20 percent. Of these, nearly 75 percent were the property of the YIVO and Strashun libraries.

When I told Horne I would leave the Depot after Pomrenze's mission, he tried to persuade me to stay, to finish my identification of the Yiddish and Hebrew books. In the next two weeks, I received a series of letters intended to encourage me to stay. They were written by Horne's various superiors in MFA&A and praised me for my past work. They all expressed the hope that I'd stay on till I finished examining all the unidentified books. The last was from Richard F. Howard, chief, MFA&A Section, Restitution Branch, OMGUS, Berlin, thanking me for "the great amount of time, effort, care, and special skill" which I devoted to the books at the Depot. He hoped that I would find it possible to continue to give the MFA&A the benefit of my "specialized knowledge."

At that time, I was urging Horne to propose to Berlin to liquidate the Depot and transfer the remaining heirless Jewish property, identified or not, to the Jewish Cultural Reconstruction. That was an organization created on the initiative of Professor Salo W. Baron, which represented a broad spectrum of Jewish cultural institutions throughout the world. Its purpose was to take title to heirless Jewish cultural property and distribute it to Jewish libraries throughout the world.

On Sunday, June 15, Pomrenze arrived in Offenbach. He was a short, stocky man, sure of himself and his importance. He had a spectacular array of military orders, which enabled him to go anywhere and get anything done. He, Horne, and I spent hours that Sunday in conversation, though Pomrenze did more of the talking and we did more of the listening.

On Monday, June 16, Pomrenze came to the Depot. He had been its first director. It was familiar territory for him. He made things bustle at the Depot as I'd never seen before. The Germans moved with more speed and energy than they had ever before displayed. That morning three freight cars pulled in from Frankfurt at the Depot's railroad siding. As Pomrenze darted about, bestirring the Germans, they began to move the cases out of the Depot to the loading platforms and then onto the freight cars. The moving and loading continued through Tuesday.

According to the OAD's statistics, 420 cases of materials of the YIVO and Strashun libraries were to be shipped. It turned out that only 414 marked cases could be found. Horne told the loaders to take six cases at random to fill the quota. By 5 P.M. on Tuesday, all 420 cases had been loaded on the freight cars. On Wednesday morning, they chugged off from the Depot on their way to Frankfurt, with Pomrenze aboard.

There they were to be attached to the mail train leaving for Bremen that night. Pomrenze traveled with the train, accompanied by a contingent of American MP security guards.

The ship on which the books were to travel was due in Bremerhaven on Thursday and on that same day, June 19, the 420 cases were loaded on the S.S. *Pioneer Cove,* U.S. Lines Co., which sailed from Bremen at noon on Saturday, June 21. After the cases were loaded on the ship, Pomrenze returned to Offenbach. In the interim, I had had time to get to the PX and buy my liquor ration. We drank to the successful conclusion of his mission. He didn't know it, but I was drinking also to the successful conclusion of mine.

A few days later, I returned to Munich and was given a new assignment in the British zone. I had decided that I would stay just long enough to fulfill the conditions of my contract with the JDC. Once the YIVO library had been shipped to New York, I felt that I had laid to rest those ghosts of Vilna that had haunted me since 1939. I had realized the obsessive fantasies of rescue which had tormented me for years. I had in fact saved a few remnants of Vilna, even if they were just books, mere pieces of paper, the tatters and shards of a civilization.

The sweet memories of Vilna and of the people I had known and loved were still intact in my mind. I knew that nothing more was left to me. My fevered feelings of guilt for having abandoned them had died away. I was ready now to move ahead. I was ready now to start a new life.

Index

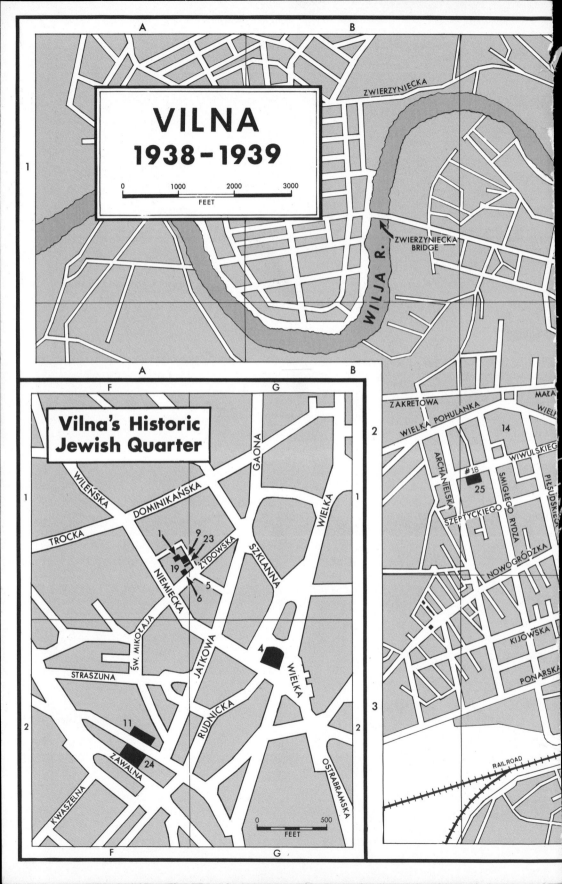